Forever Saul Leiter

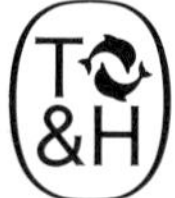

One of the things photography has
allowed me is to take pleasure in looking.

Contents

1

The World of Saul Leiter

I see this world simply. It is a source of endless delight.

Sedan, 1950s

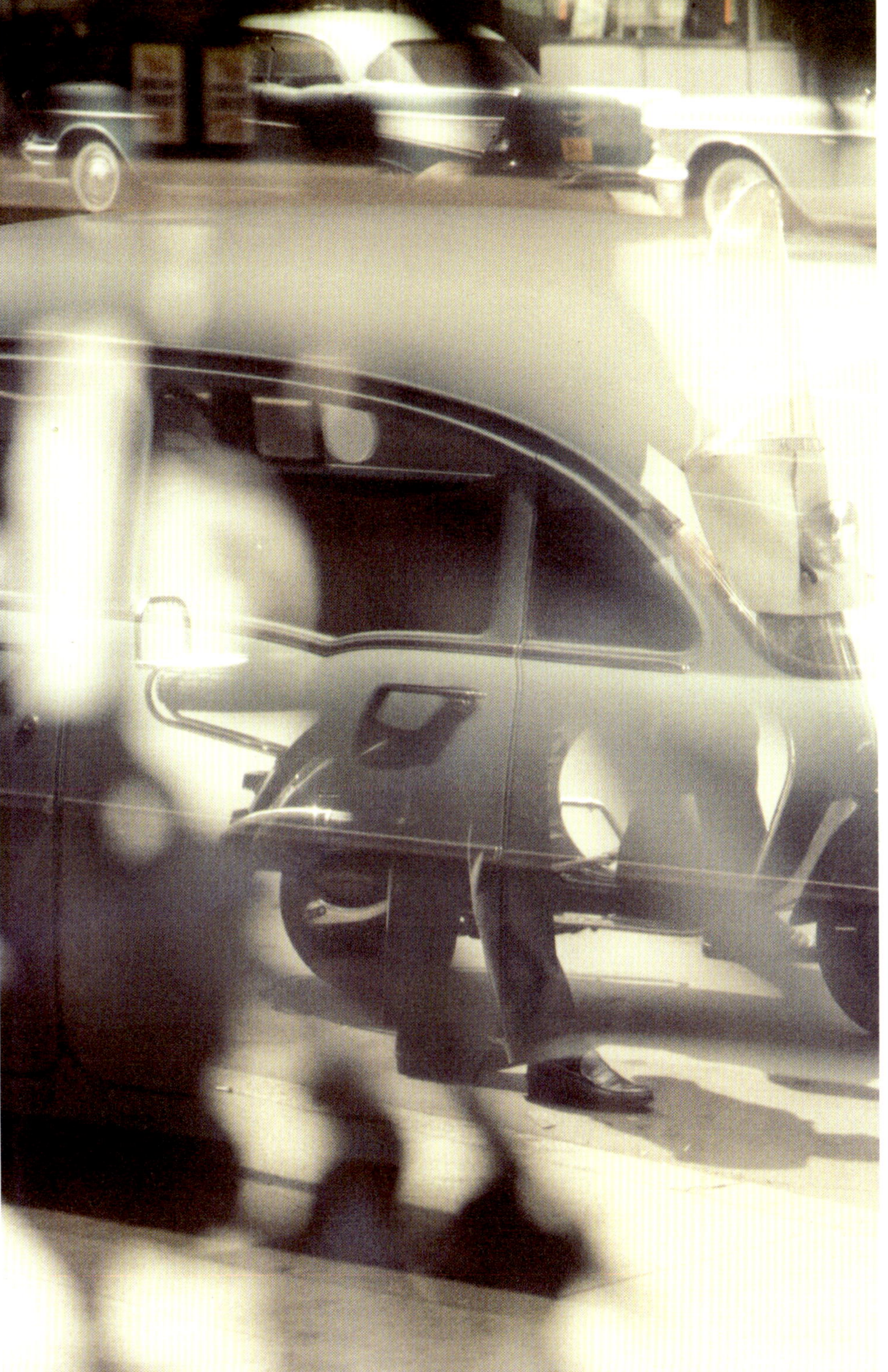

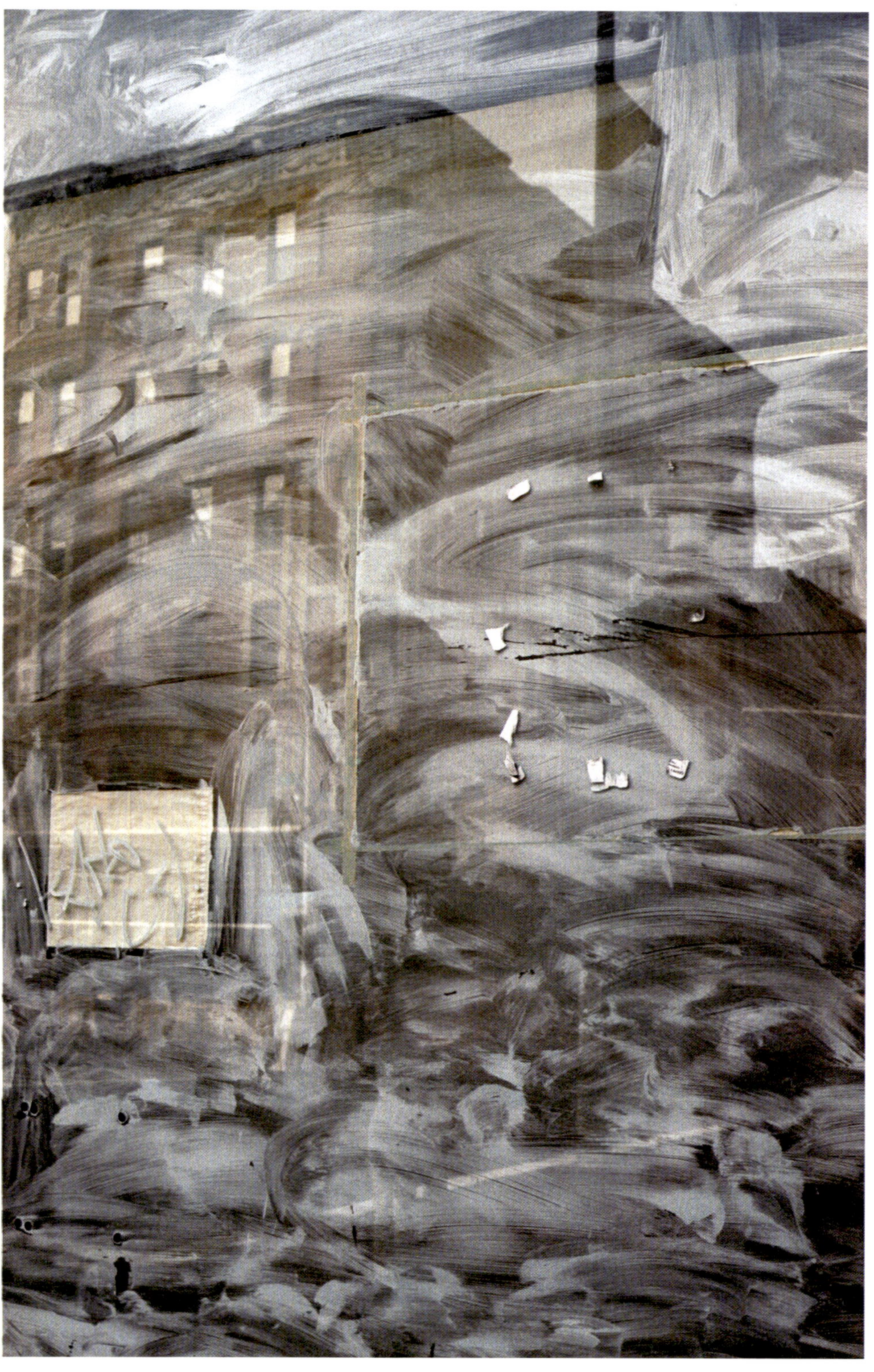

I did things because I liked doing it.
When I'm asked: Why did you do certain things?
Because I liked it!

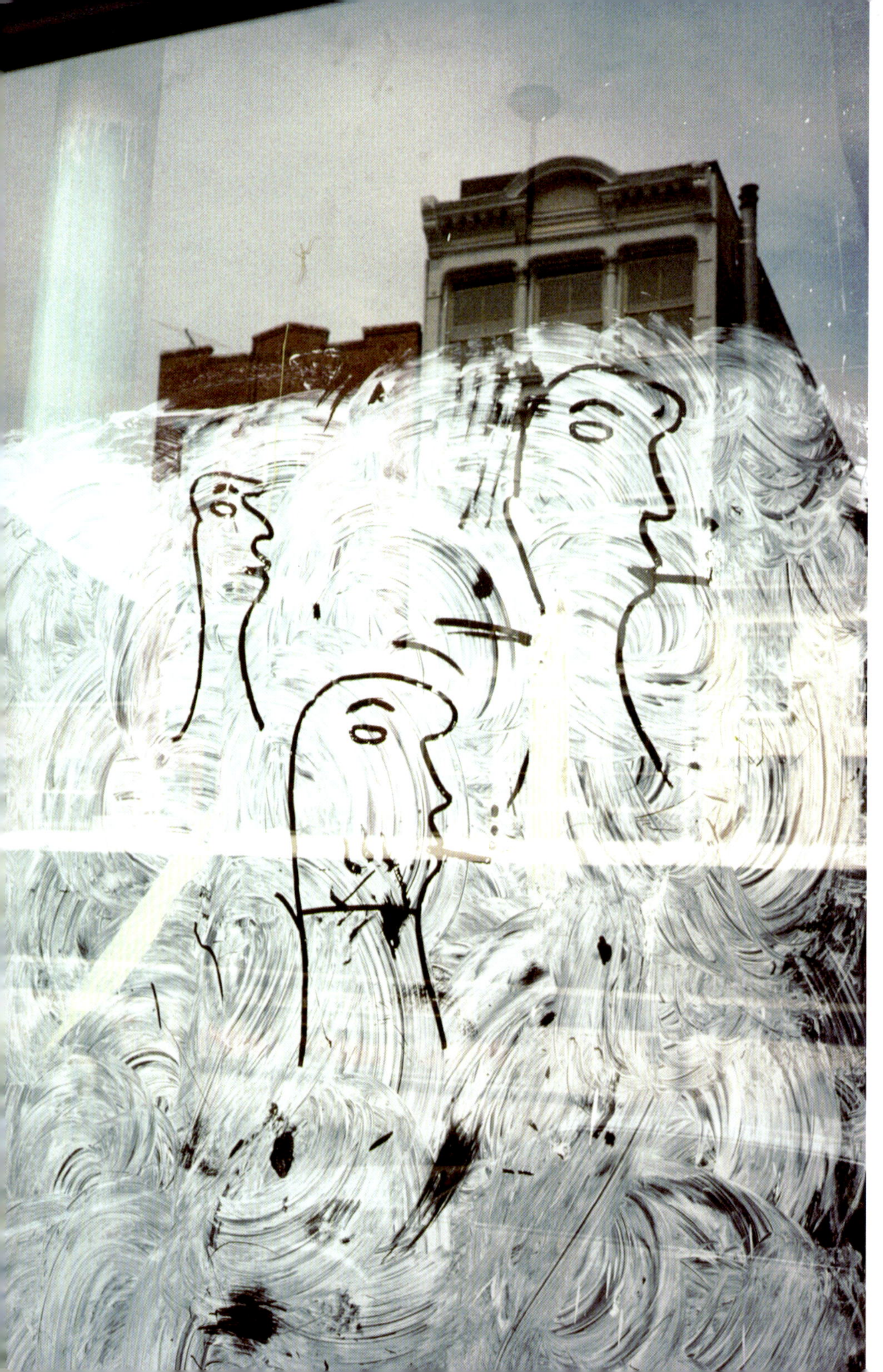

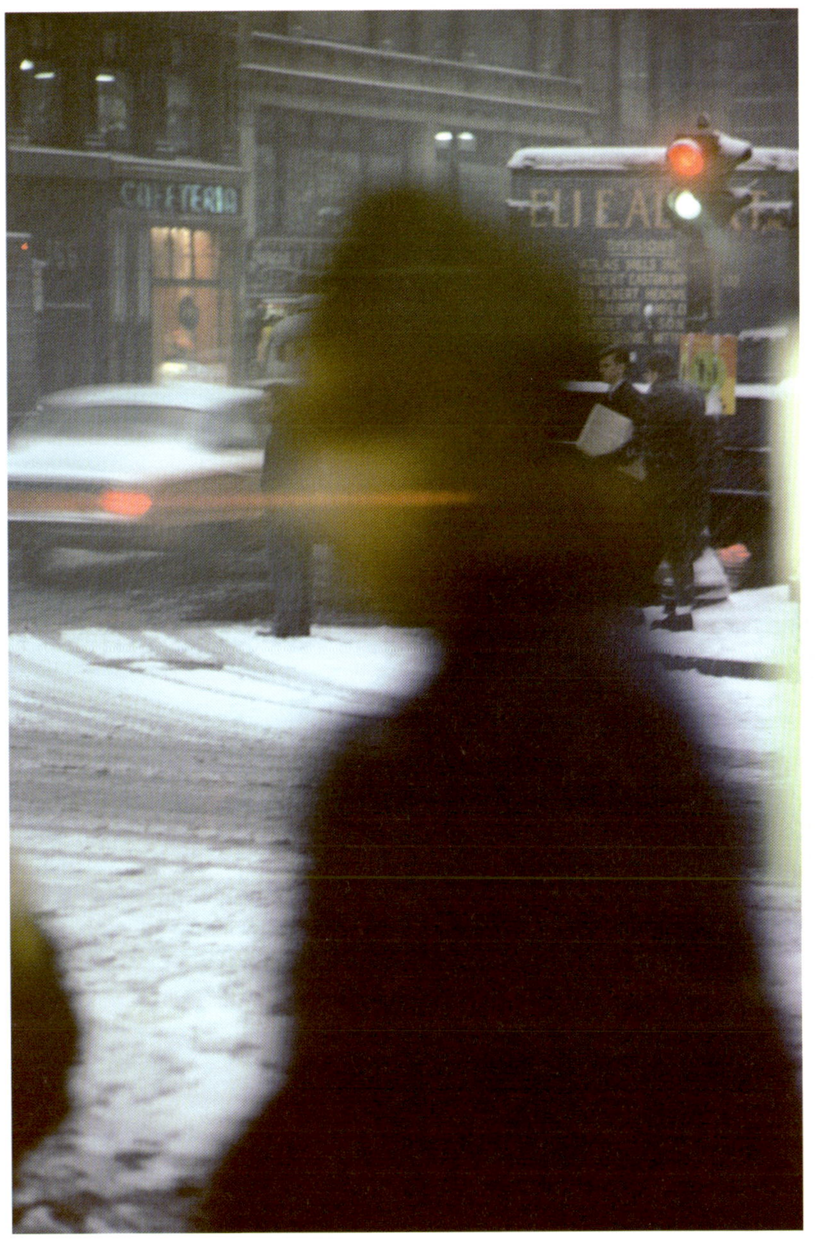

Graffiti Heads, 1950

Untitled, 1960s

pp. 12–13: Untitled, undated

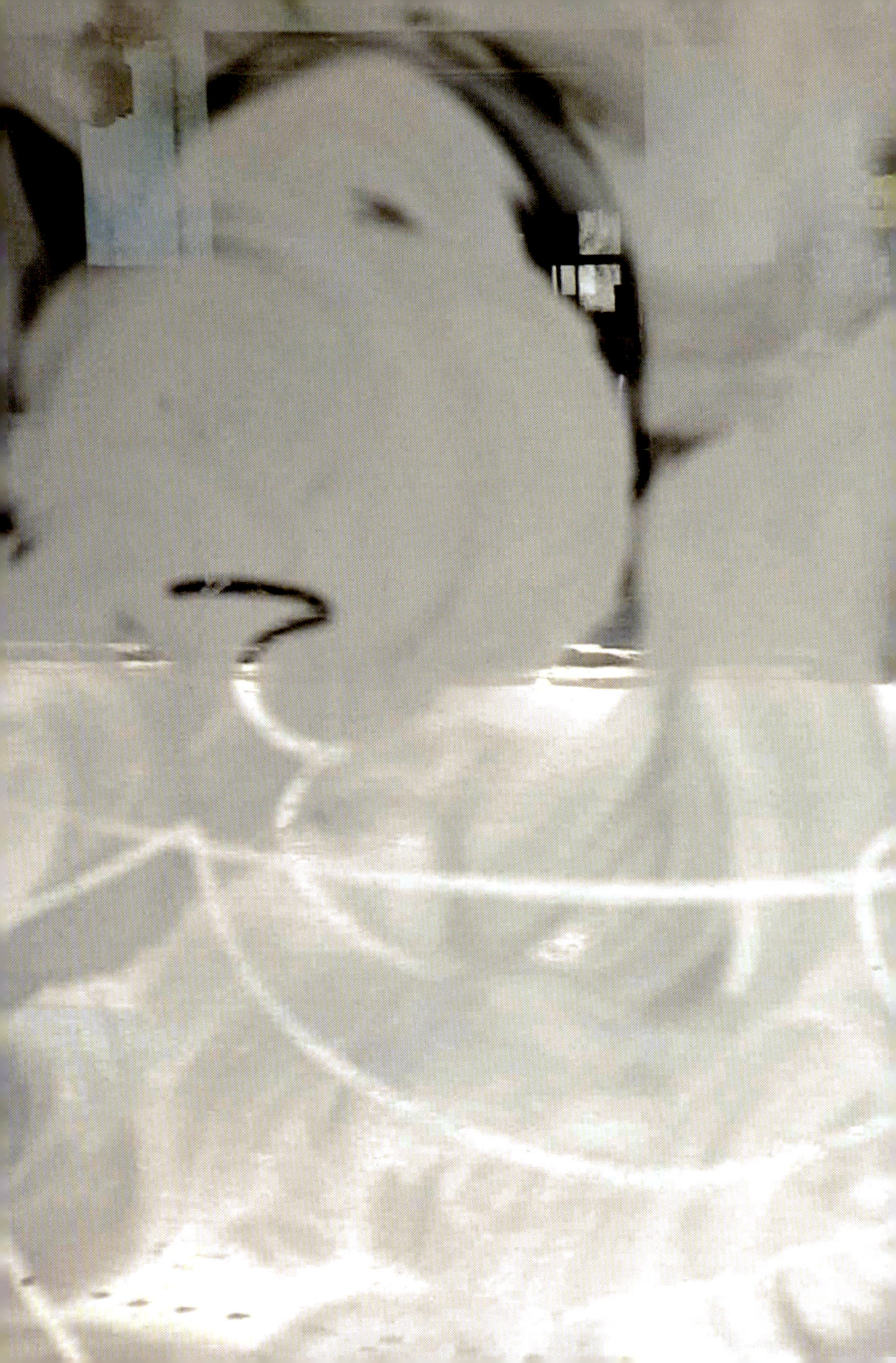

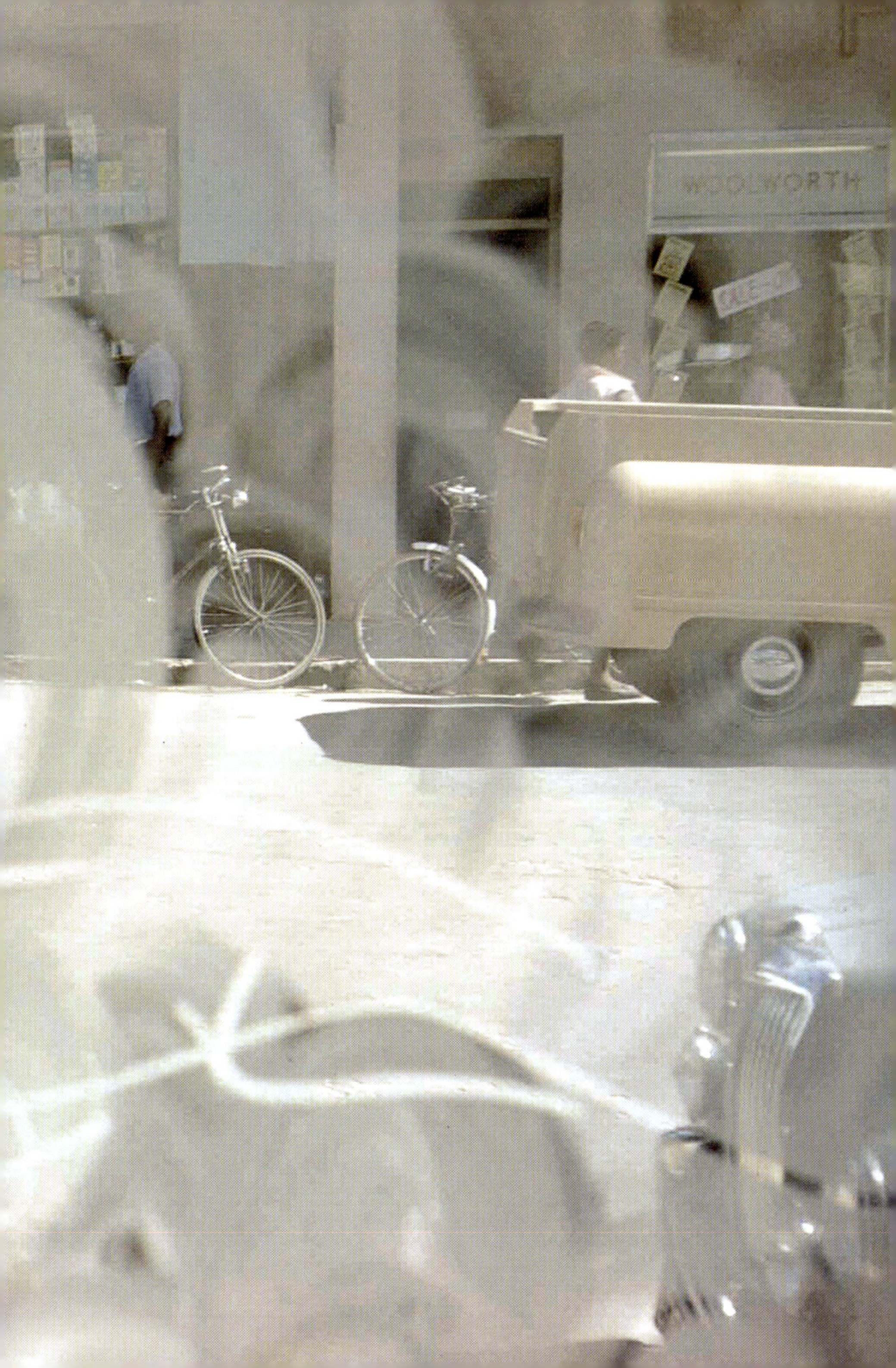

WOOLWORTH

I don't recall planning to photograph certain things.

Sidewalk, 1950s

pp. 16–17: Untitled, undated

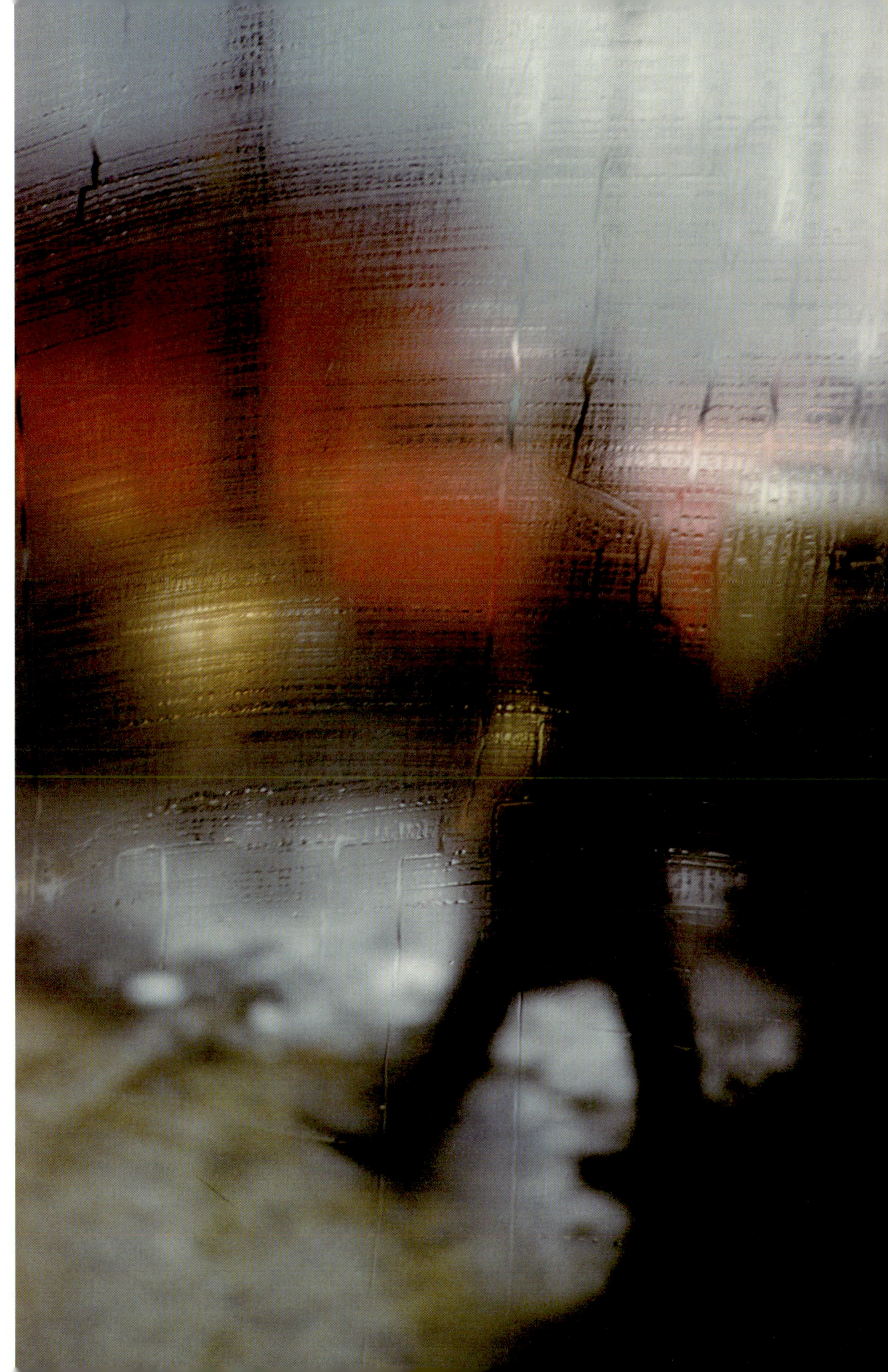

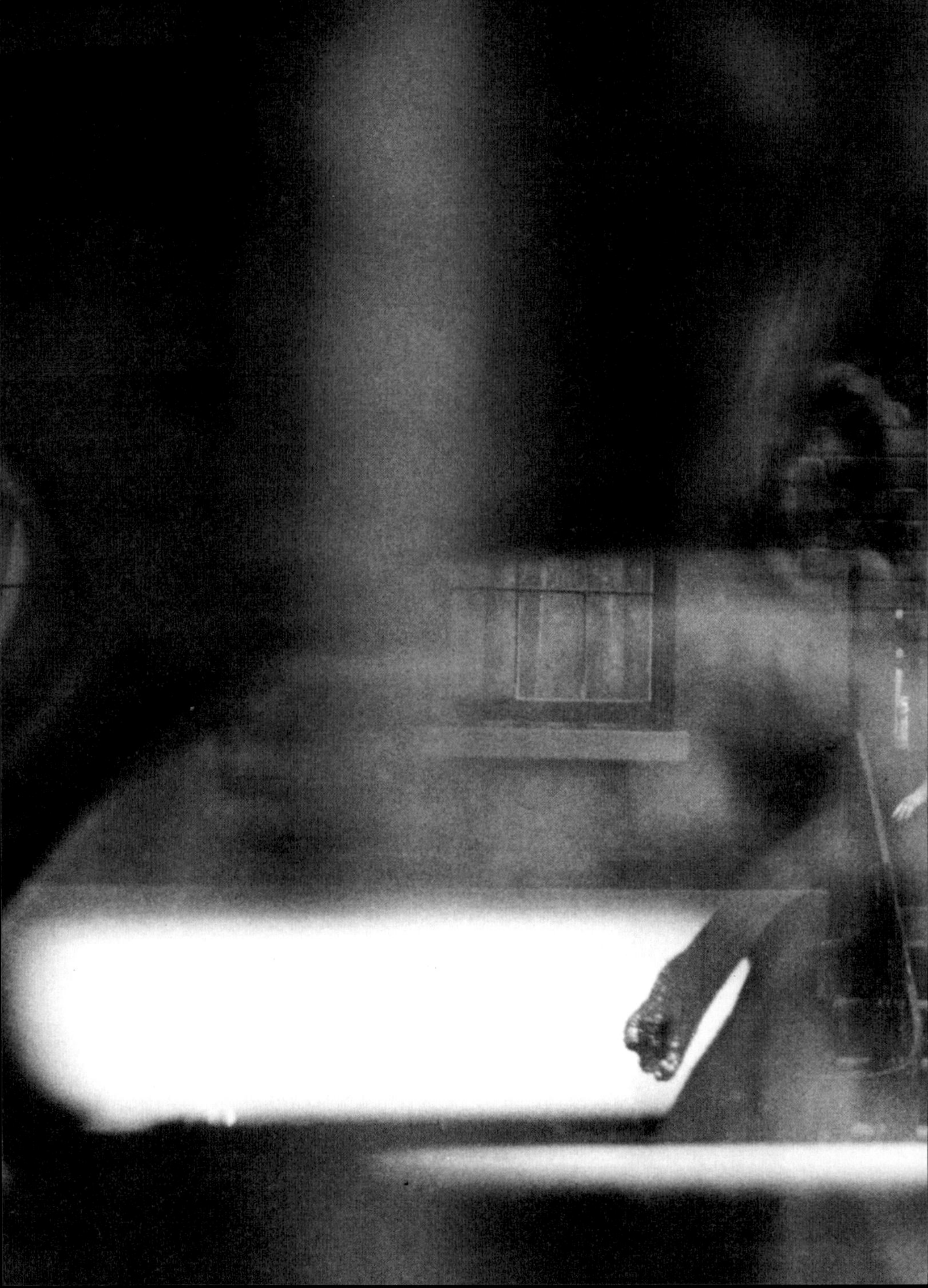

Right now, somewhere, someone is taking a very fine photograph.

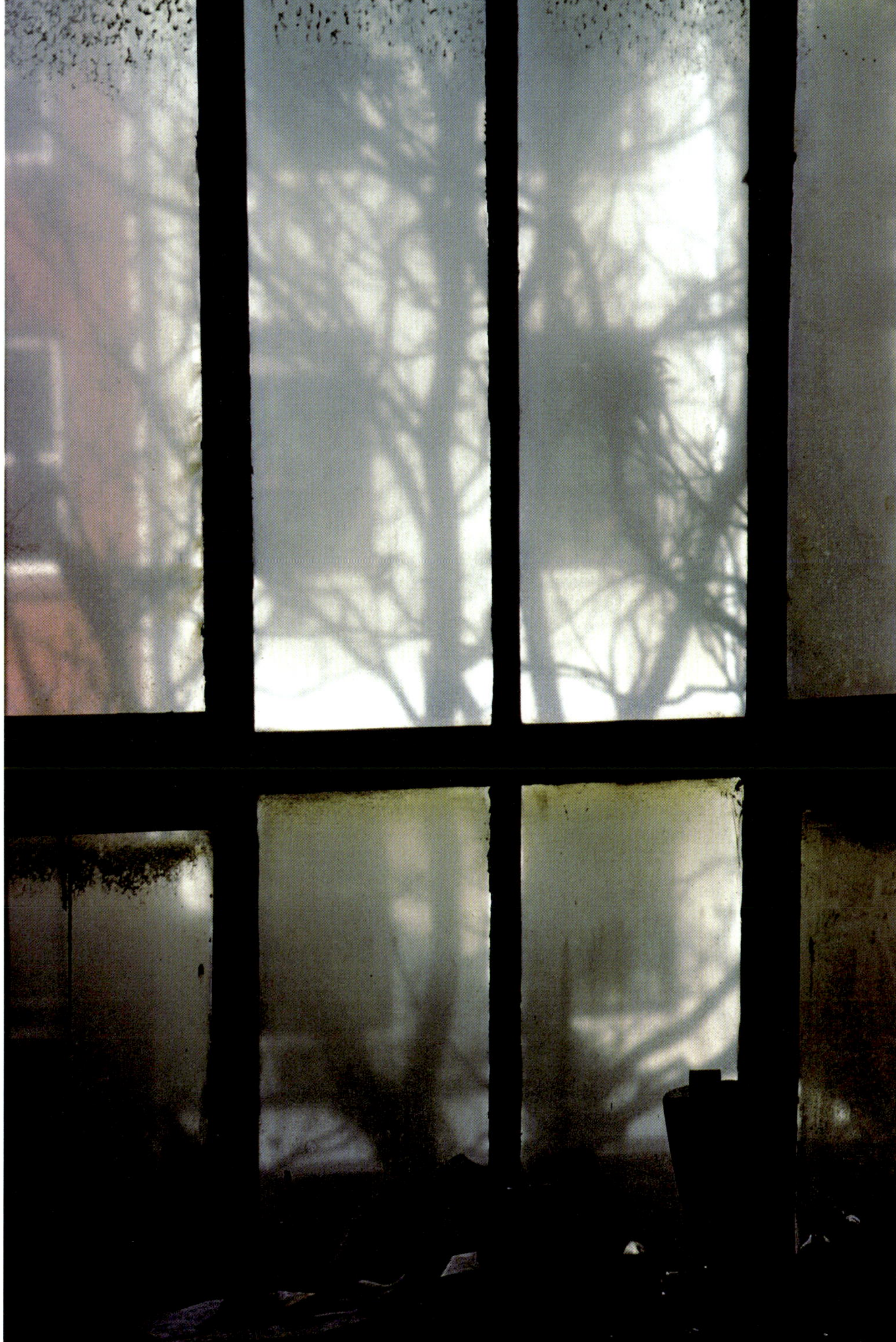

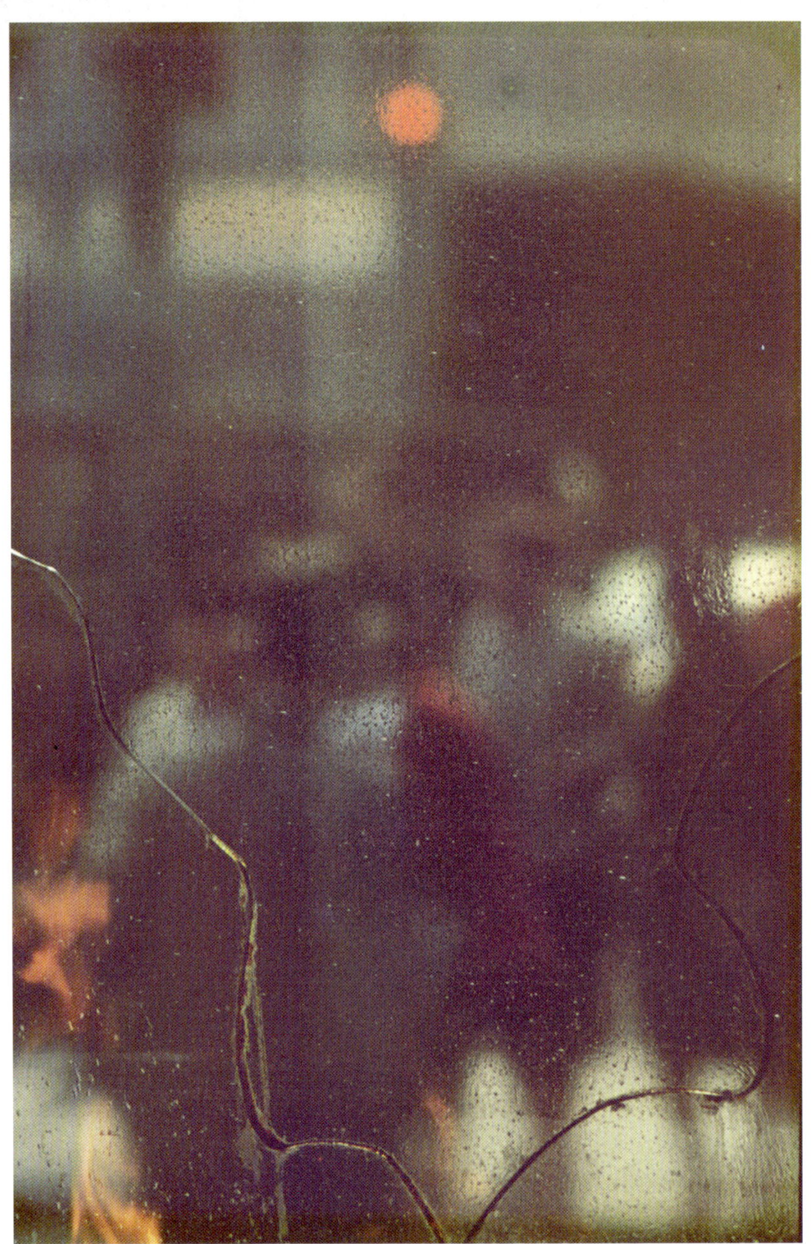

Untitled, 1950s

Window, 5817 Beacon Street, c. 1942

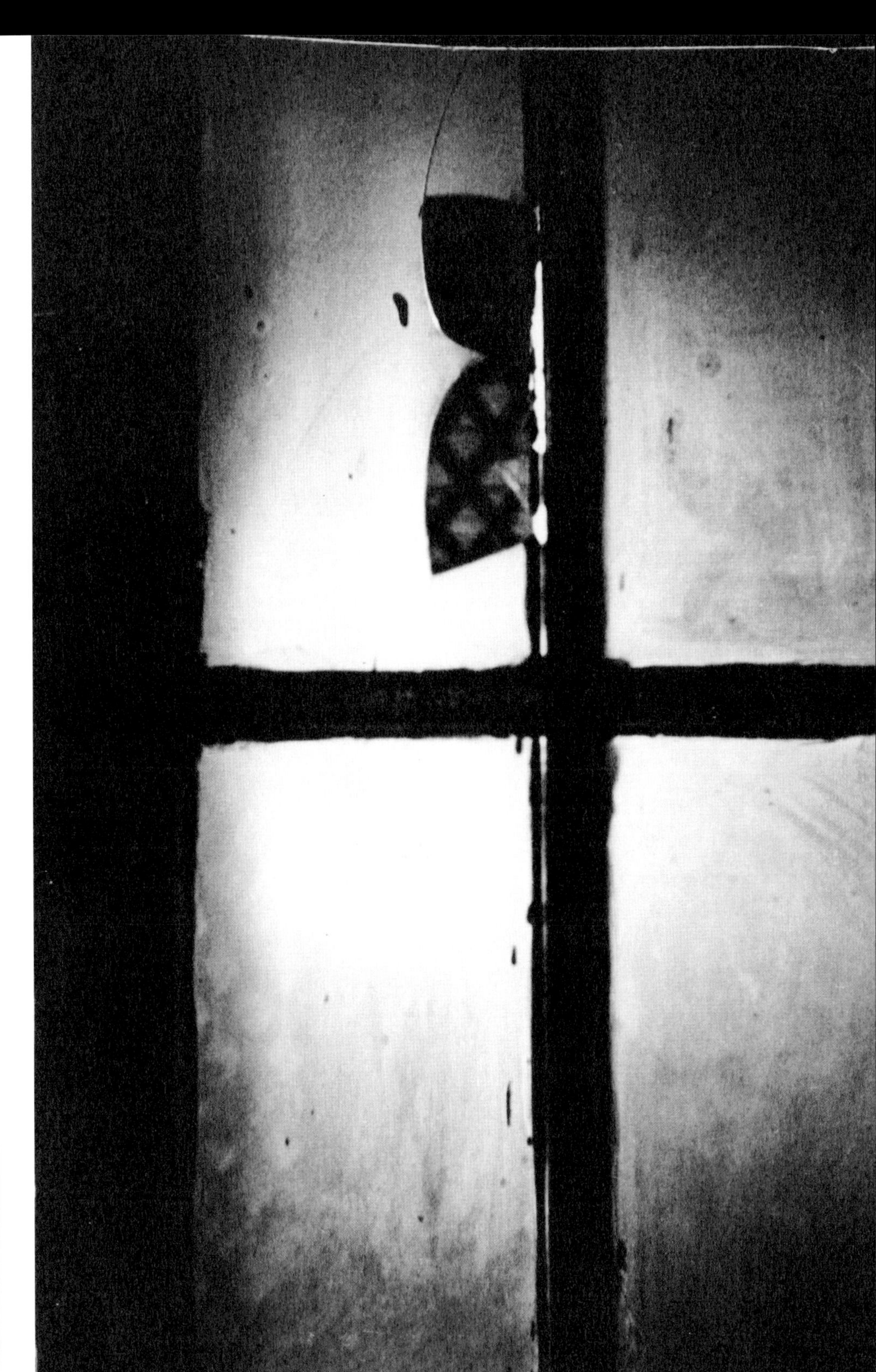

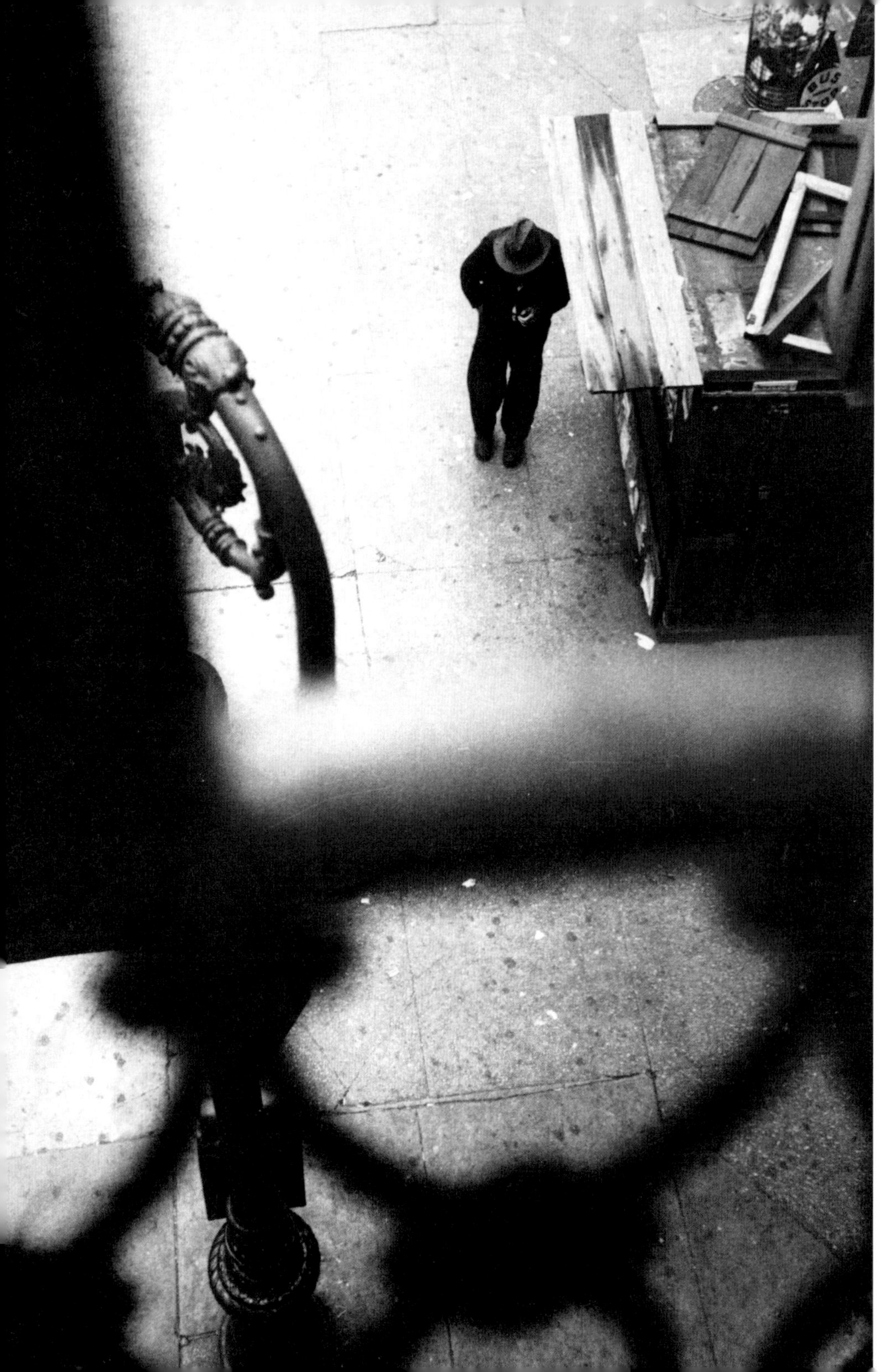

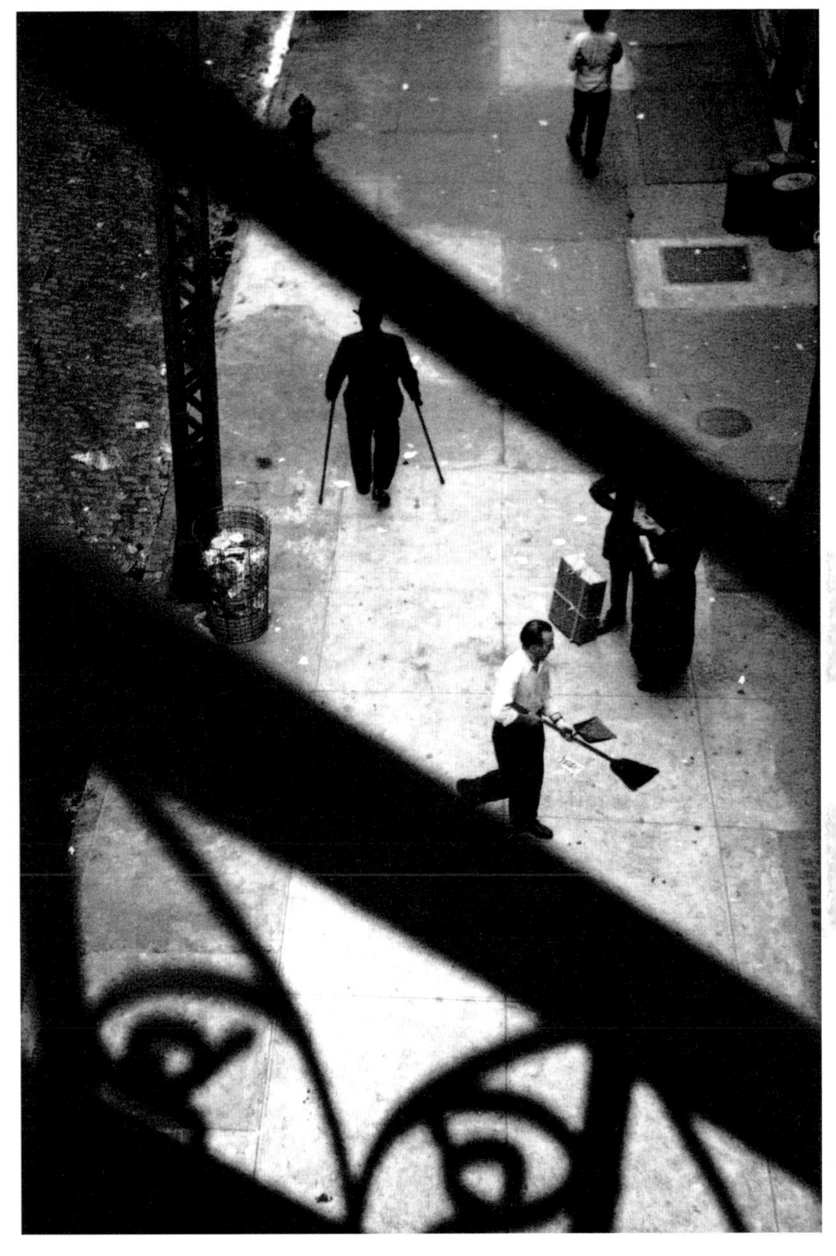

From the El, c. 1955

I have sometimes overlooked the fact
that something was actually of some importance.

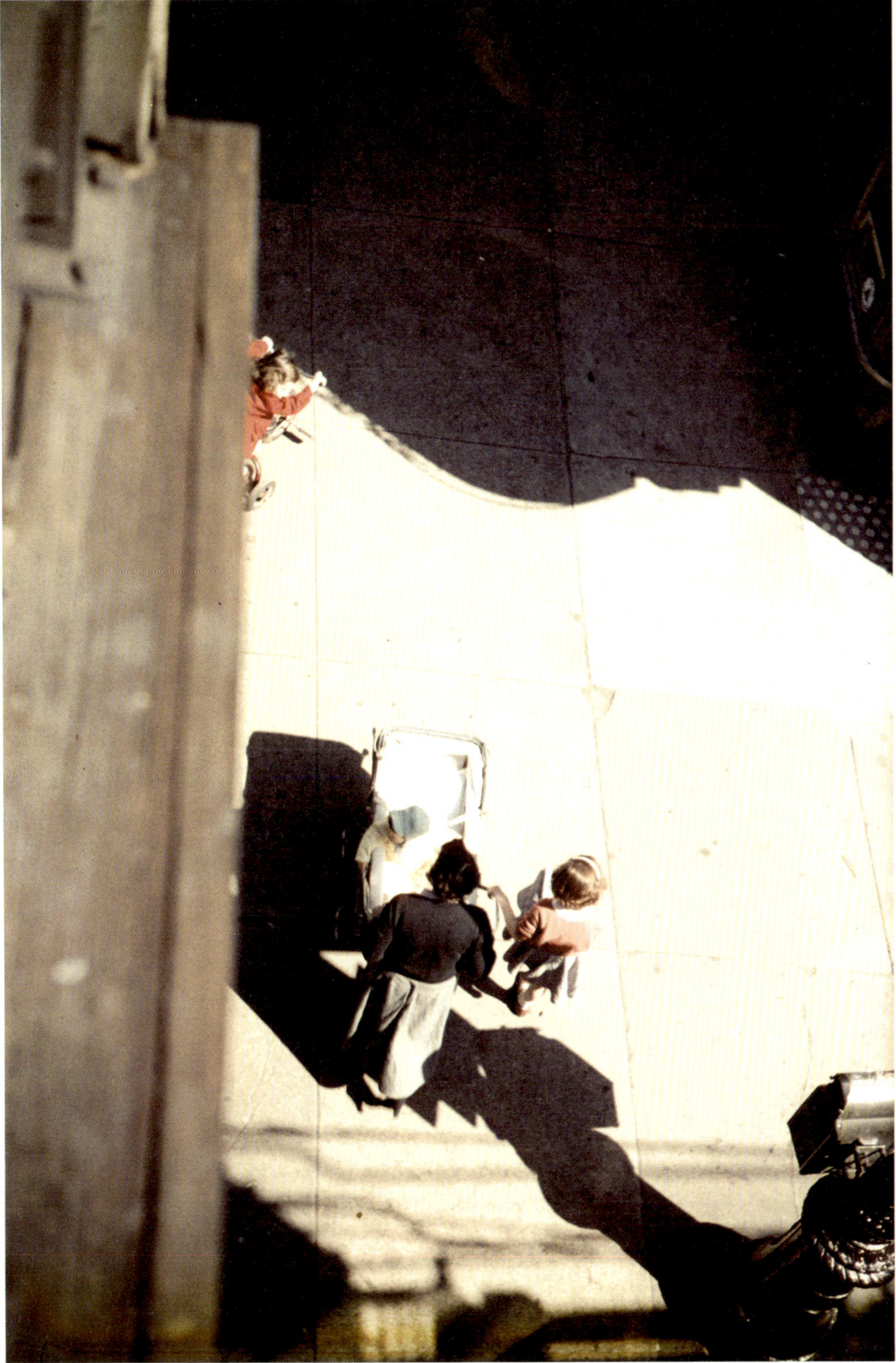

Walking, c. 1955

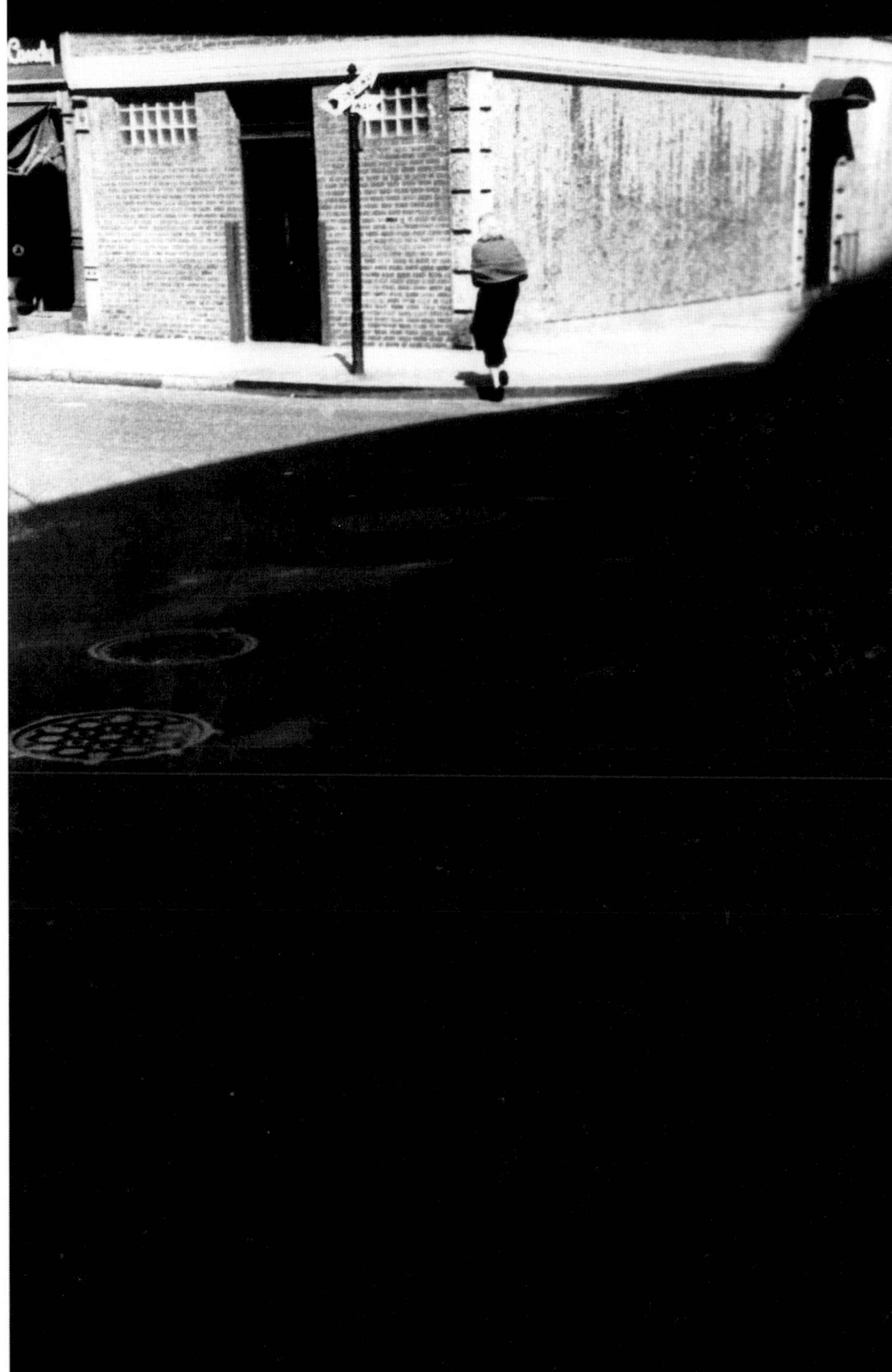

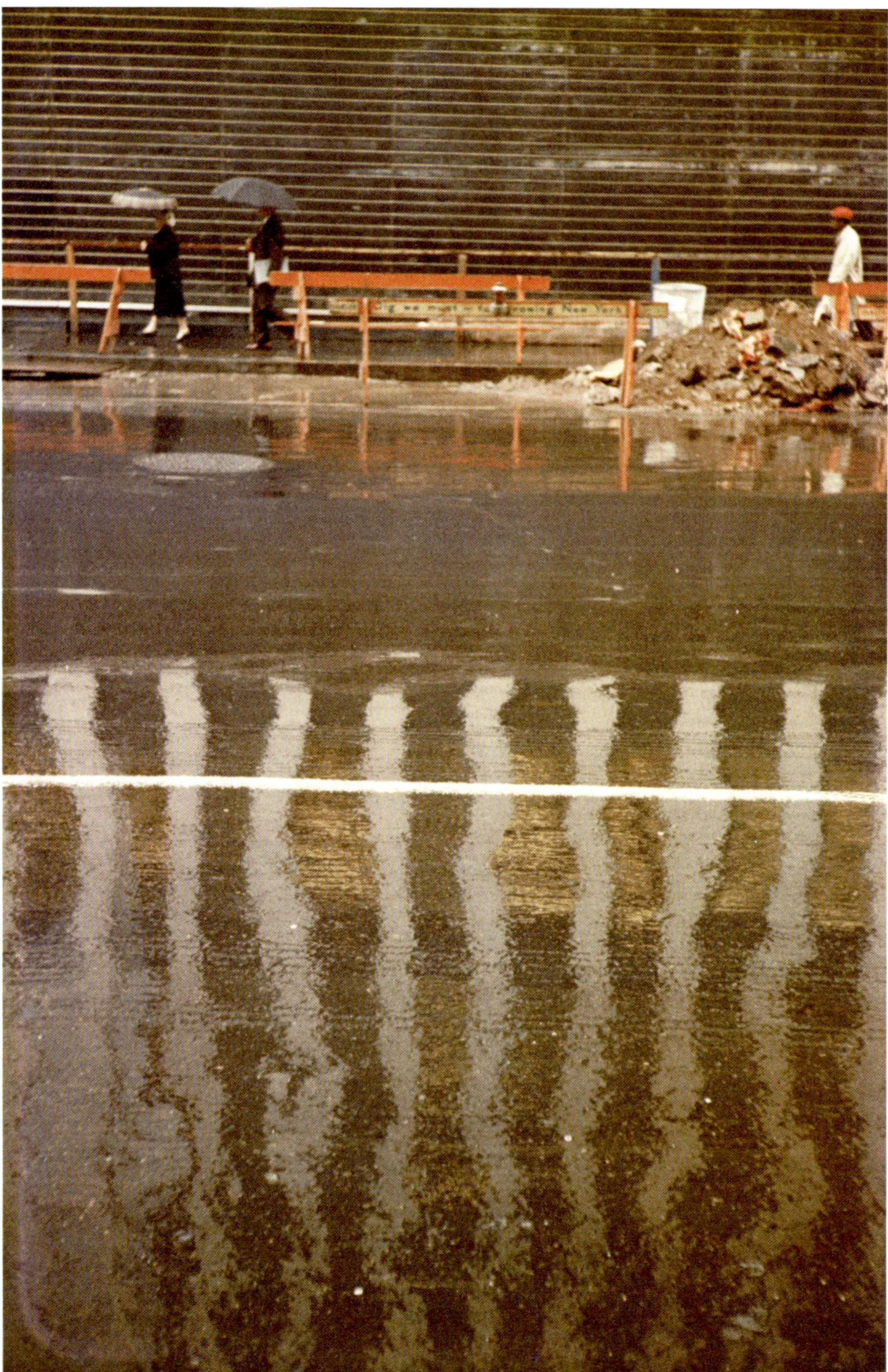

I happen to believe in the beauty of simple things.
I believe that the most uninteresting thing can be very interesting.

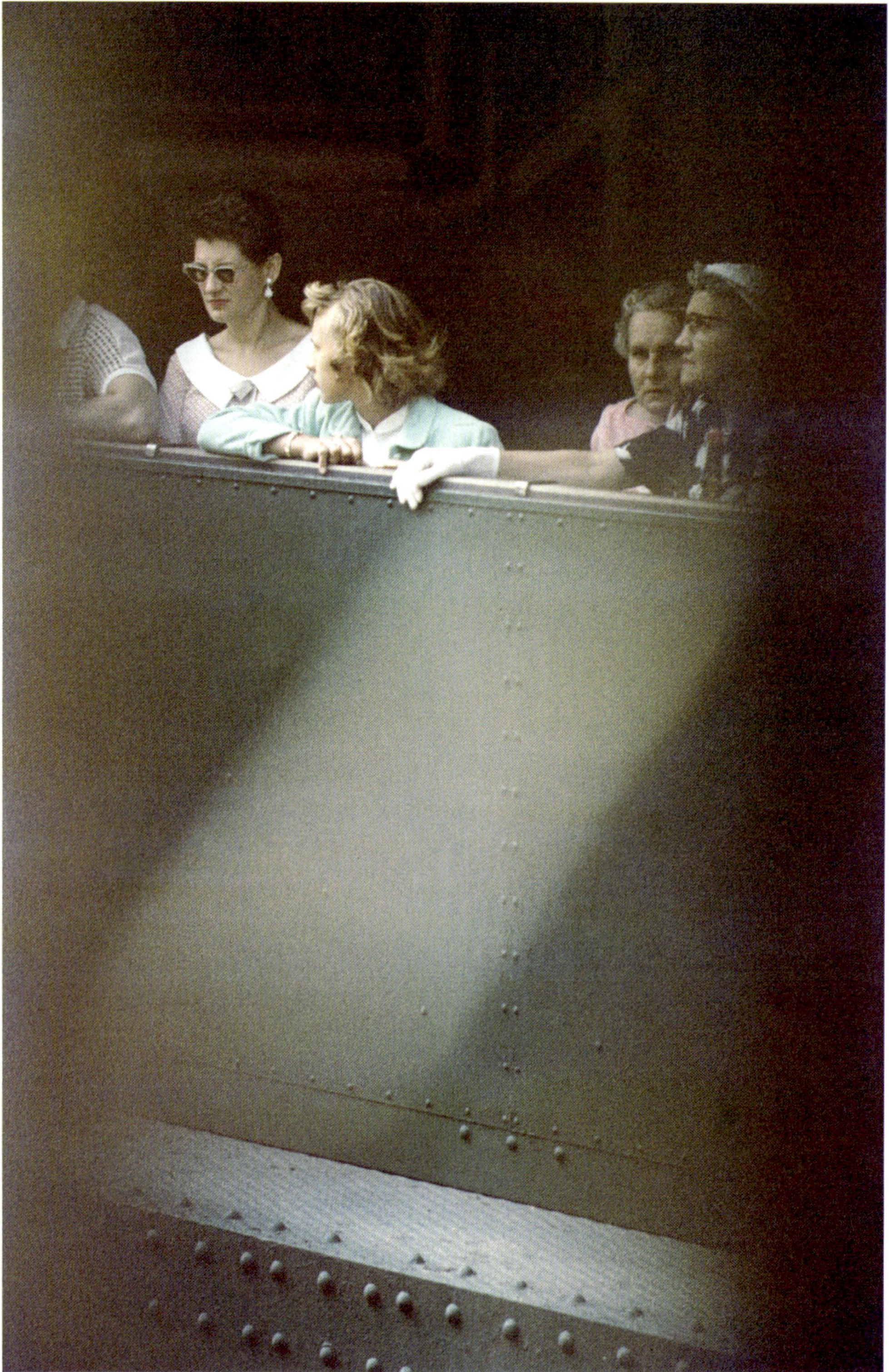

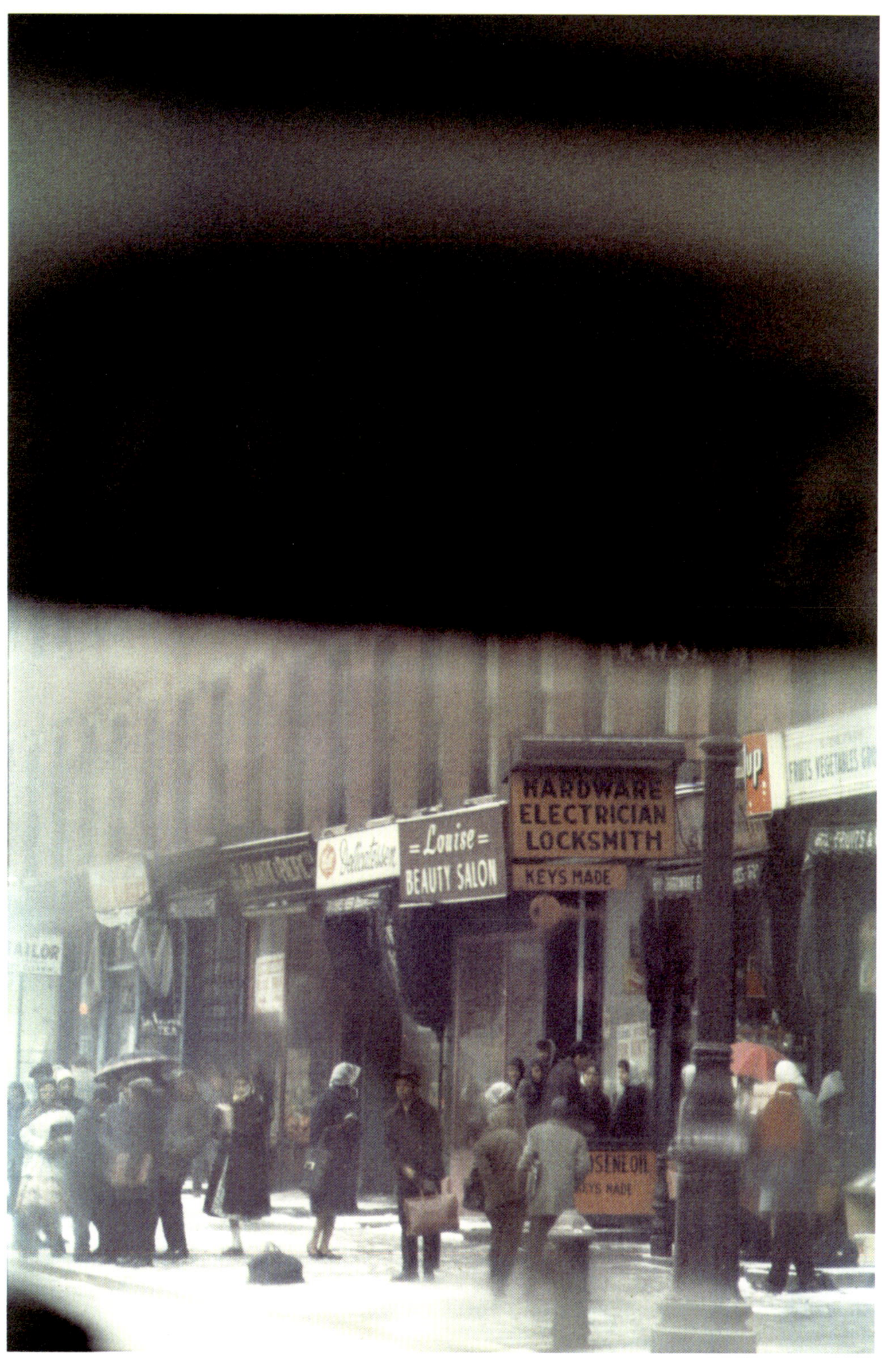

Louise
BEAUTY SALON
HARDWARE
ELECTRICIAN
LOCKSMITH
KEYS MADE
FRUITS VEGETABLES
UP
TAYLOR
KEYS MADE

Untitled, 1950s

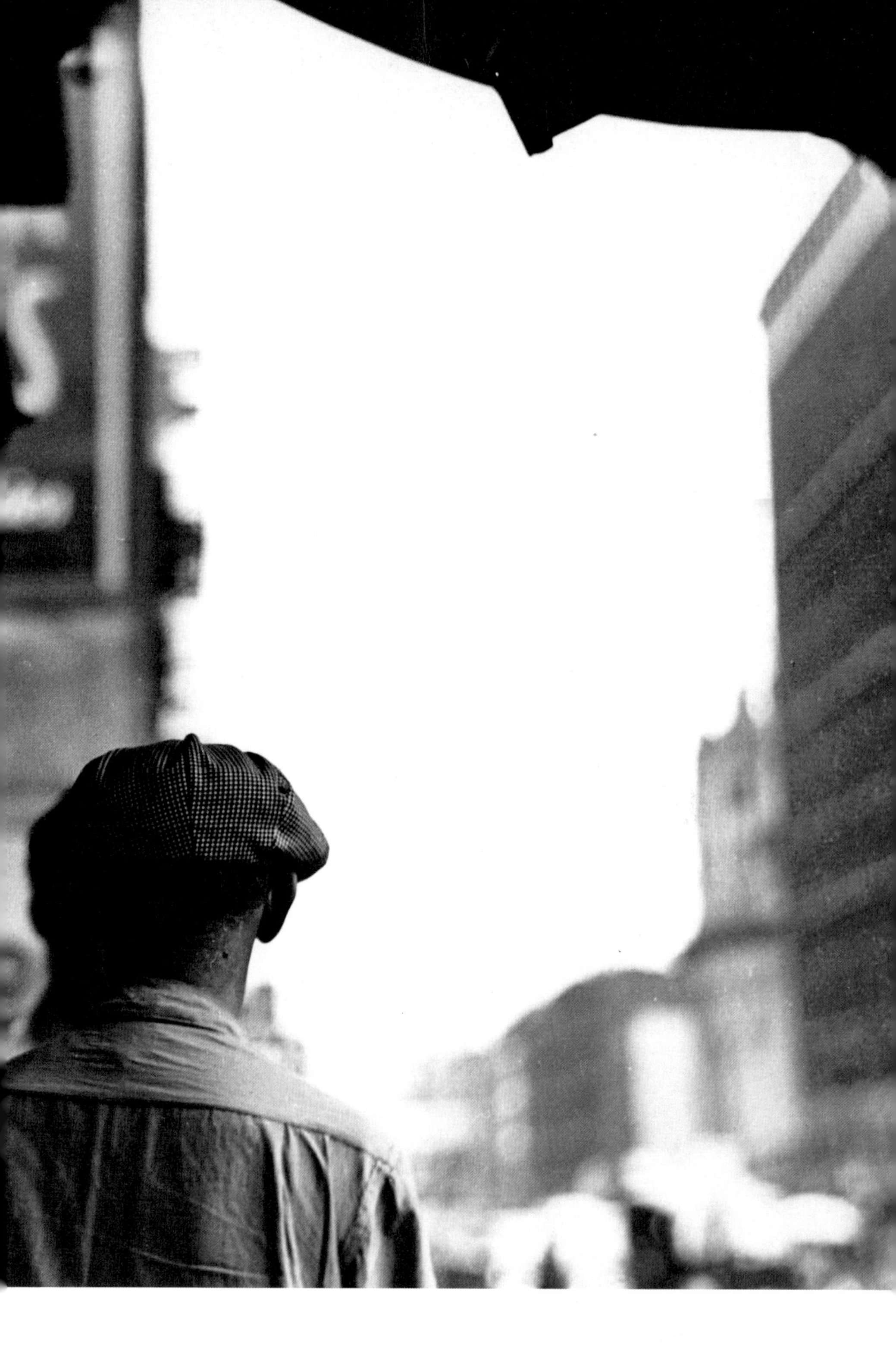

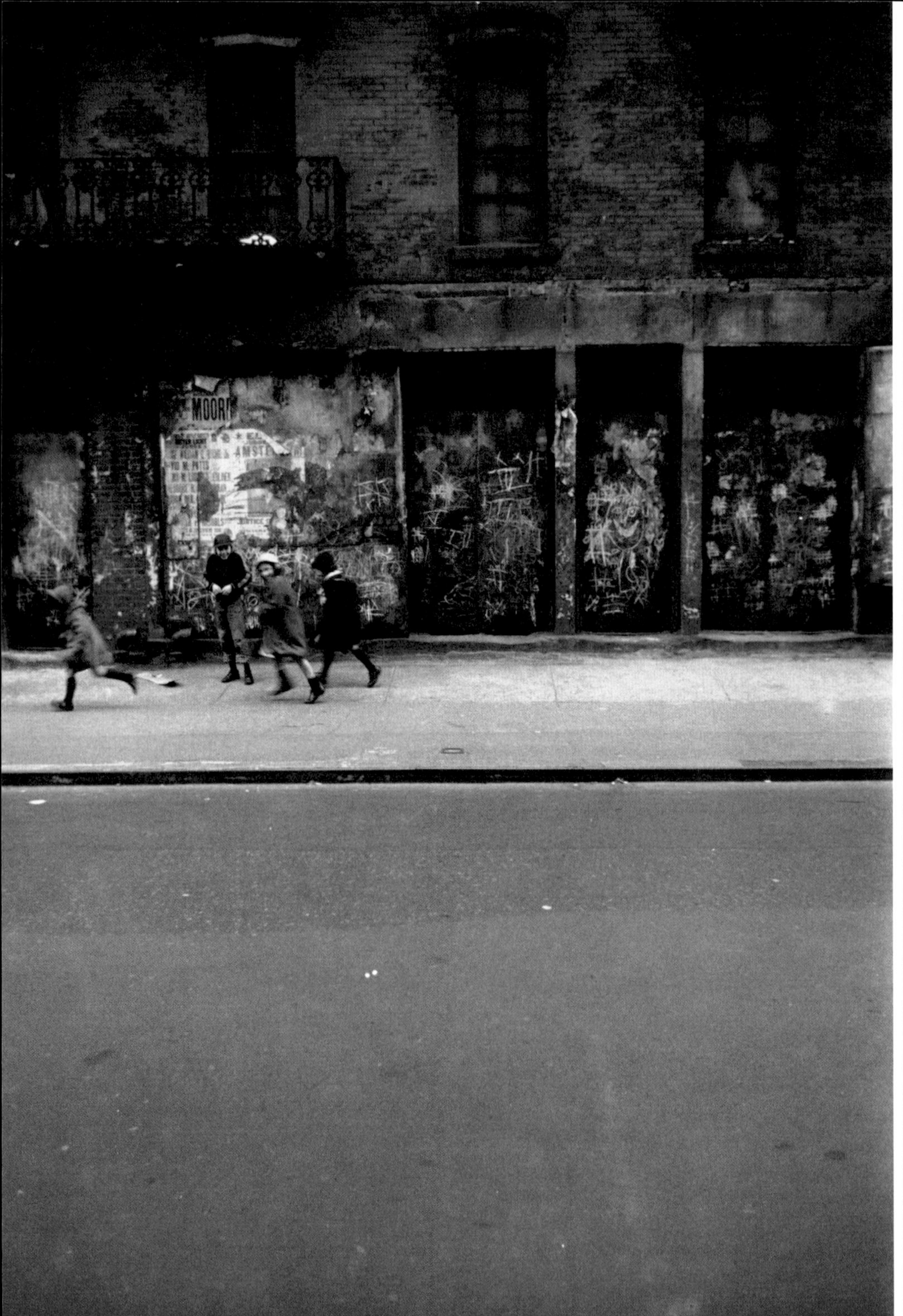
MOORT

Even though I've lived in New York most of my life,

I can't say that I know New York.

Occasionally when I'm in the street and people ask me for directions,

I tell them I don't live here.

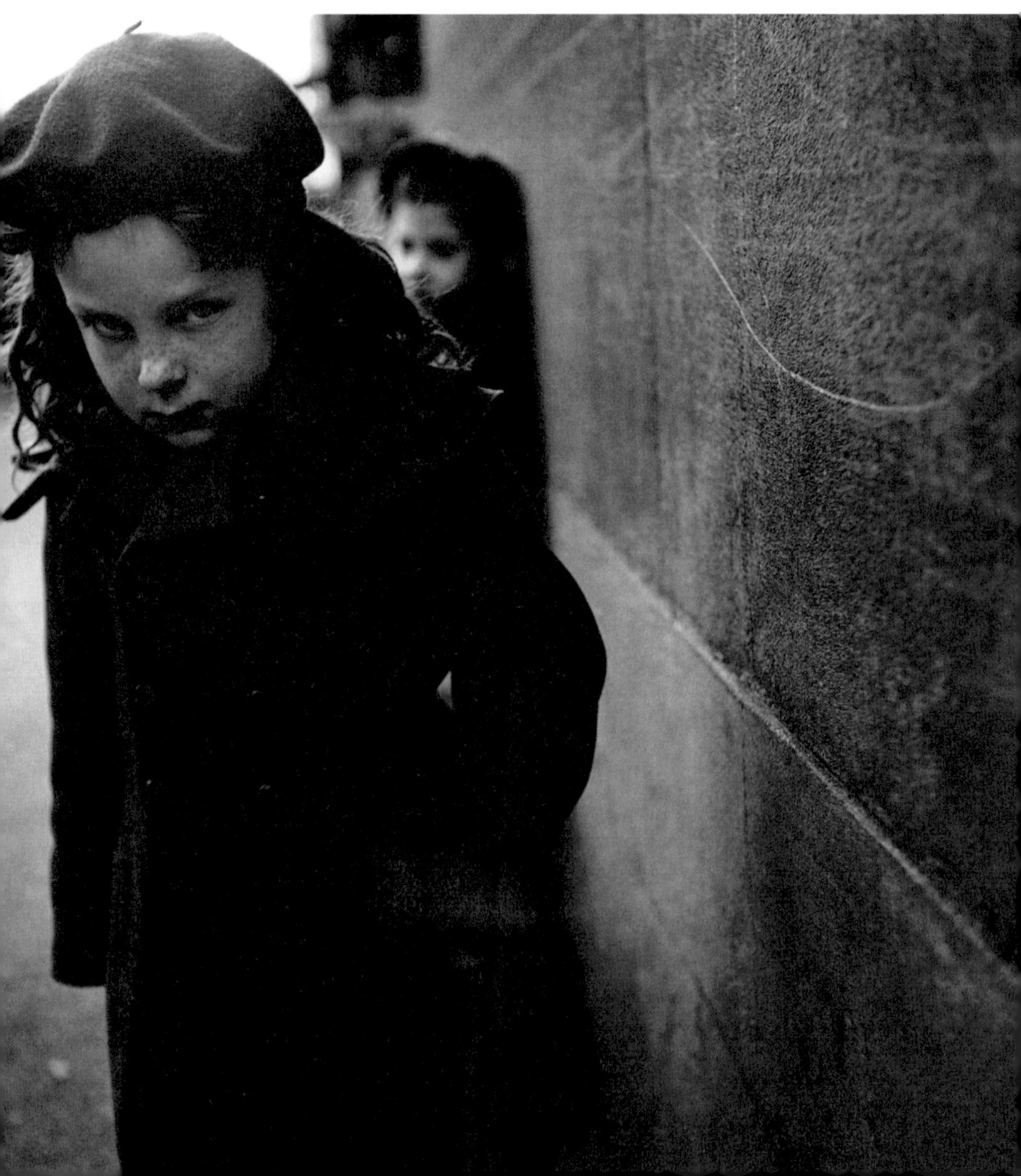

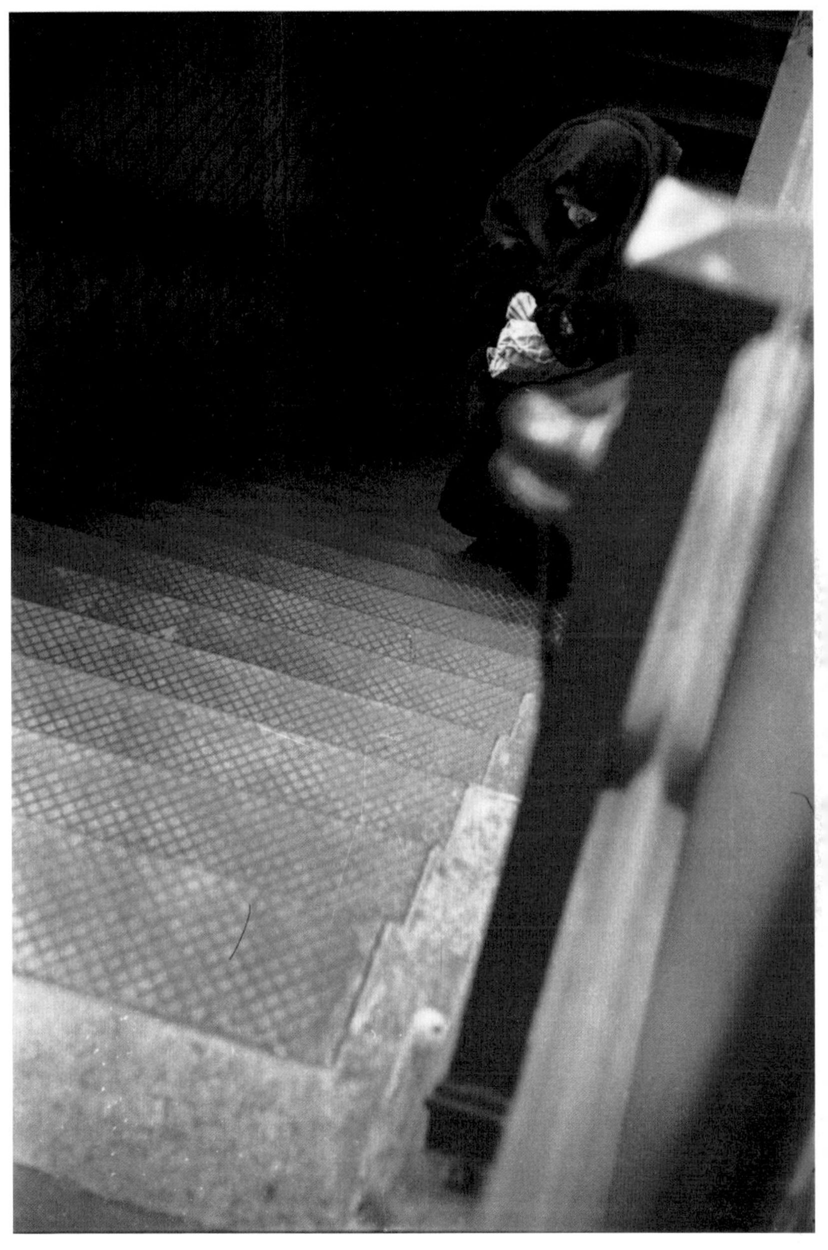

Freckles, c. 1958   Subway, c. 1958

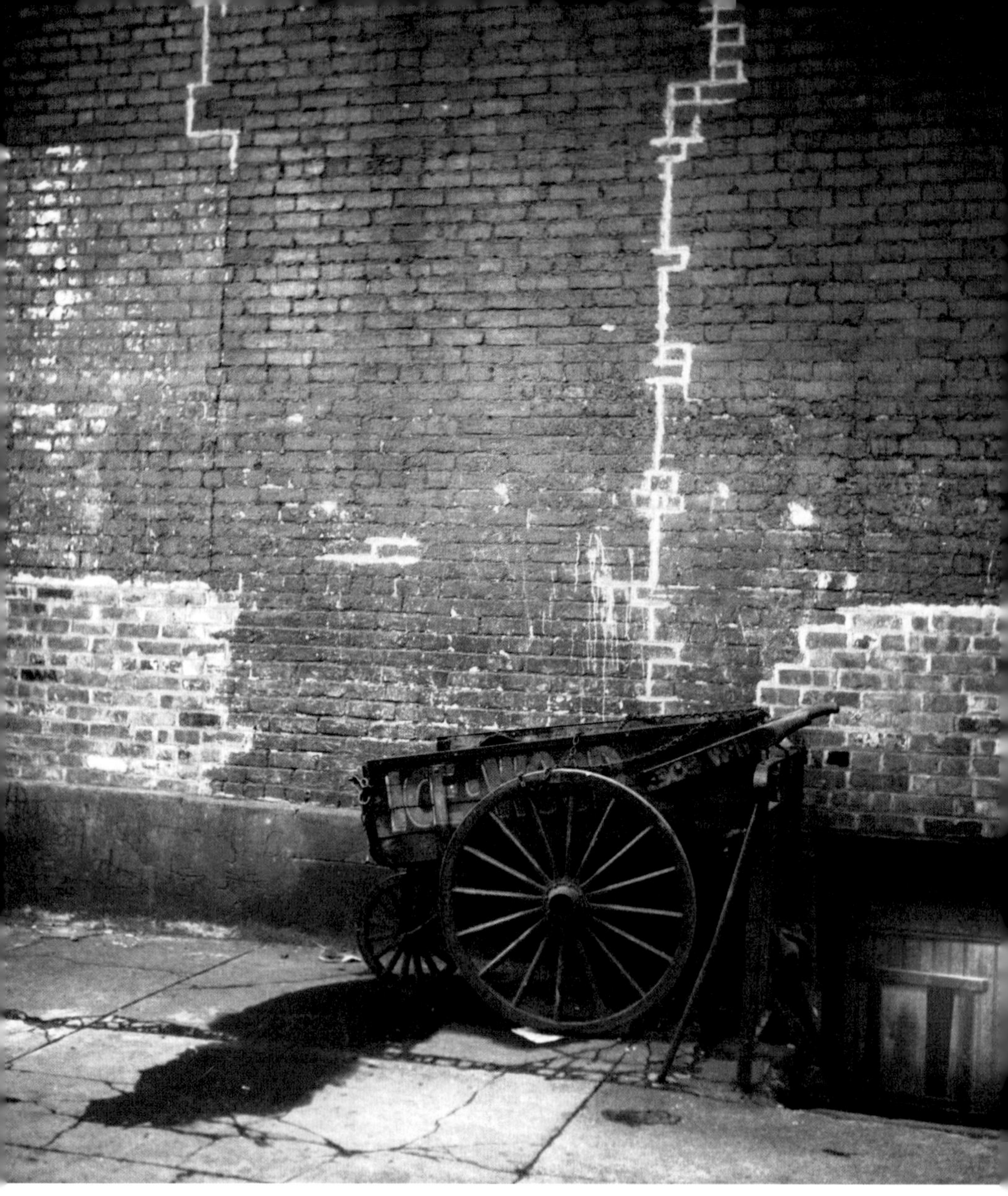

I do like photographs where sometimes everything's lost

and in some corner something's going on and you're not quite sure what it is.

Cart, c. 1948

Begging, c. 1952
From the El, c. 1955

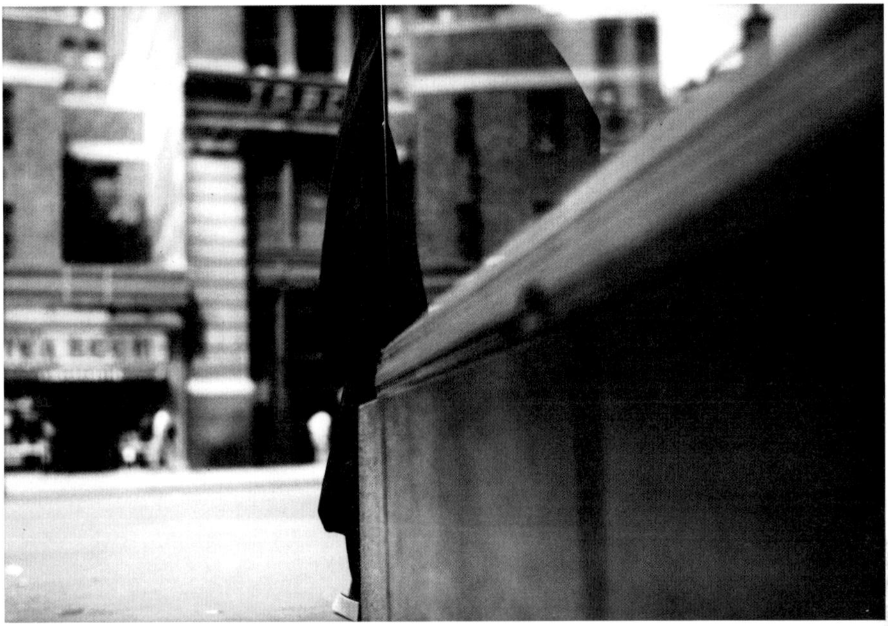

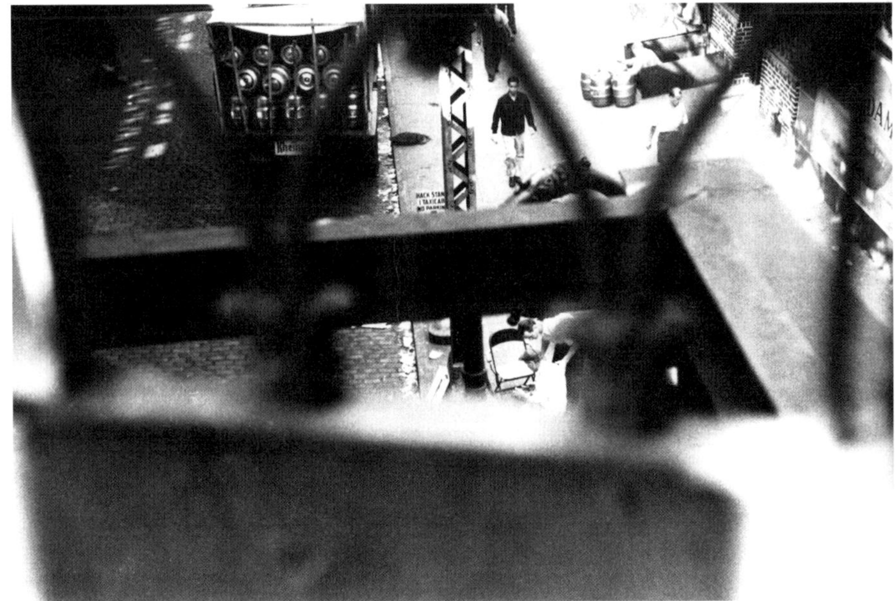

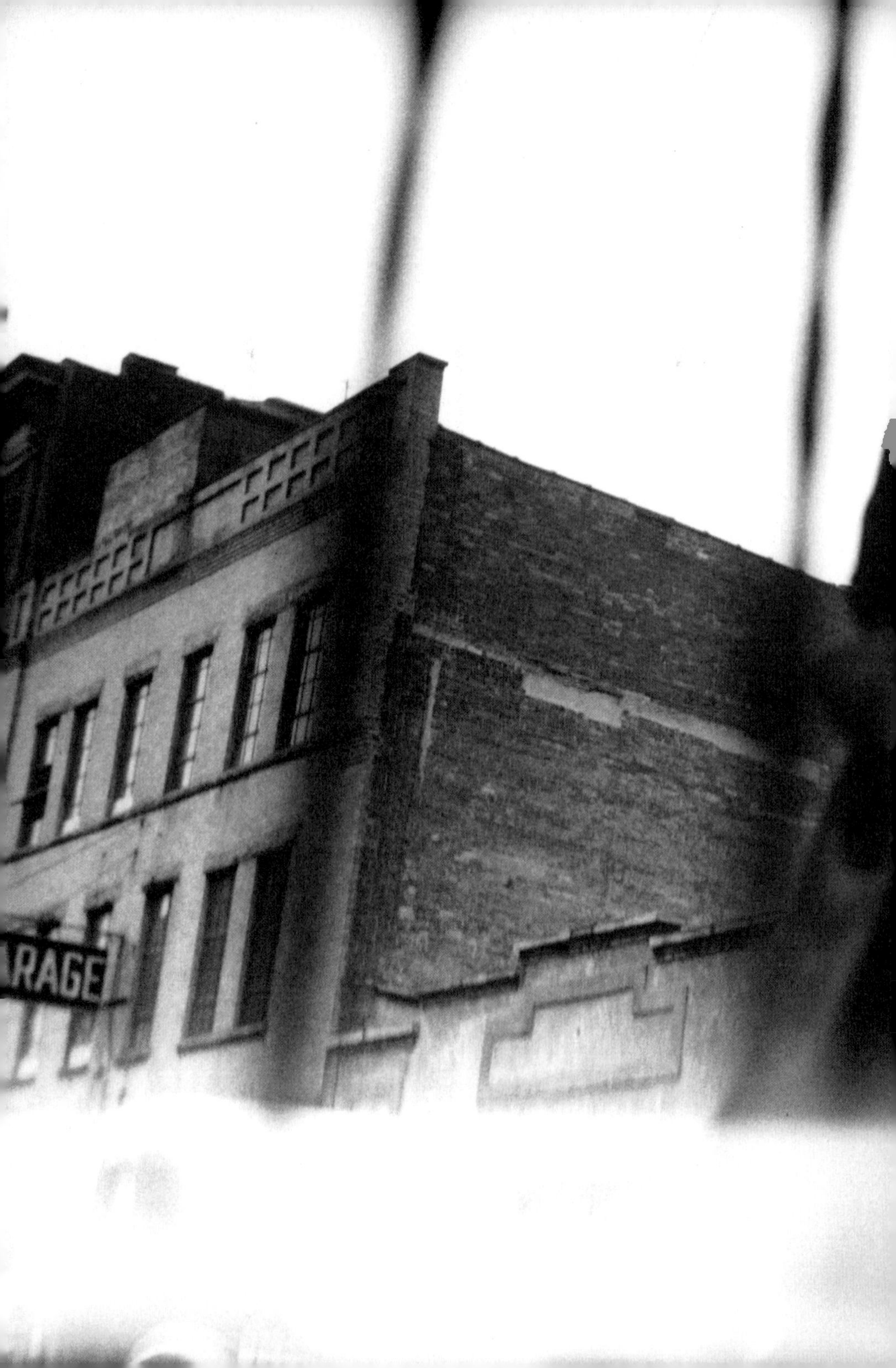
RAGE

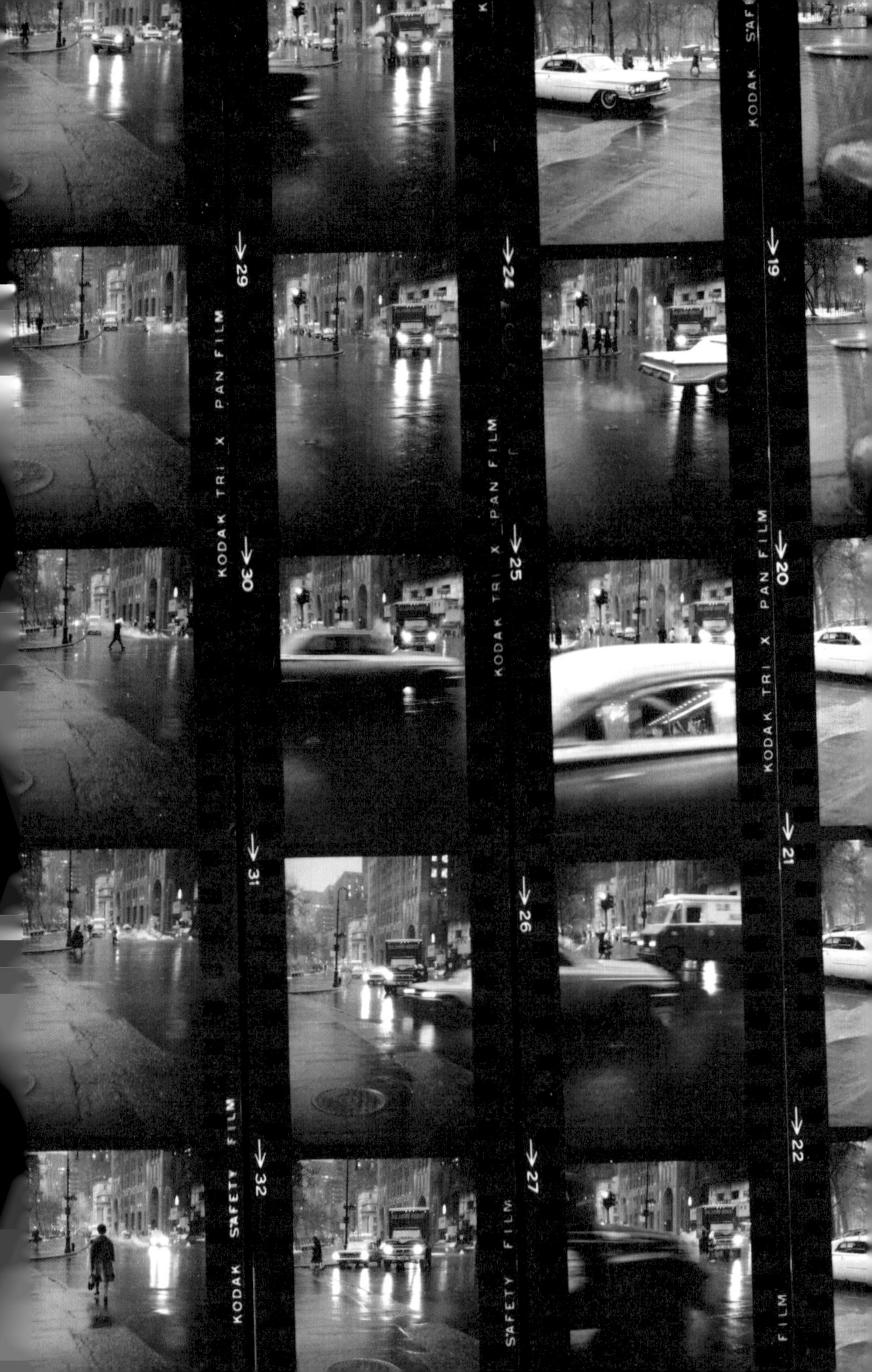

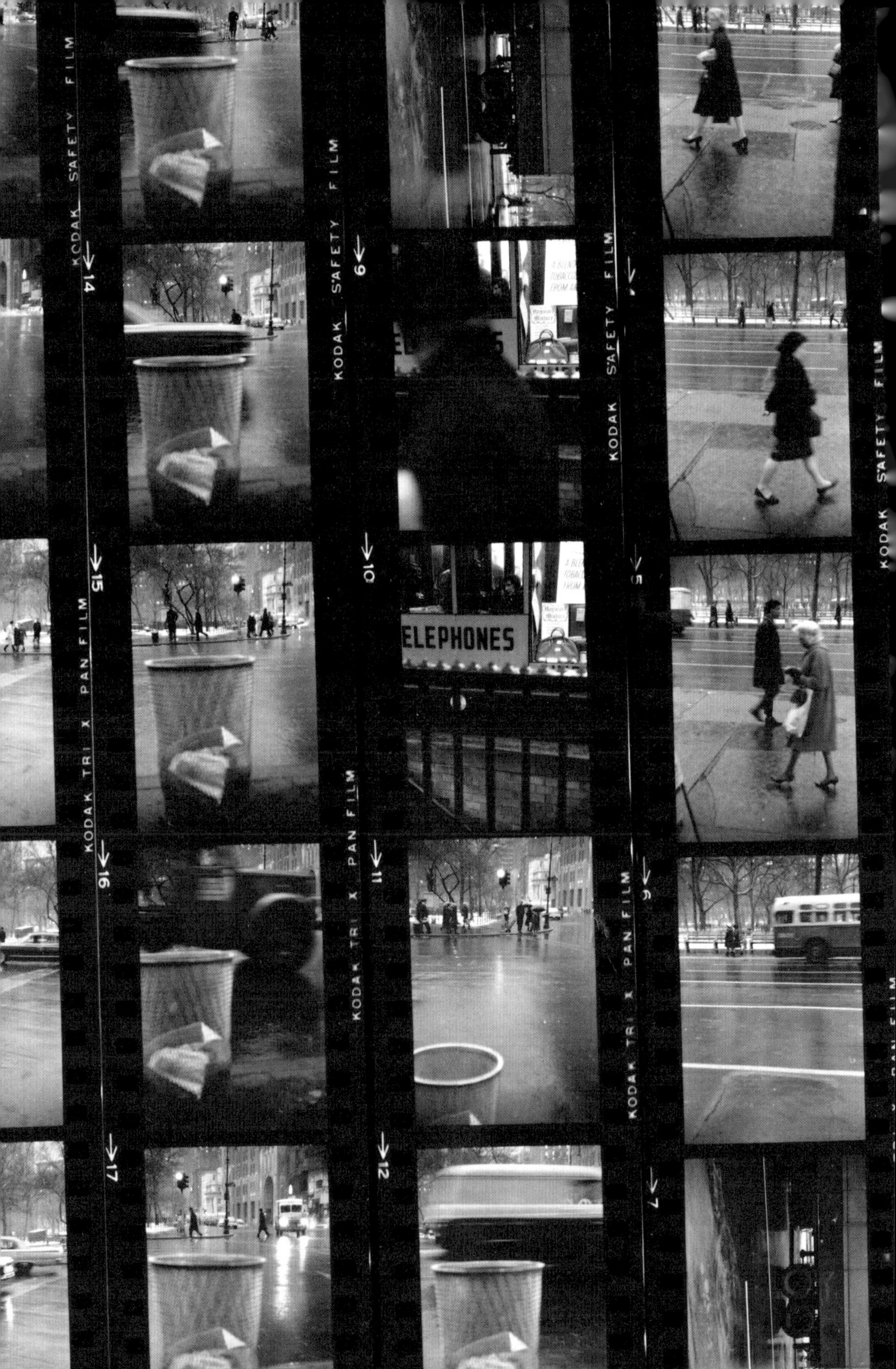
KODAK SAFETY FILM
KODAK SAFETY FILM
KODAK SAFETY FILM
KODAK SAFETY FILM
KODAK TRI X PAN FILM
KODAK TRI X PAN FILM
TELEPHONES

To be an important person involves a great deal of effort.
Quite often it's not worth it.

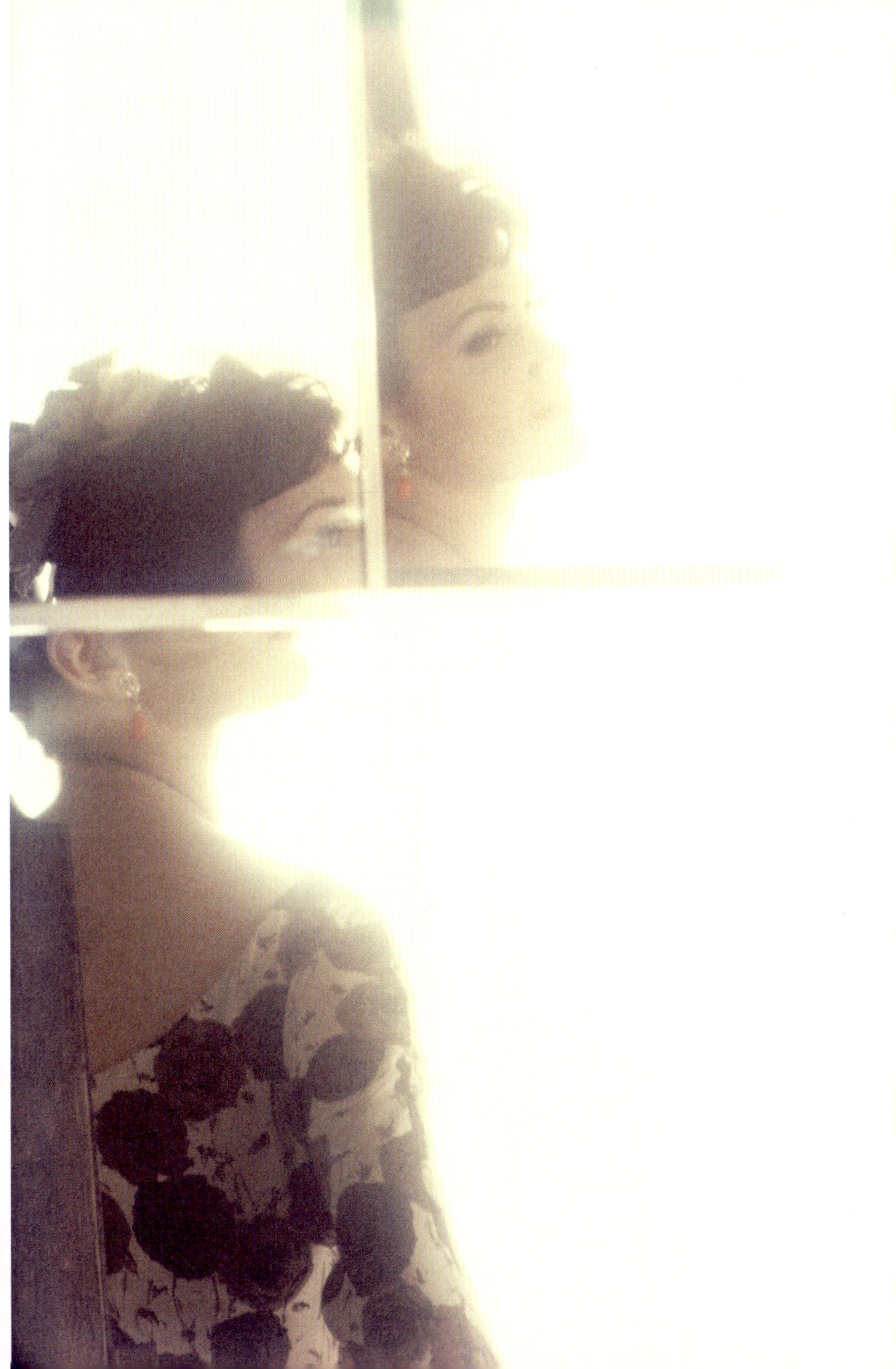

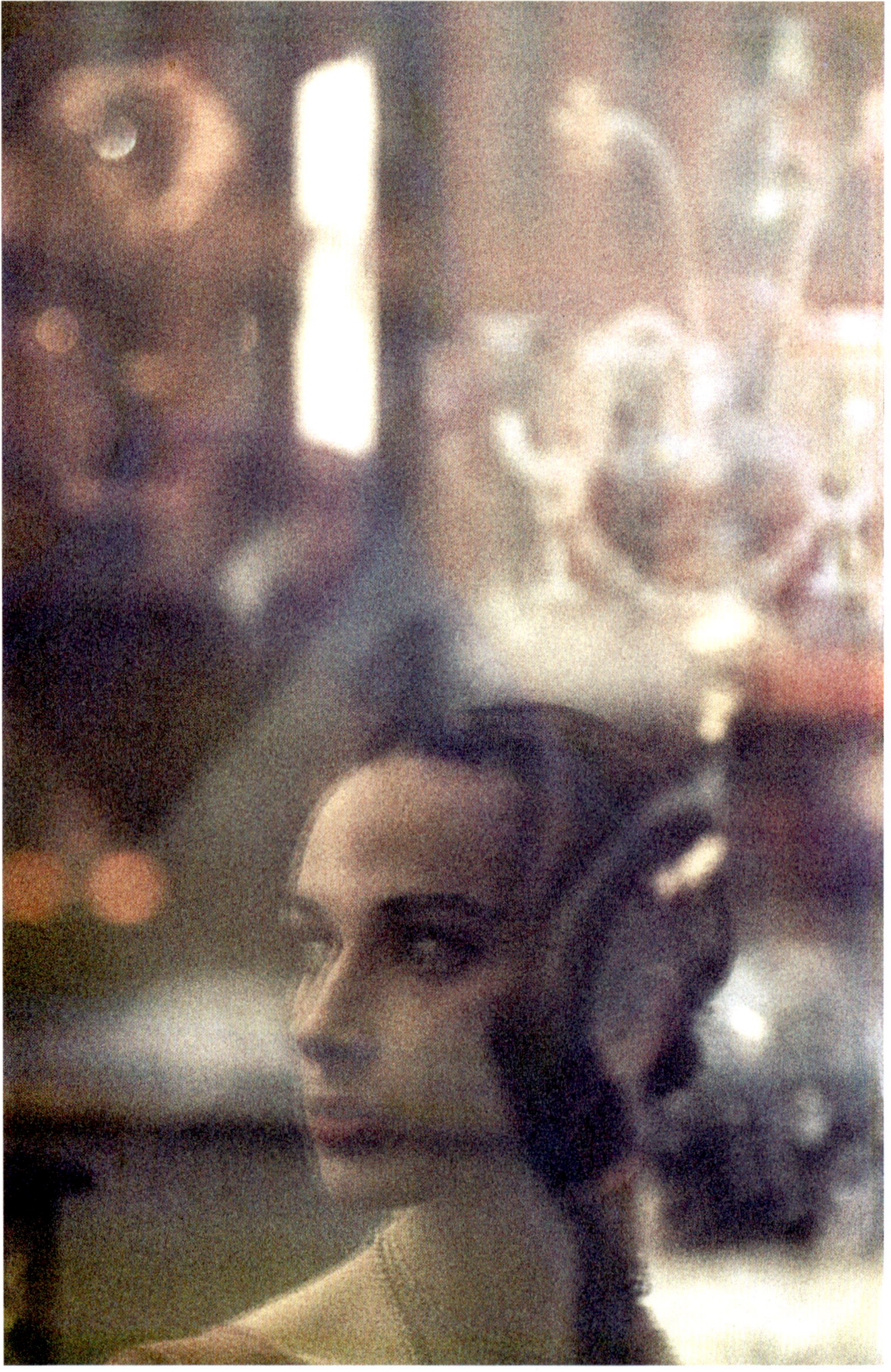

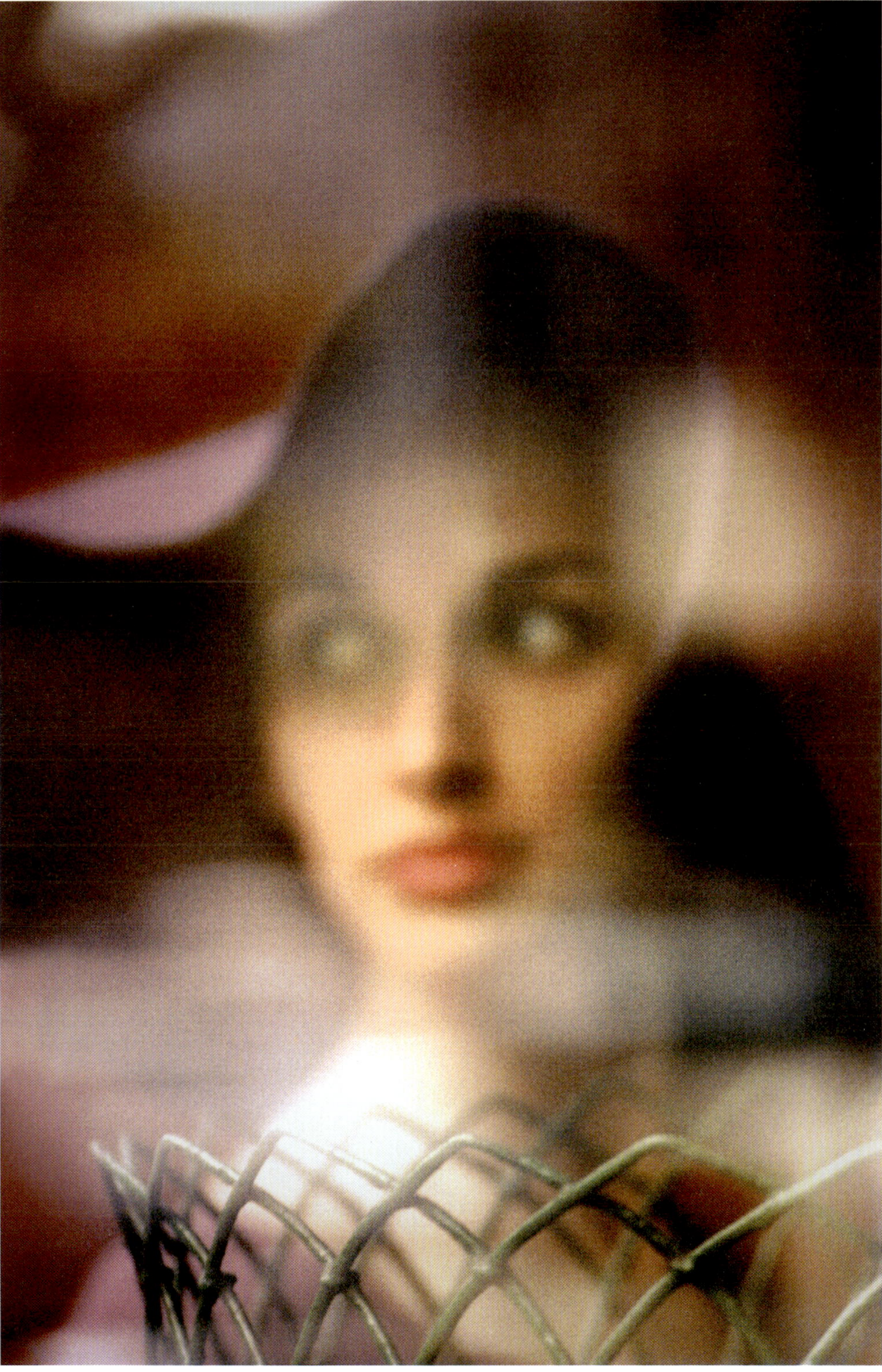

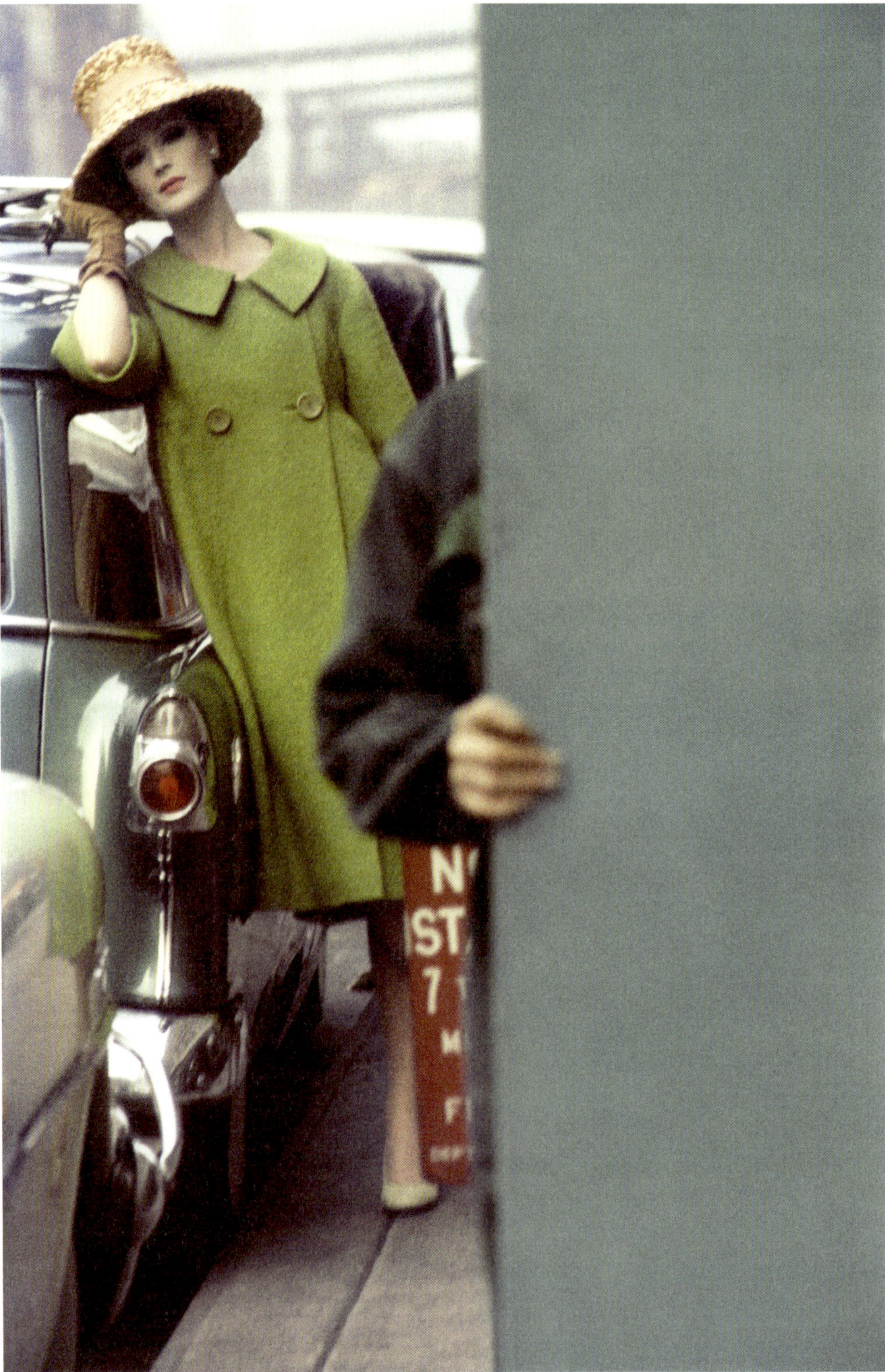

NO
STA
7 1
M
F

p. 46: Carol Brown, *Harper's Bazaar*, c. 1959
p. 47: Fashion Test, 1960s

Harper's Bazaar, February 1959

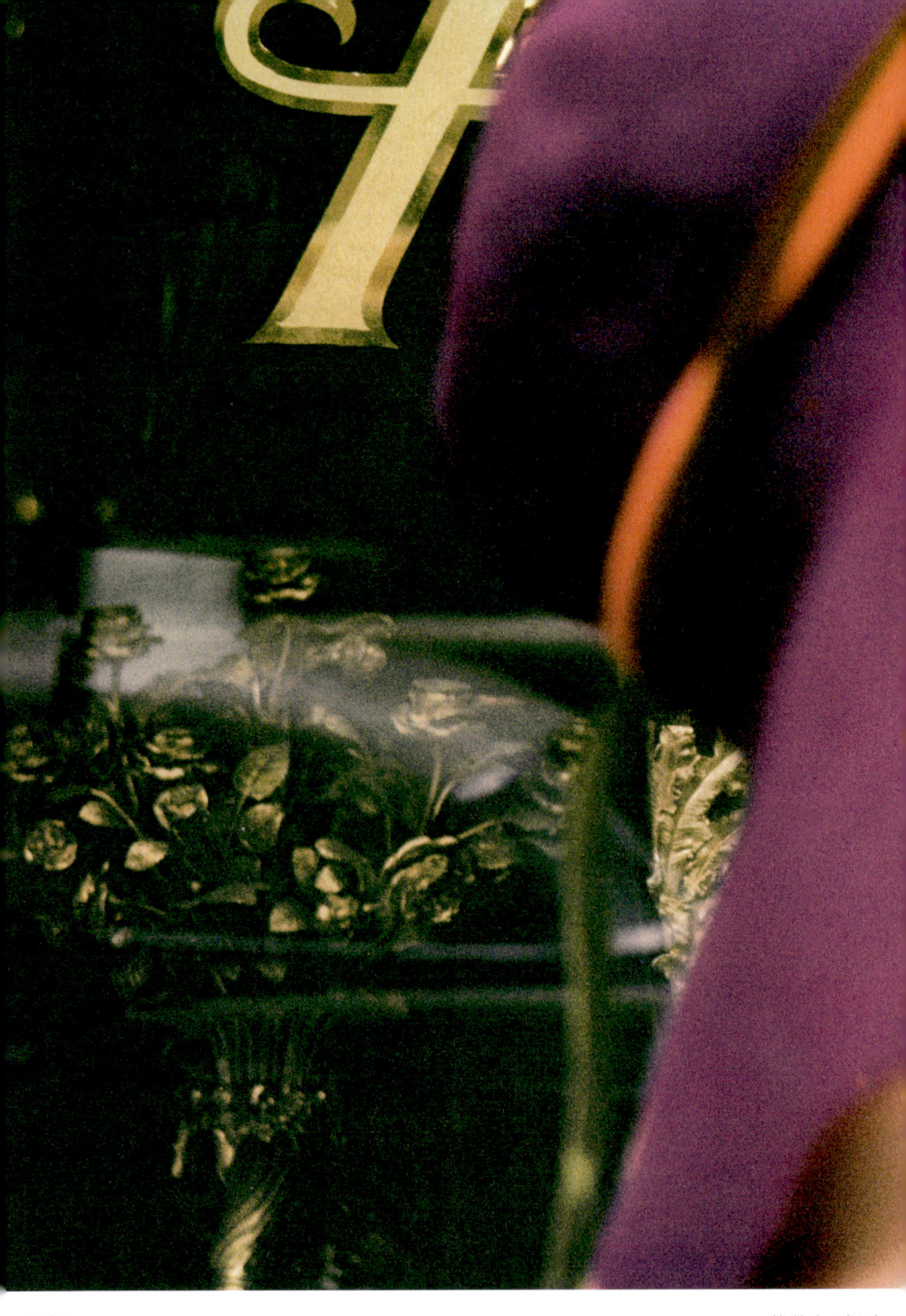

Untitled, undated

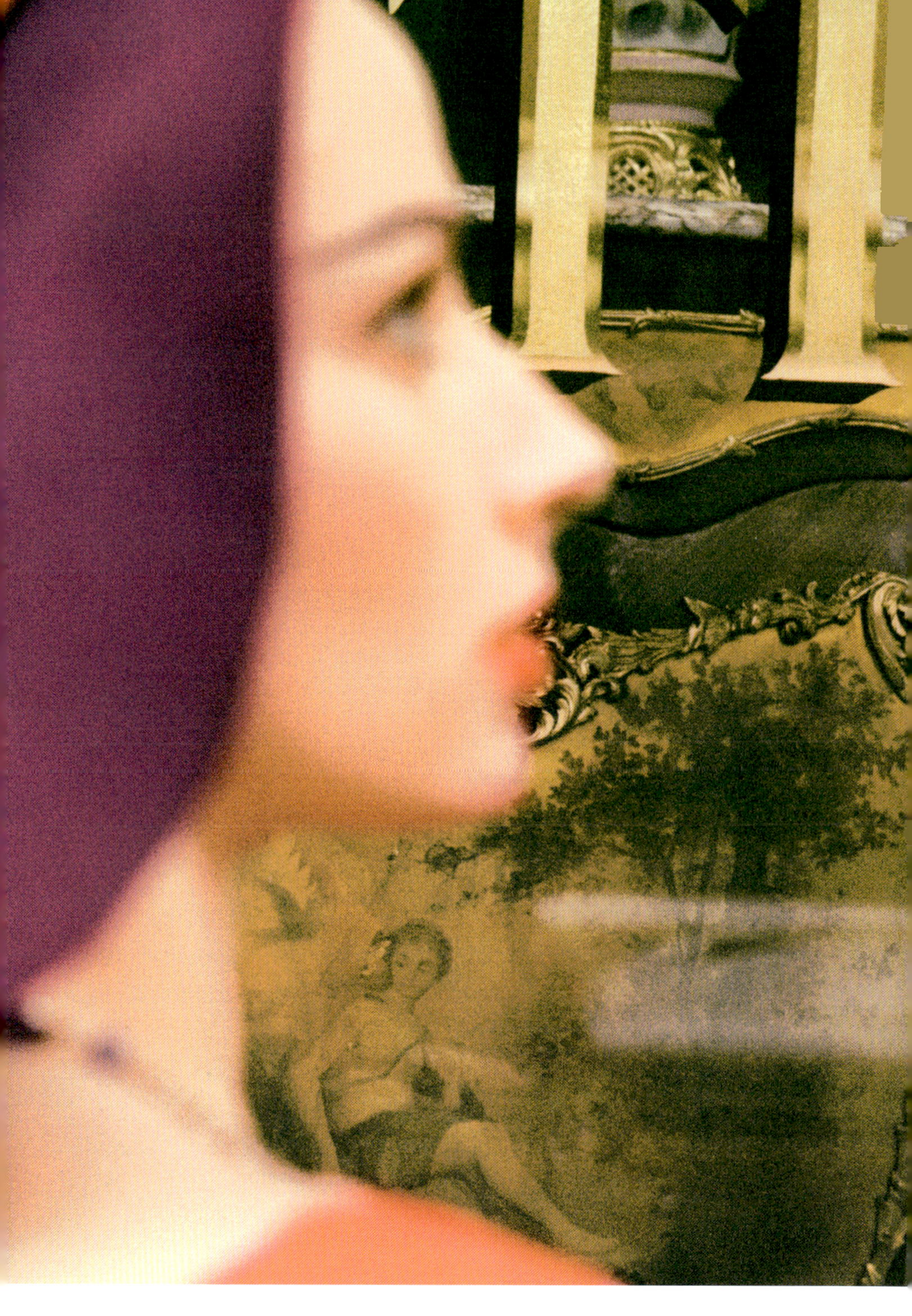

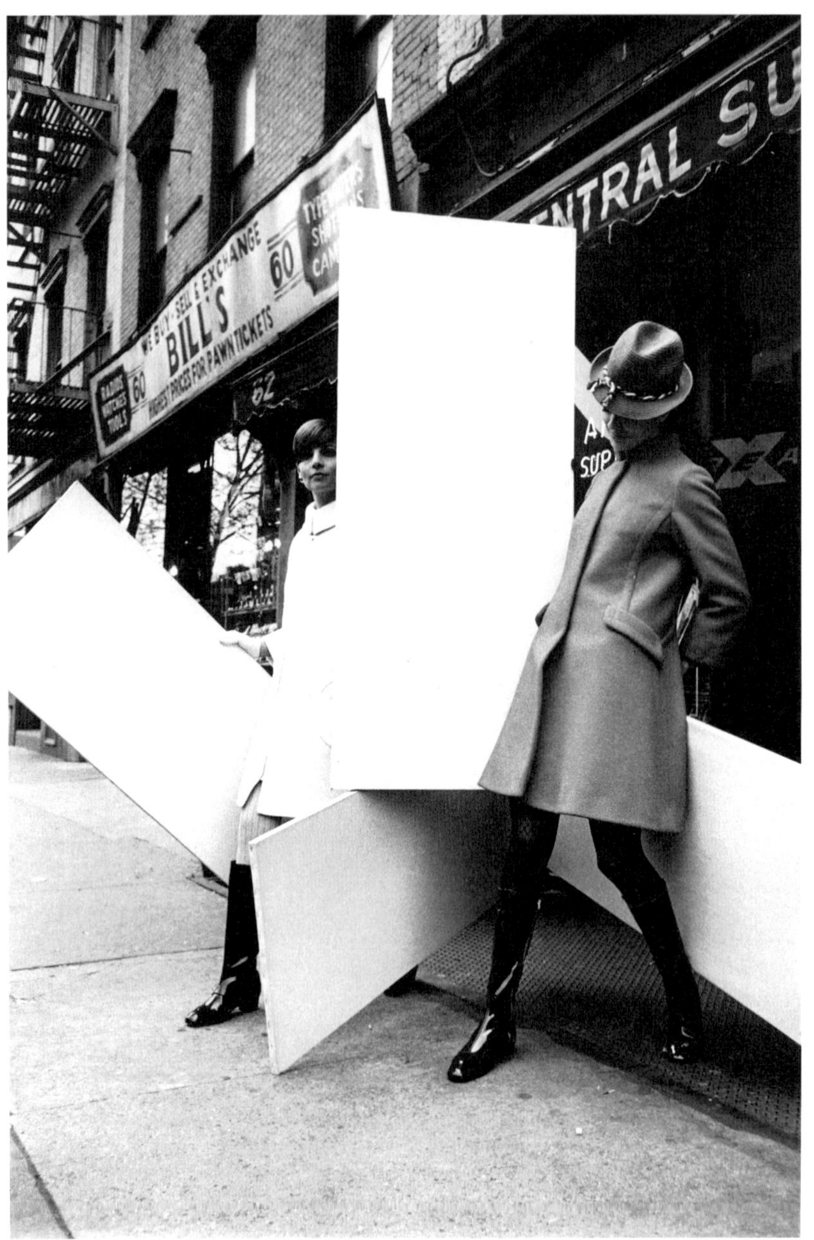

CENTRAL SU
BILL'S
WE BUY · SELL & EXCHANGE
HIGHEST PRICES FOR PAWN TICKETS
60
60
62

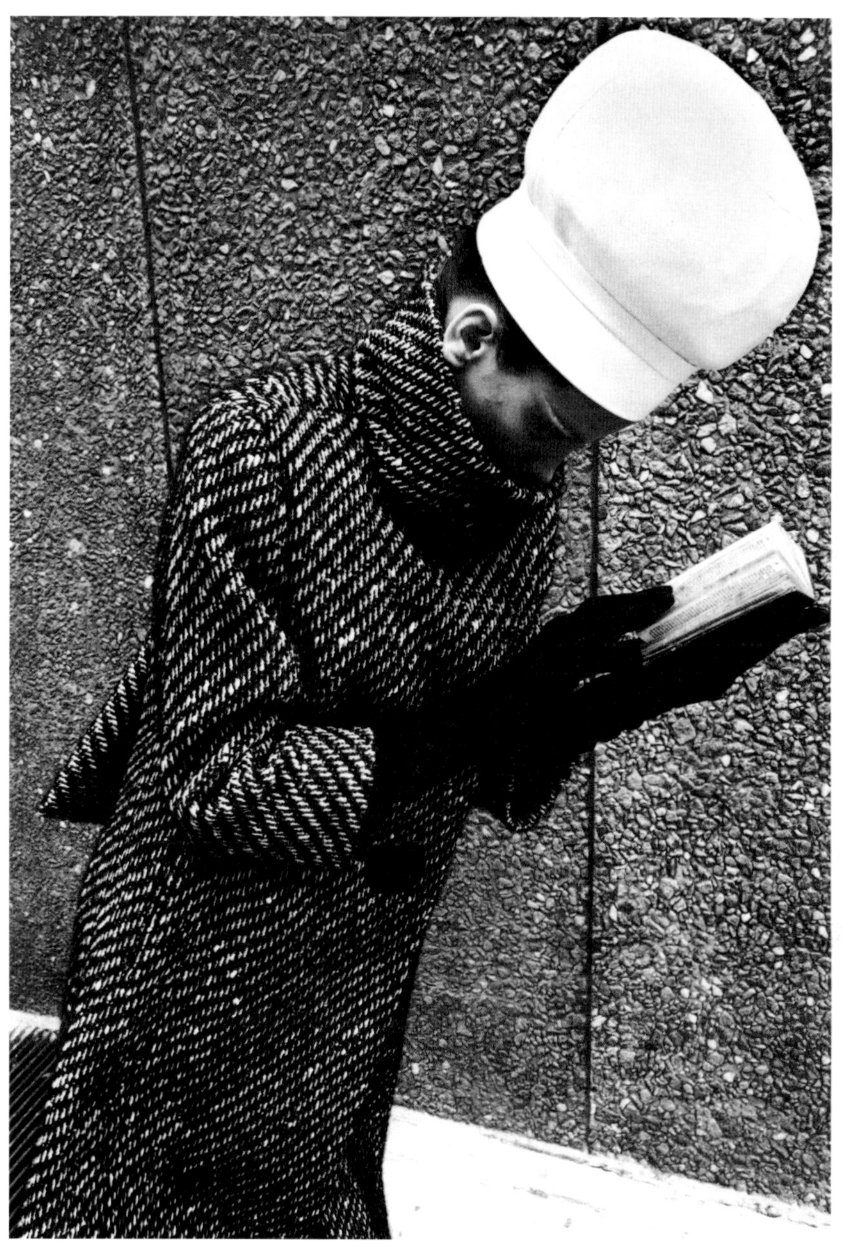

Harper's Bazaar, c. 1960

I have a great regard for certain notions of beauty even though to some,
it is an old-fashioned idea.
I do not think that misery is more profound than happiness.

Harper's Bazaar, c. 1960

p. 56: Contact sheet, undated
p. 57: Contact sheet, undated

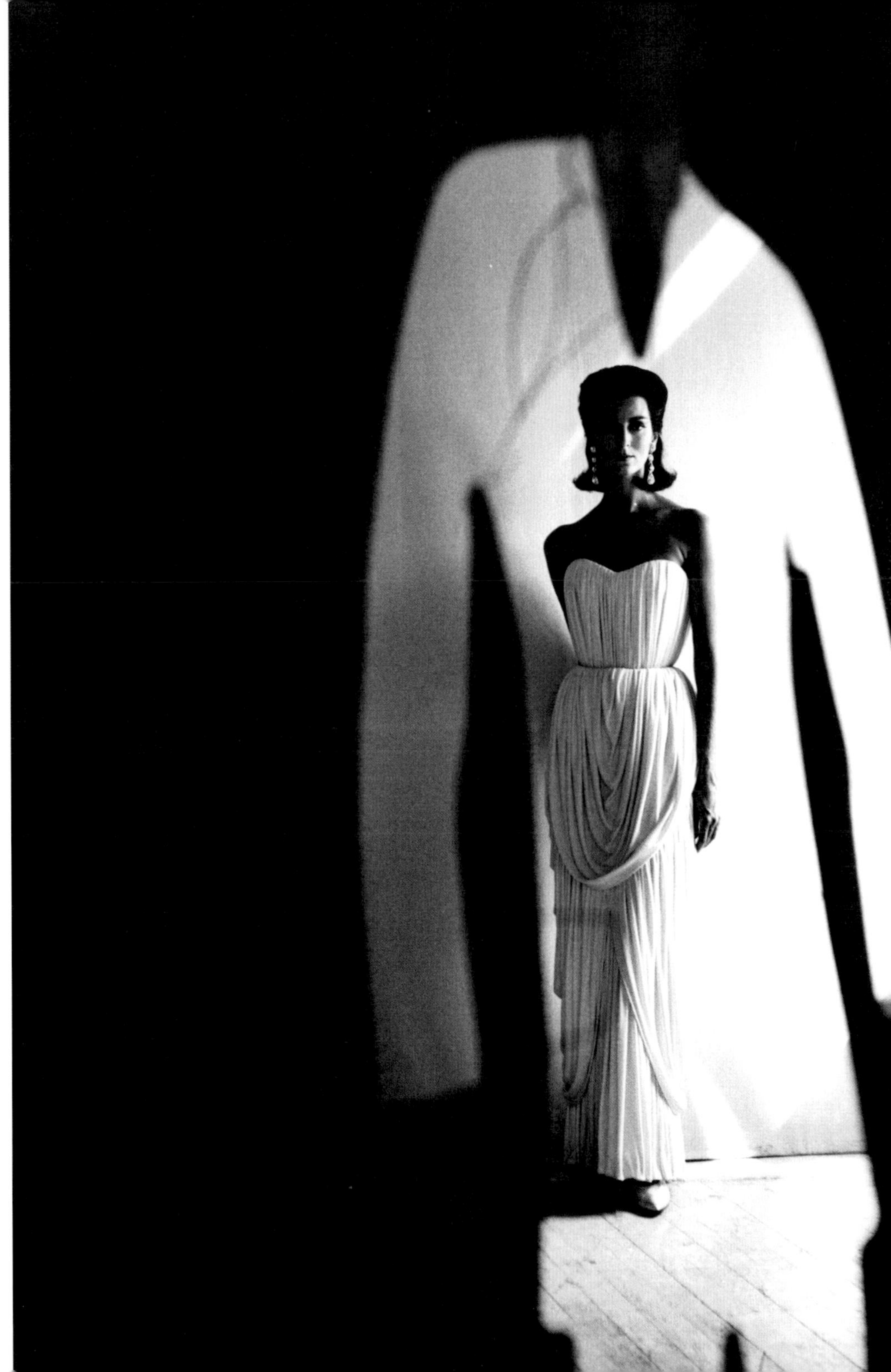

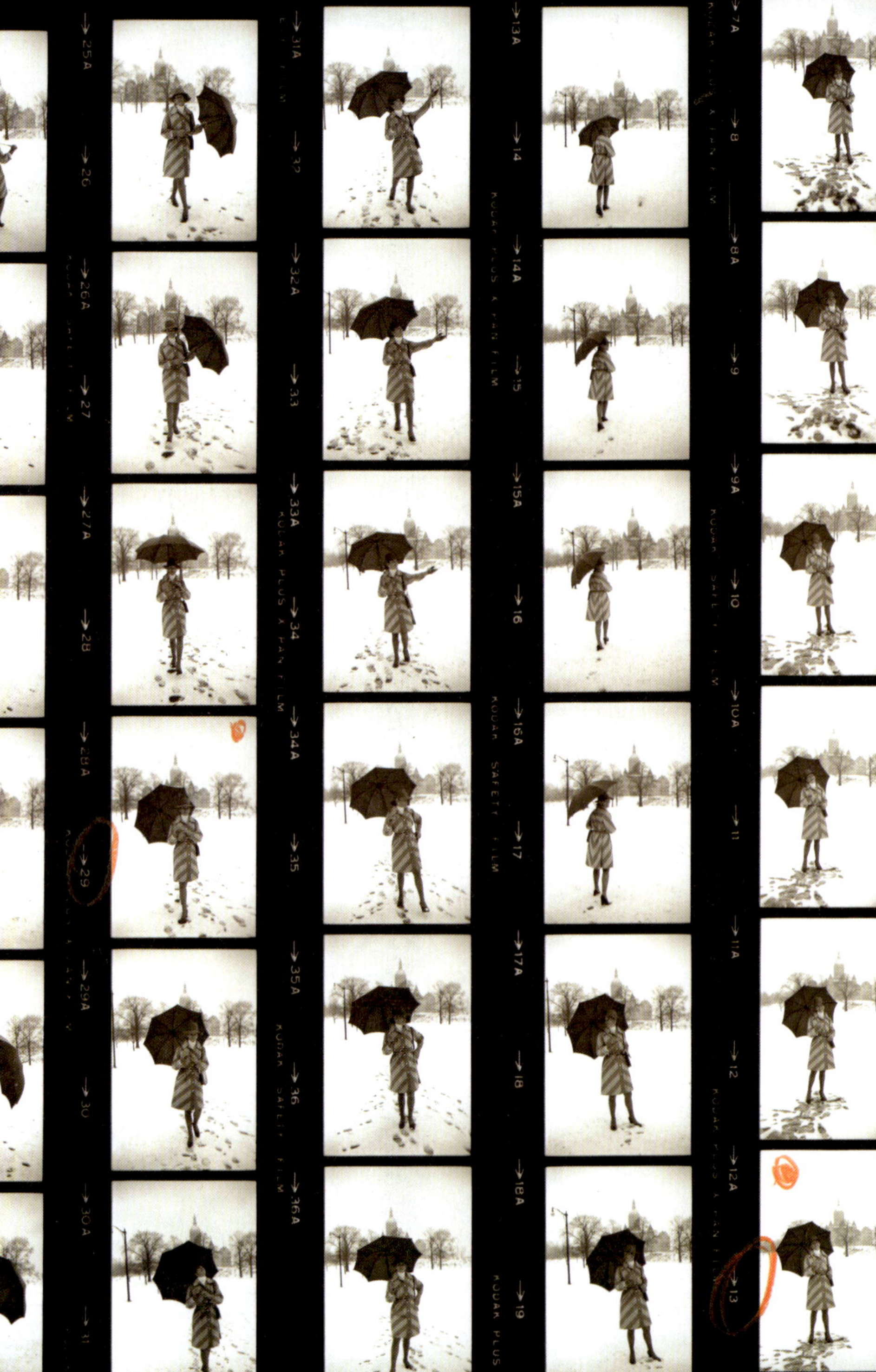

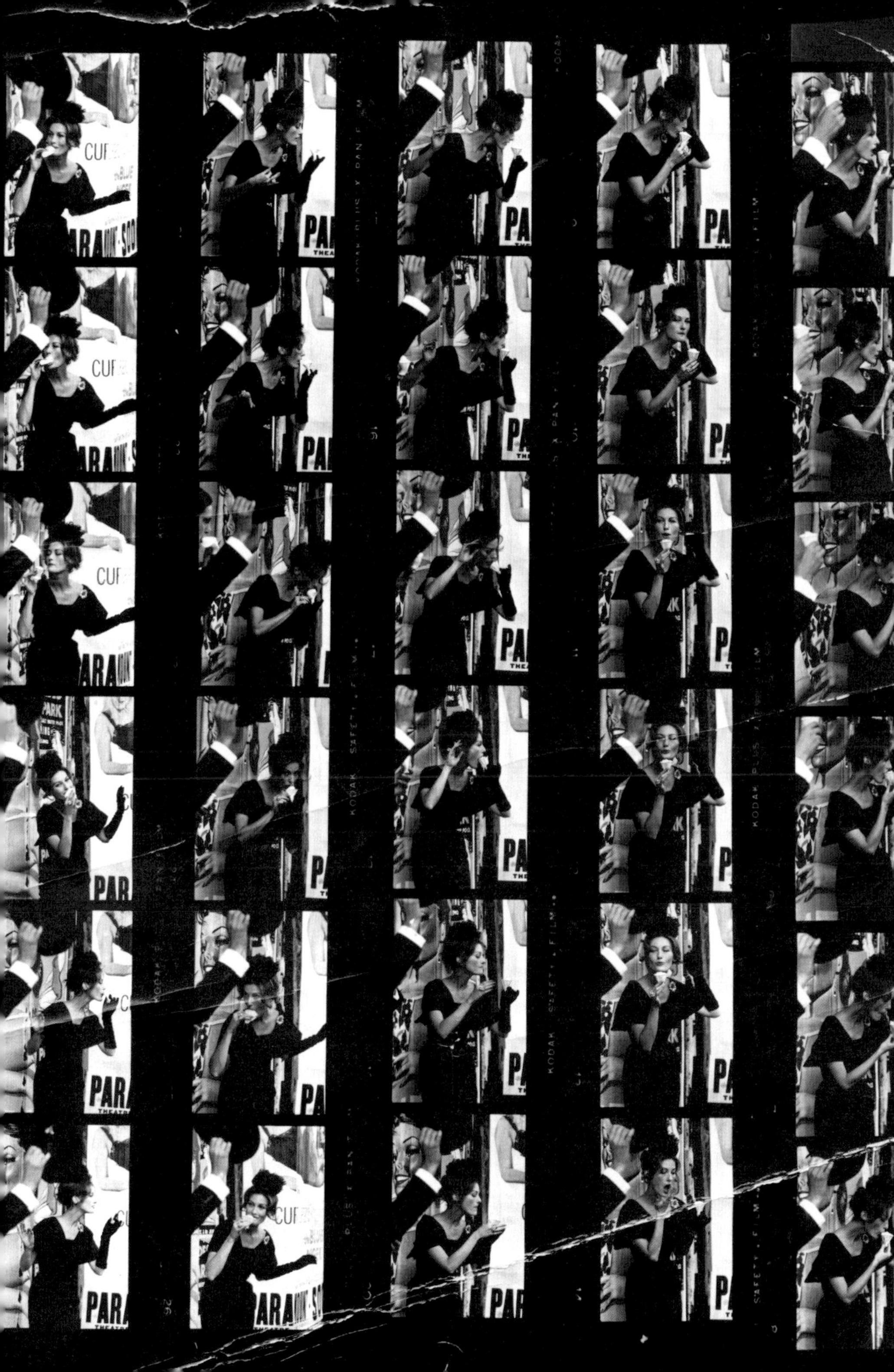

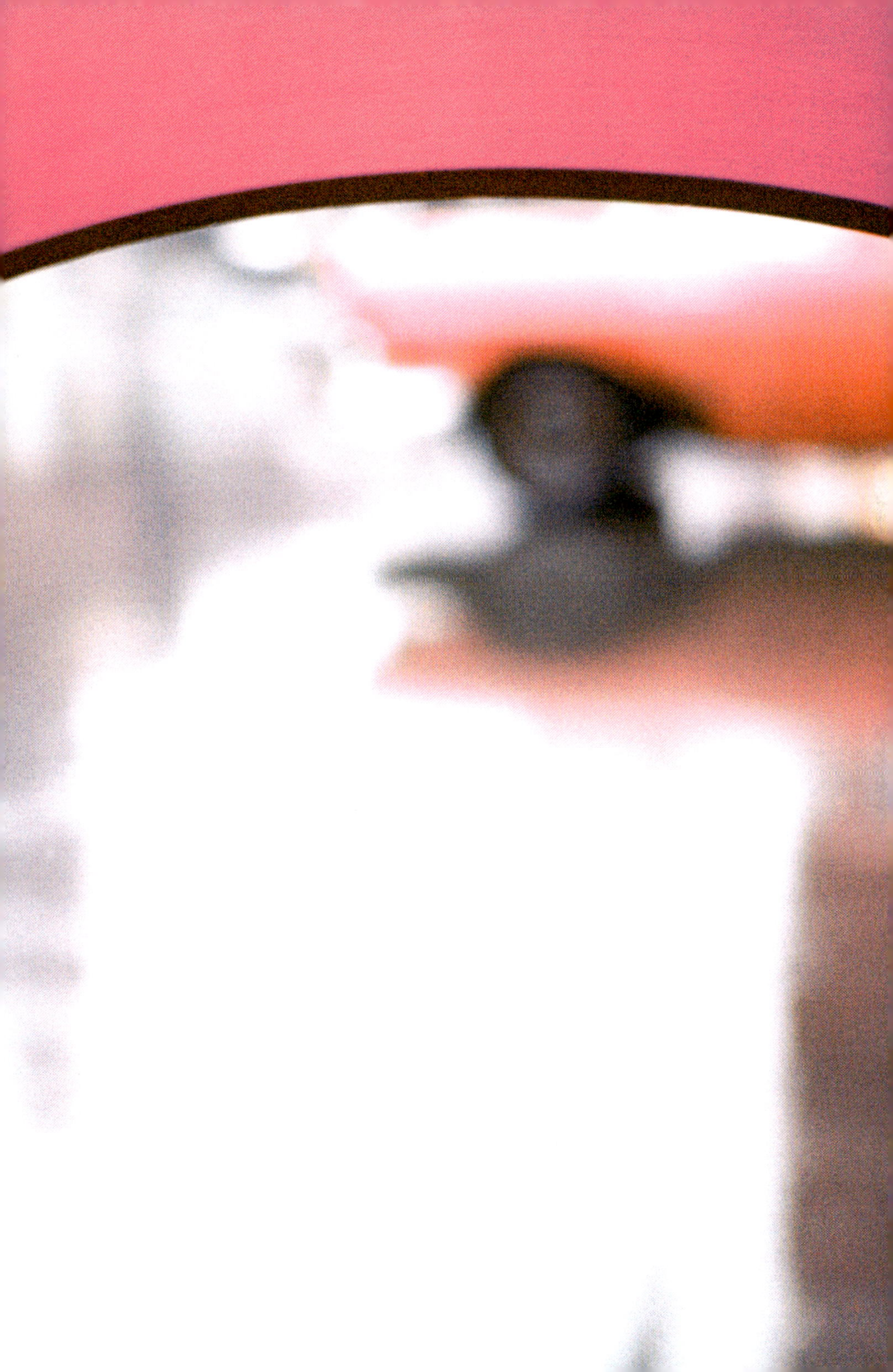

pp. 58–59: Purple Umbrella, 1950s

Some of the good work that I did, I did right in my own neighborhood.
The street is like a ballet.
You never know what is going to happen.

Cap, c. 1960

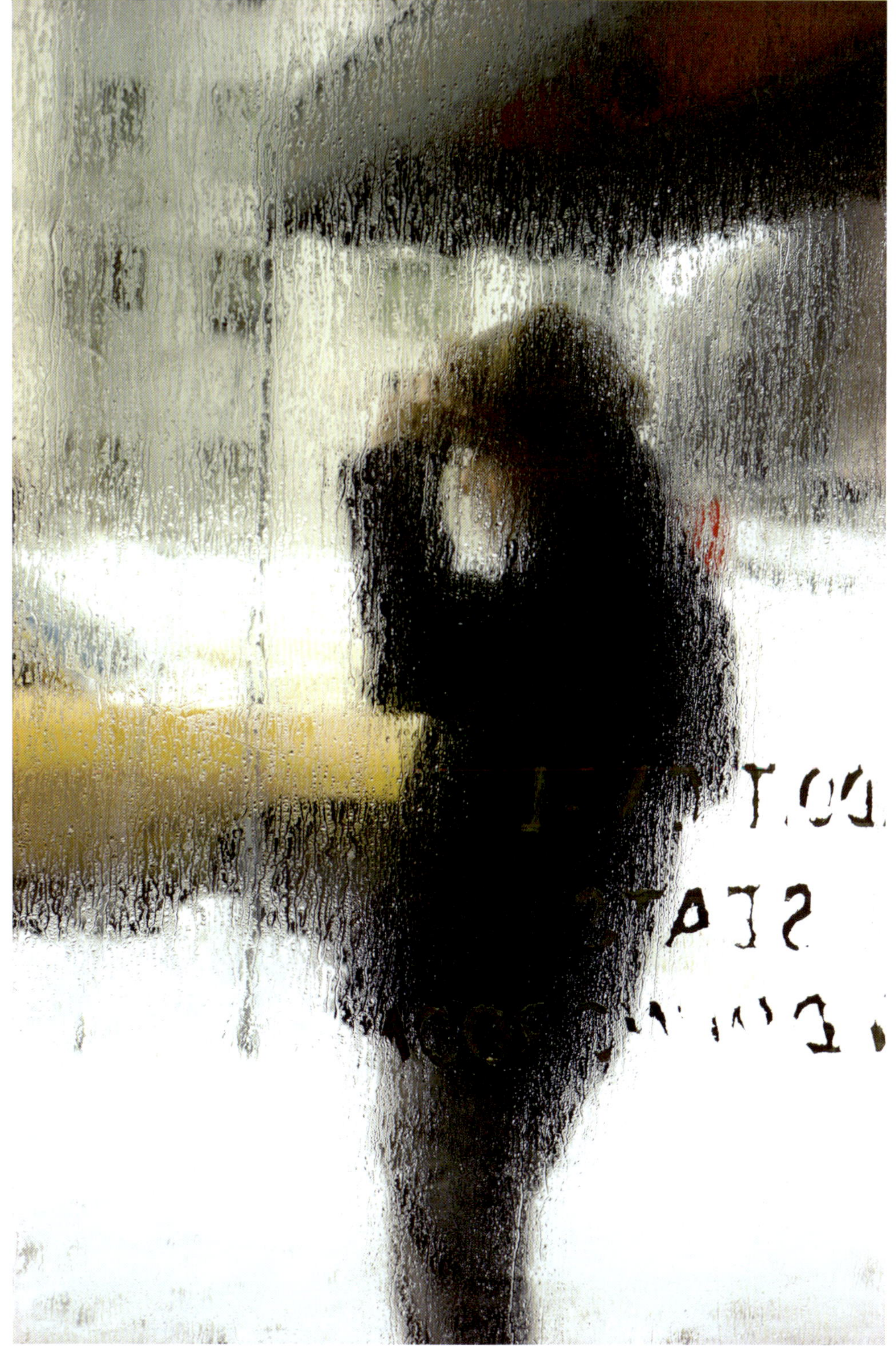

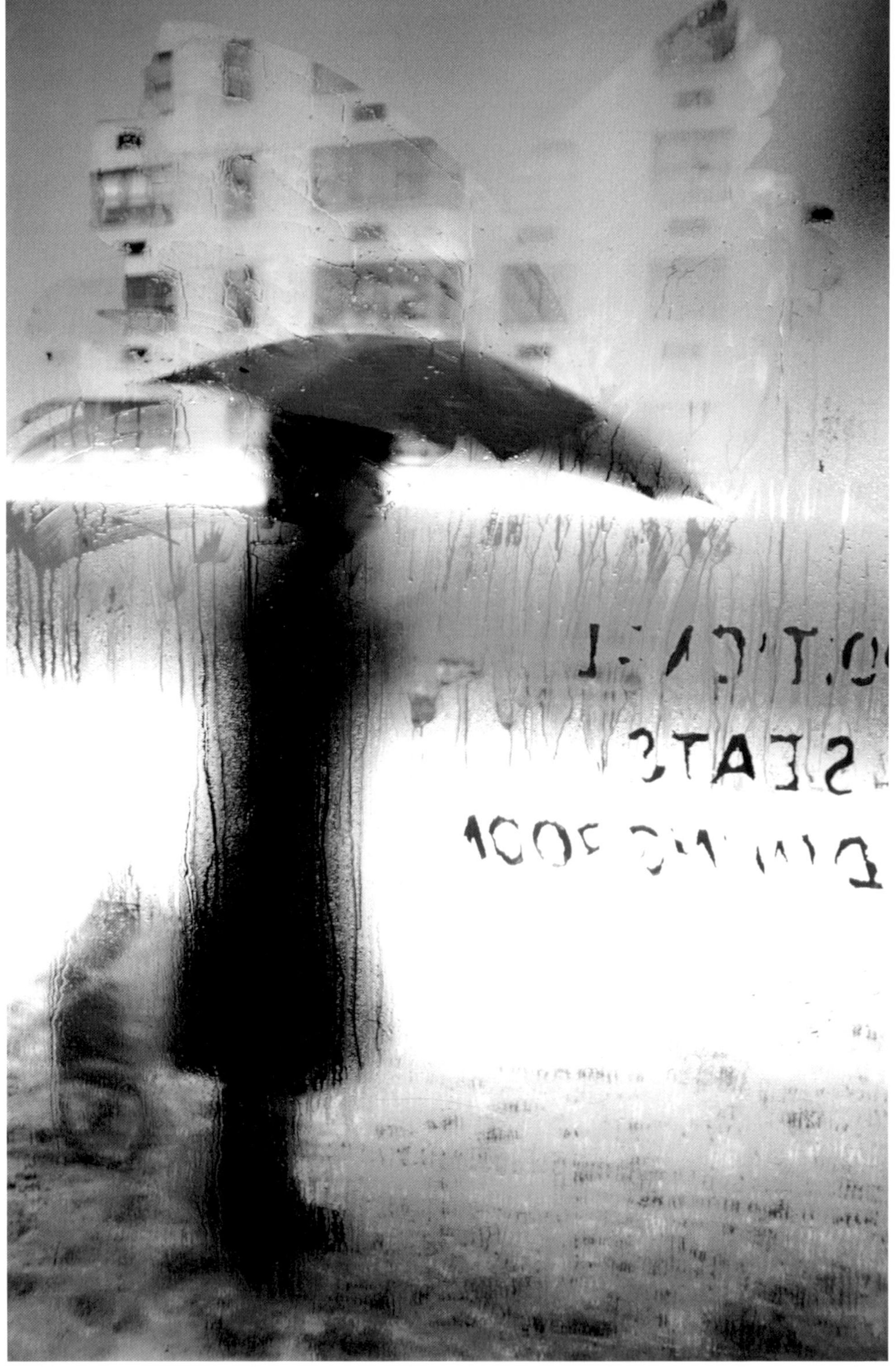

Snow, 1970

When I look at certain things, I find them attractive or interesting or beautiful, and I take pictures.
Sometimes they're good, sometimes they're not so good…

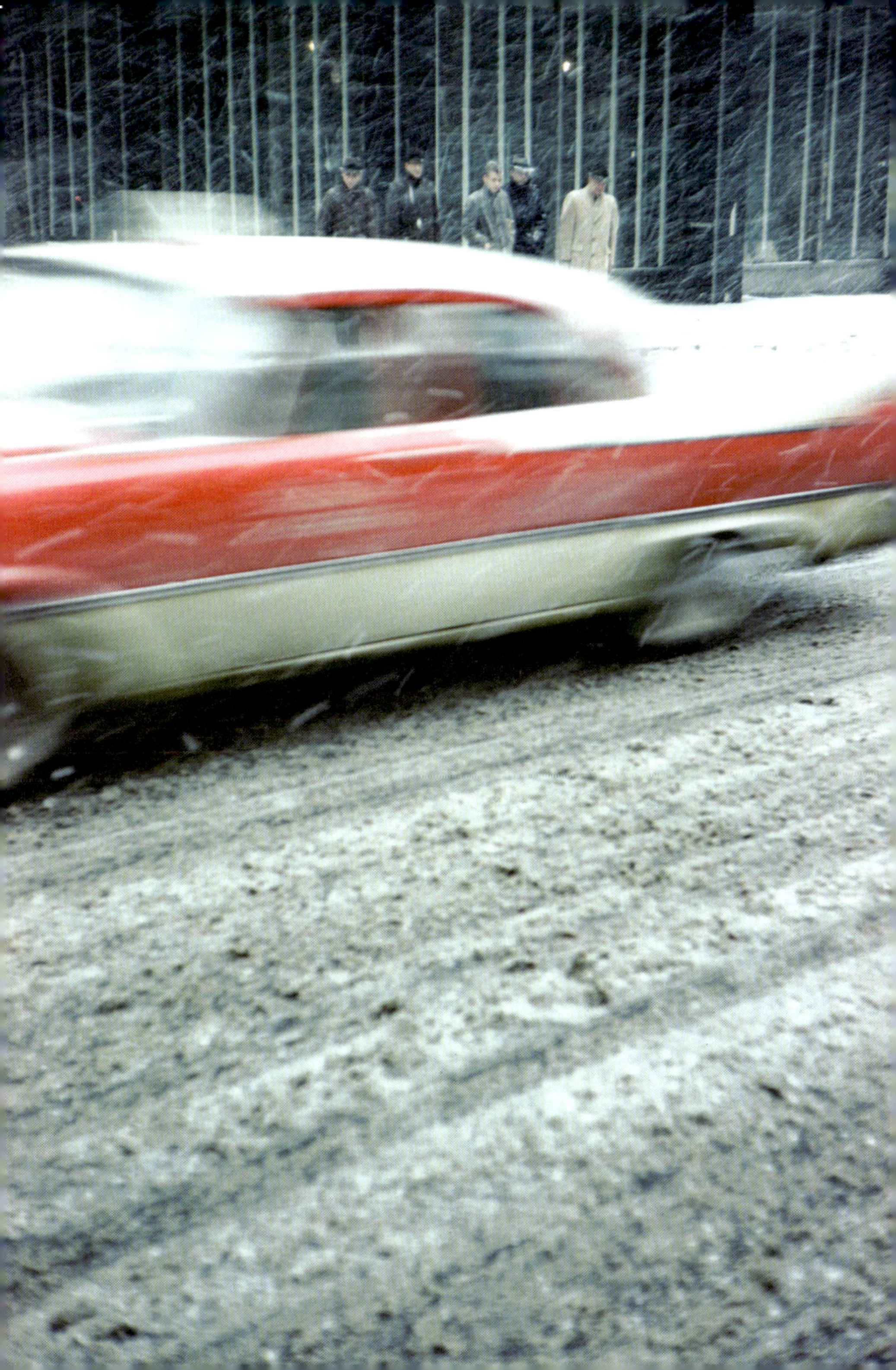

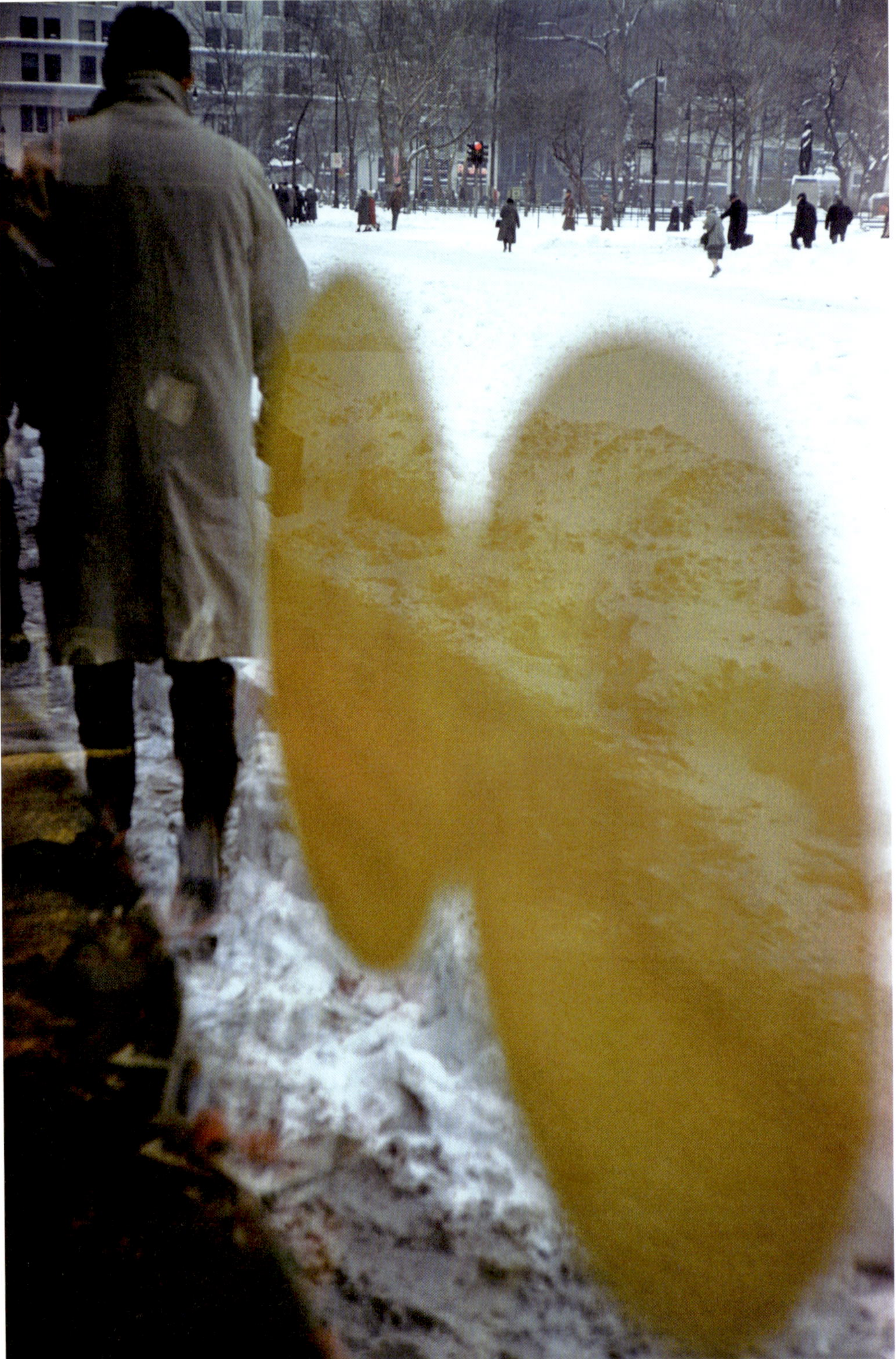

My life is full of unused opportunities.

Just a few days ago I found a letter that I had slipped into a book.

It remained there for about thirty years.

I opened it—it was an invitation to participate in an exhibition.

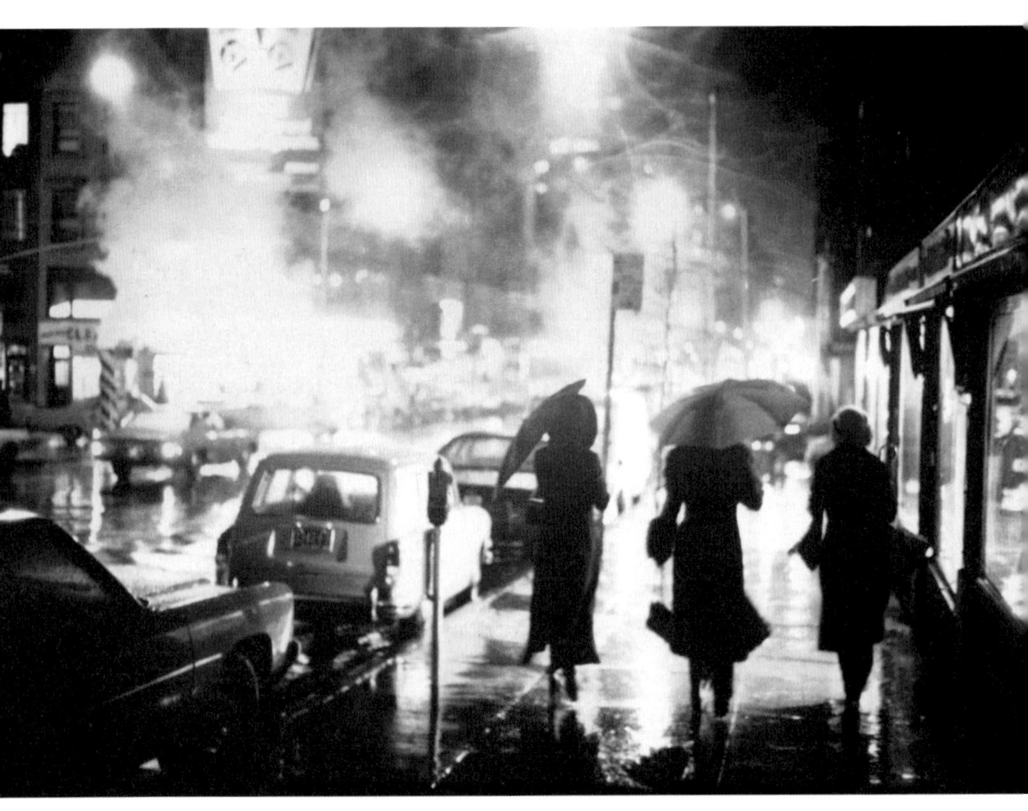

Untitled, undated

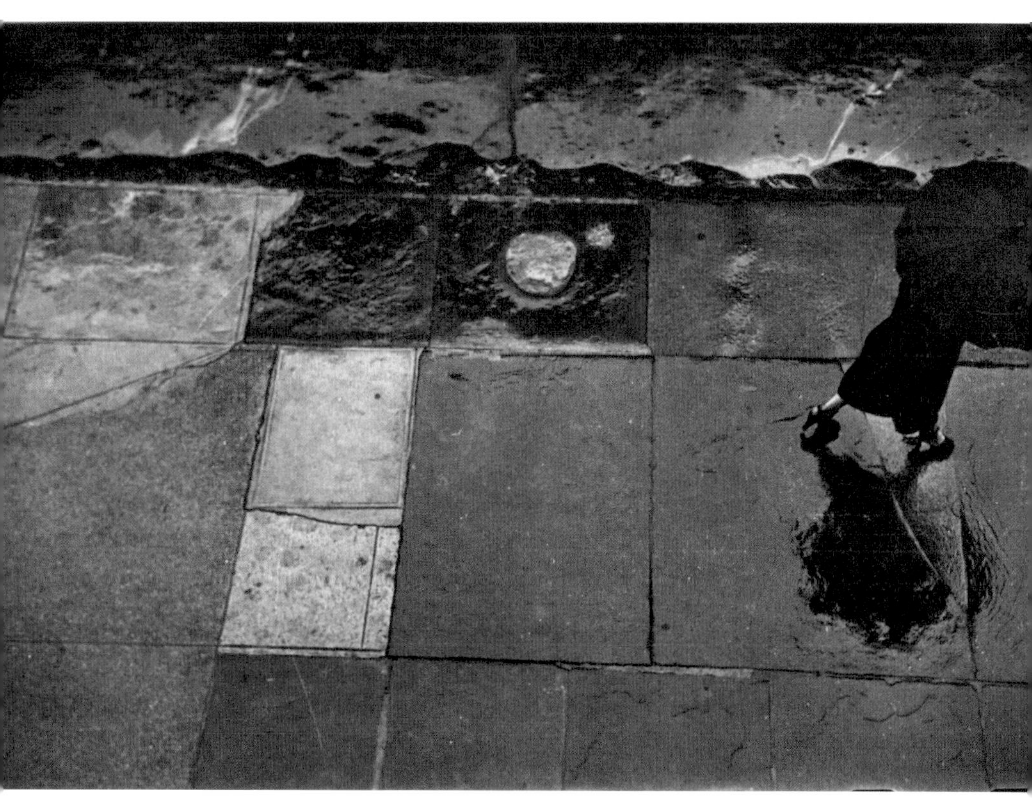

Untitled, 1950s

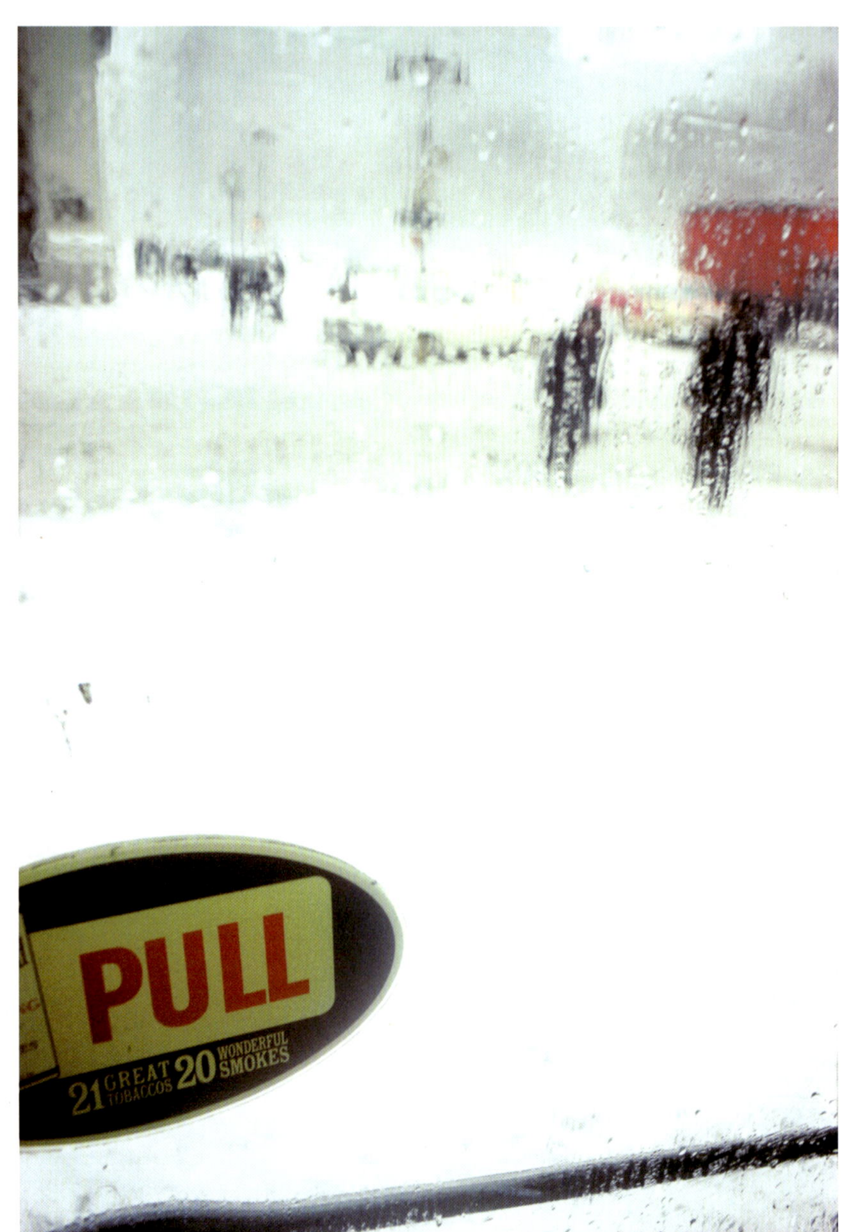

Pull, c. 1960

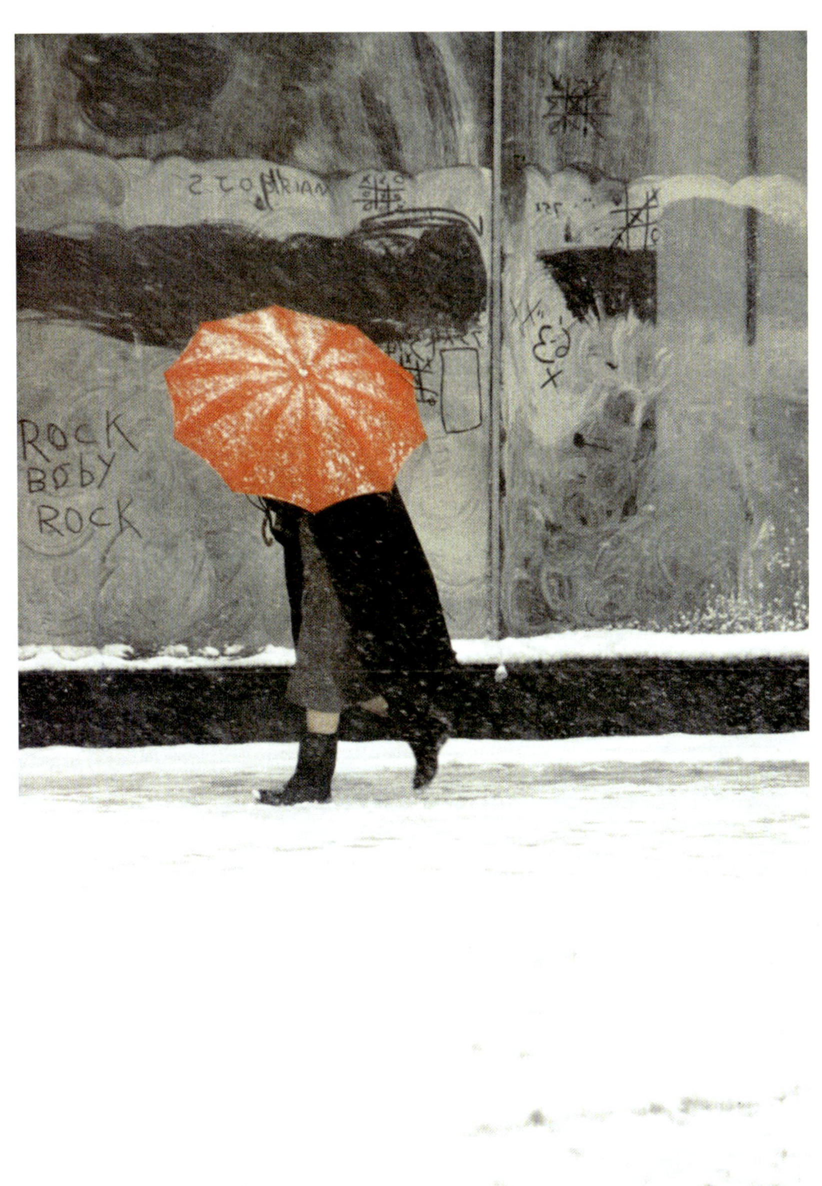

Red Umbrella, c. 1958

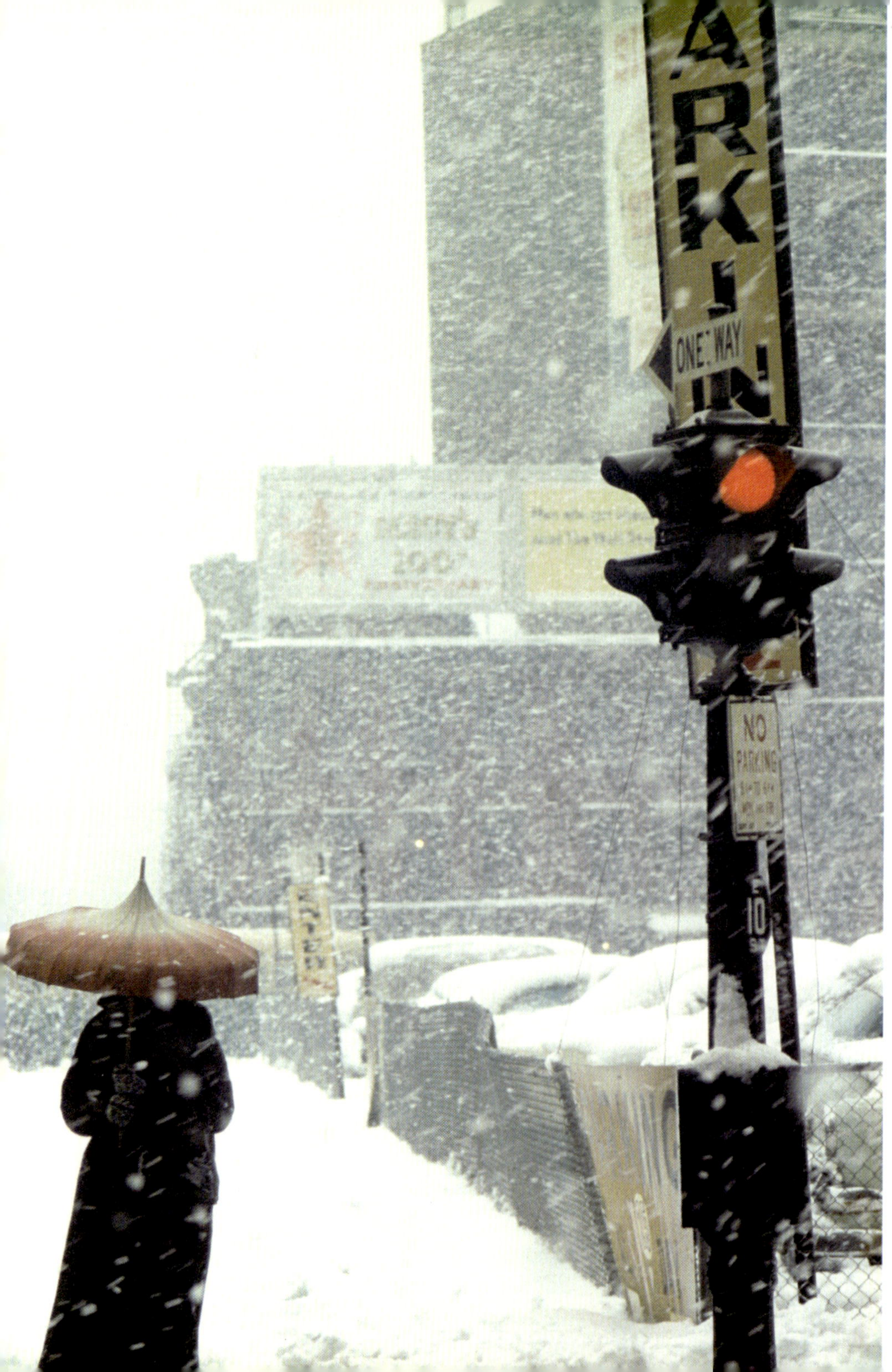

ARKIN
ONE WAY
NO PARKING

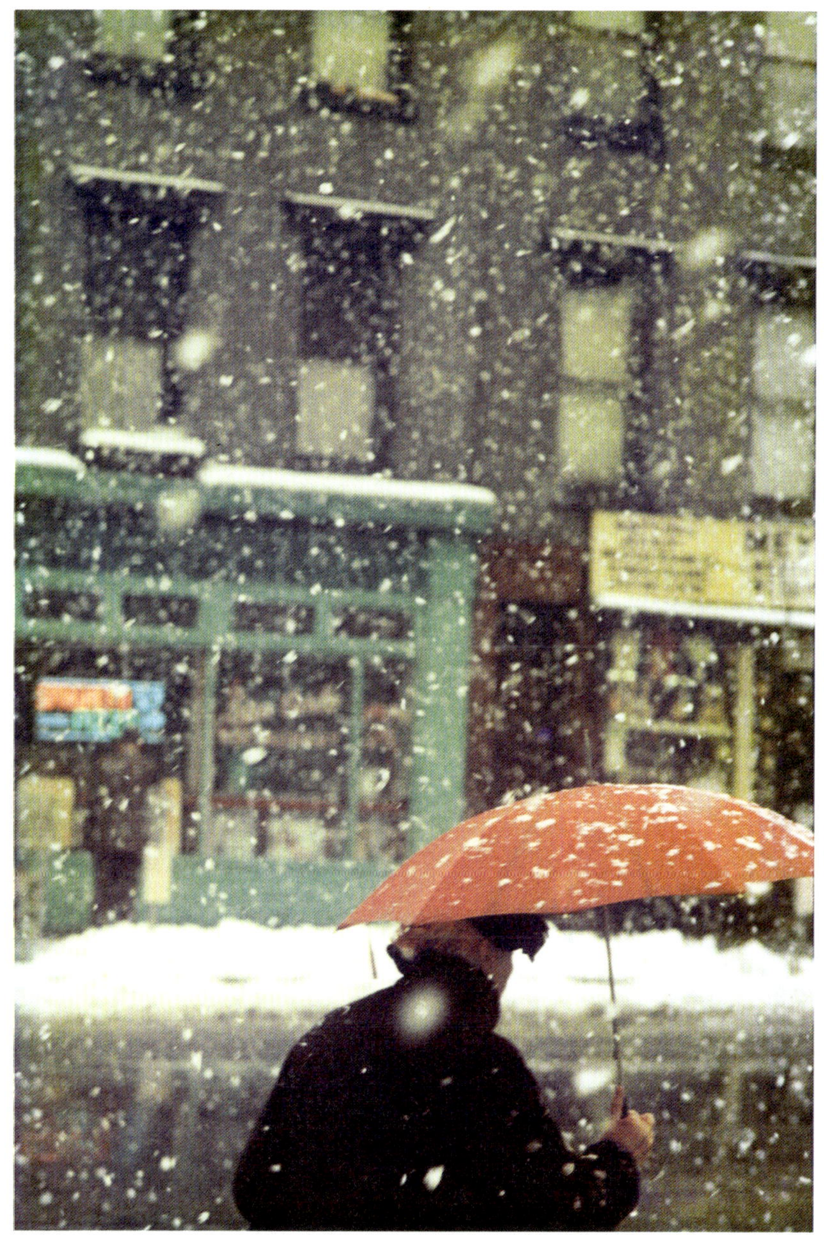

Parking, 1950s   Untitled, c. 1955

When you consider many of the things that people treat very seriously,
you realize that they don't deserve to be treated that seriously.
And many of the things that people worry about are not really worth worrying about.

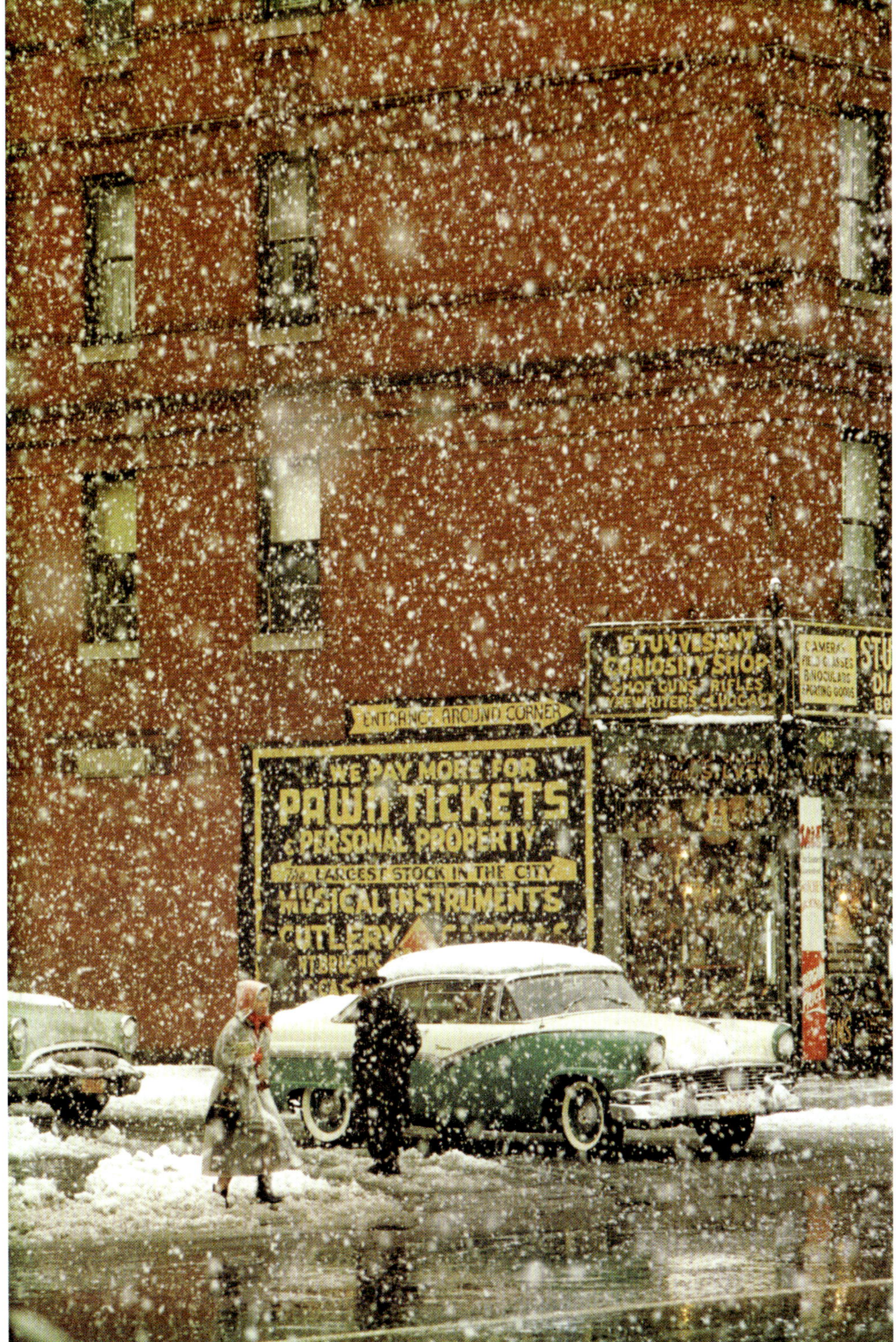

STUYVESANT
CURIOSITY SHOP
SHOT GUNS RIFLES
TYPEWRITERS LUGGAGE
CAMERAS
FIELD GLASSES
BINOCULARS
SPORTING GOODS
ENTRANCE AROUND CORNER
WE PAY MORE FOR
PAWN TICKETS
& PERSONAL PROPERTY
LARGEST STOCK IN THE CITY
MUSICAL INSTRUMENTS
CUTLERY

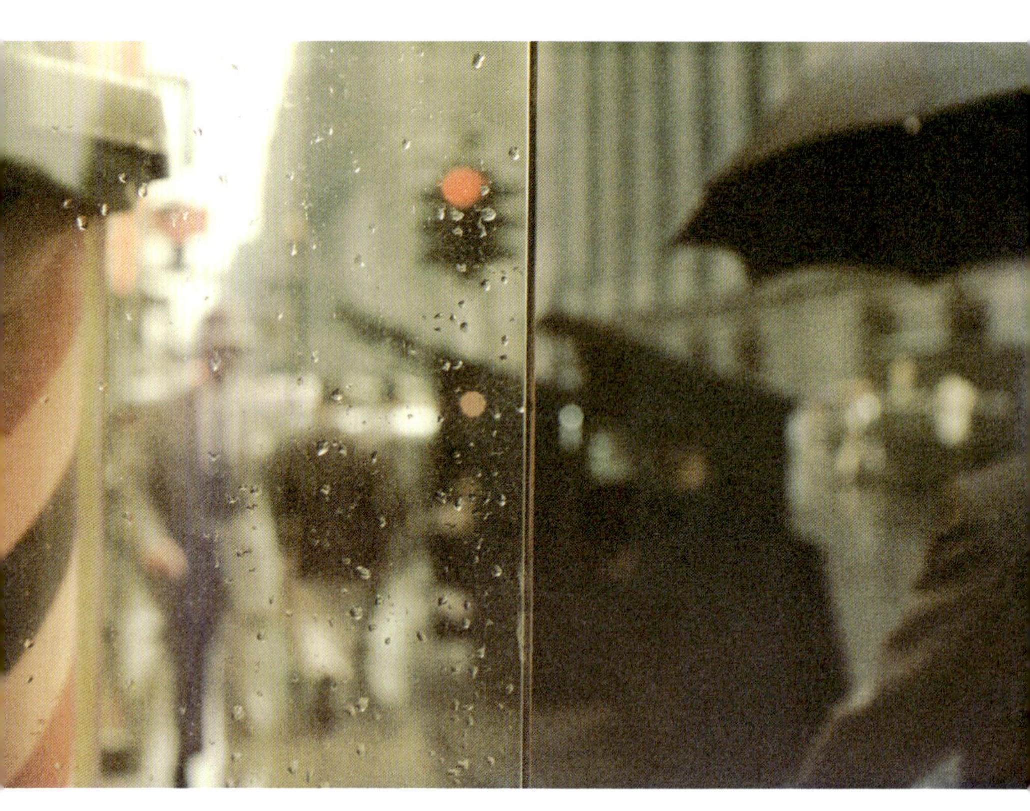

Untitled, 1950s

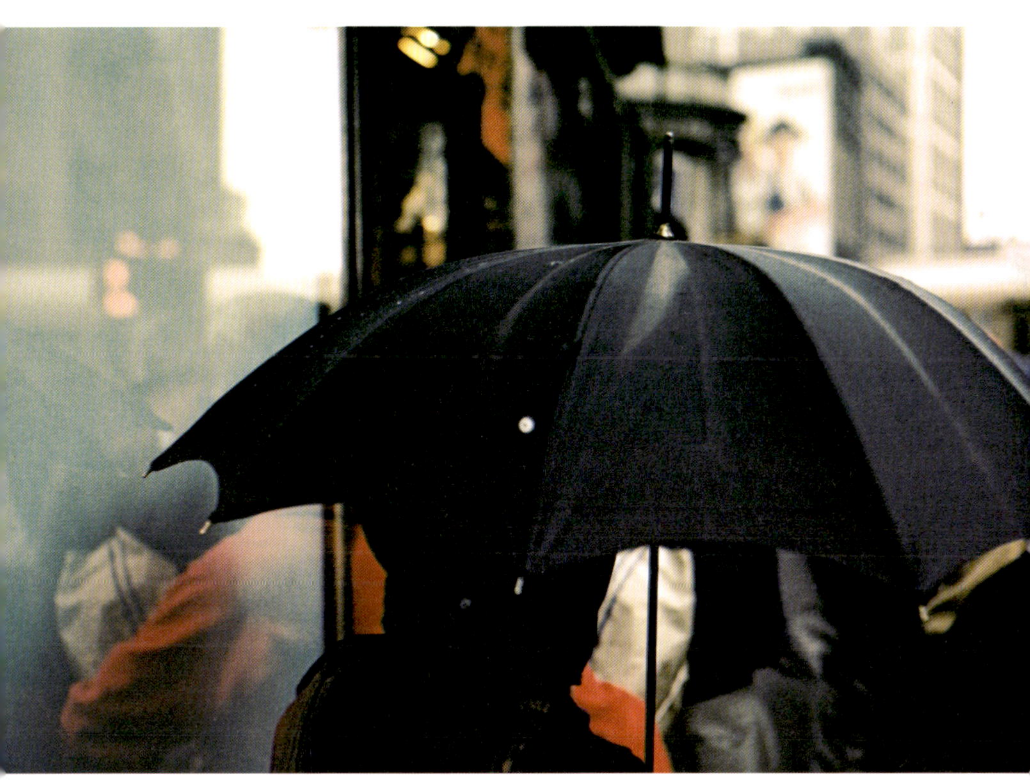

Umbrella, c. 1950

When I did photography, I wasn't thinking of painting.
Photography is about finding things, and painting is different:
It's about making something.

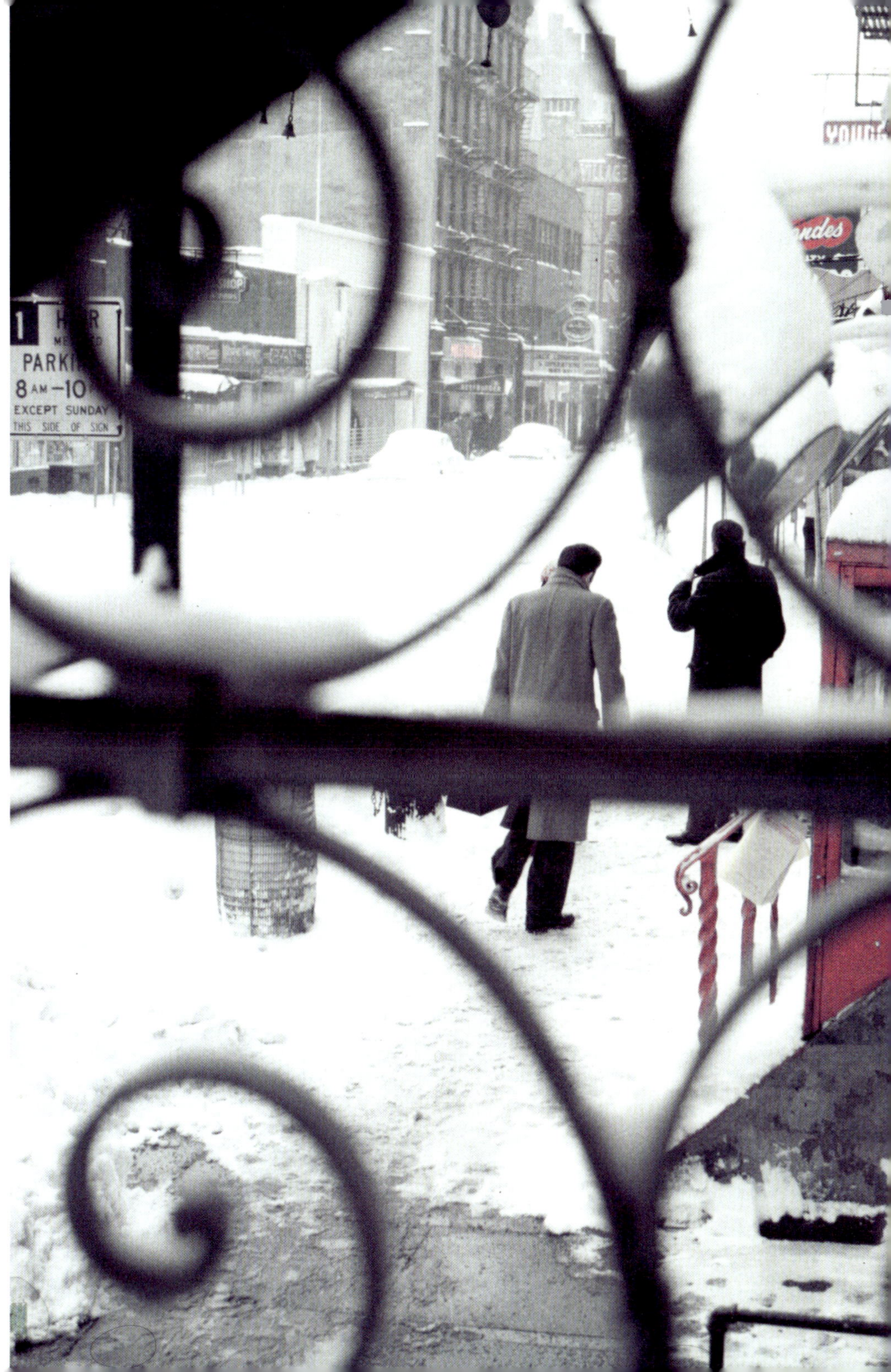

1 HOUR
METERED
PARKING
8 AM — 10
EXCEPT SUNDAY
THIS SIDE OF SIGN

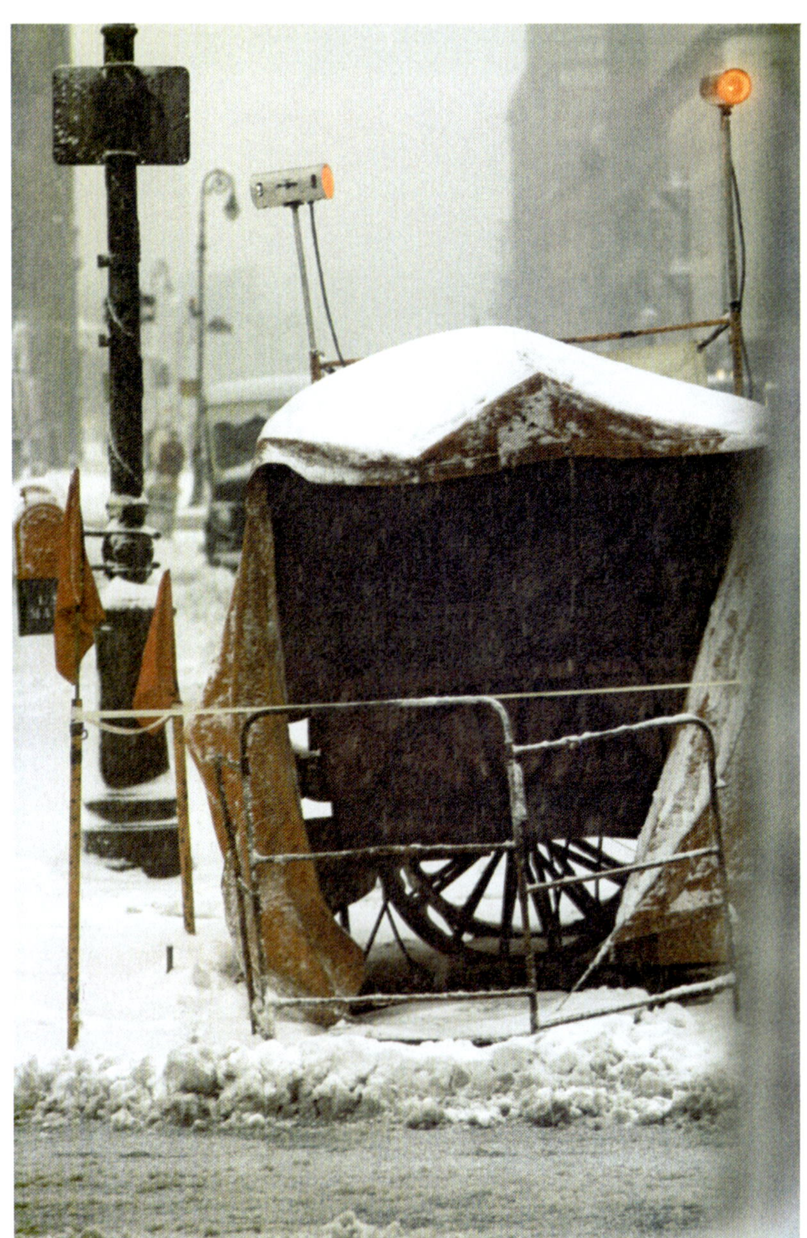

Red Lights, 1957   Untitled, 1950s

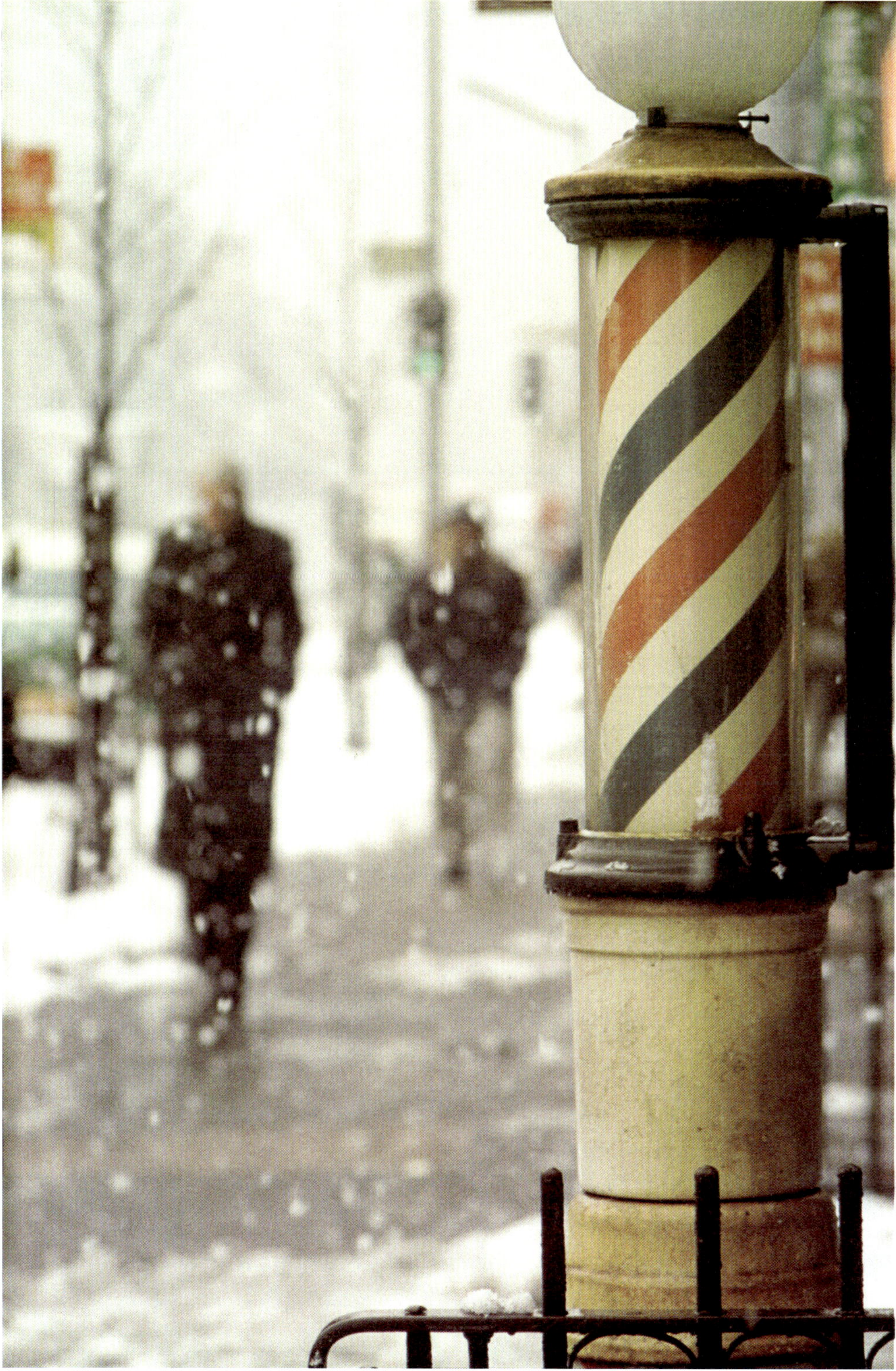

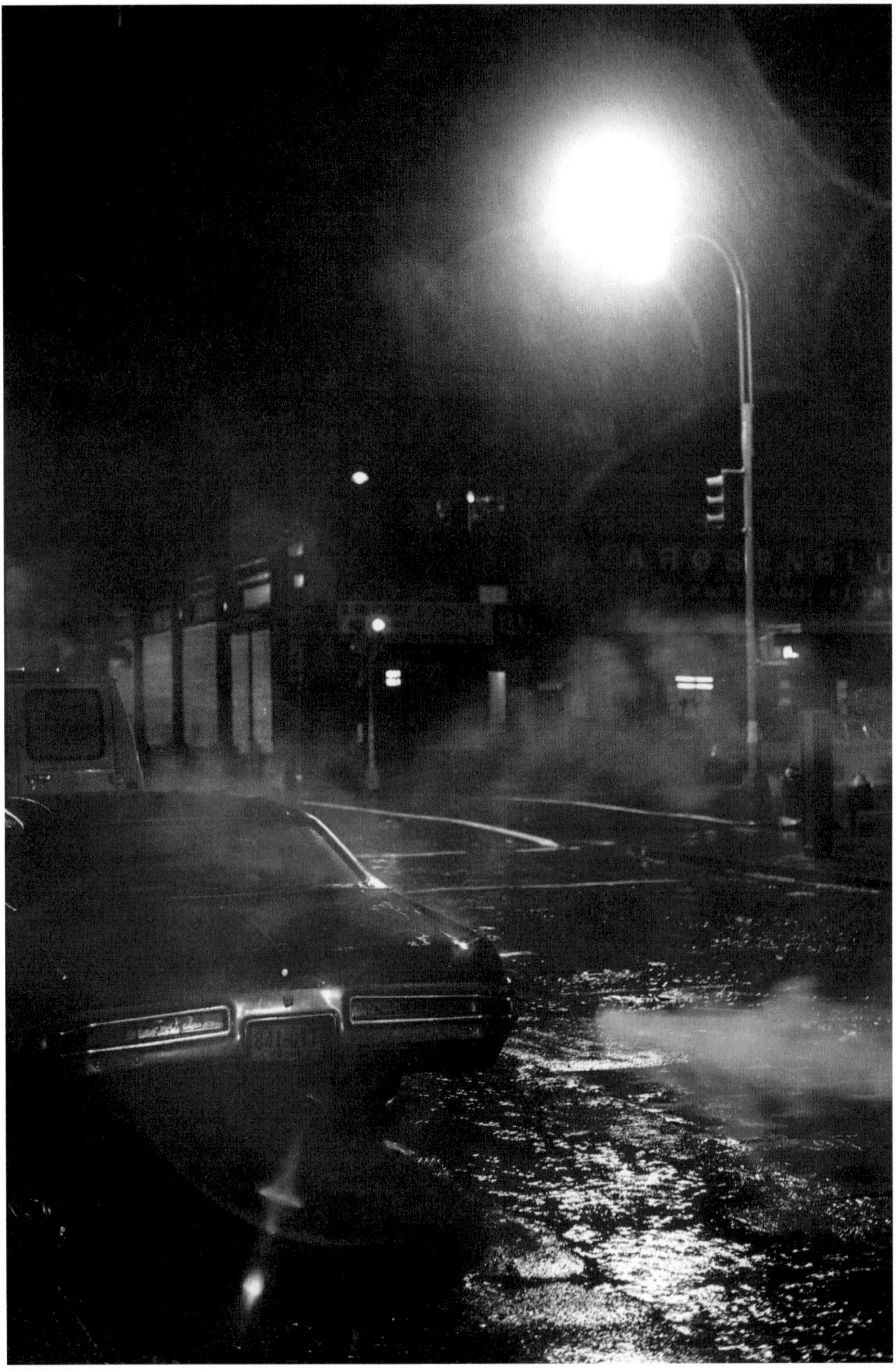

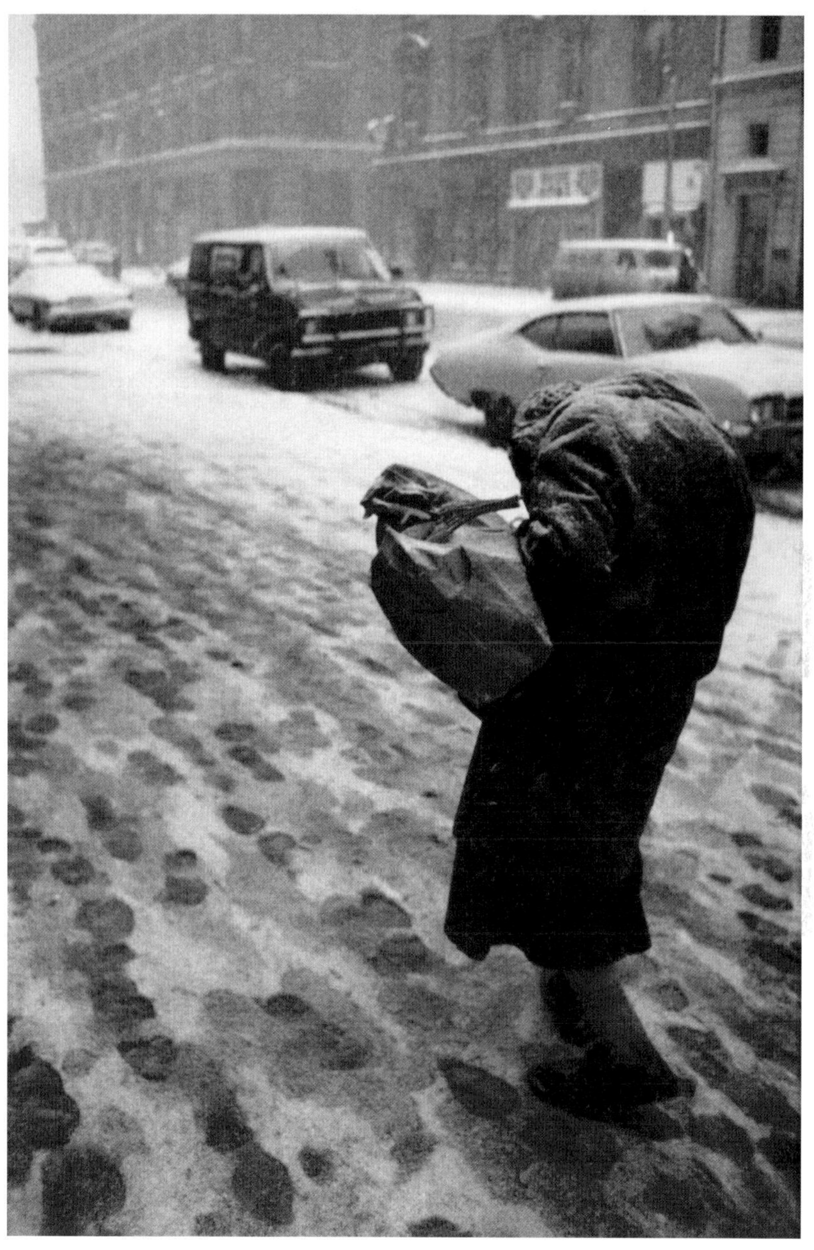

Untitled, 1970s   Untitled, c. 1970   pp. 84–85: Contact sheet, 1960s

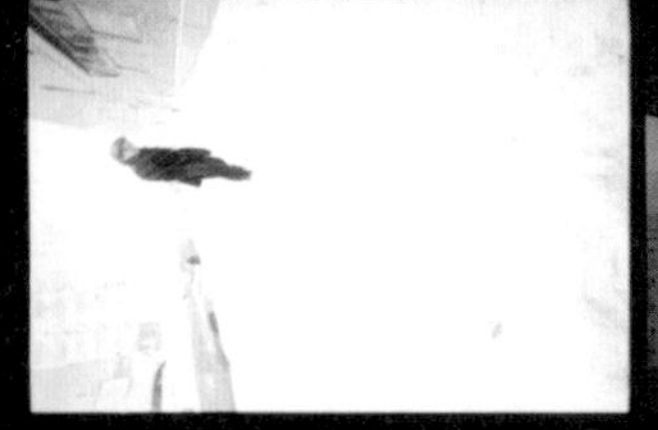
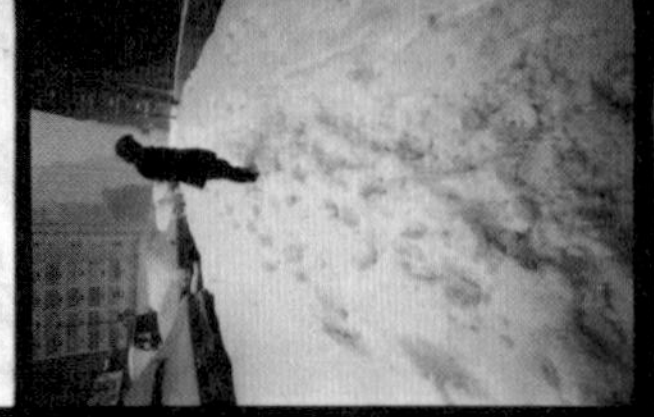
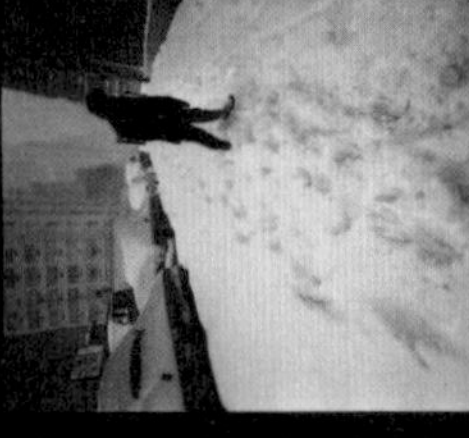
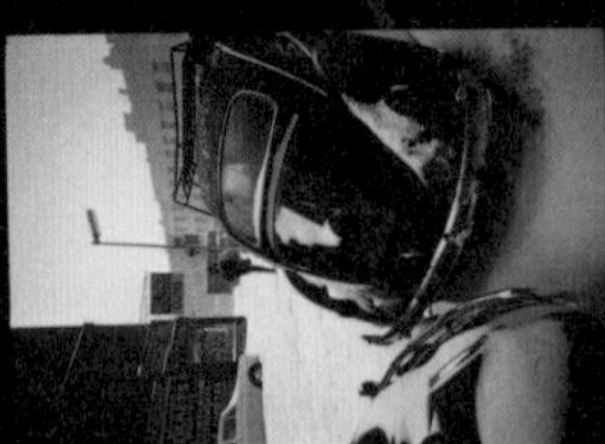
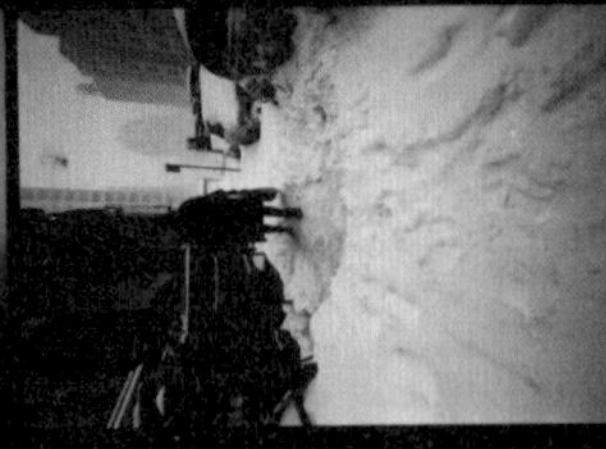
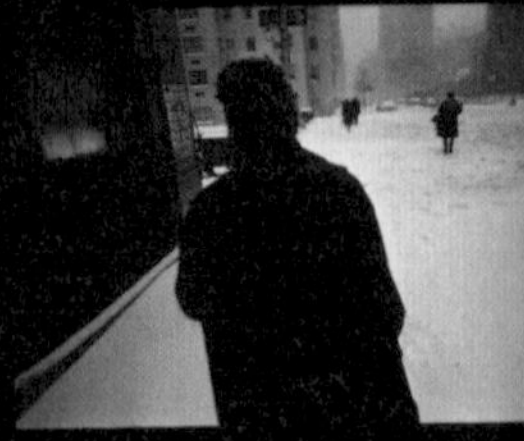
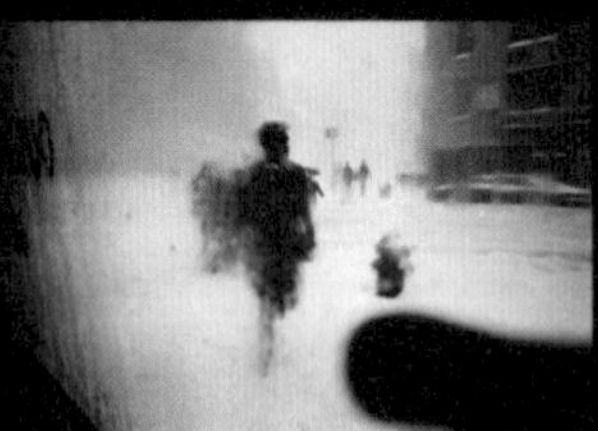
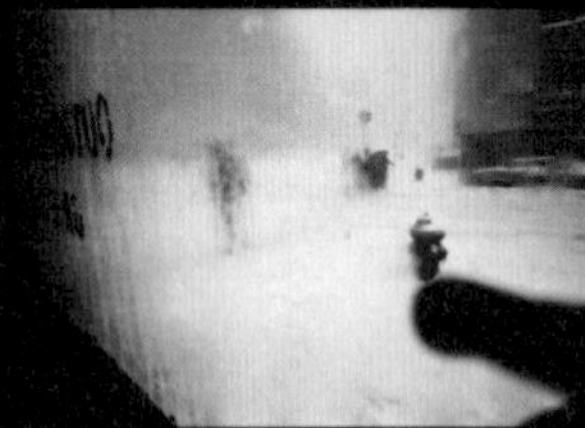
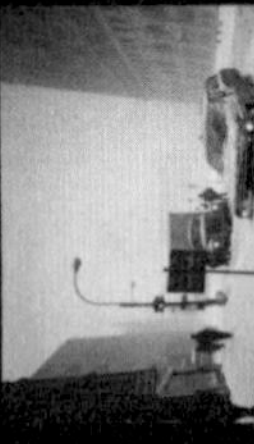
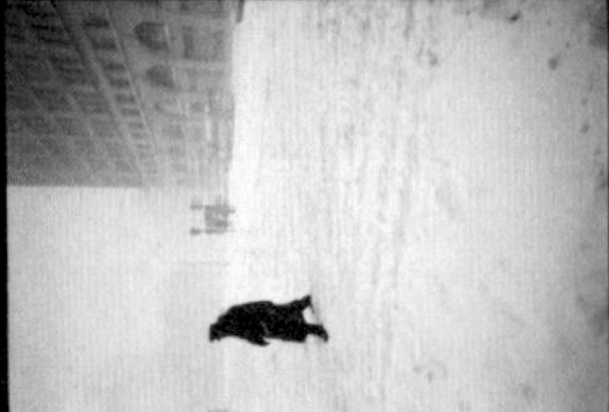
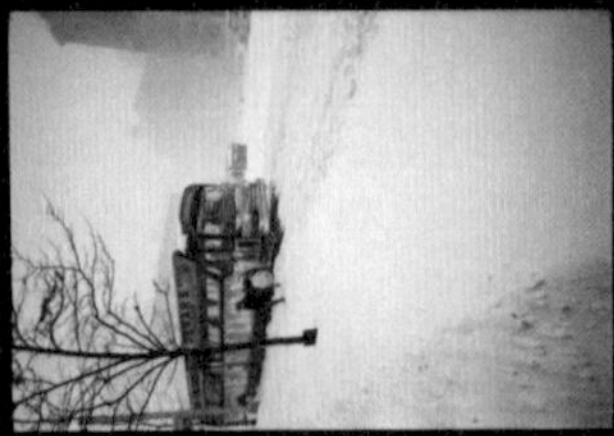

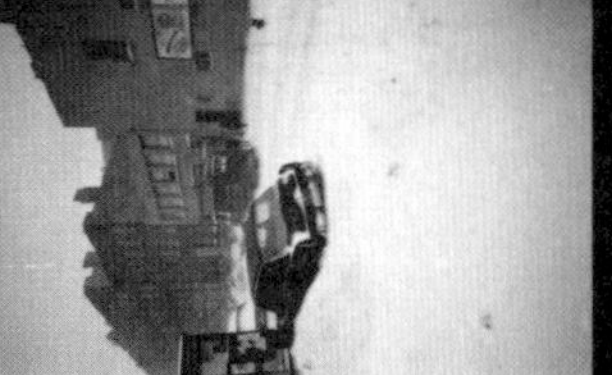
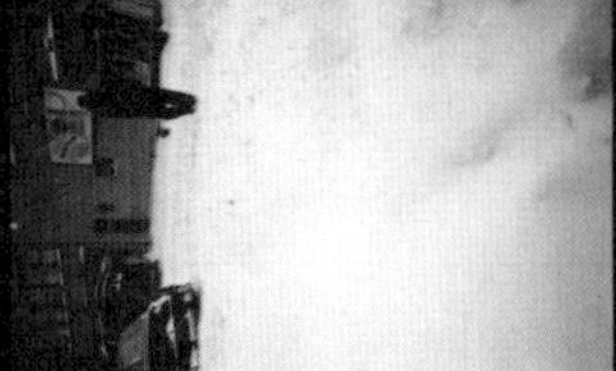
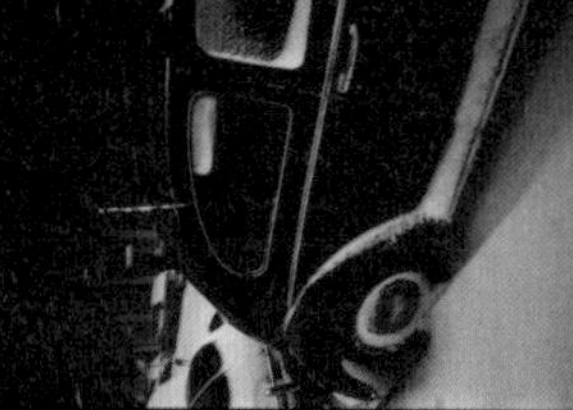

→4   →4A   →5   →5A   →6   →6A
KODAK   SAFETY   FILM

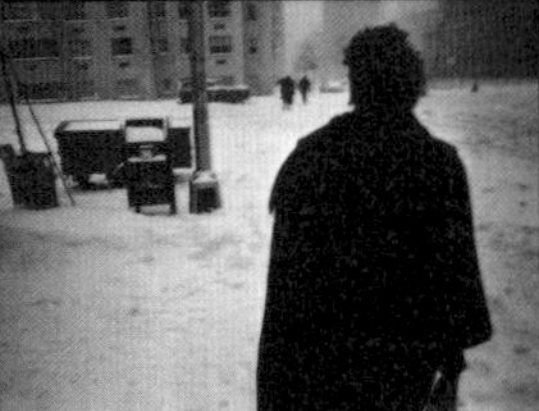
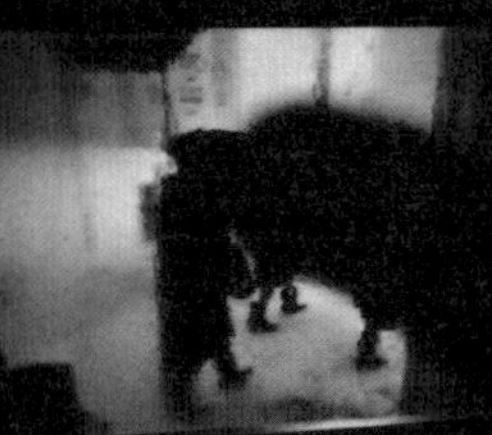
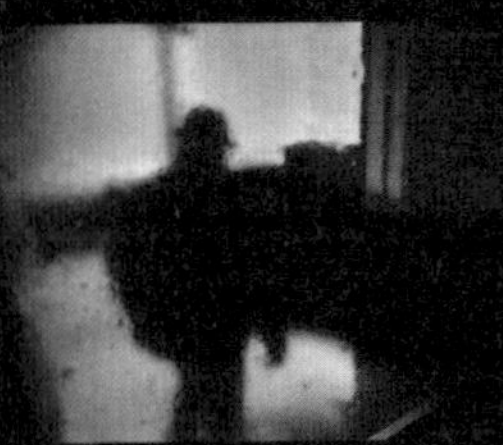

→10   →10A   →11   →11A   →12   →12A
KODAK   SAFETY   FILM

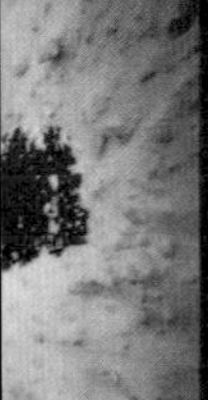
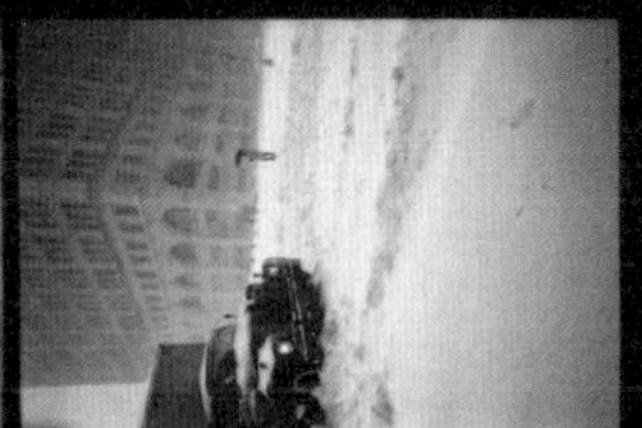
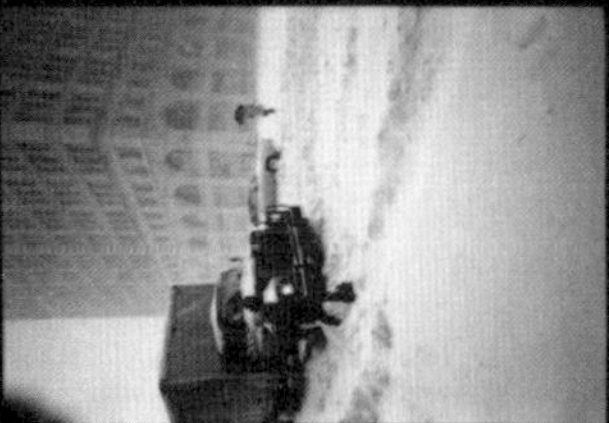

6A   →16   →16A   →17   →17A

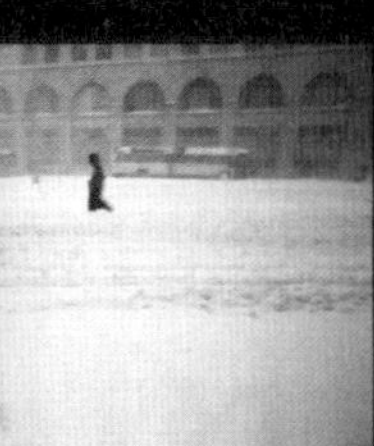
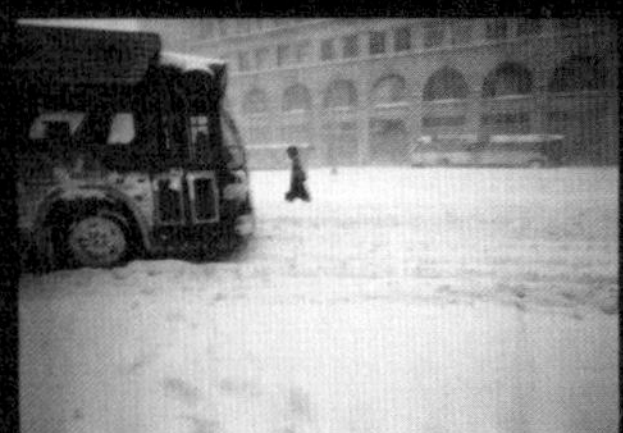

→20A

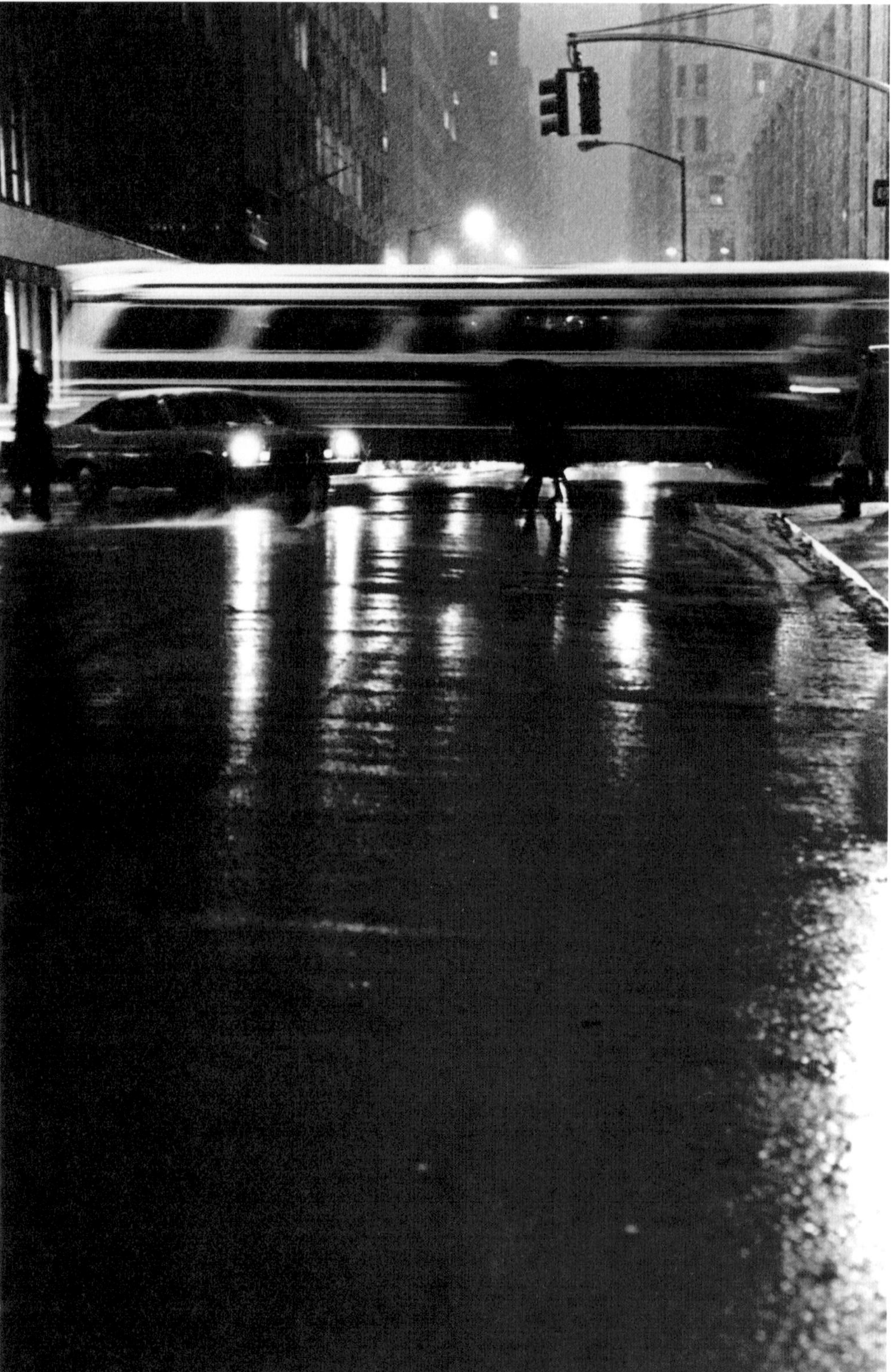

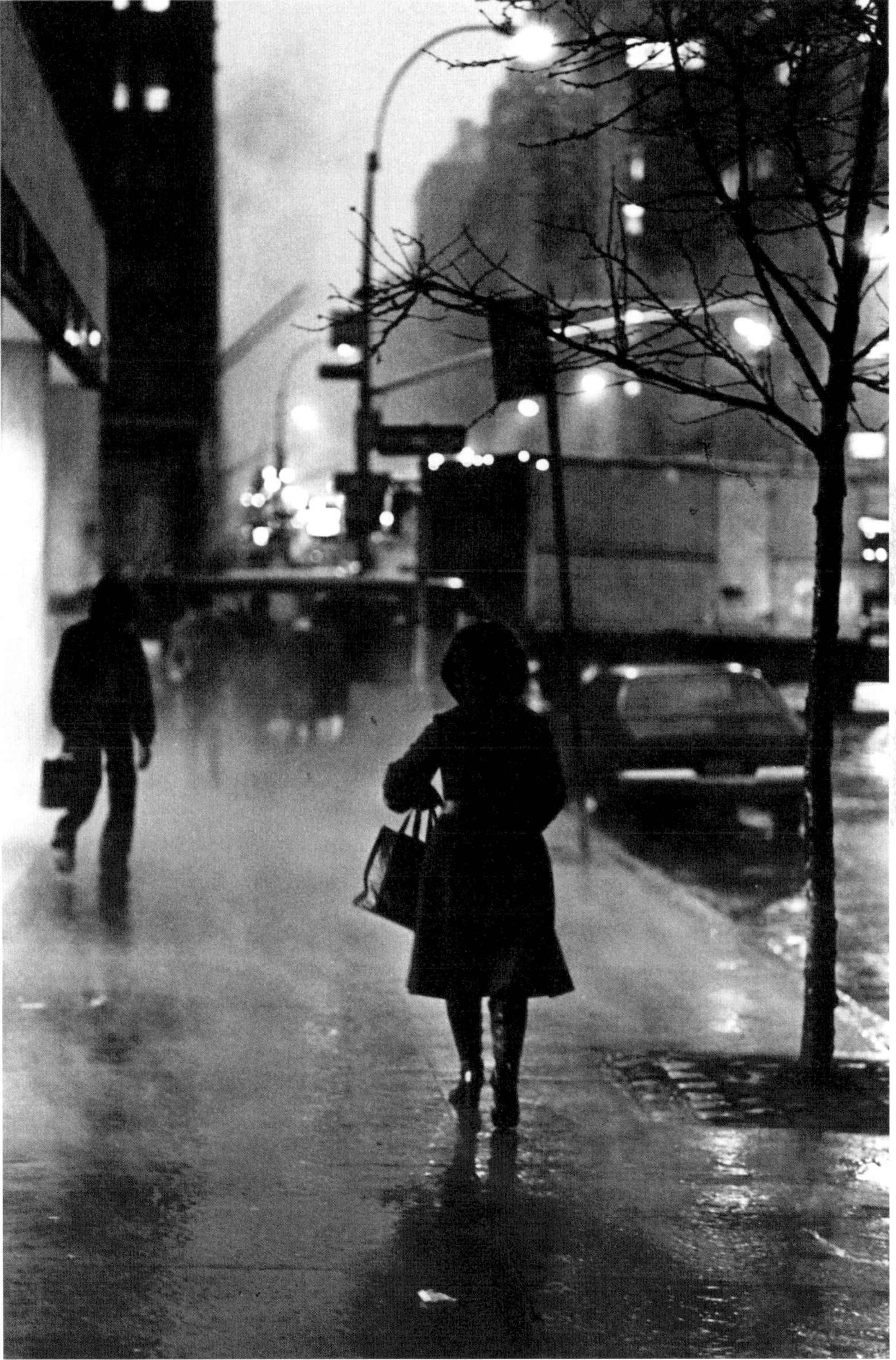

p. 86: Fifth Avenue, 1970s
p. 87: Fifth Avenue, 1970s

I am sometimes irresponsible.
Instead of paying my taxes, I buy some books.

Untitled, 1960s

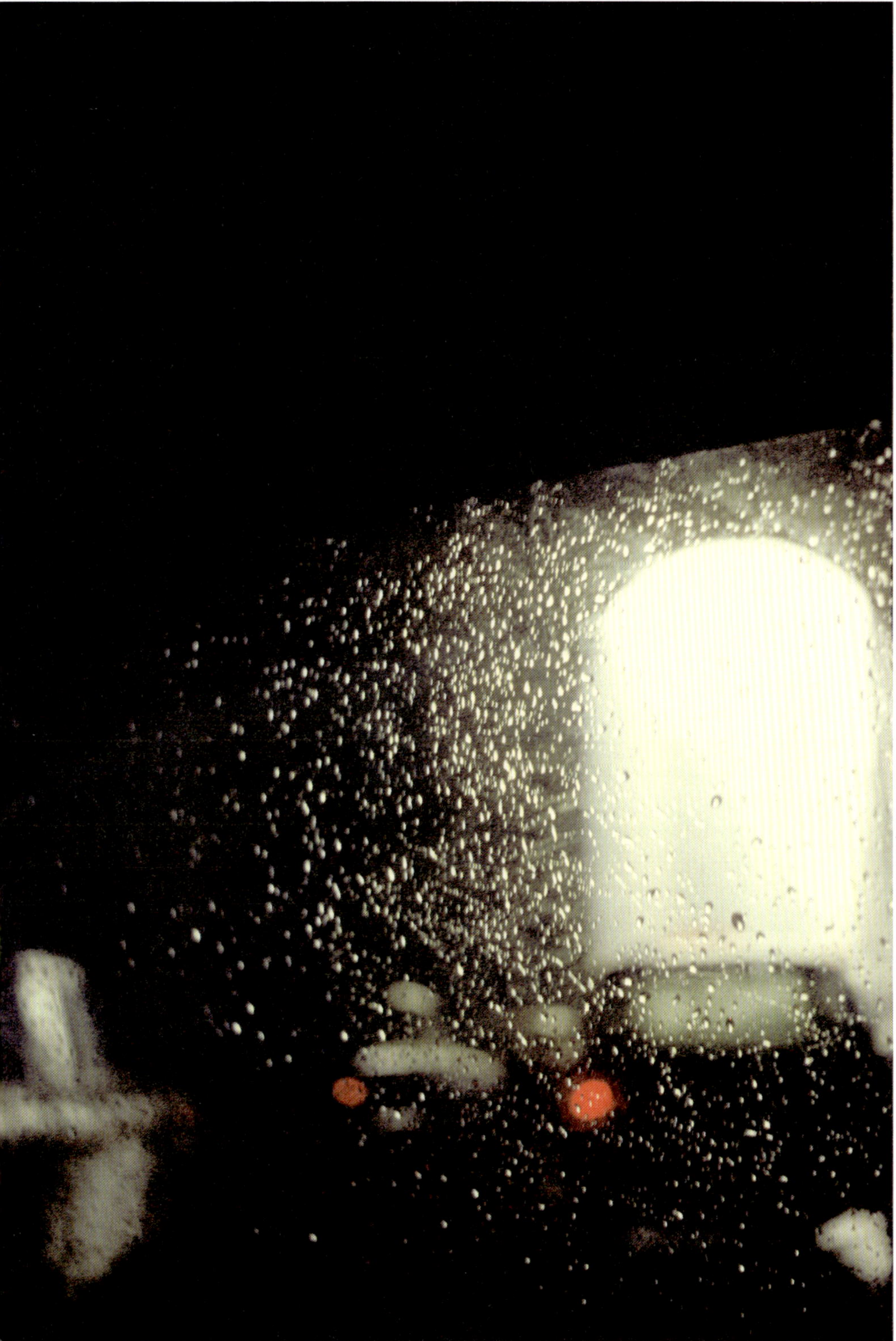

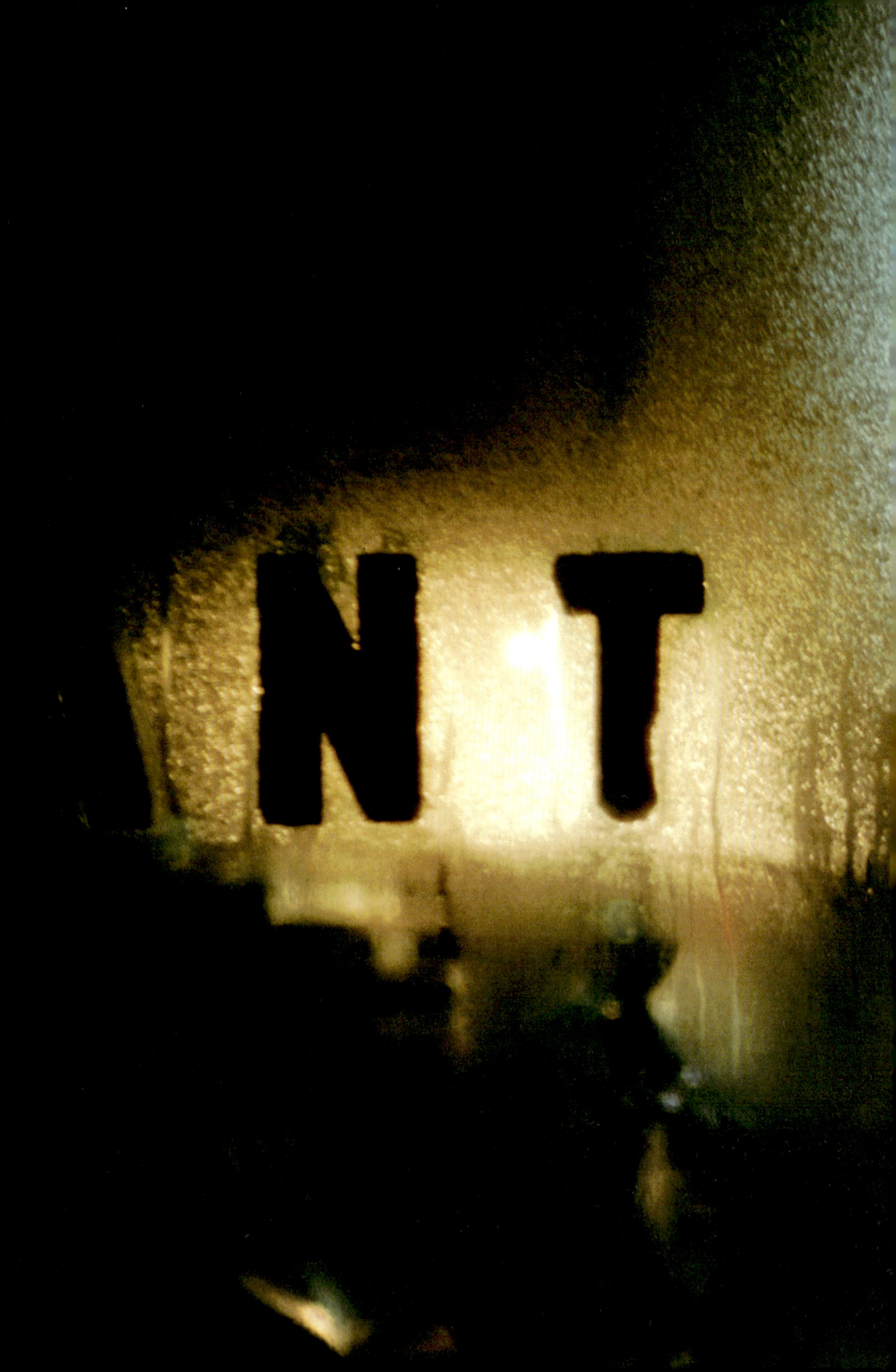
N T

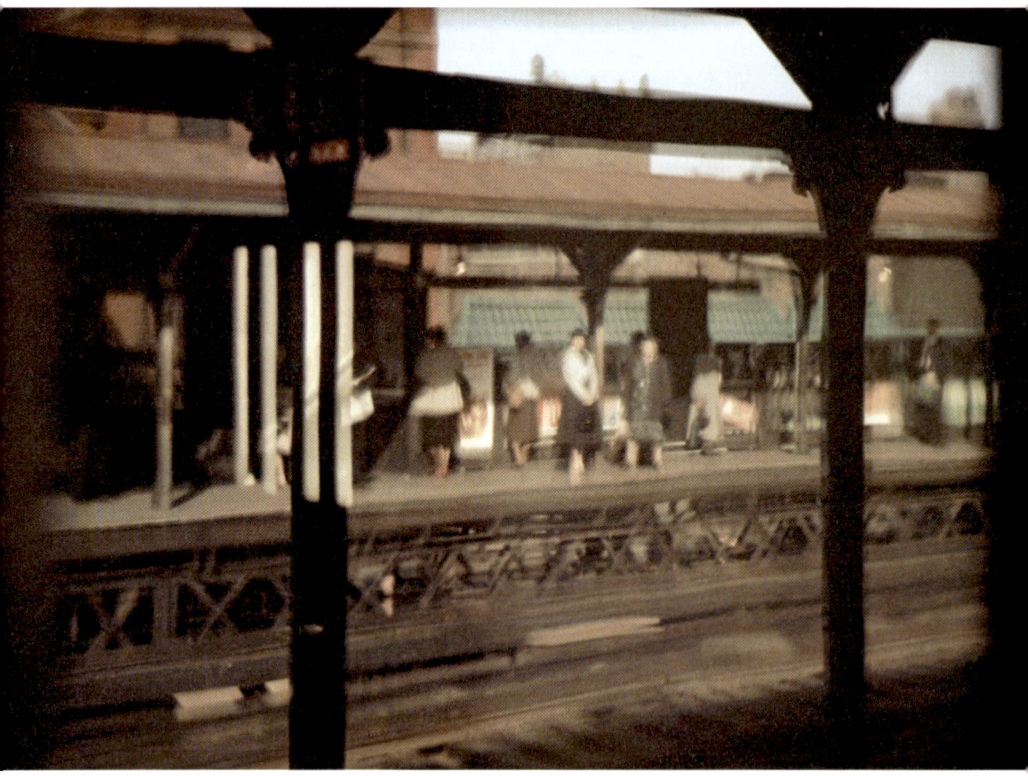

El, 1954

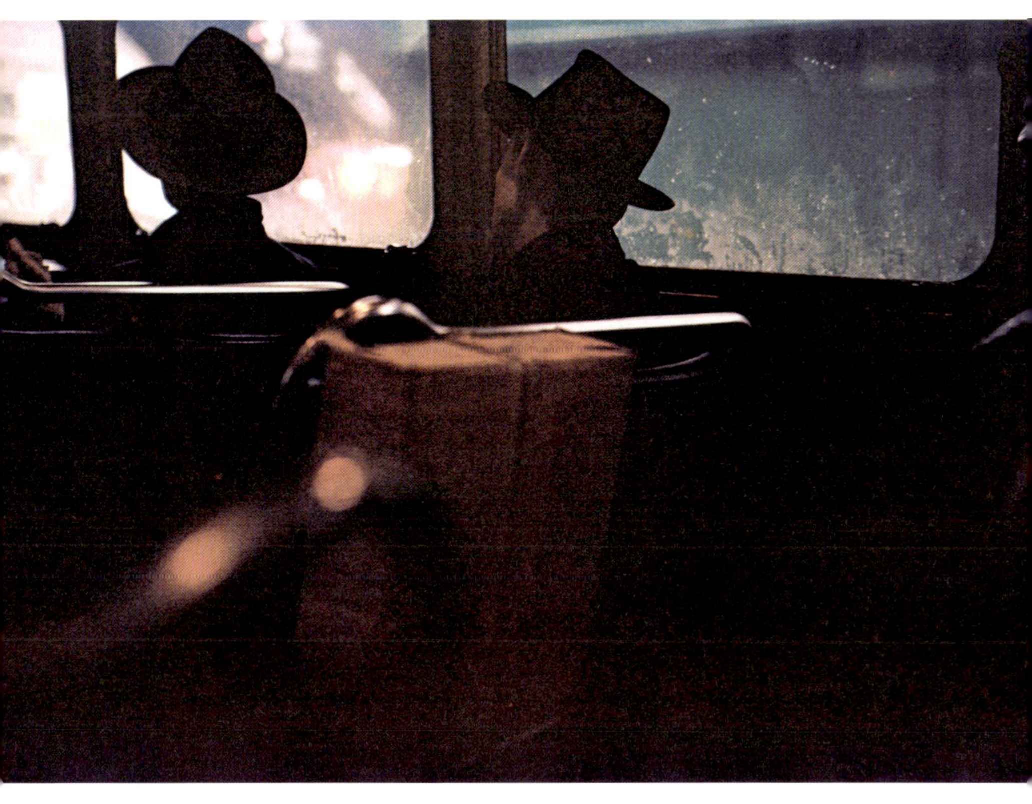

Bus at Night, 1950s

Round Mirror, 1950s

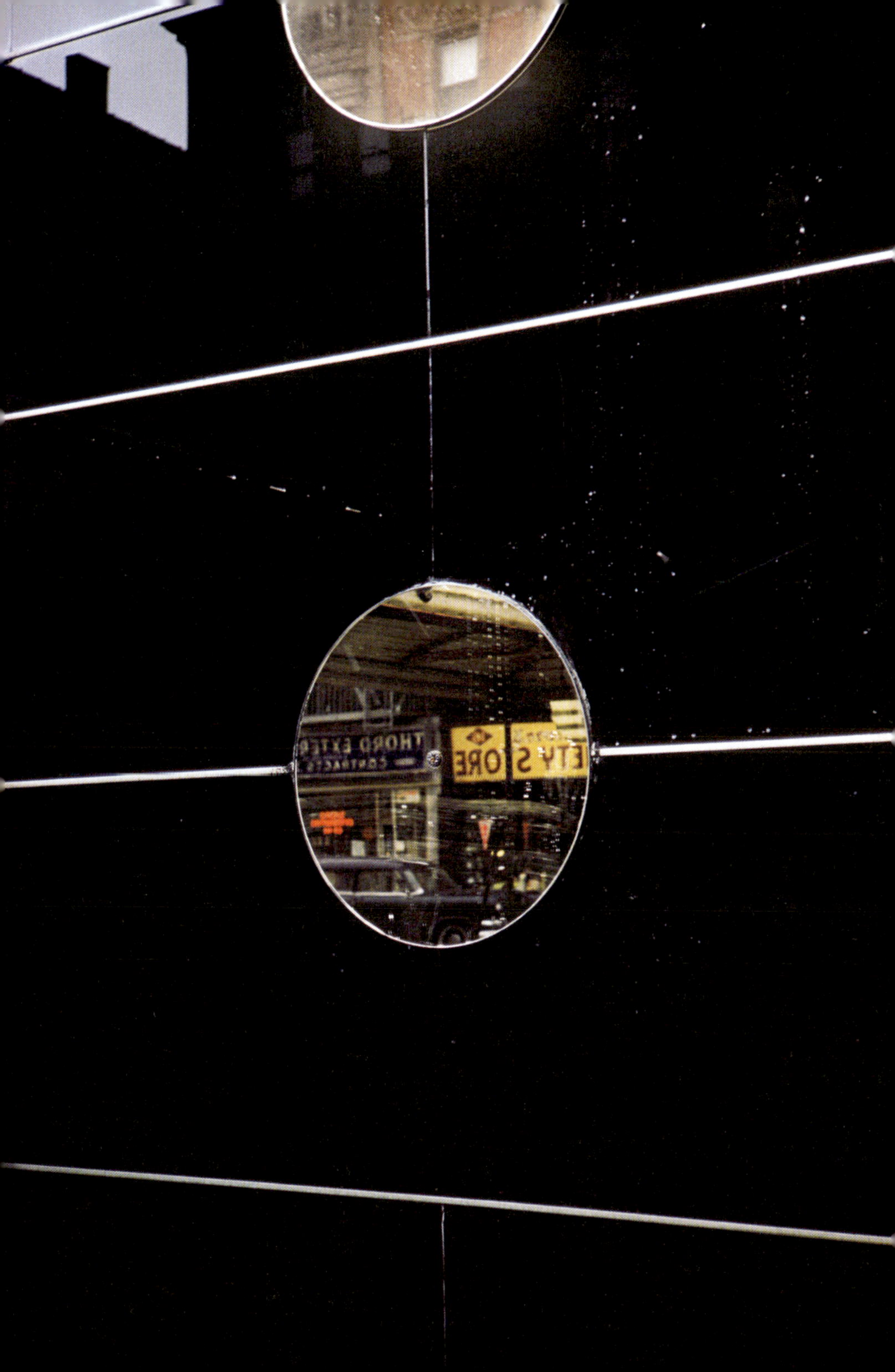

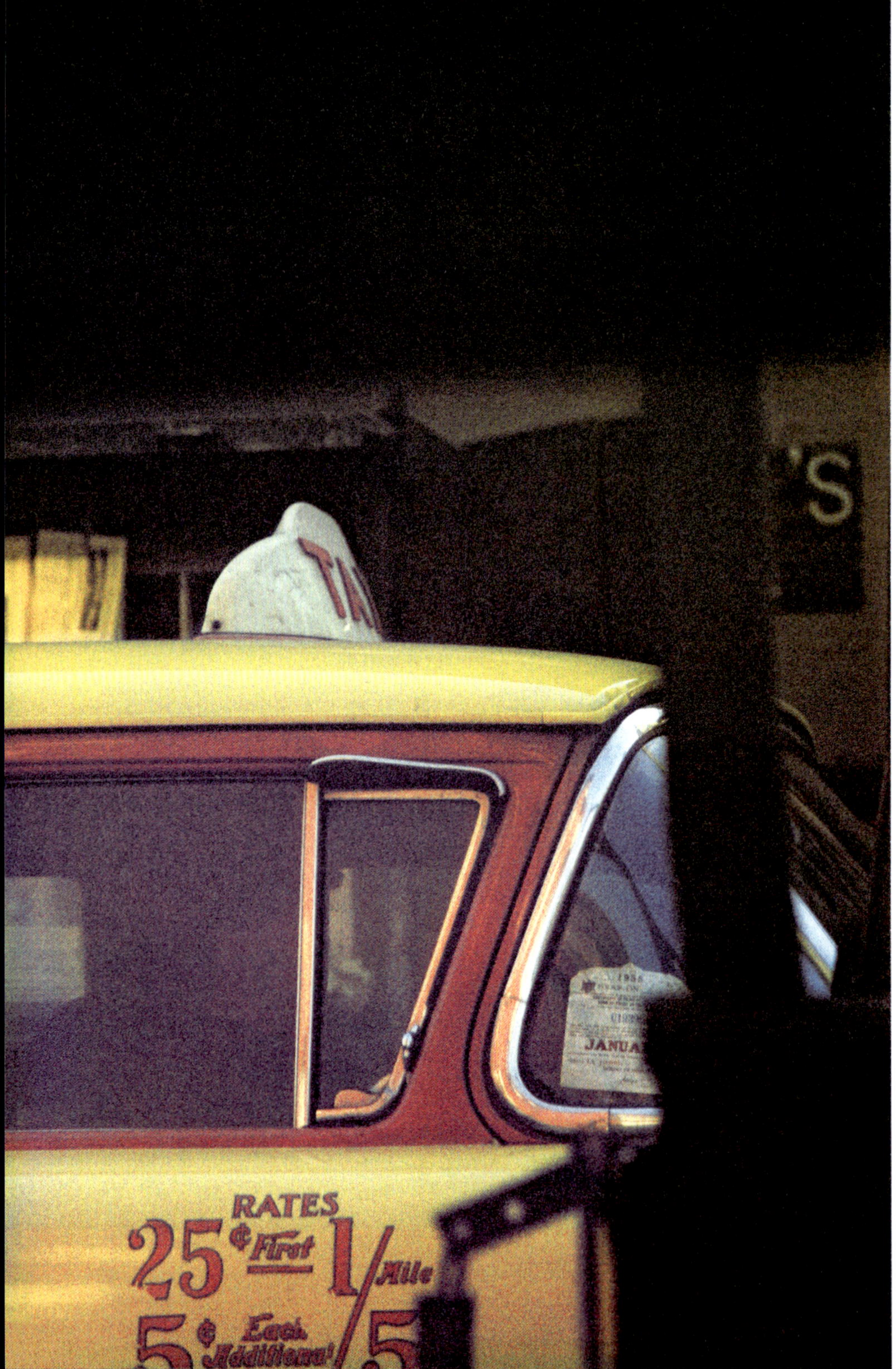
'S
RATES
25¢ First 1/ Mile
5¢ Each Additional 1/5

We live in a world of color.
We're surrounded by color.

Taxi, c. 1960

Window, 1957

Tanager Steps, 1952

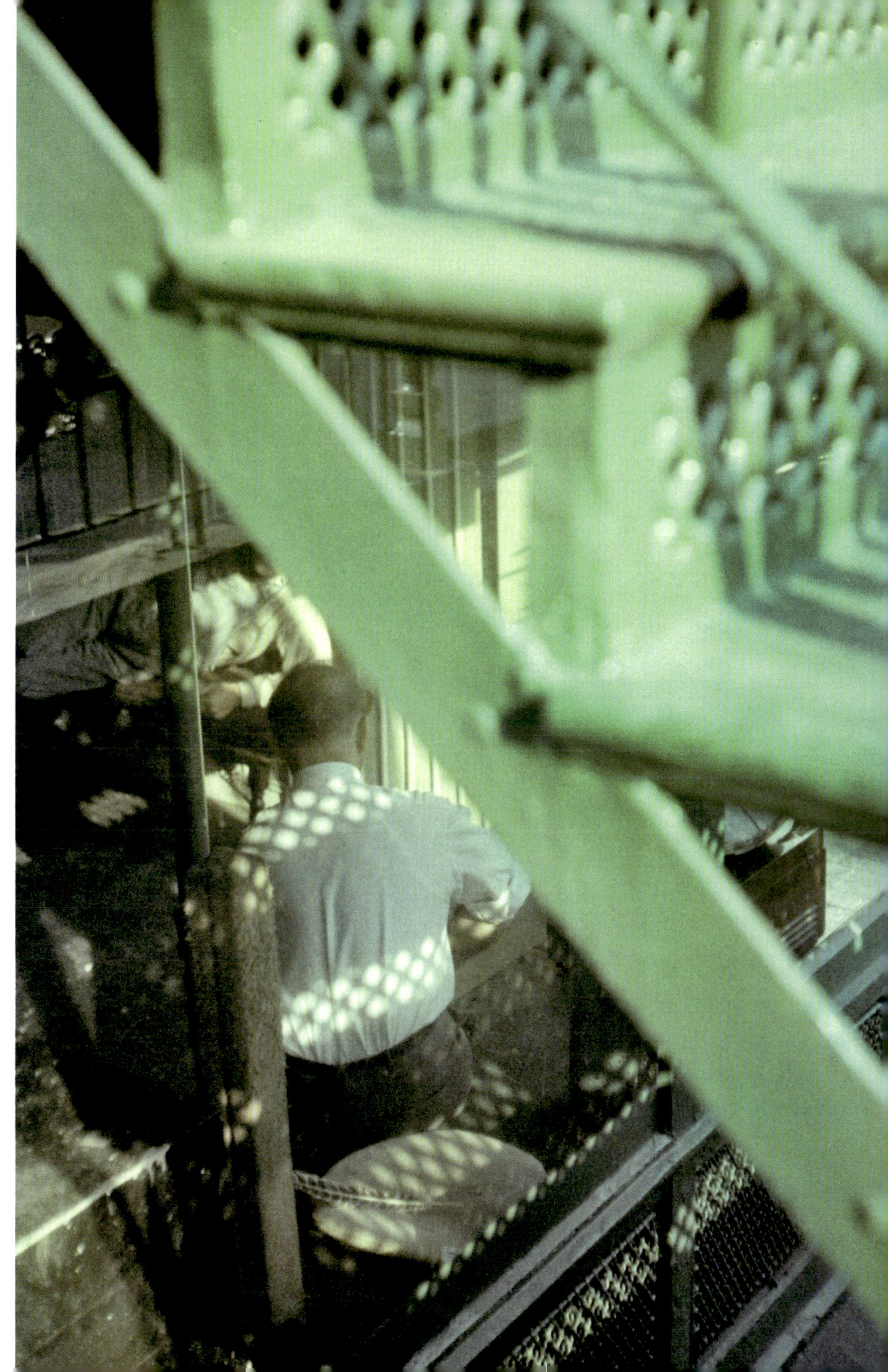

Untitled, 1962

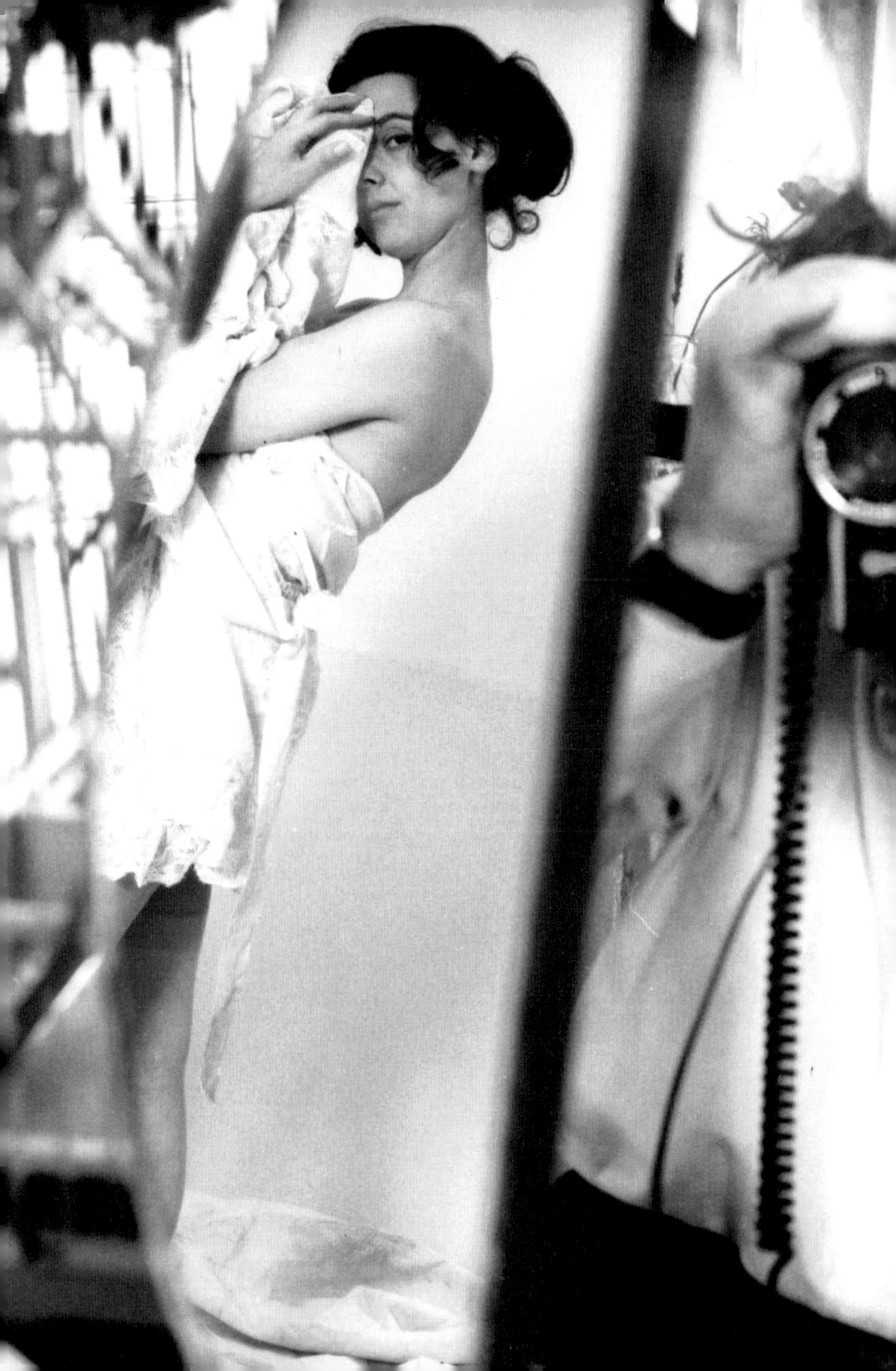

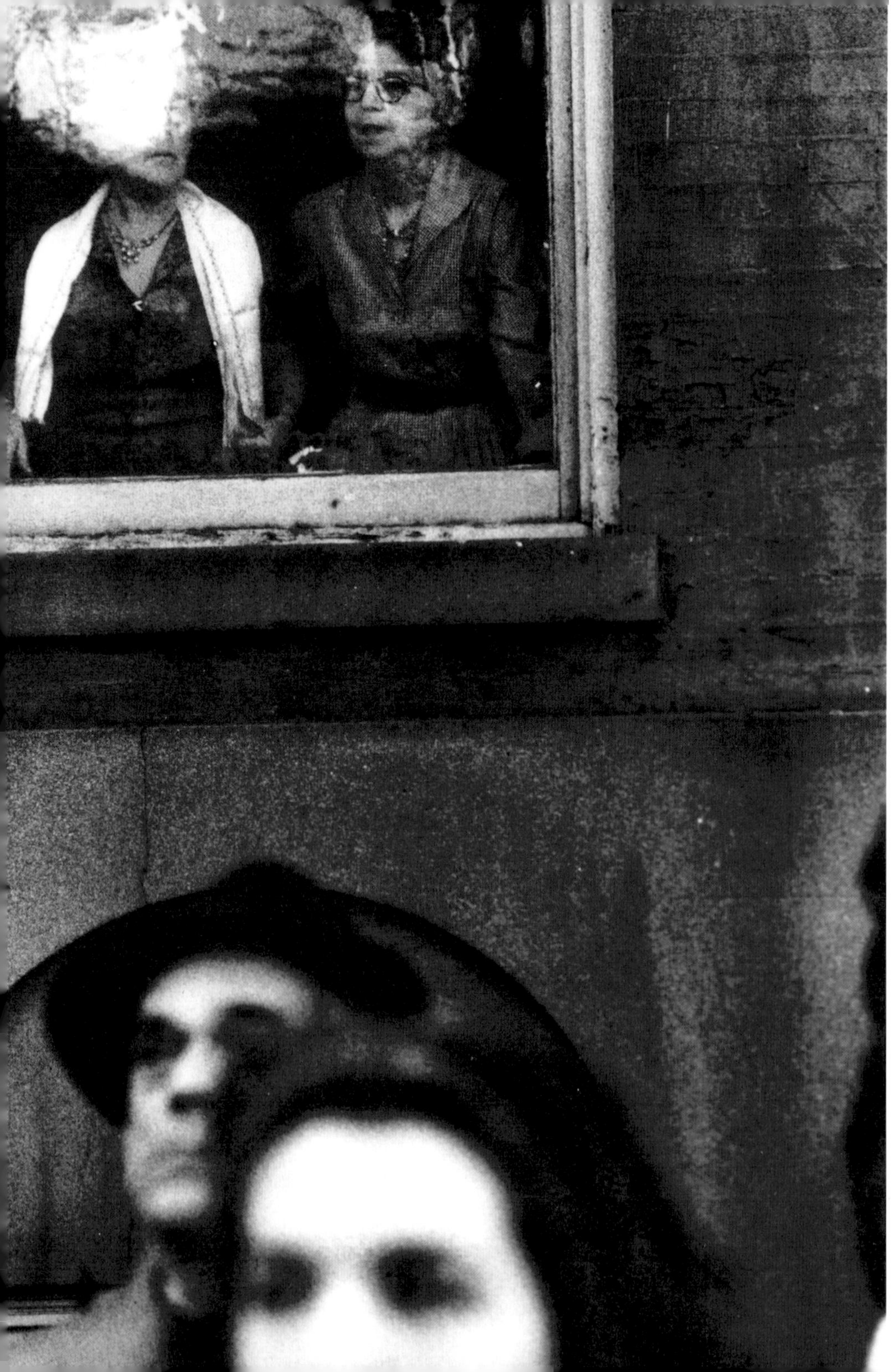

I have avoided profound explanations of what I do.

MacArthur Parade, 1951

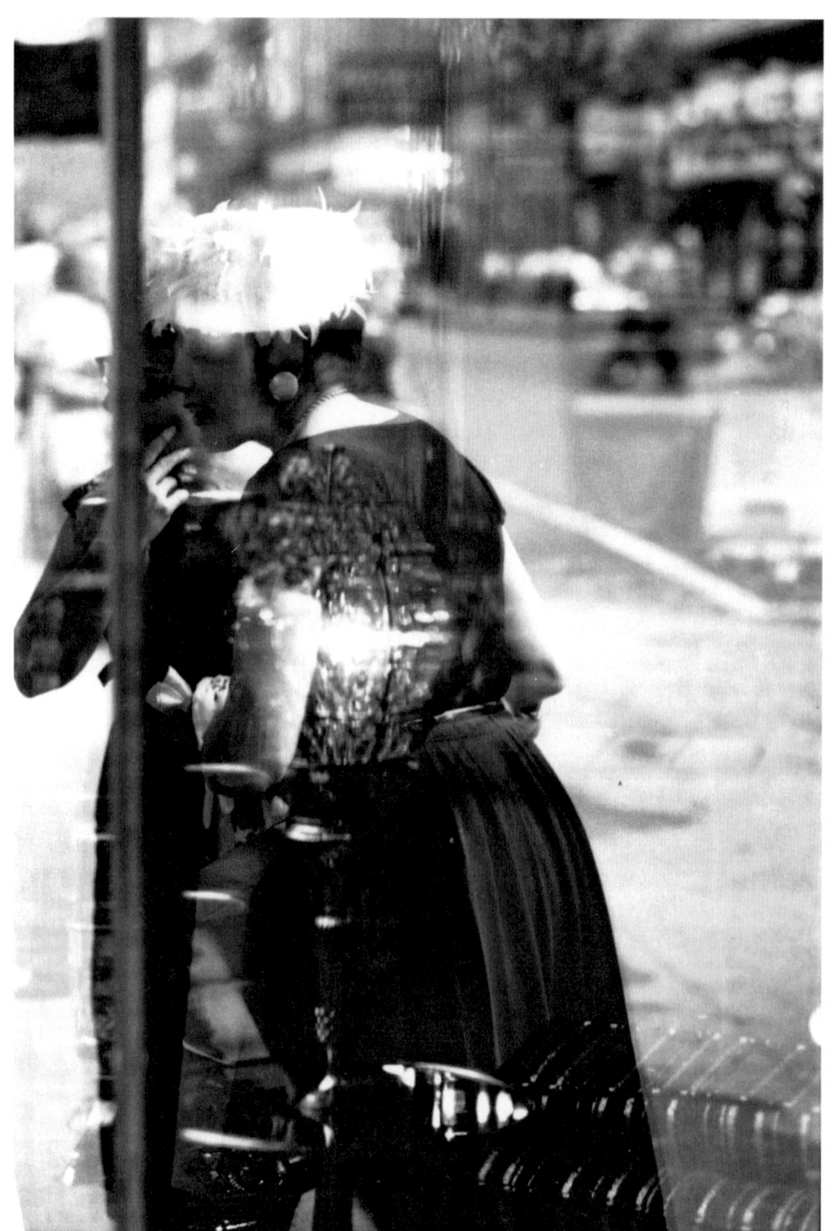

Shopping, 1958   Reading, c. 1955

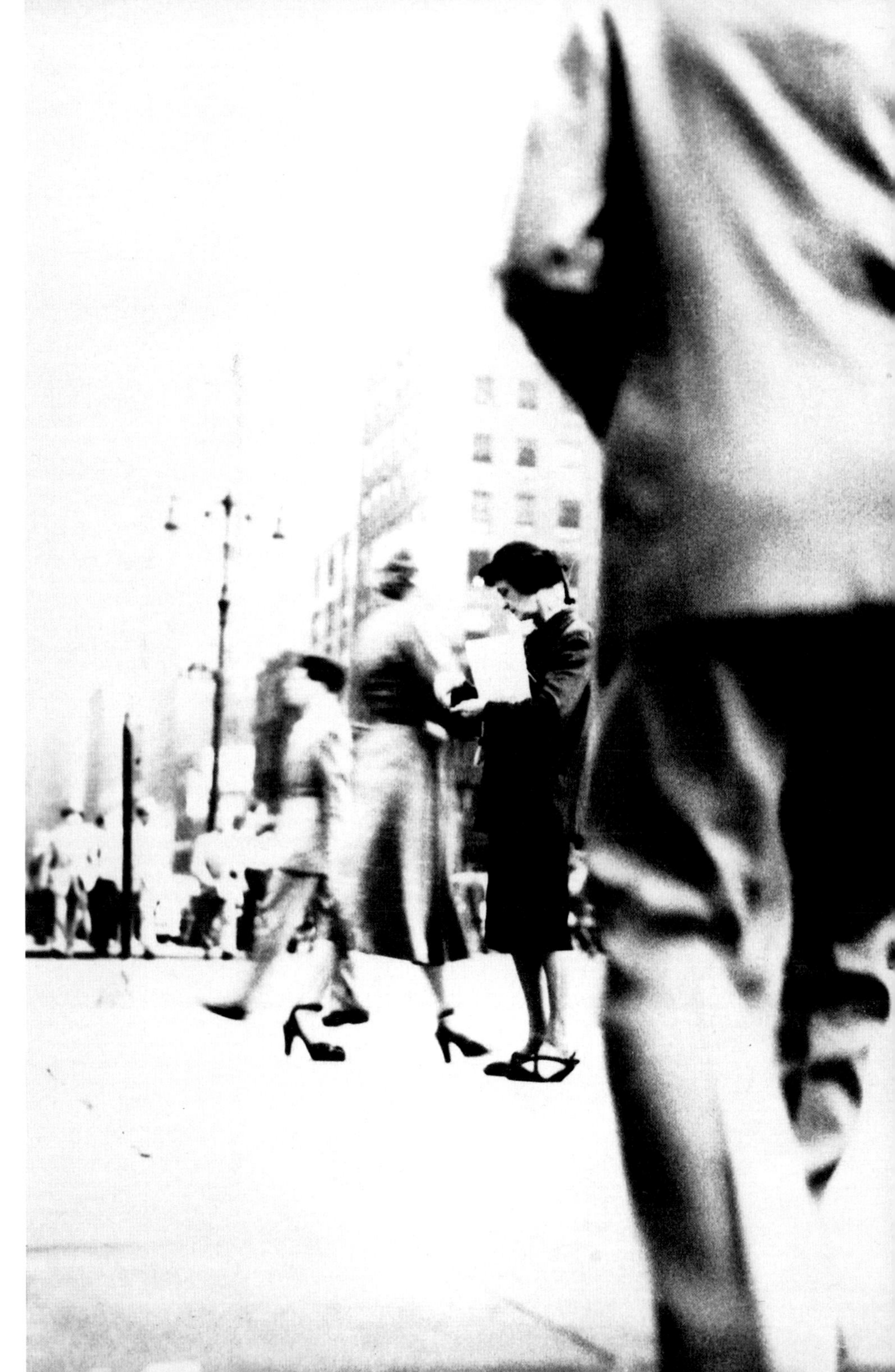

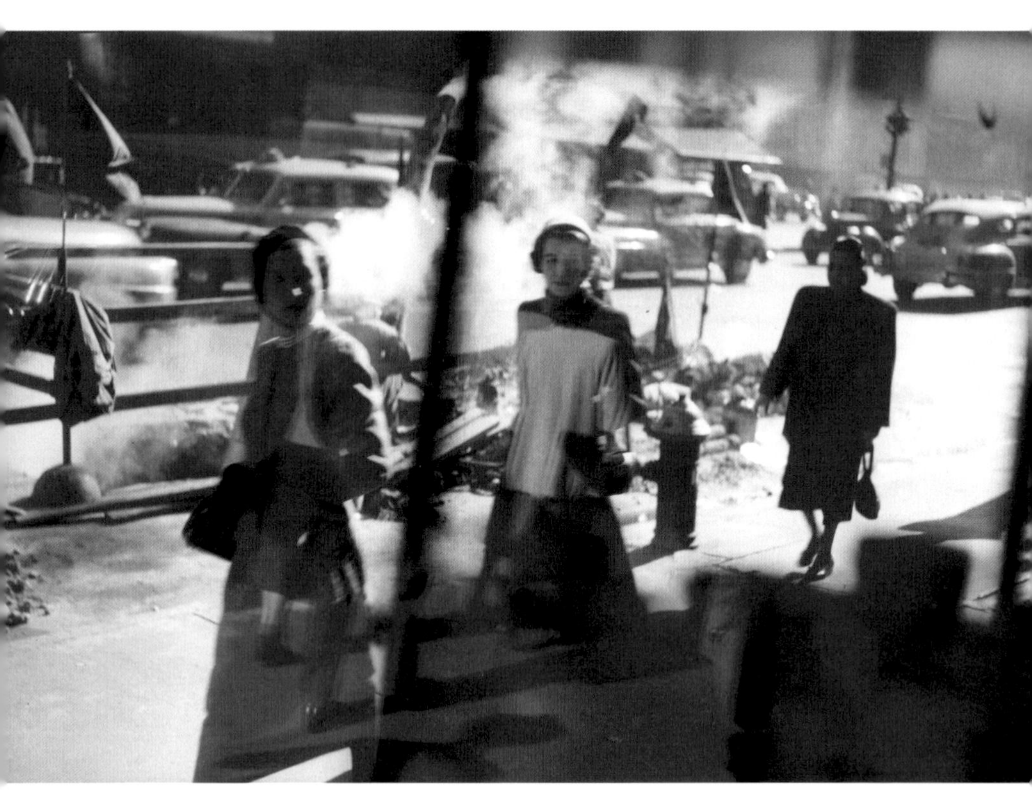

Construction Site, 1950s

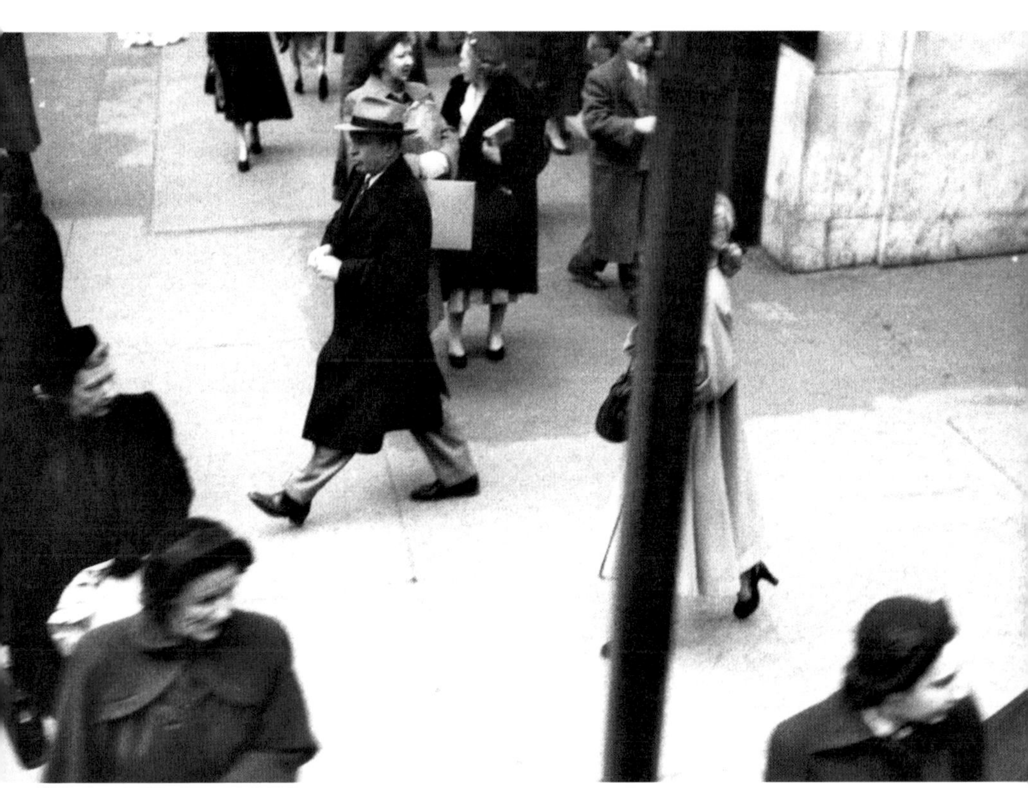

Dottie, 1950s

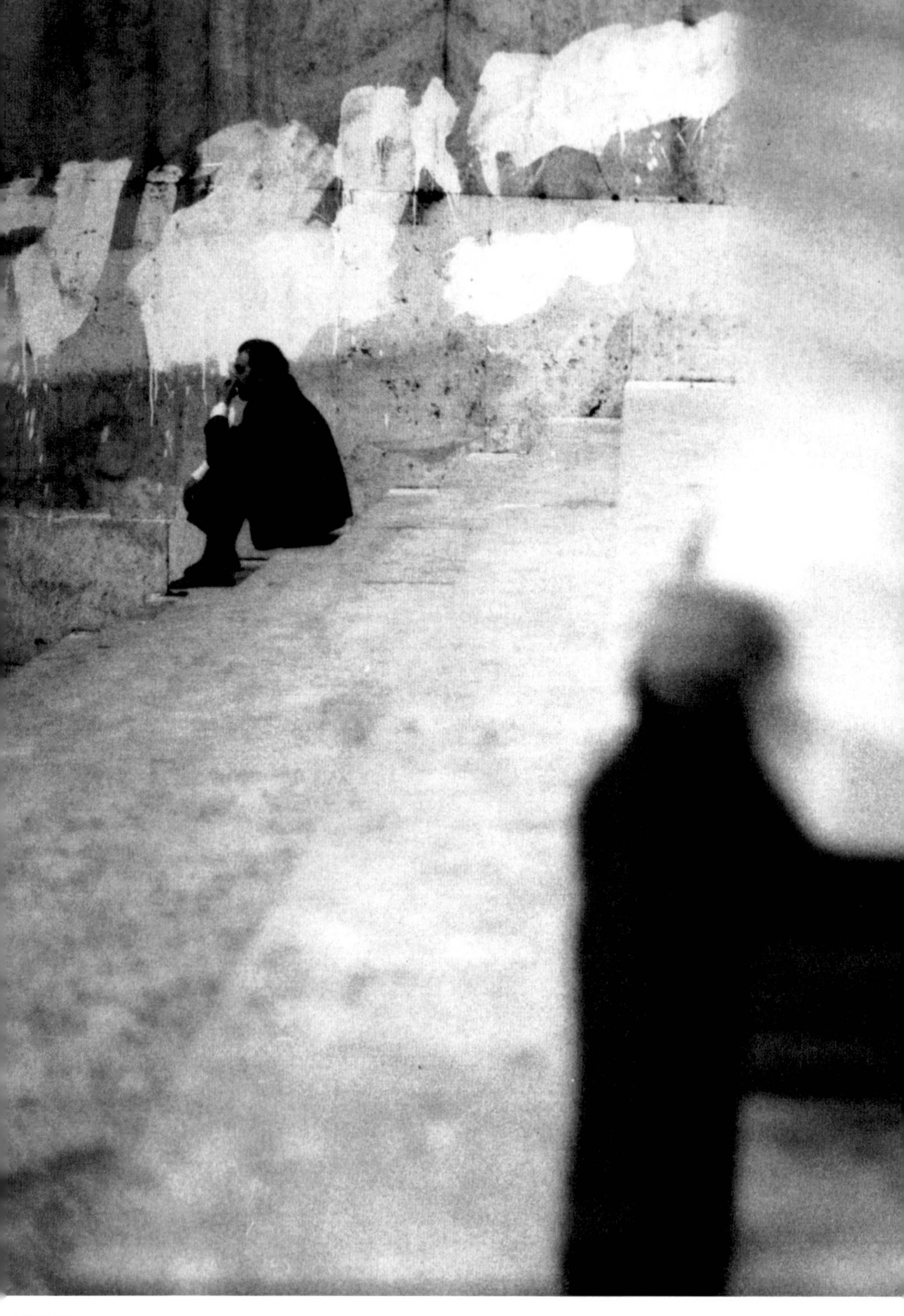

Rome, 1960

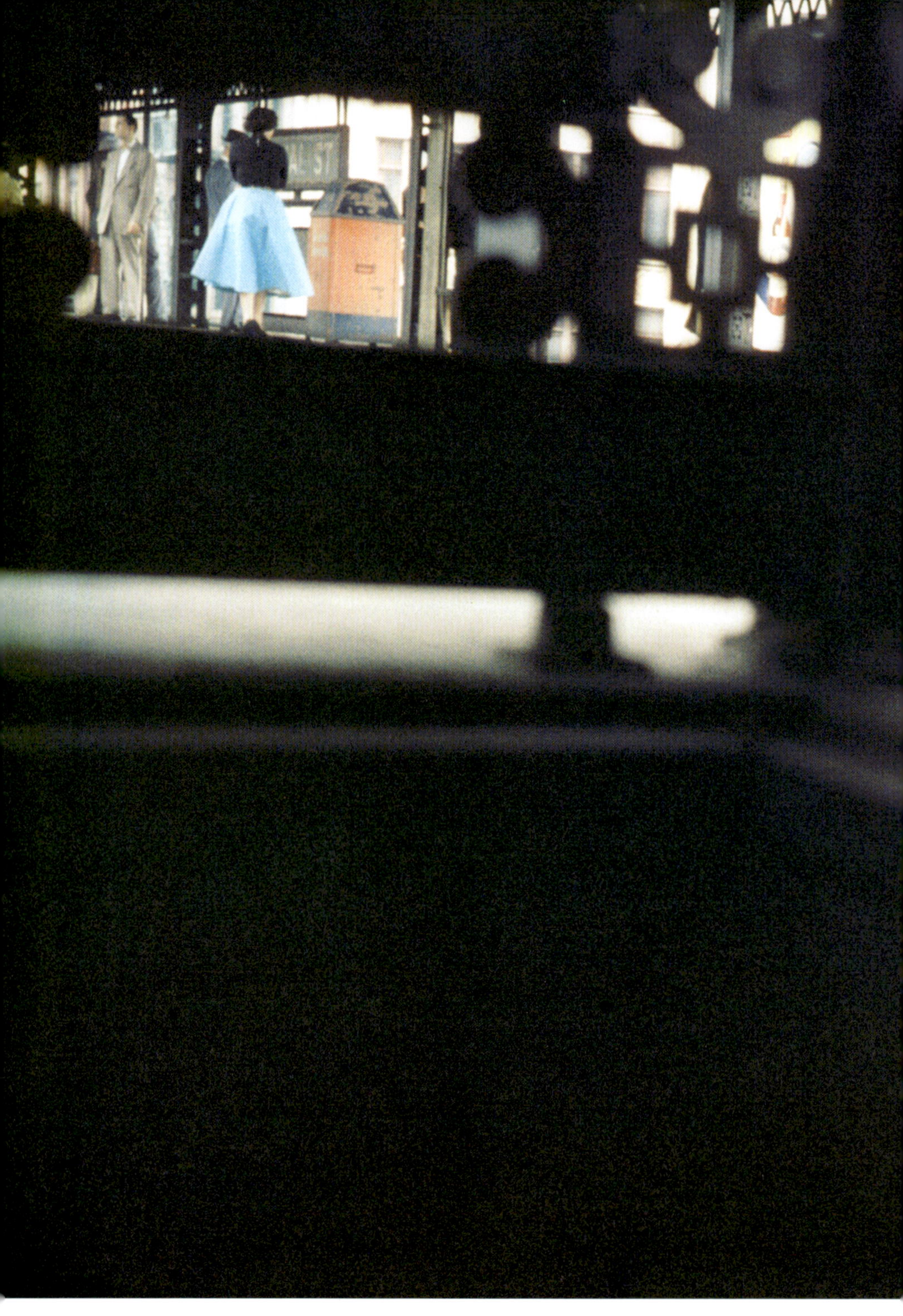

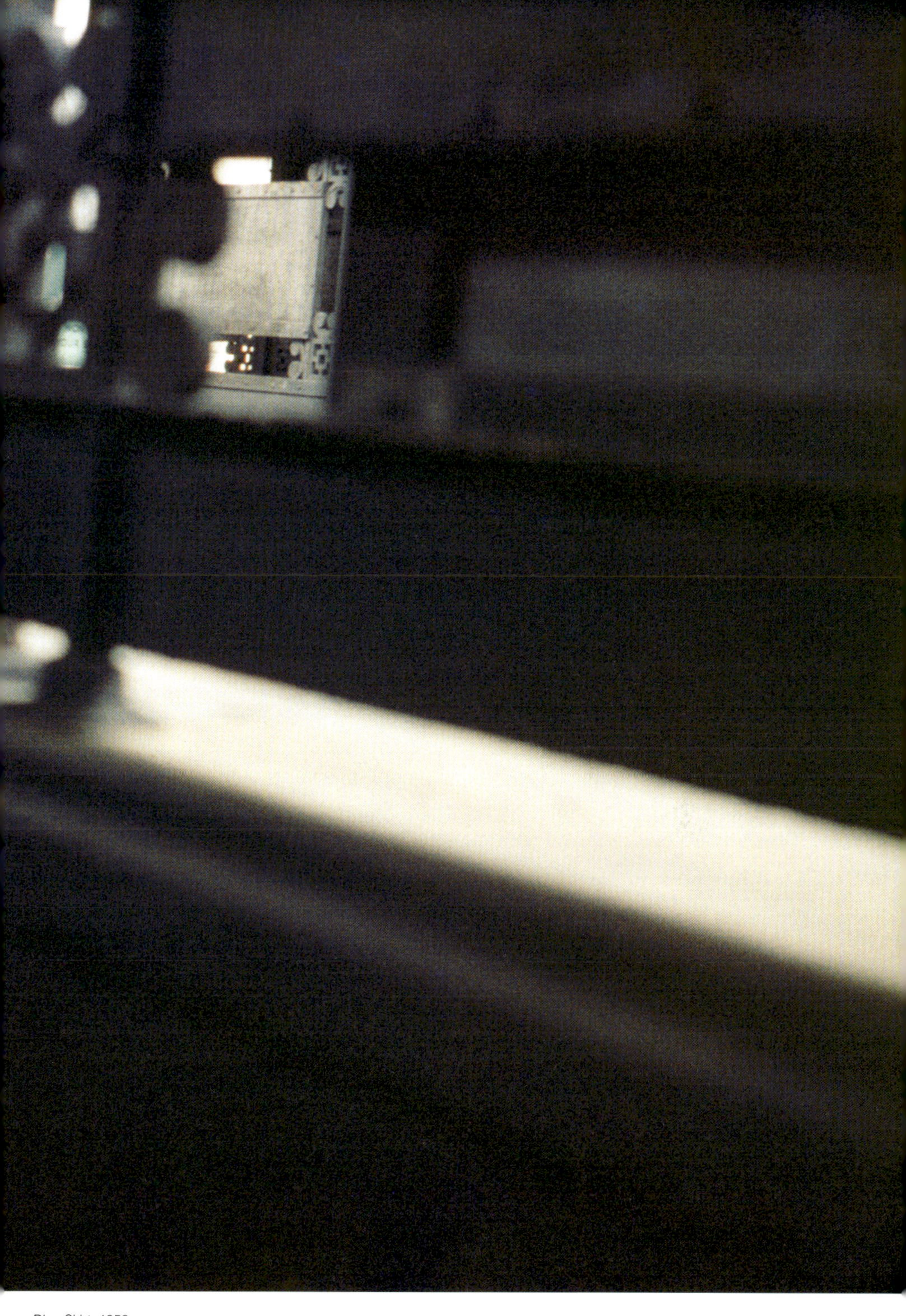

Blue Skirt, 1950s

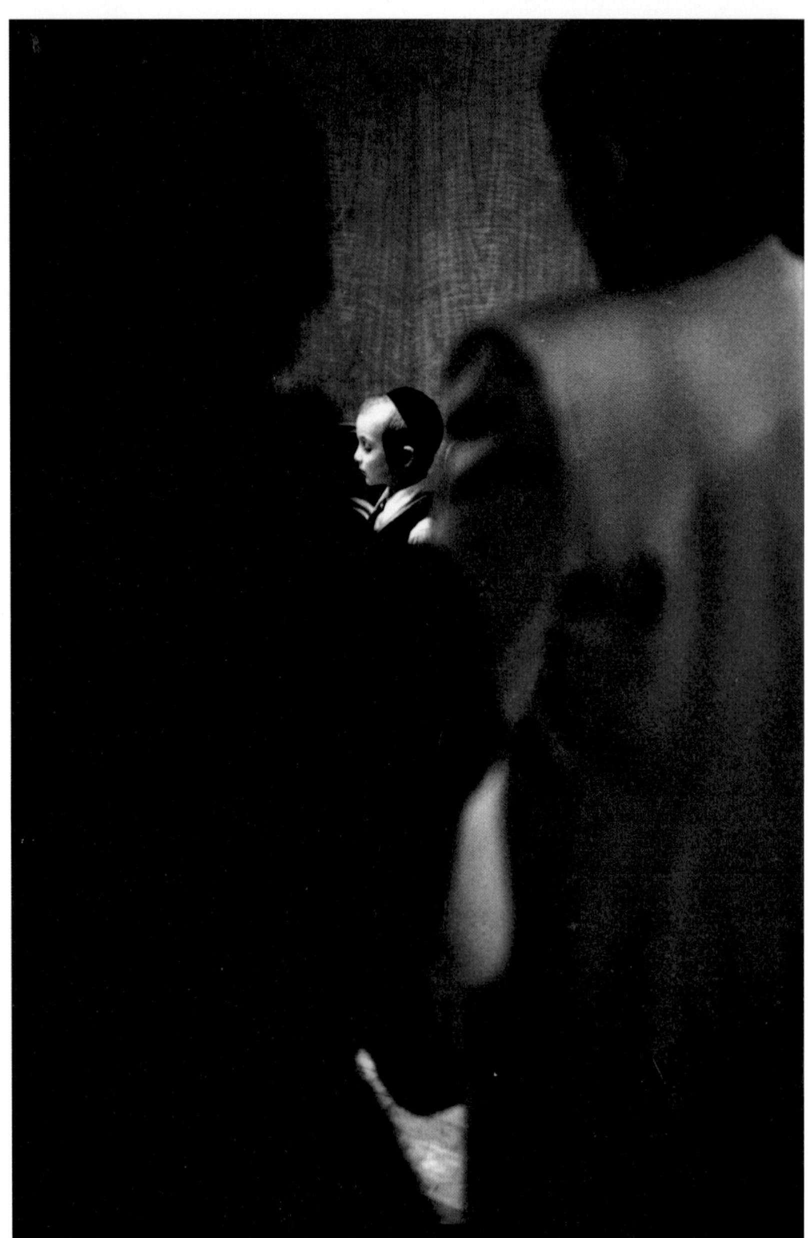

Wedding, c. 1948

Kiss, 1952
Untitled, c. 1955

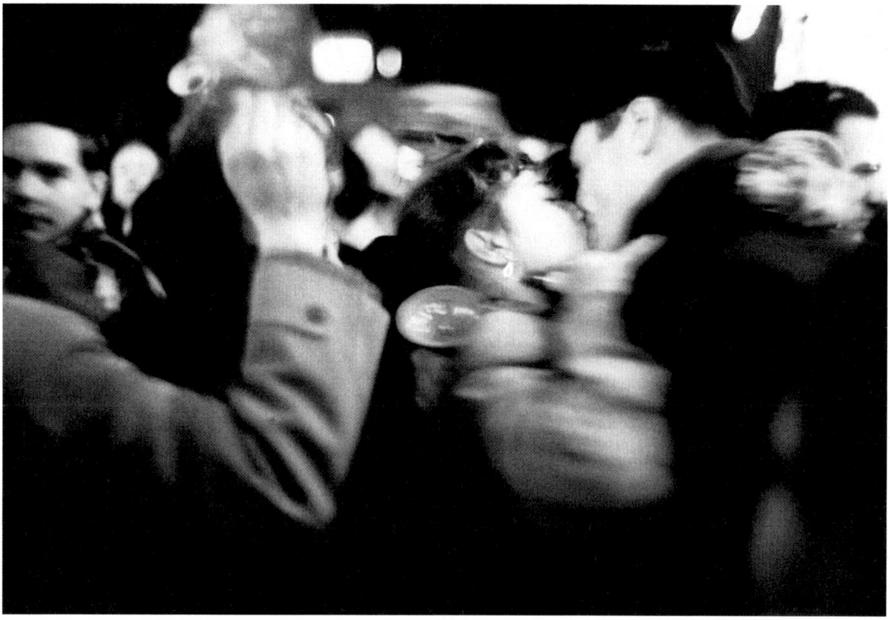

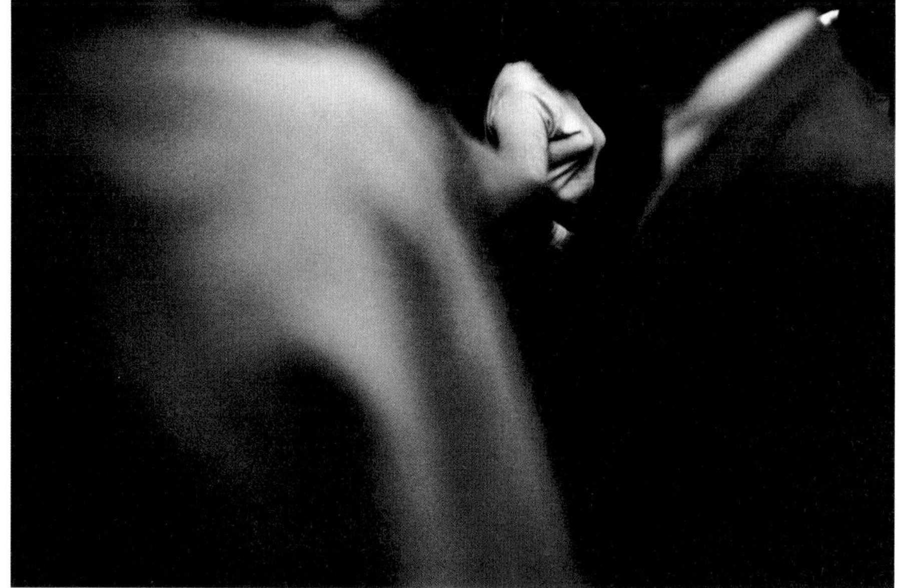

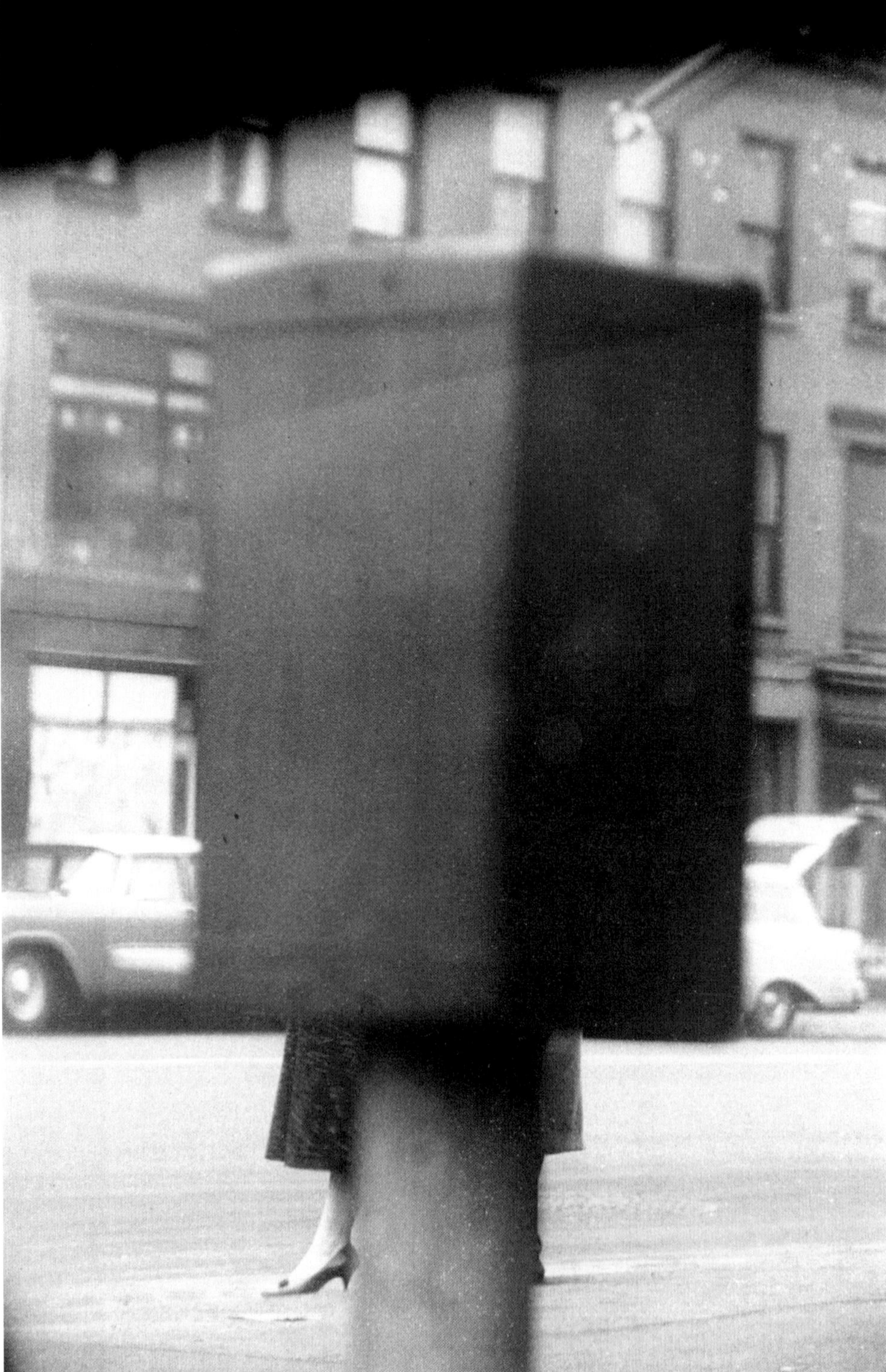

I was hoping to be forgotten.
I aspired to be unimportant.

We live in a world full of expectations,
and if you have the courage, you ignore the expectations.
And you can look forward to trouble.

Bicycle, c. 2009

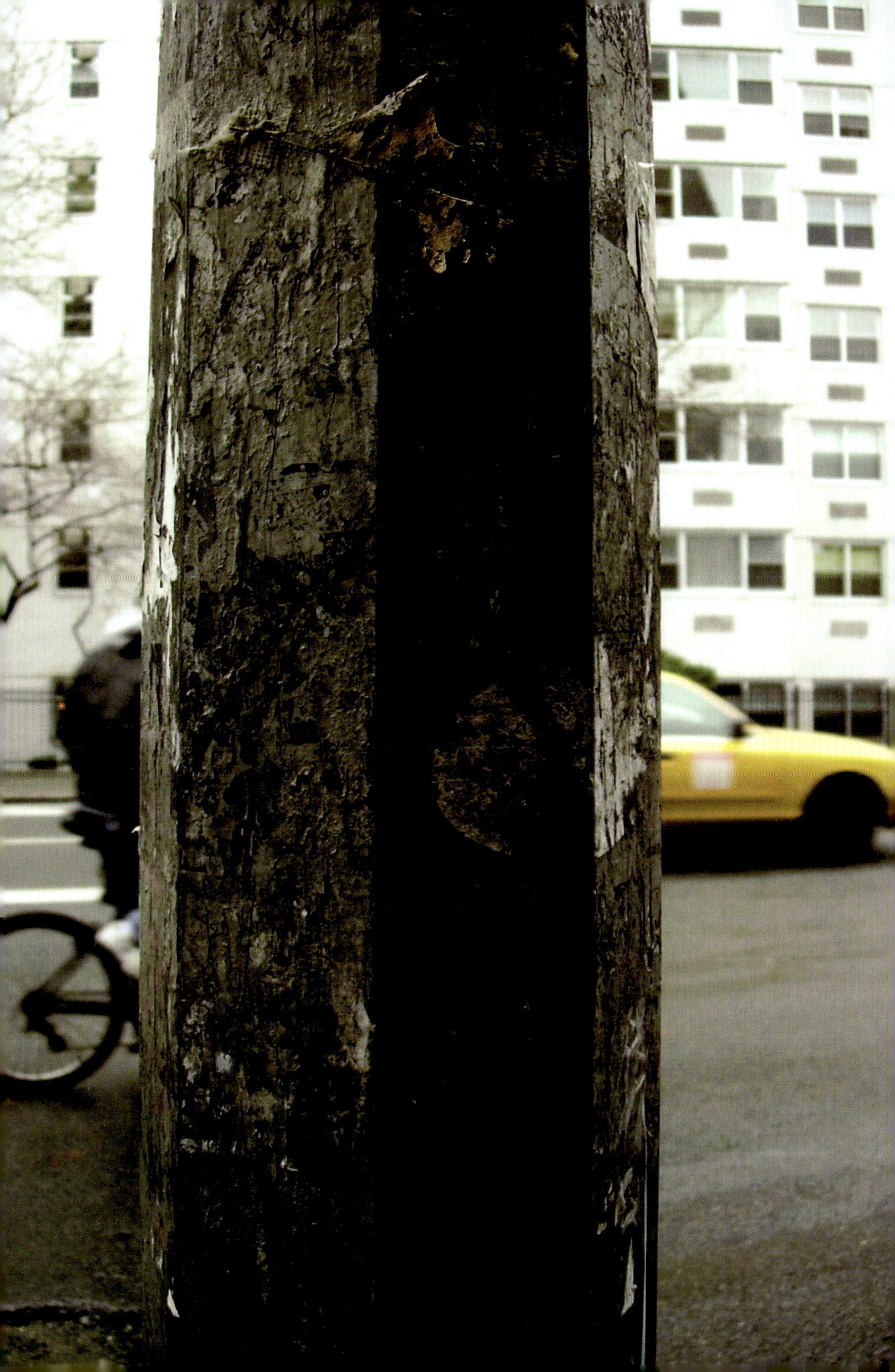

Green Dress, c. 1957

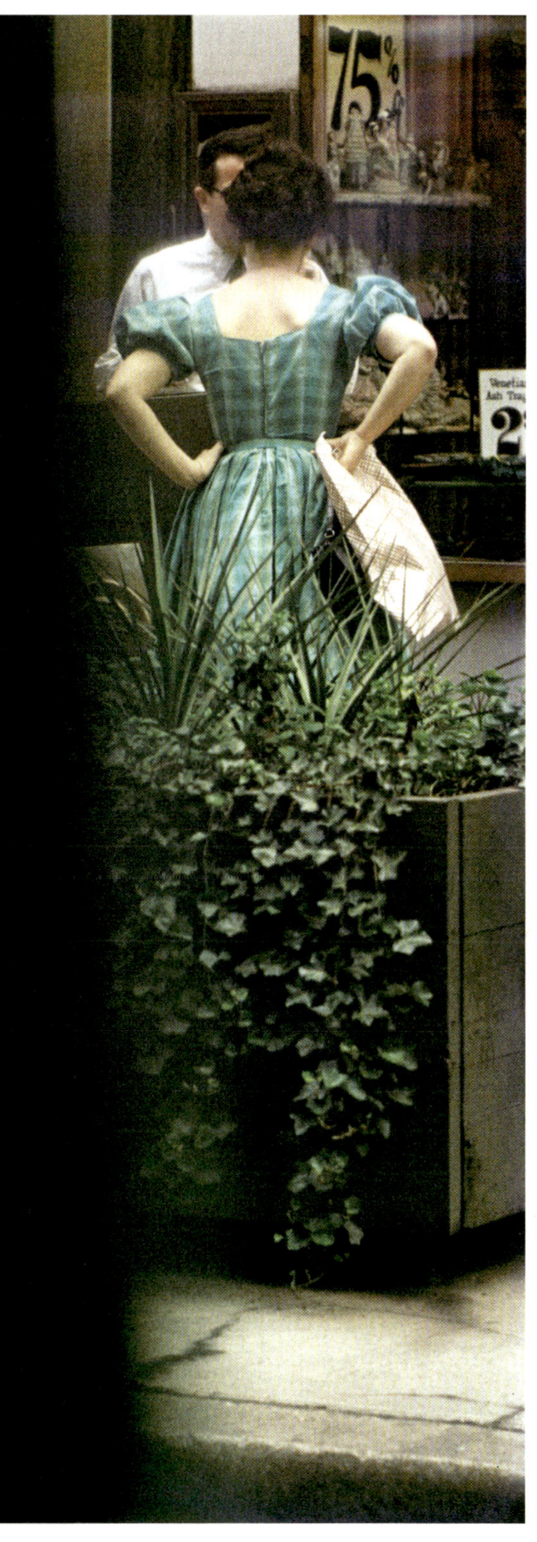

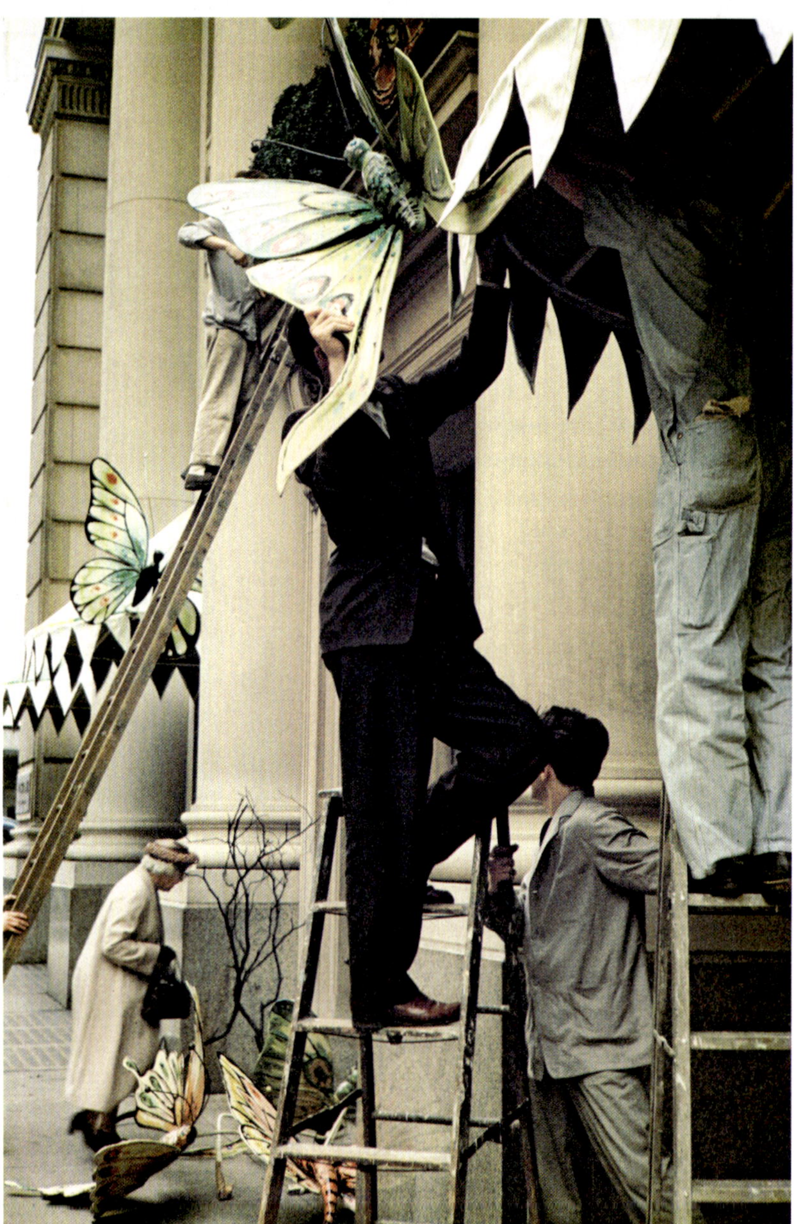

Hanging Butterflies, 1960s   Worker, 1950s

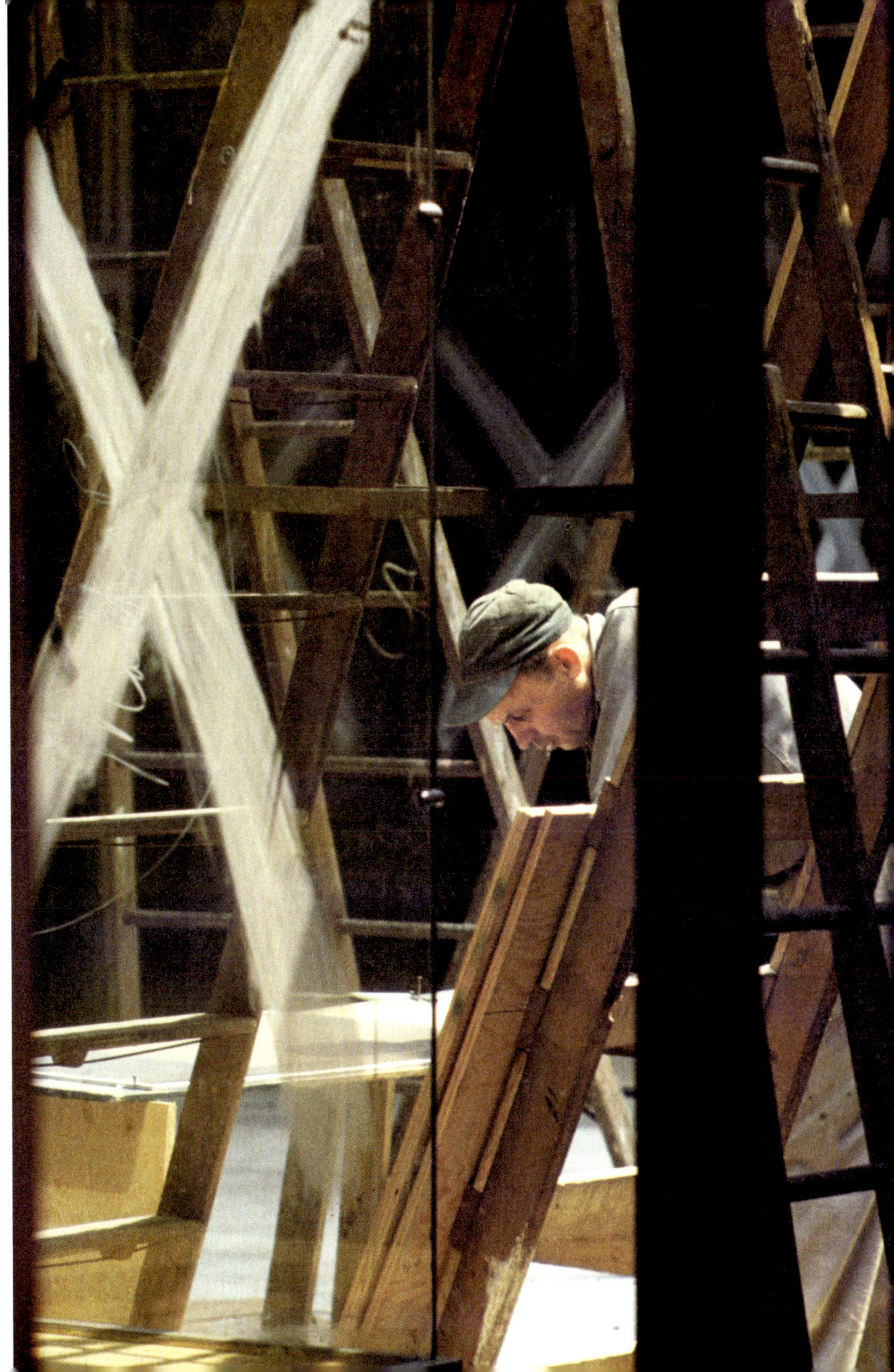

I don't see why you can't be good at something
without taking yourself so seriously.

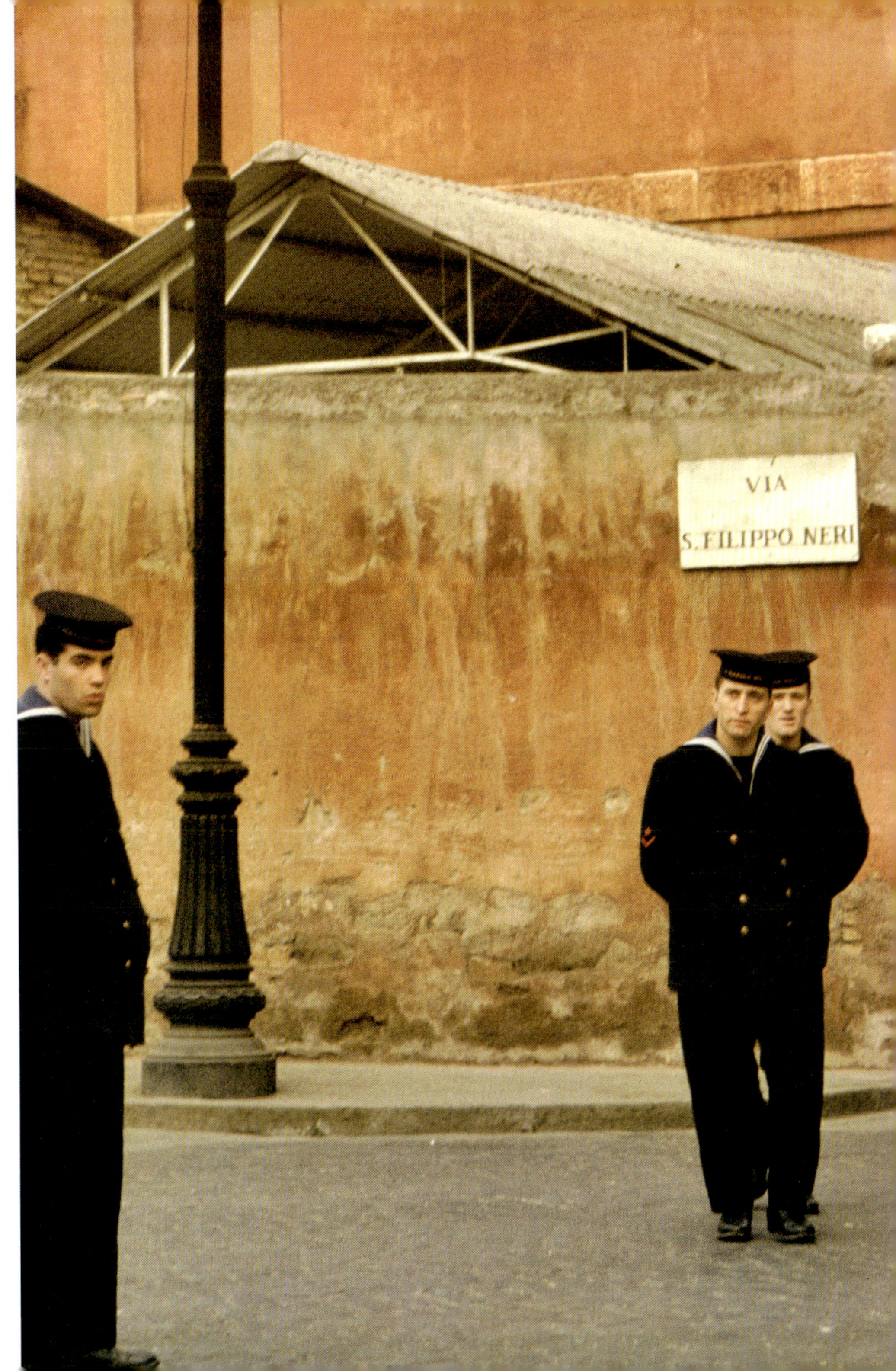

VIA
S. FILIPPO NERI

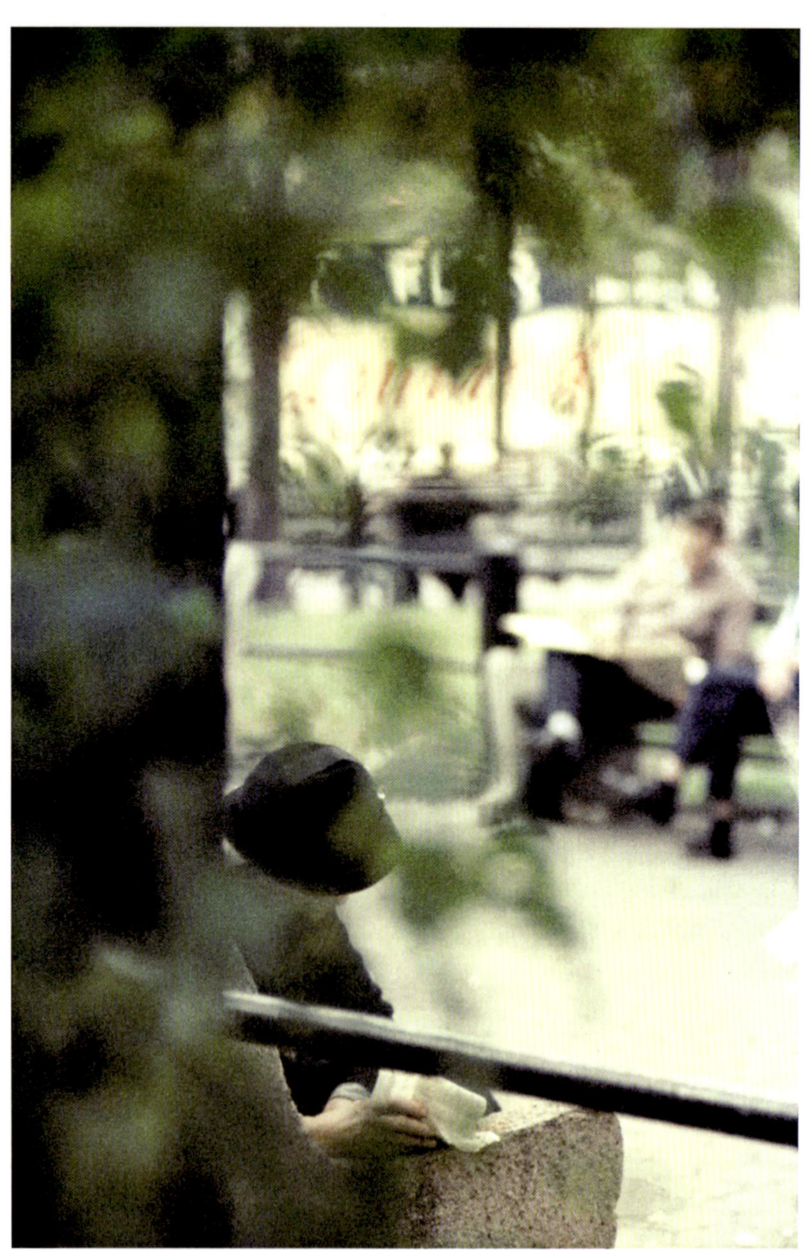

Untitled, 1950s   MR., c. 1958

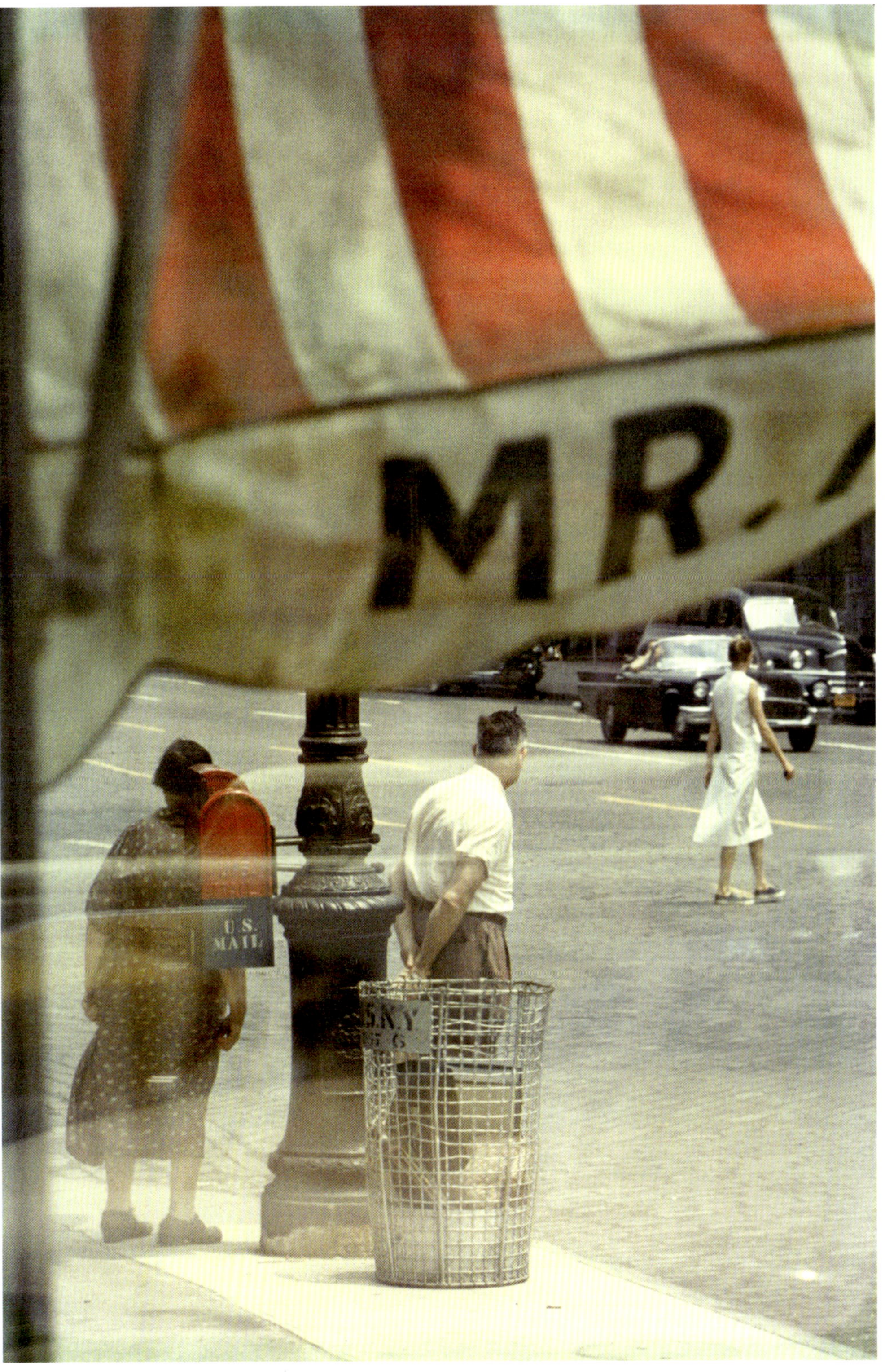
MR.
U.S.
MAIL
S.N.Y

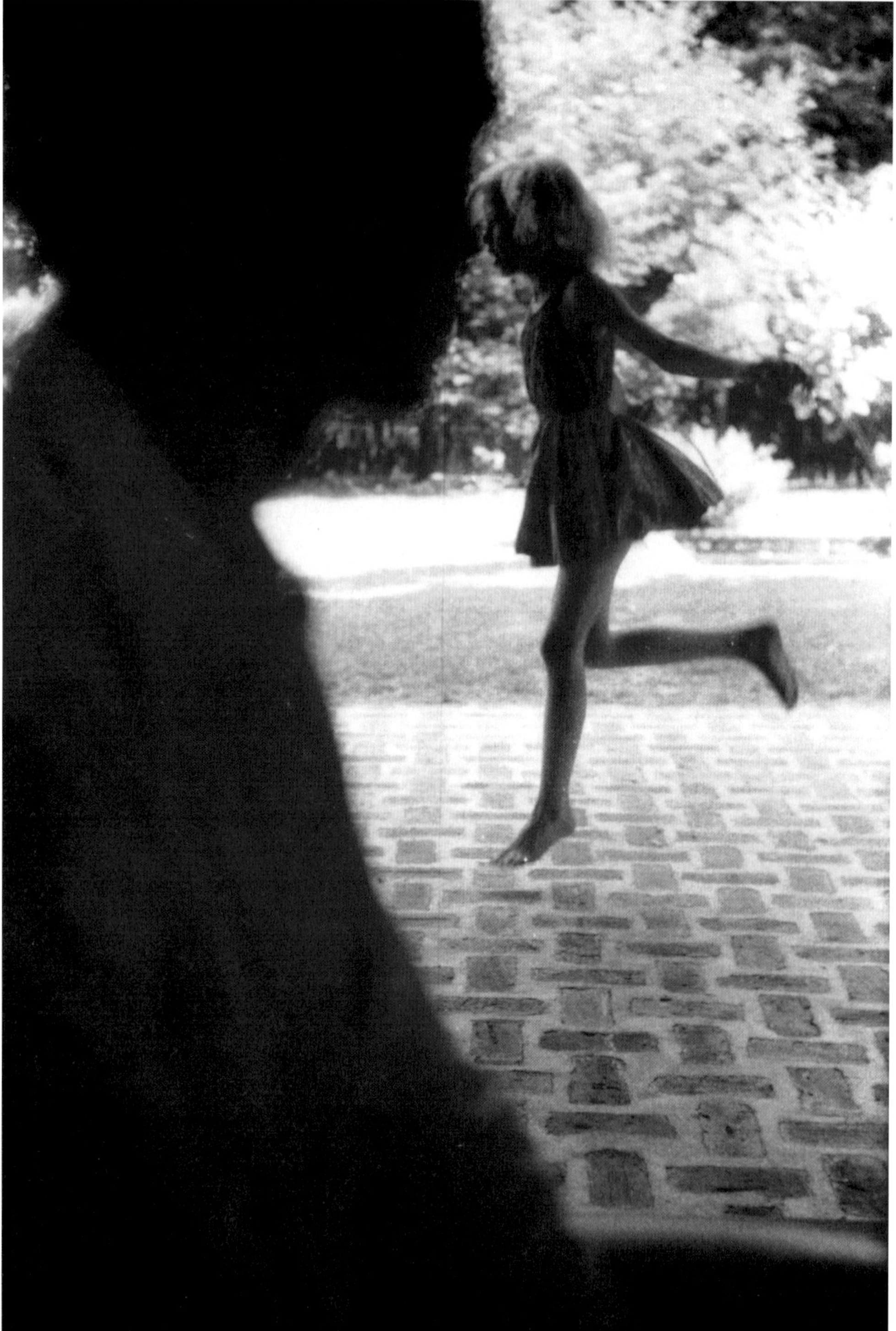

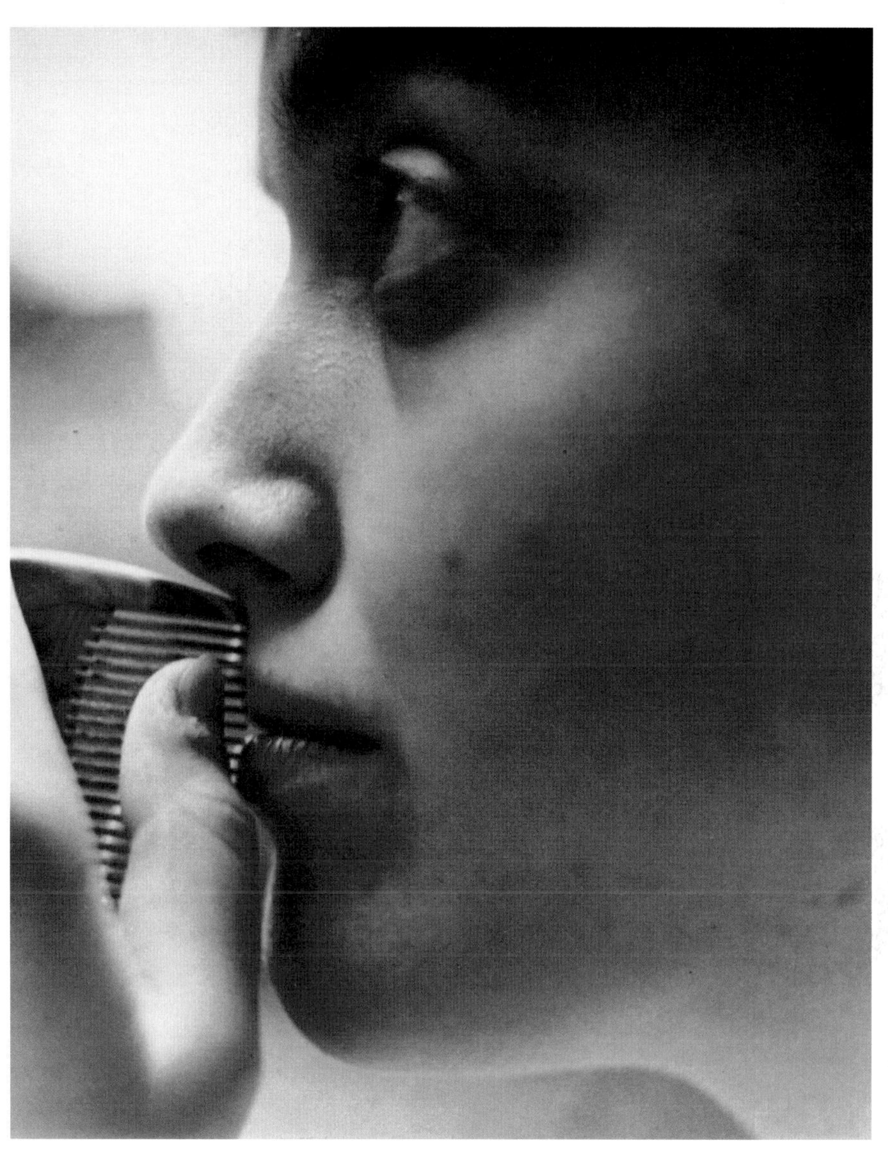

Remy, 1950s   Miriam, c. 1947

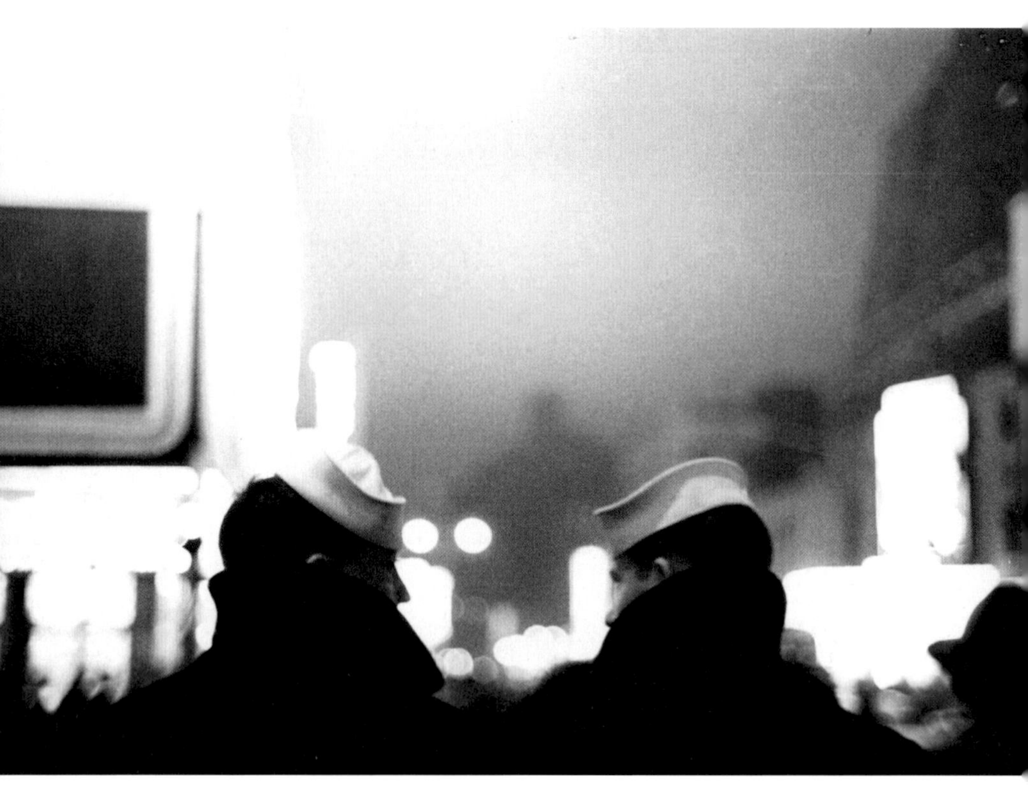

Sailors, c. 1952   Three Feet, c. 1950

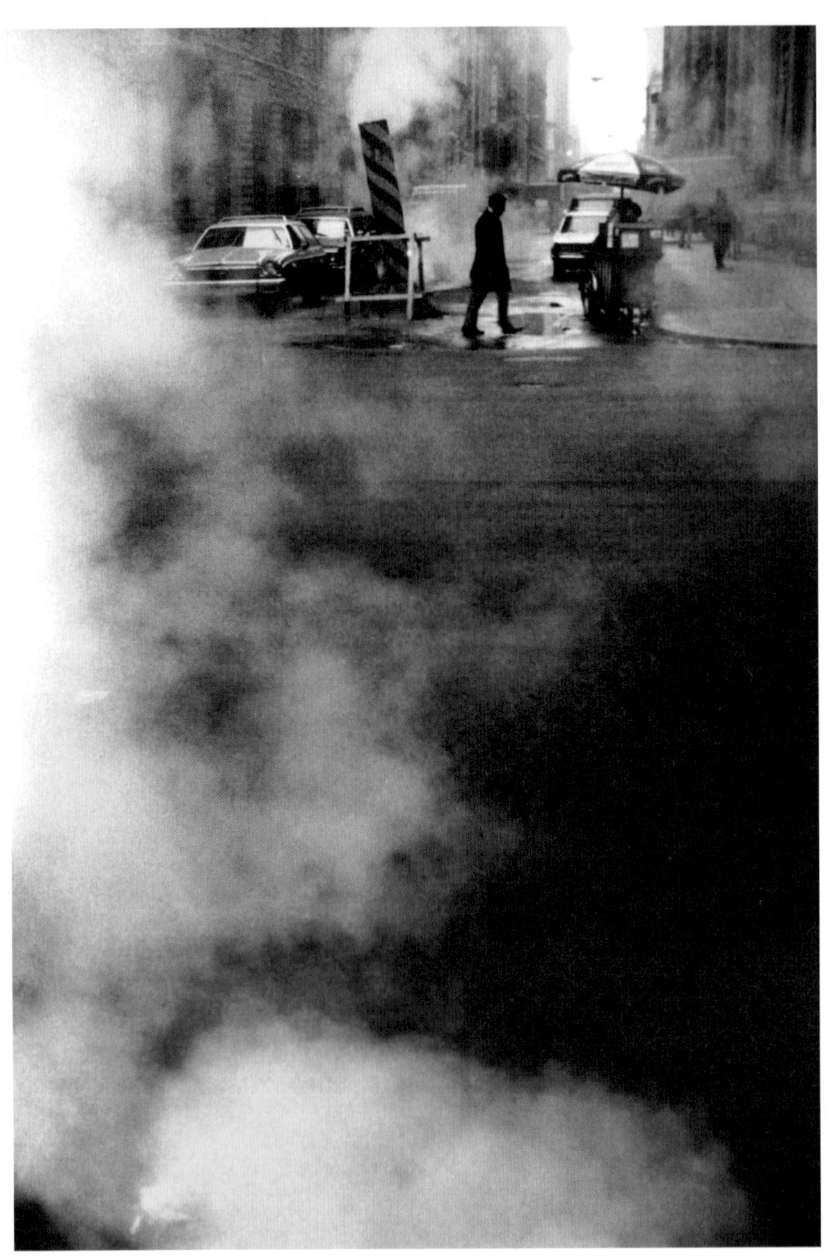

Smokestack, 1970s

Fur, c. 1950
Flower, c. 1952

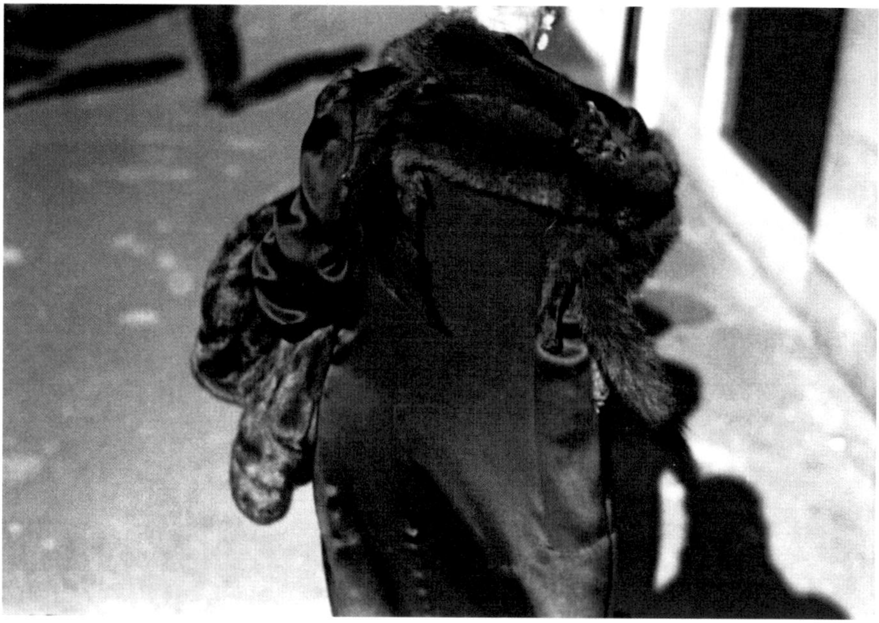

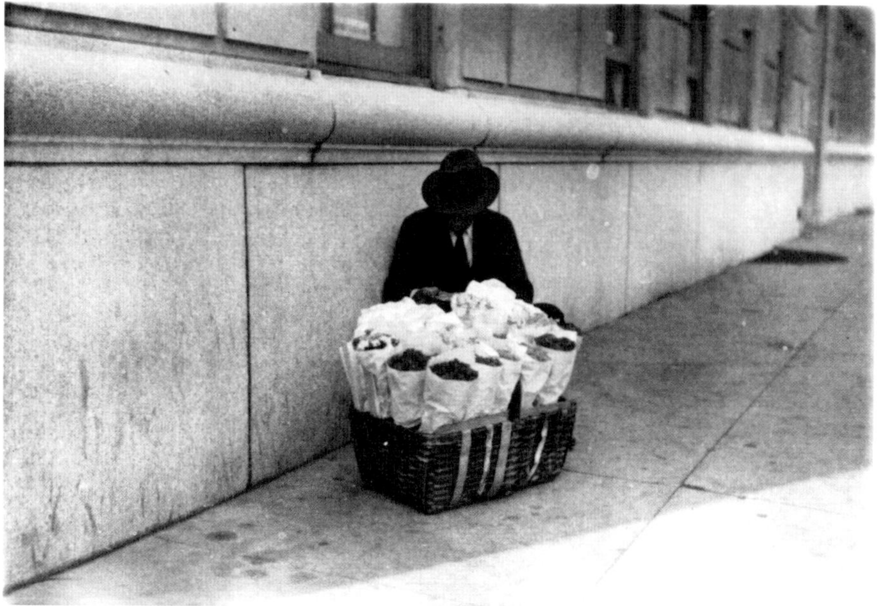

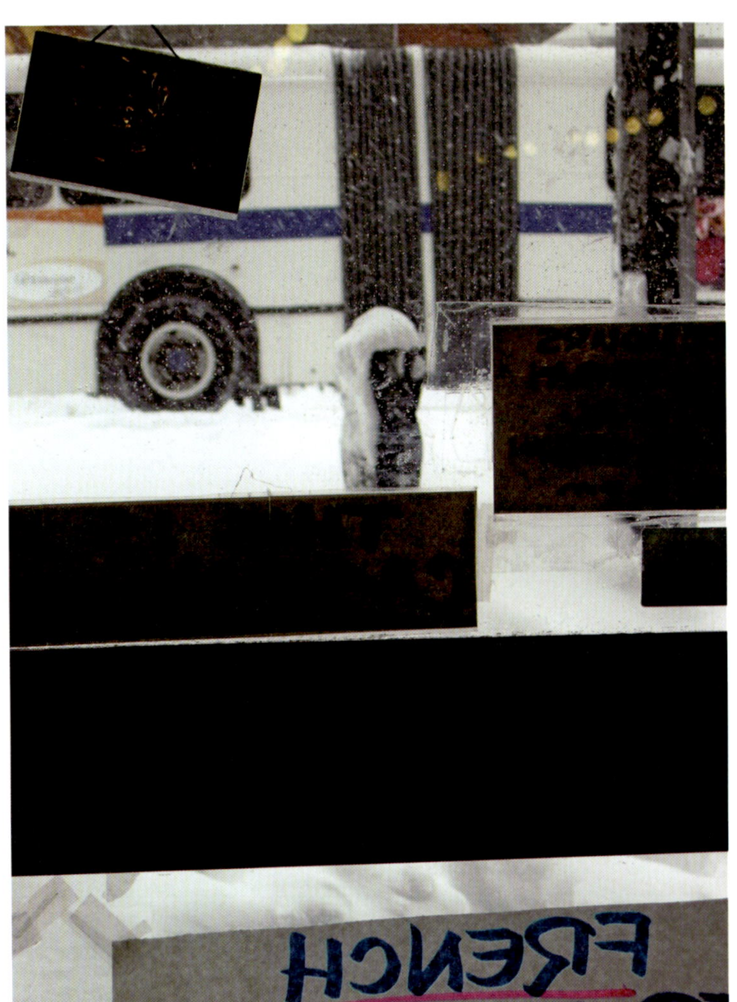

Cheese Store, c. 2008

CANAL, c. 1948

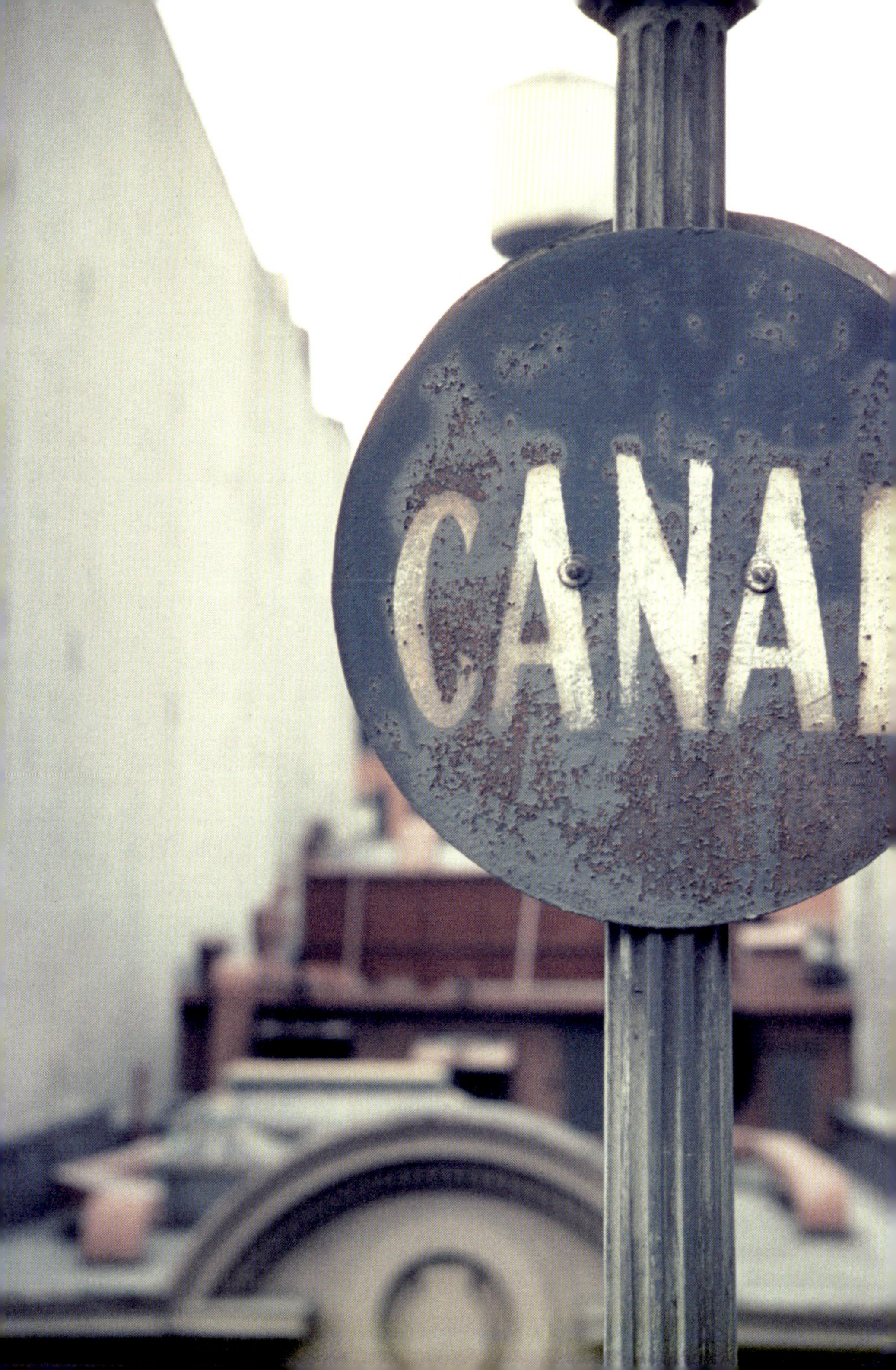
CANA

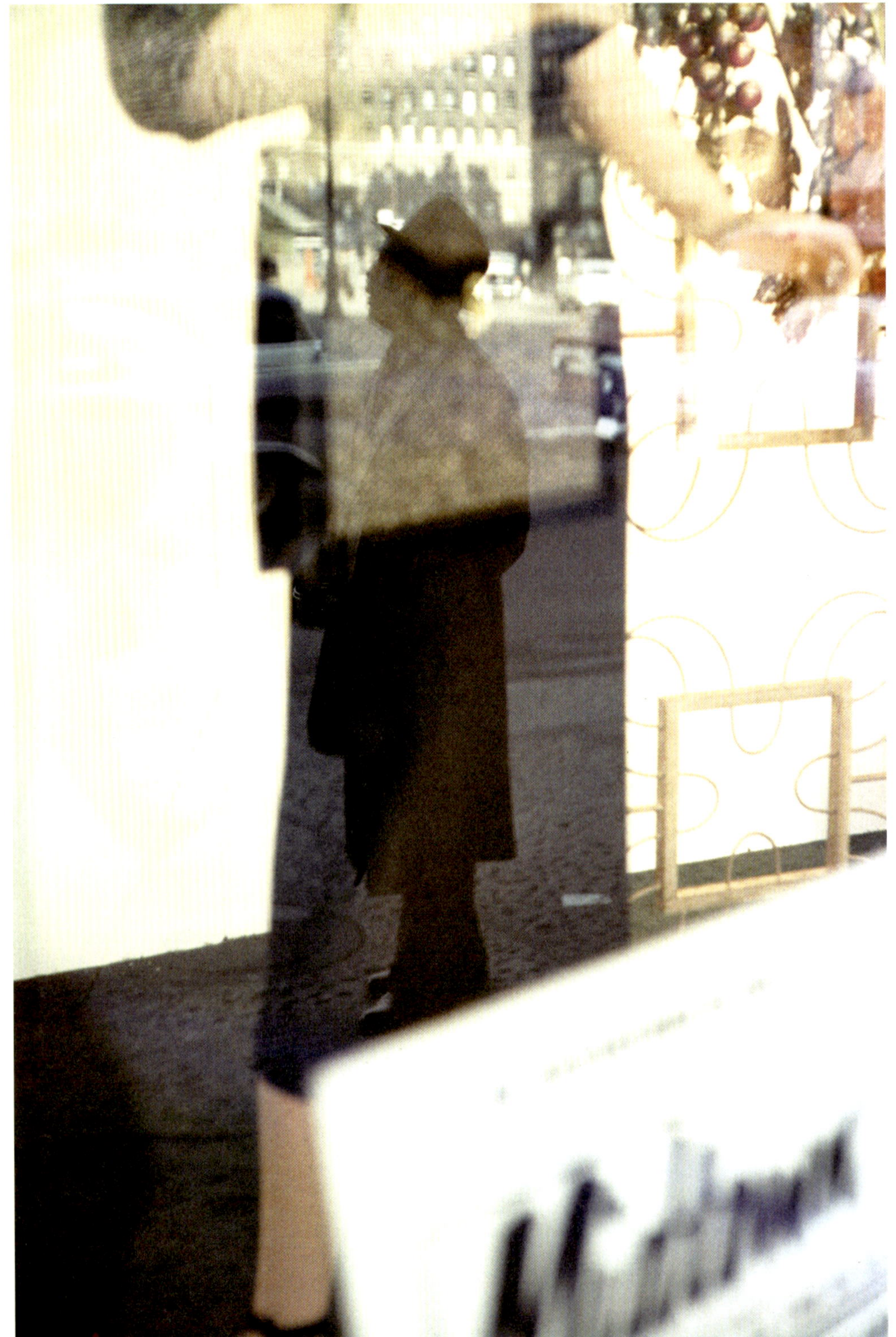

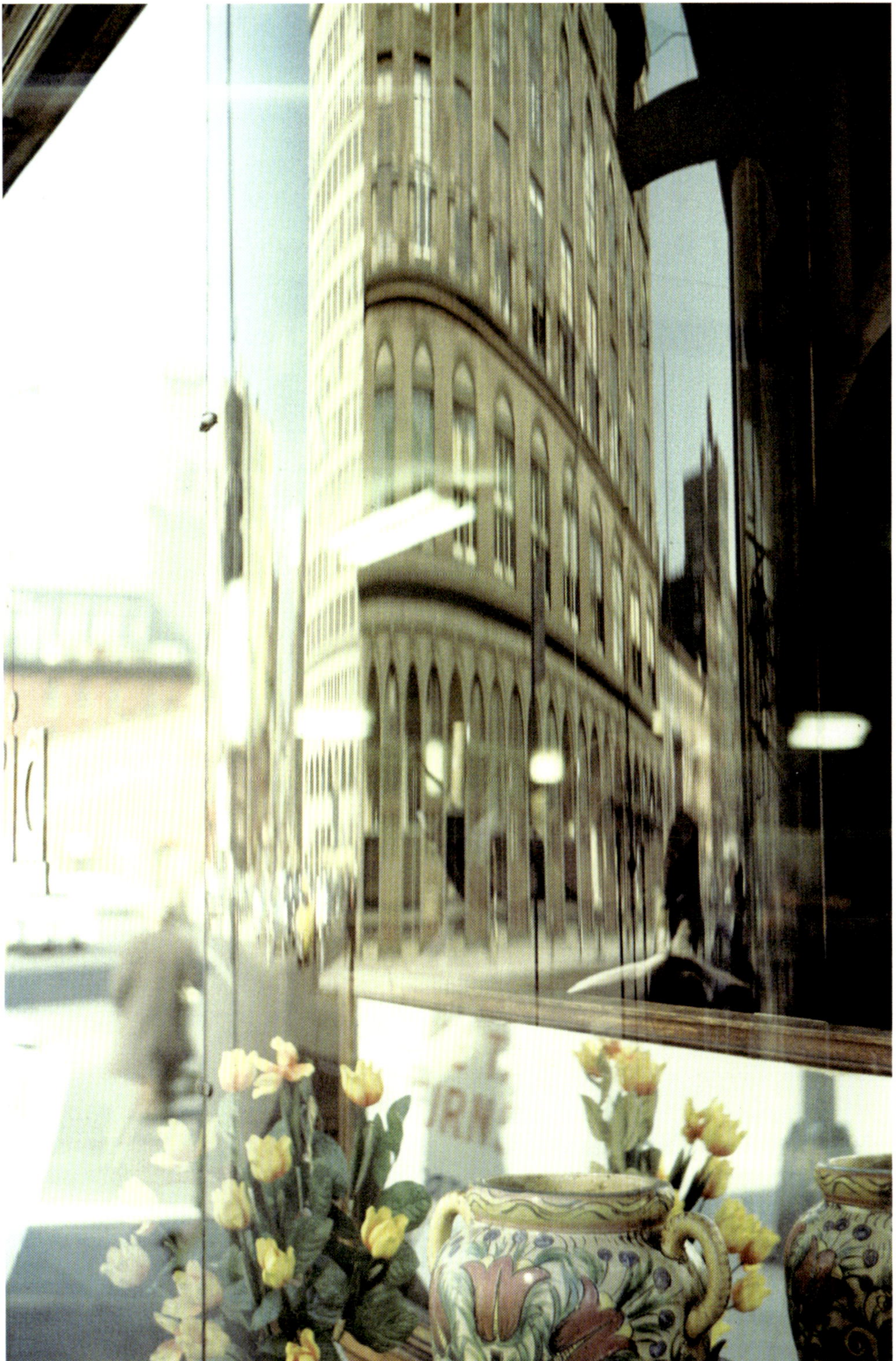

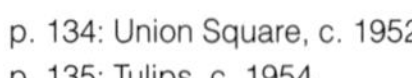

When I consider all the beautiful things that have been done,
my own achievements are rather minor.

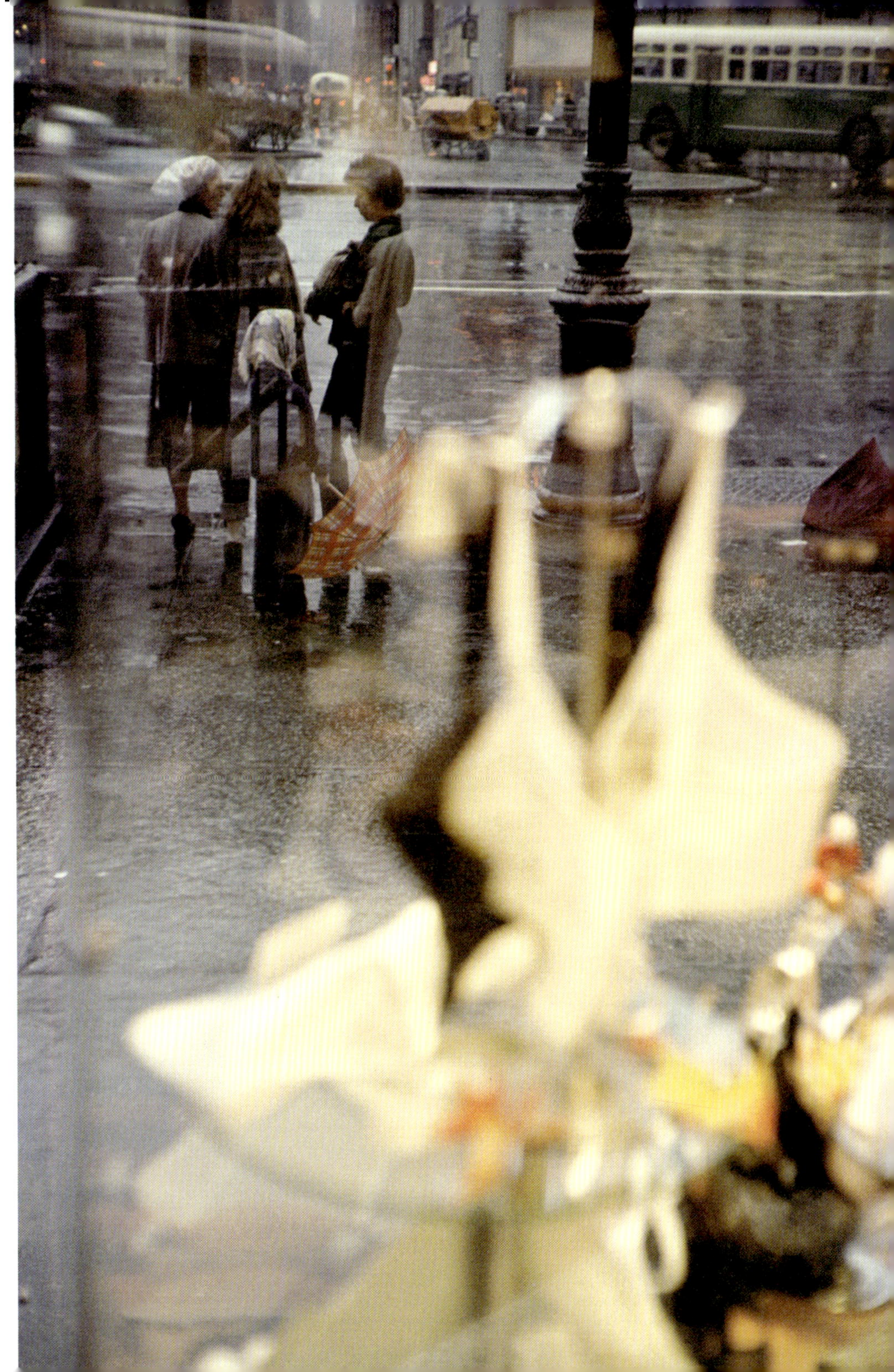

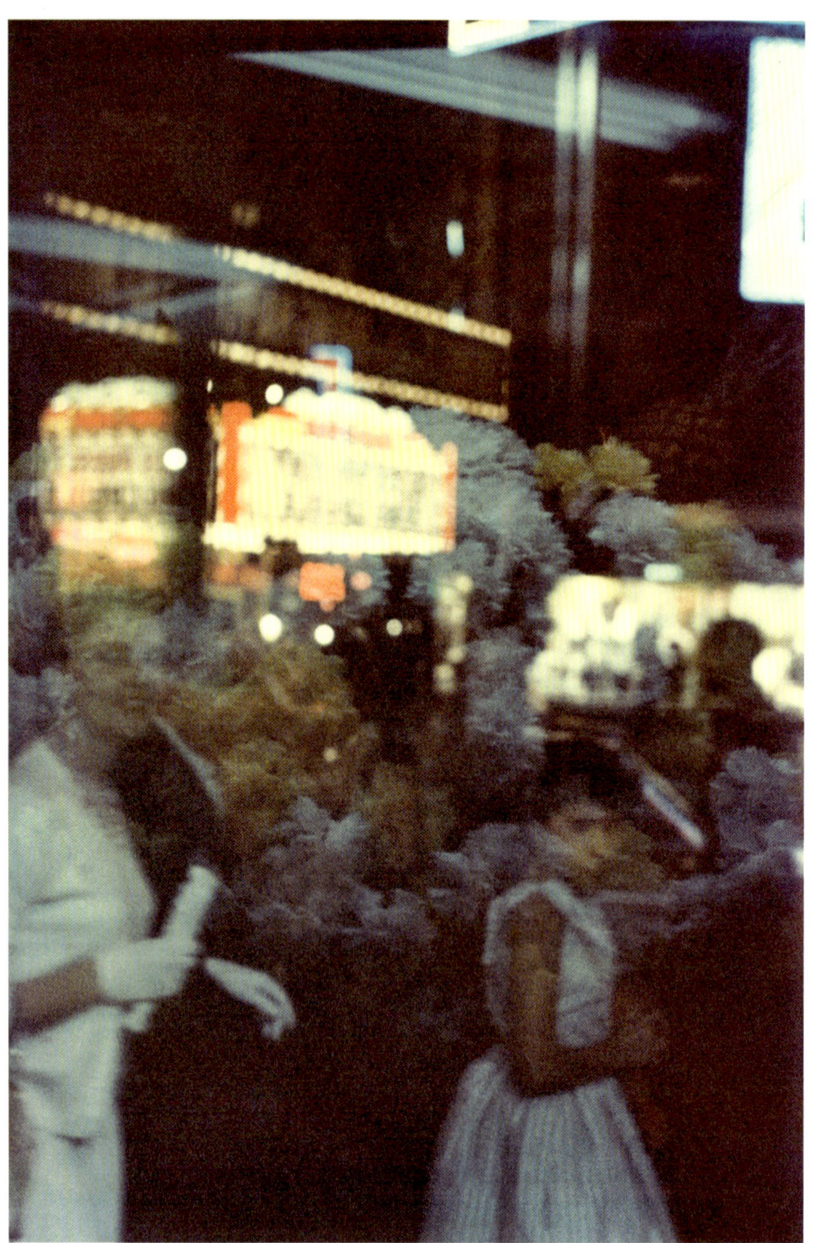

Times Square, 1950s

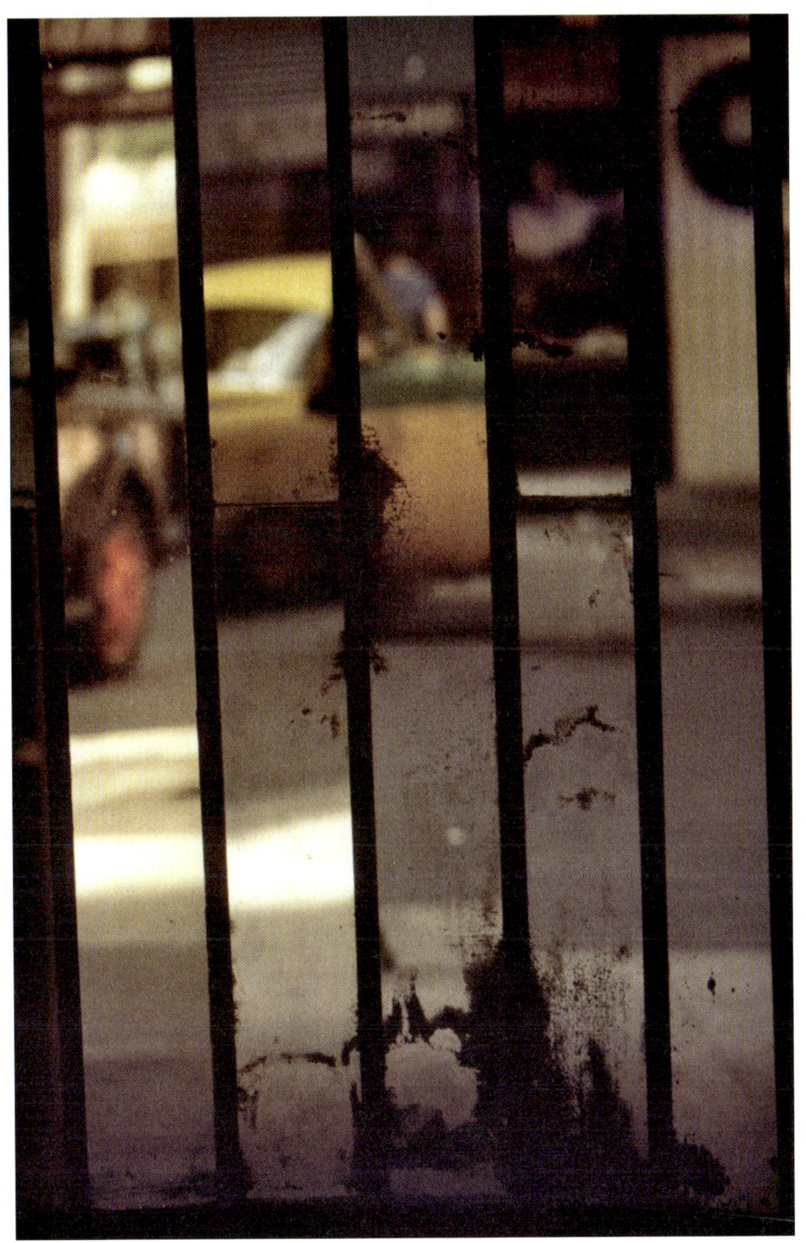

Mirrors, c. 1958

pp. 140–141: Bus, c. 2004

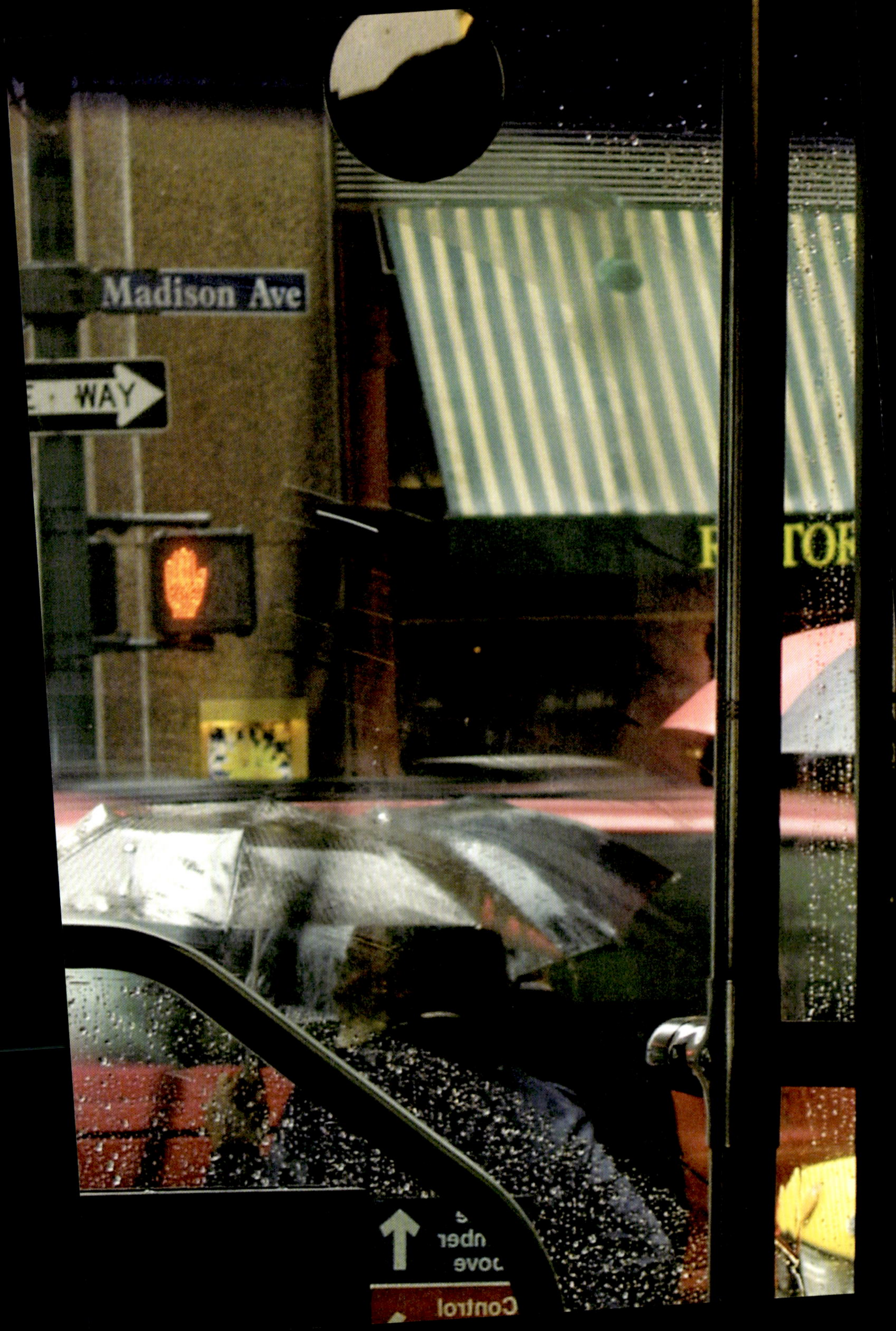

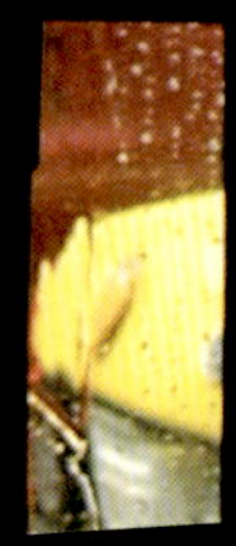

Madison Ave
WAY
Control

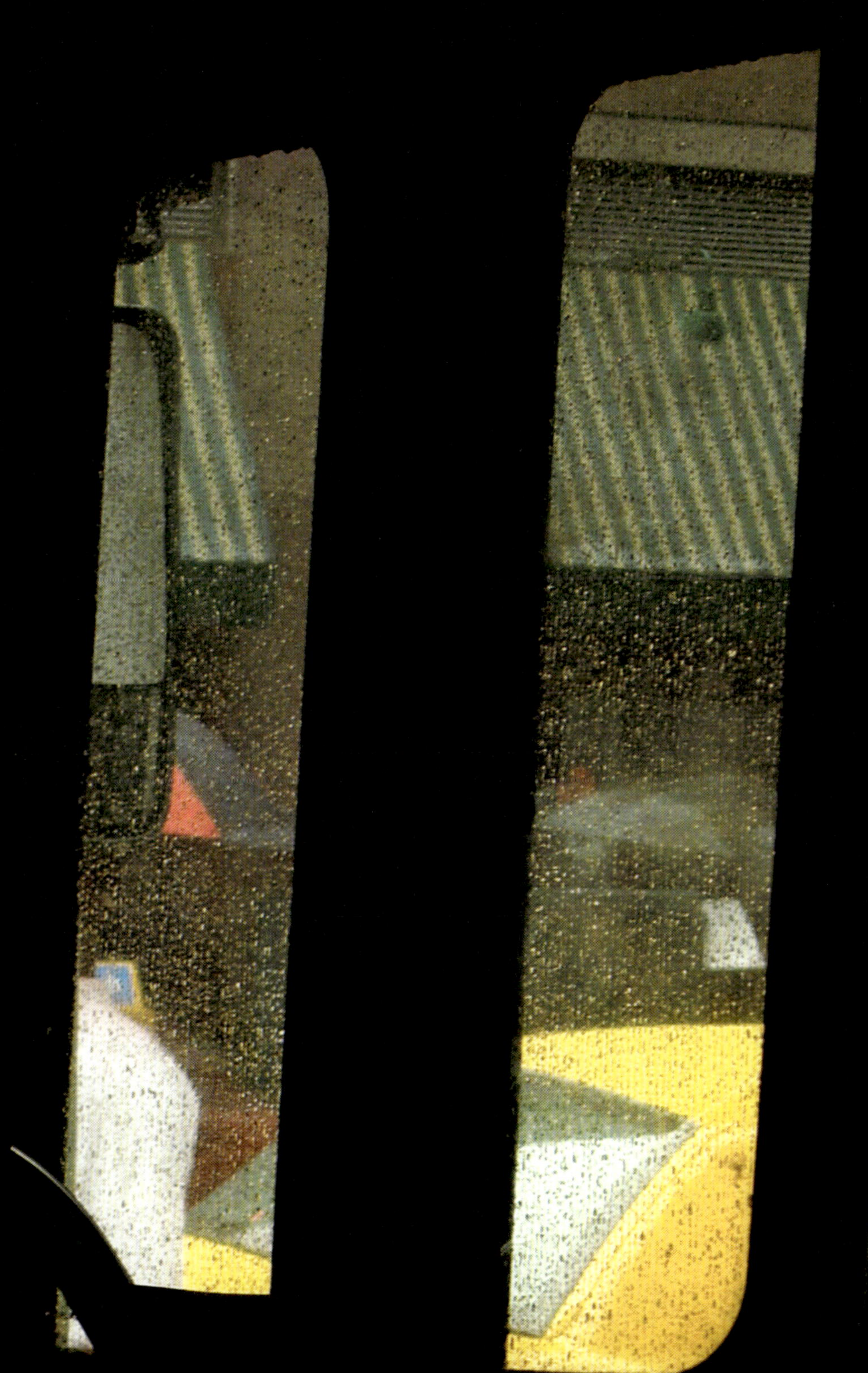

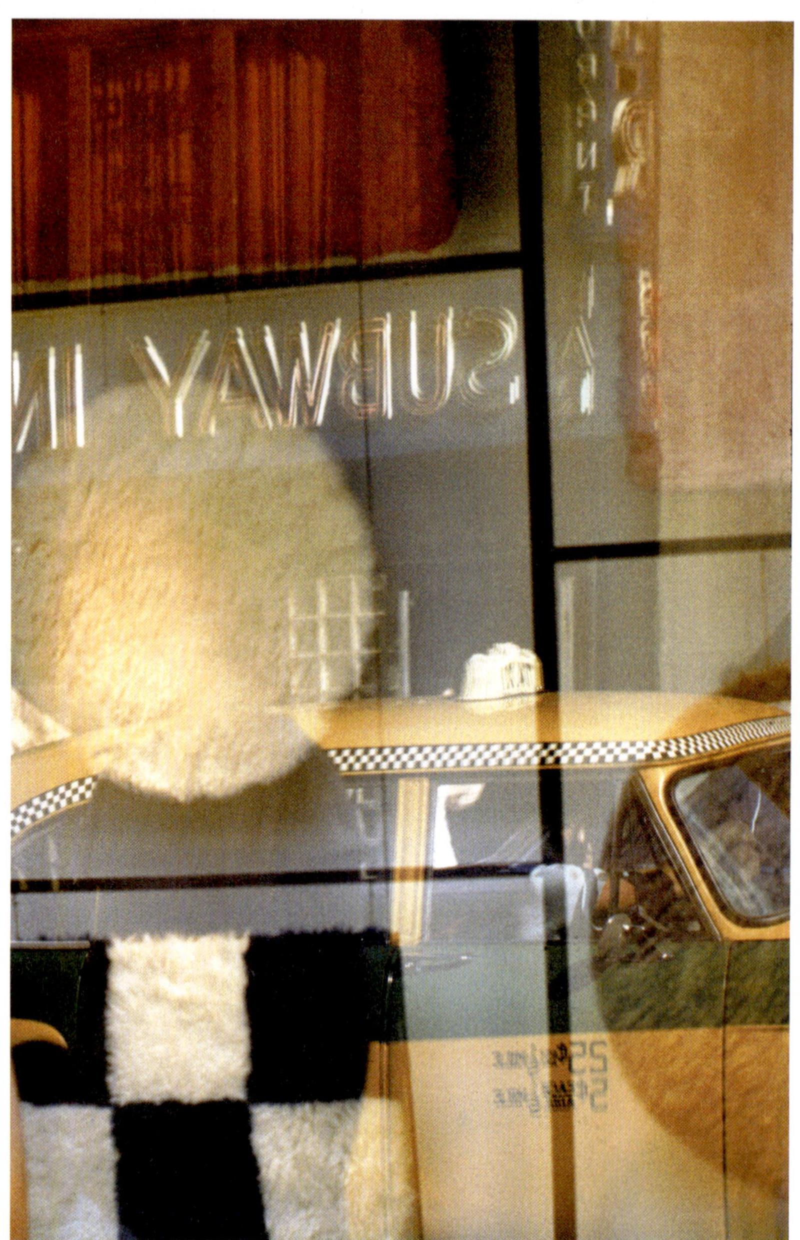

Subway Window, 1950s

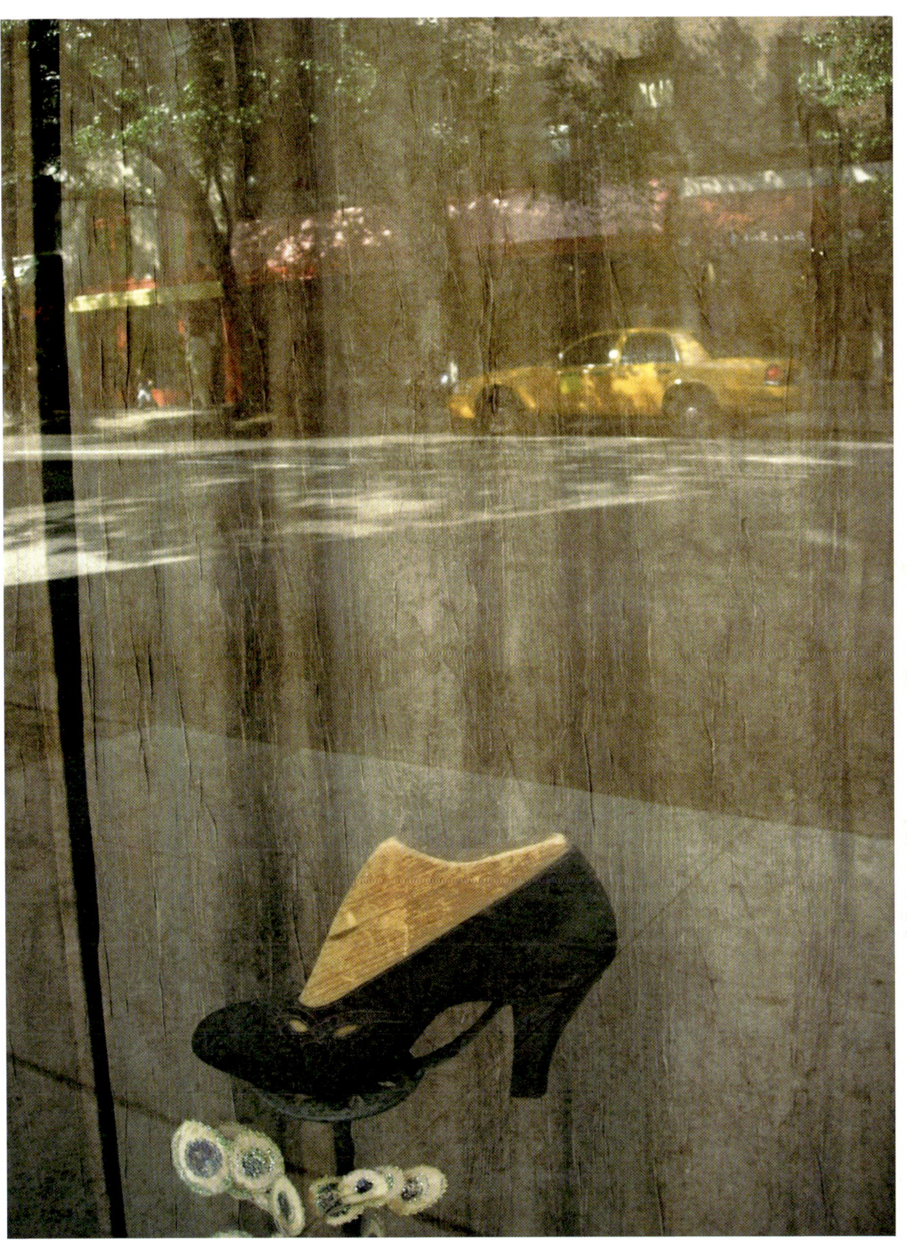

Shoe, c. 2006

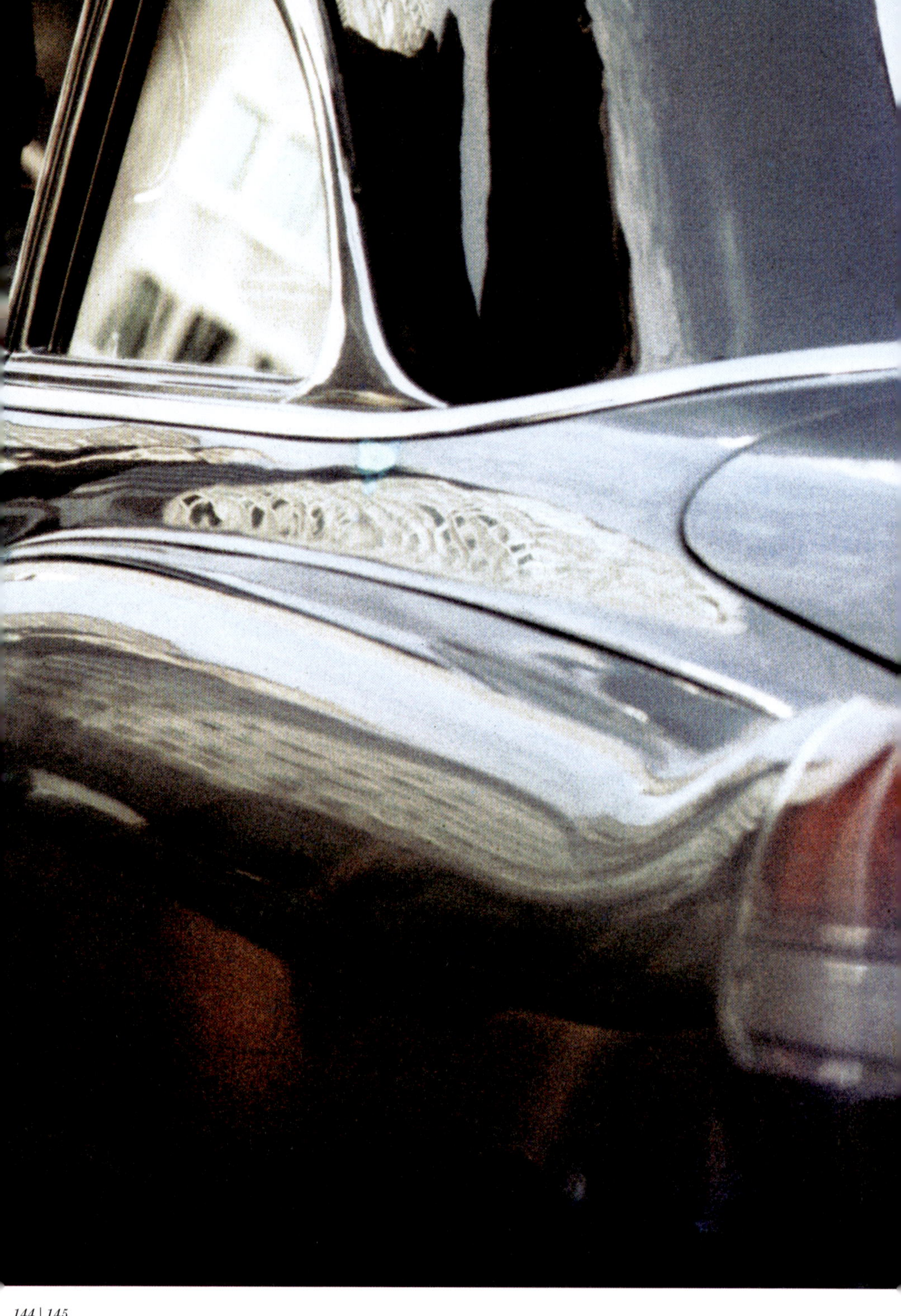

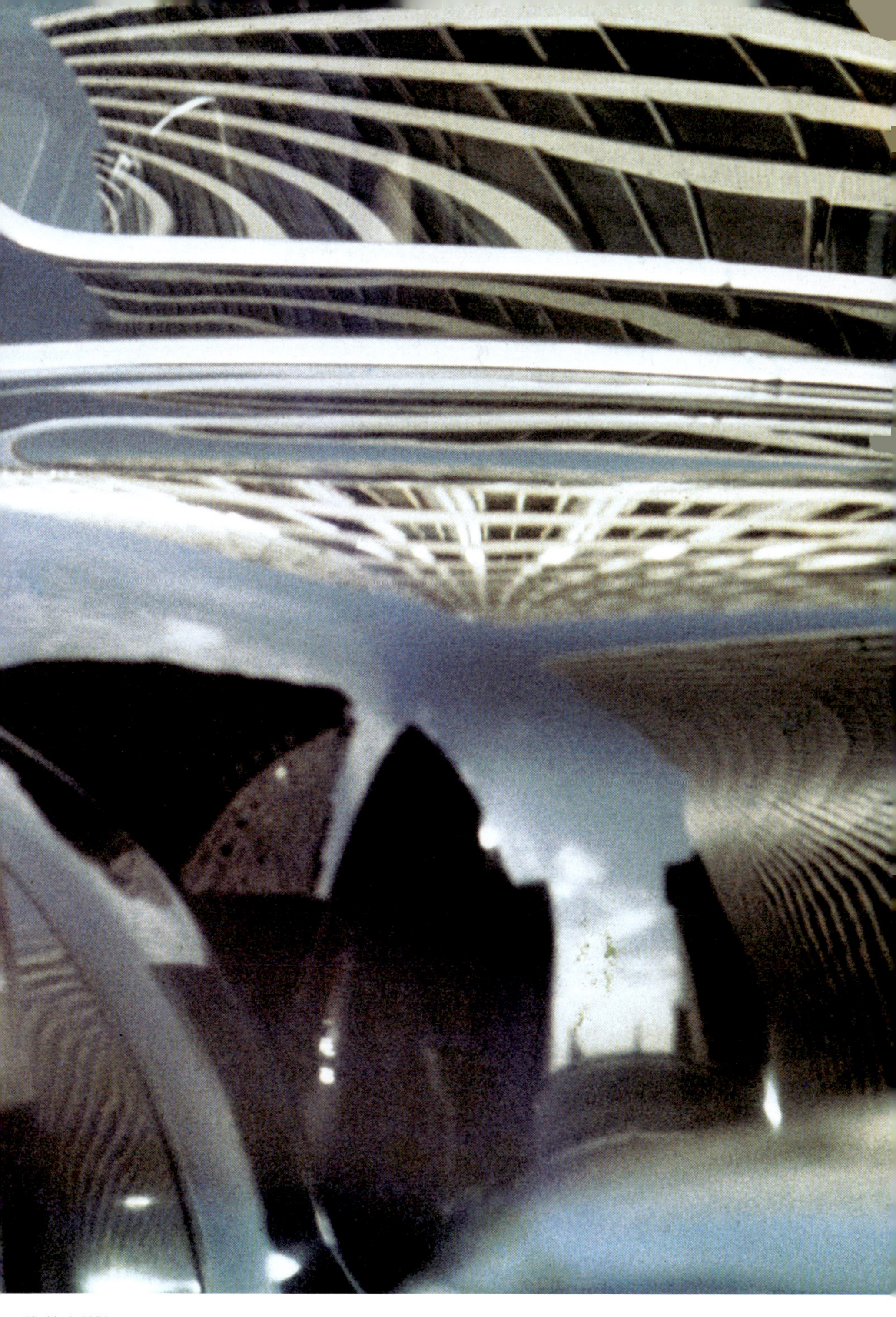

Untitled, 1950s

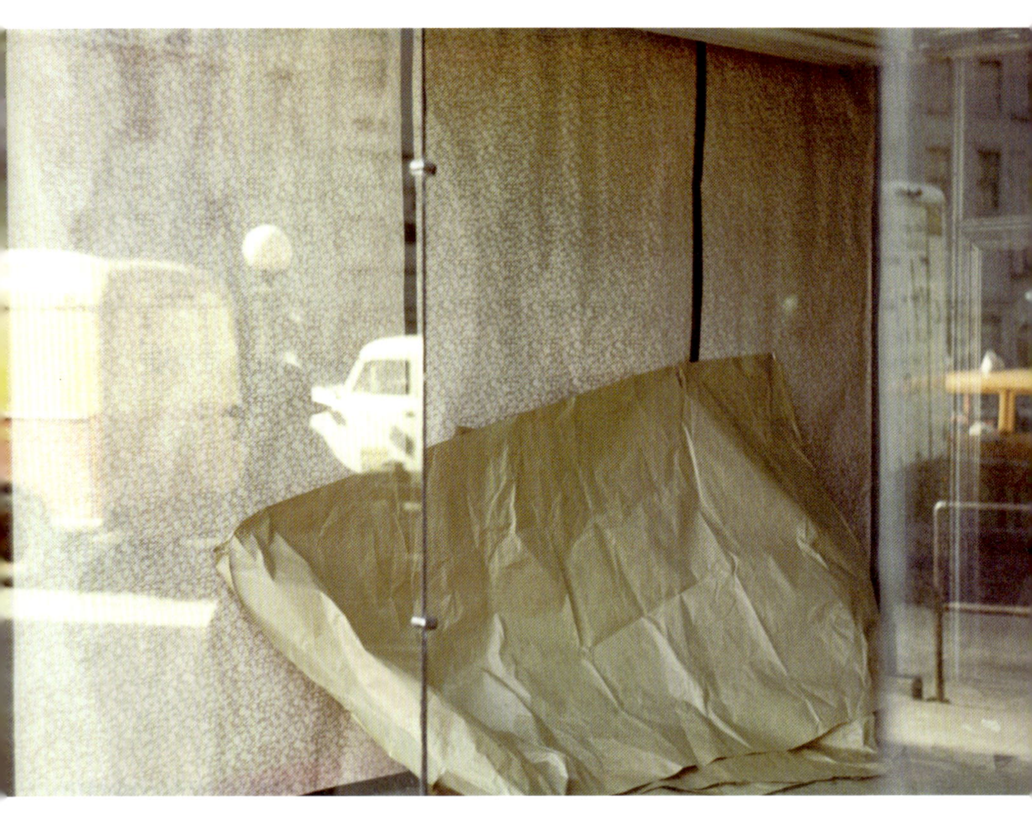

Paper, 1950s   London Map, c. 2008

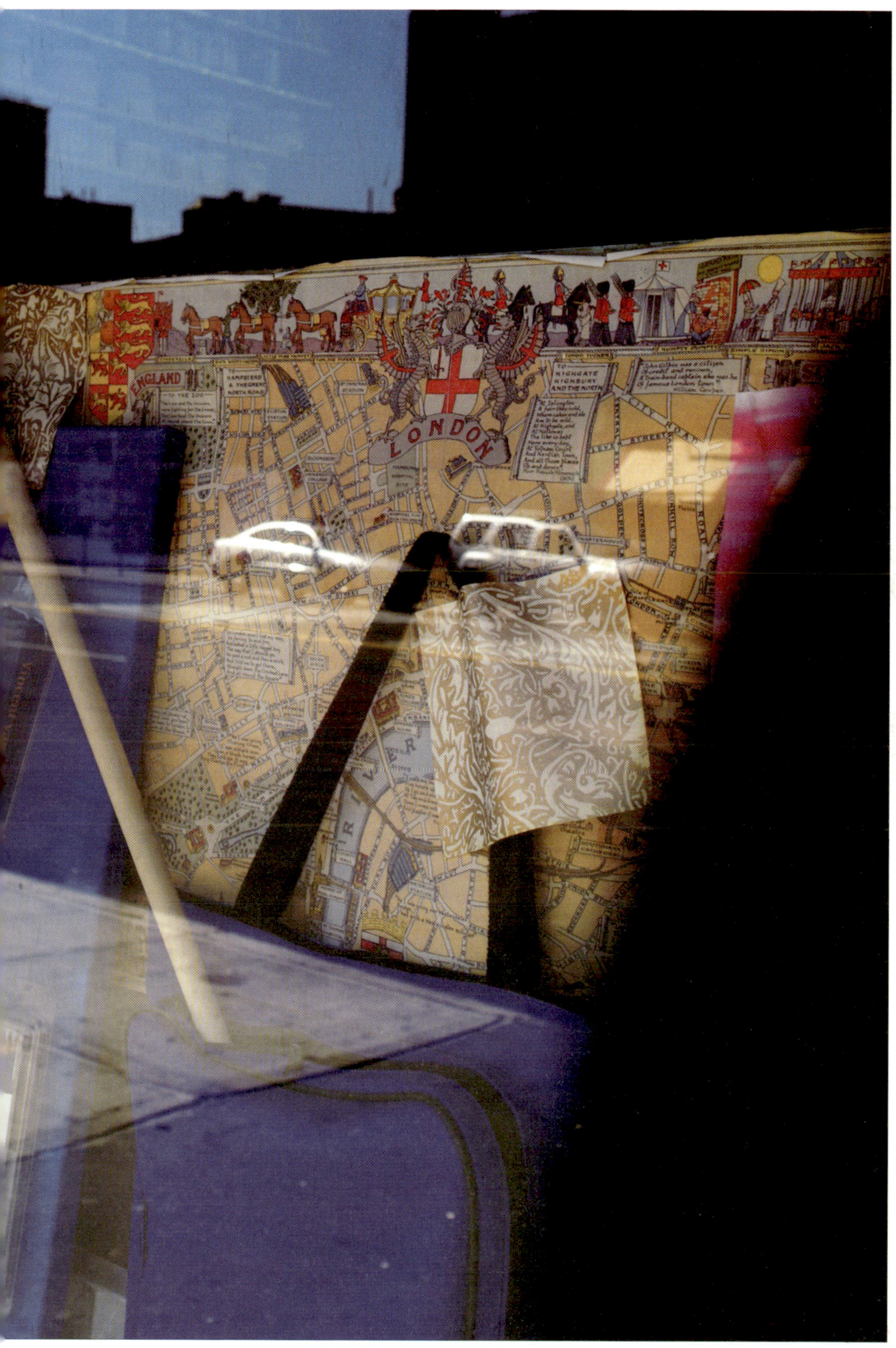

ENGLAND
LONDON
HIGHGATE
HIGHBURY
AND THE NORTH
HAMPSTEAD
& THE GREAT
NORTH ROAD
RIVER

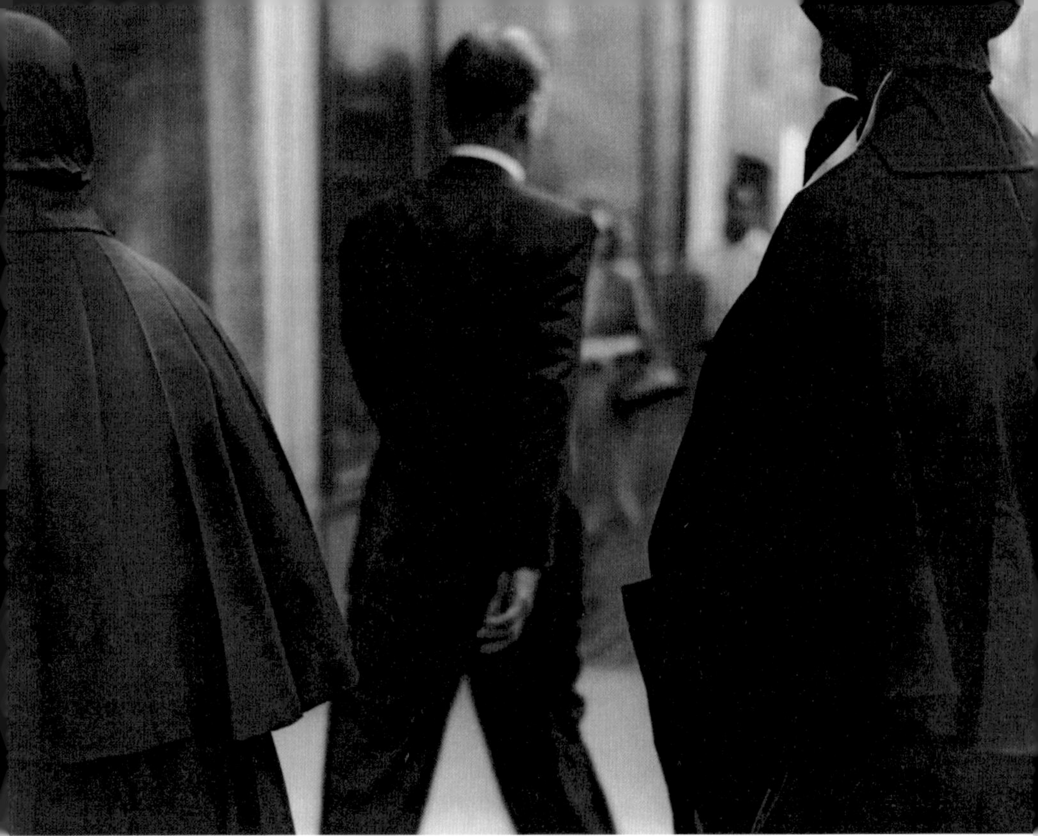

Nuns, c. 1955

Miriam, c. 1947
Kathy and Gloria, Brooklyn, c. 1948

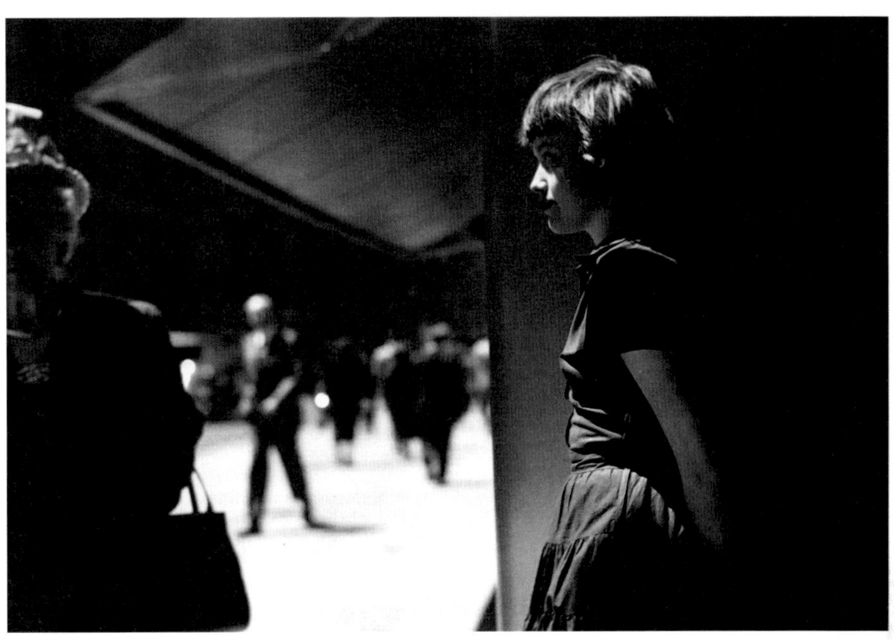

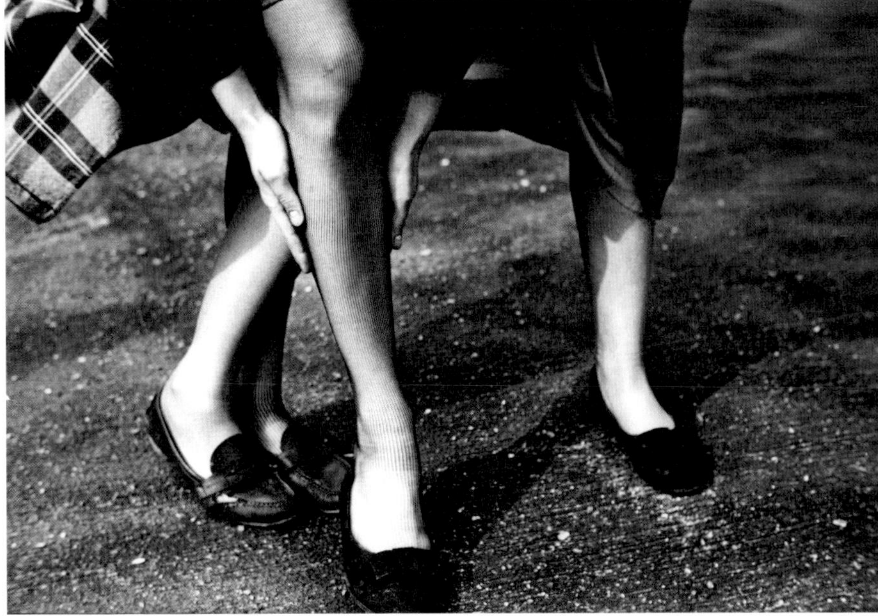

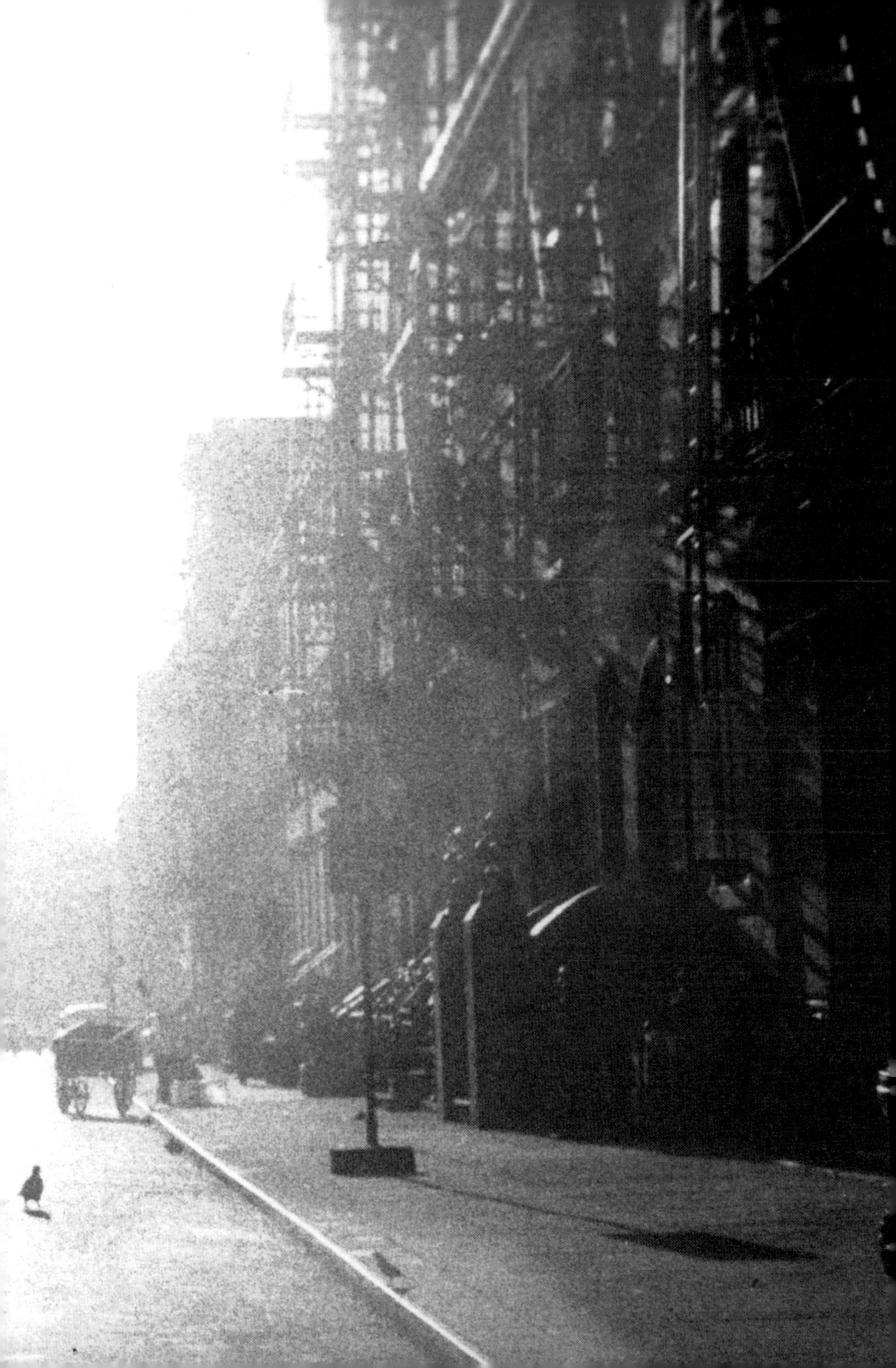

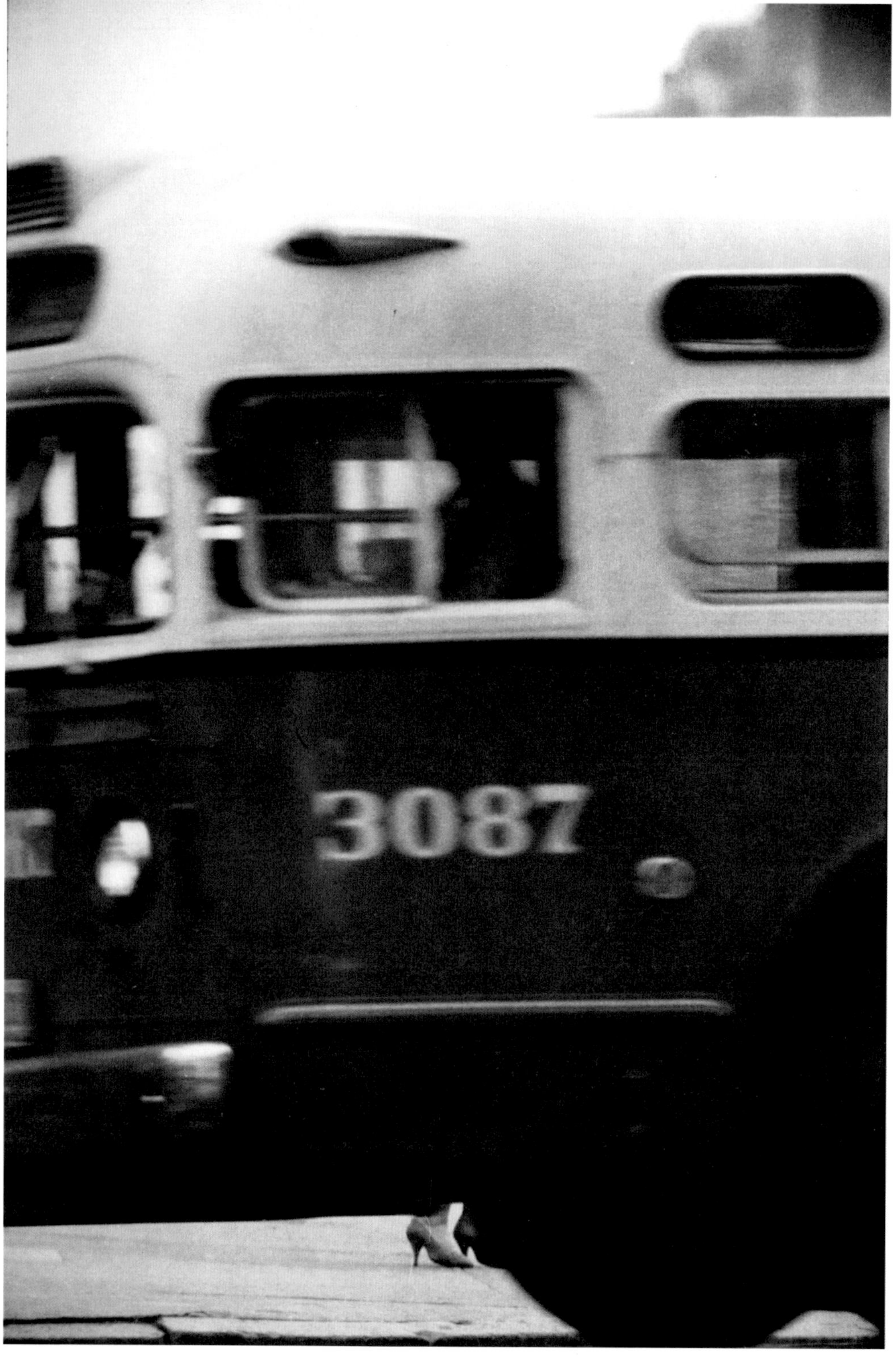
3087

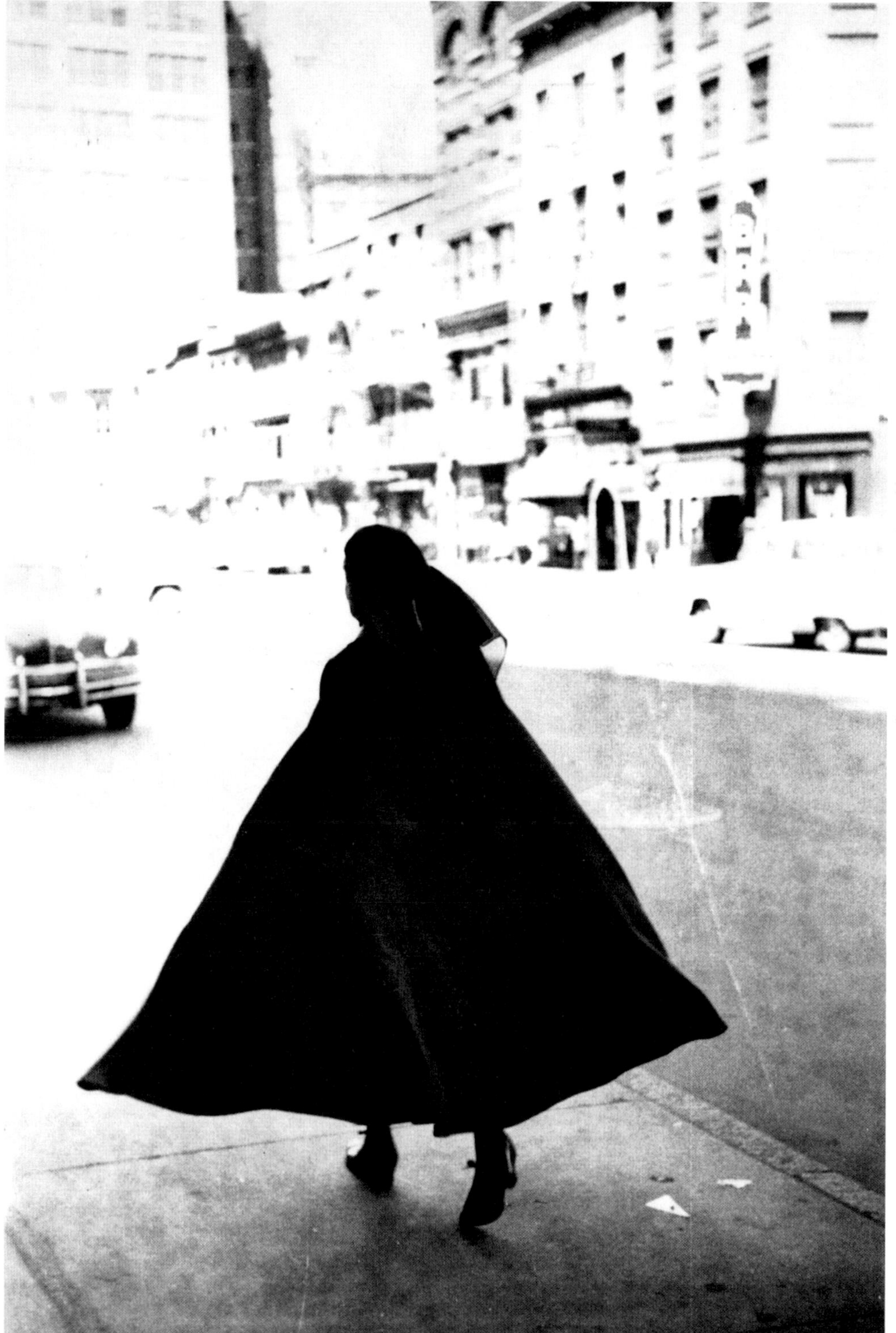

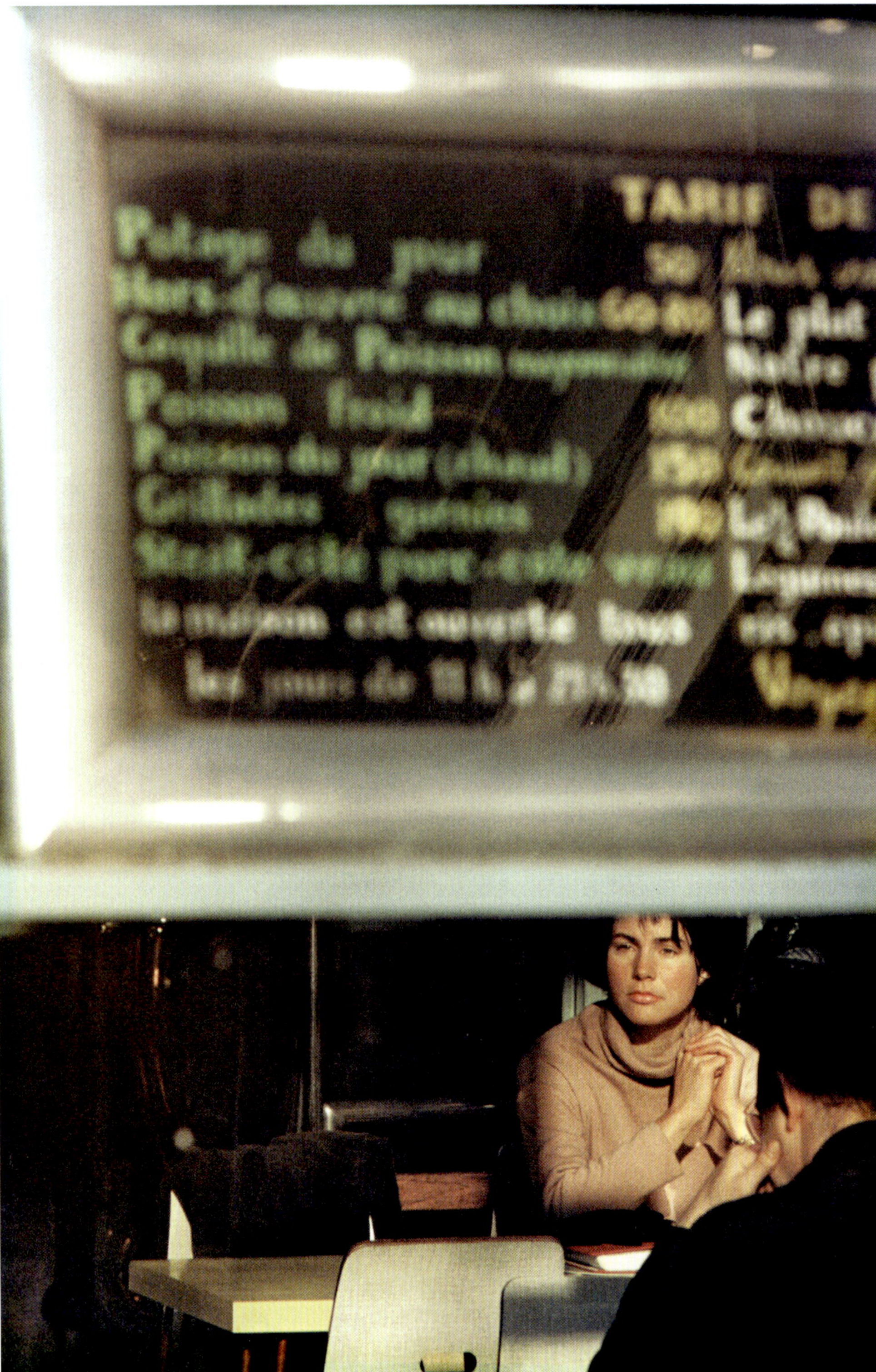

I've enjoyed having books.

I've enjoyed looking at paintings.

I've enjoyed having someone in my life that I care about who cares about me.

I attached more importance to that than I did to the idea of success.

Red Light, c. 1960

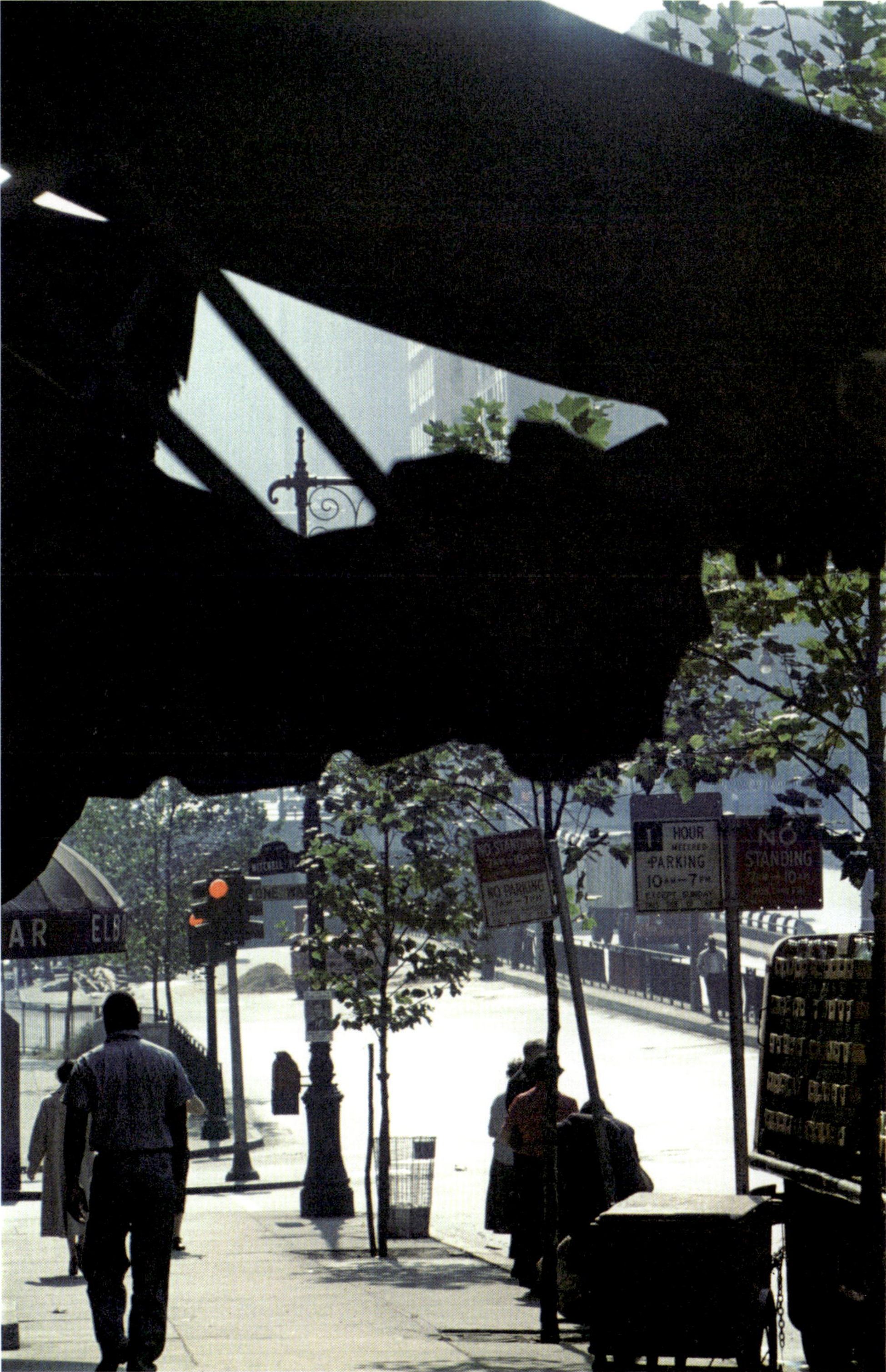

NO STANDING
NO PARKING
ONE WAY
MITCHELL PL
HOUR
METERED
PARKING
10 AM — 7 PM
EXCEPT SUNDAY
NO
STANDING
AR EL

Art consists of endless re-evaluation: Someone is great, then they're forgotten.
Then they're revived, then they're forgotten again.
And it goes on and on and on.

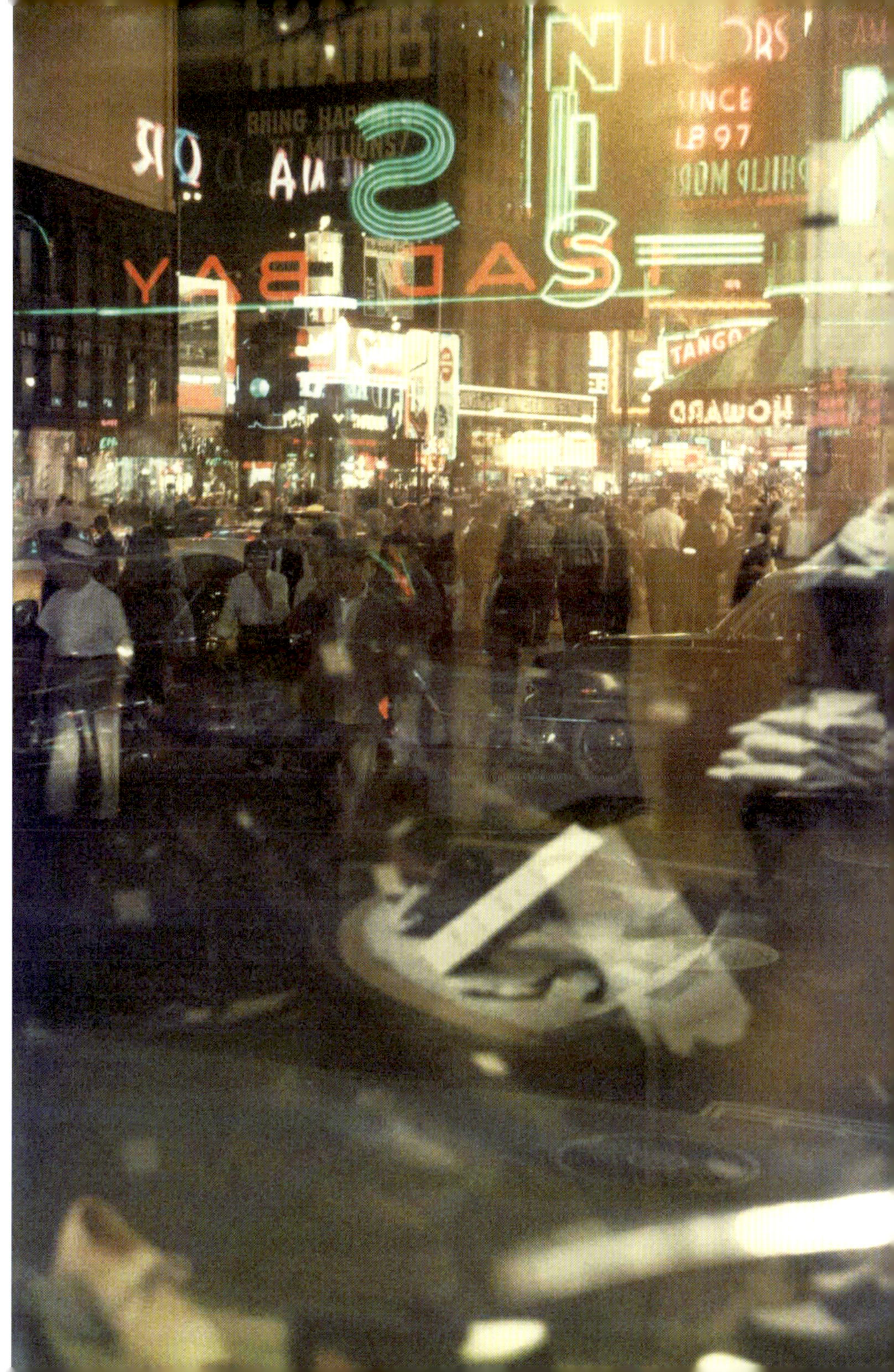

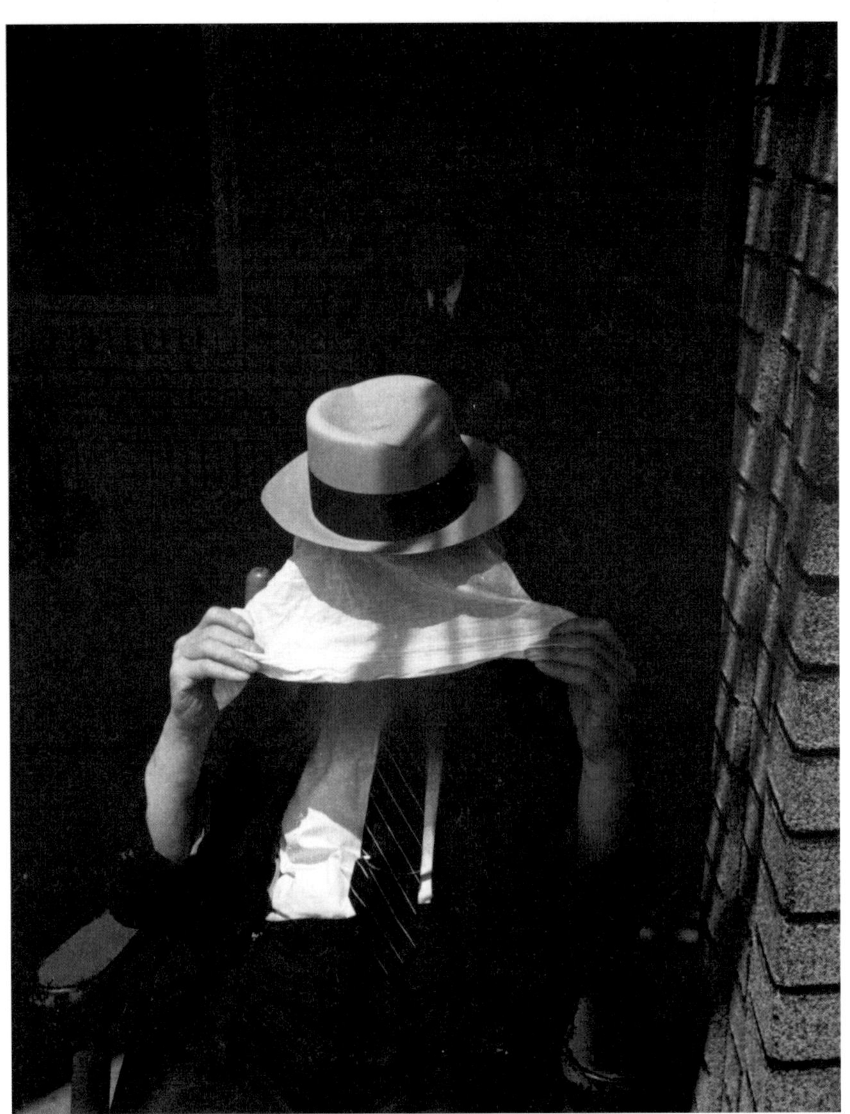

Hiding, c. 1936

Perry Street, c. 1946
Perry Street, 1946

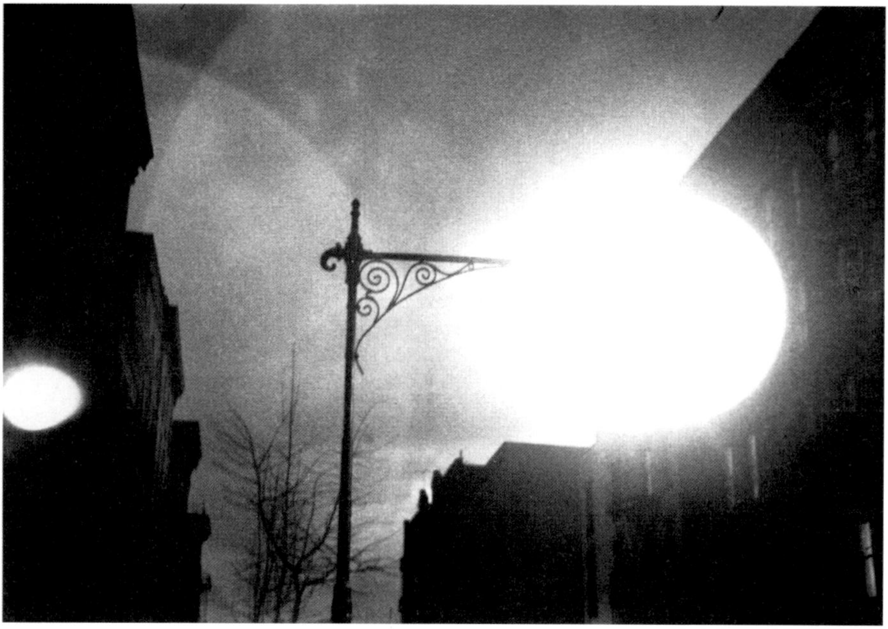

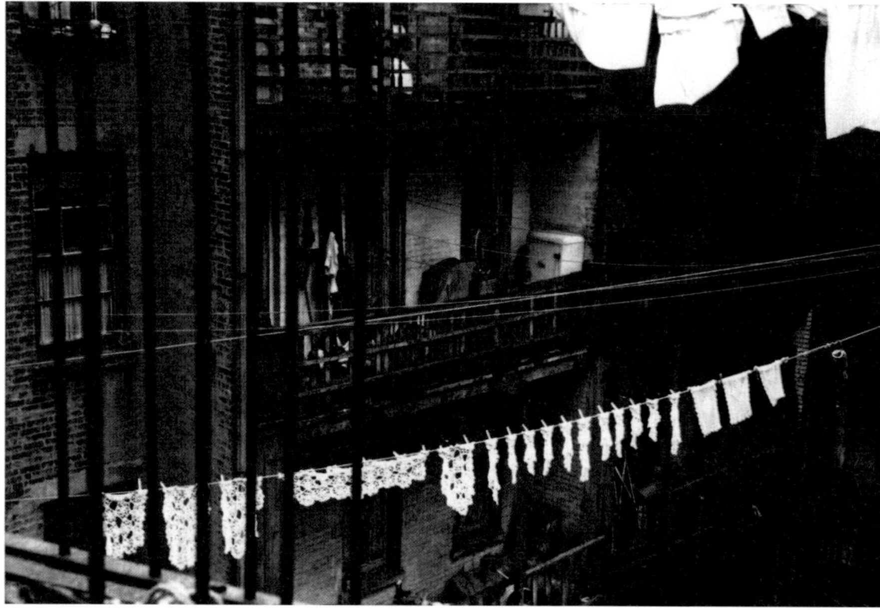

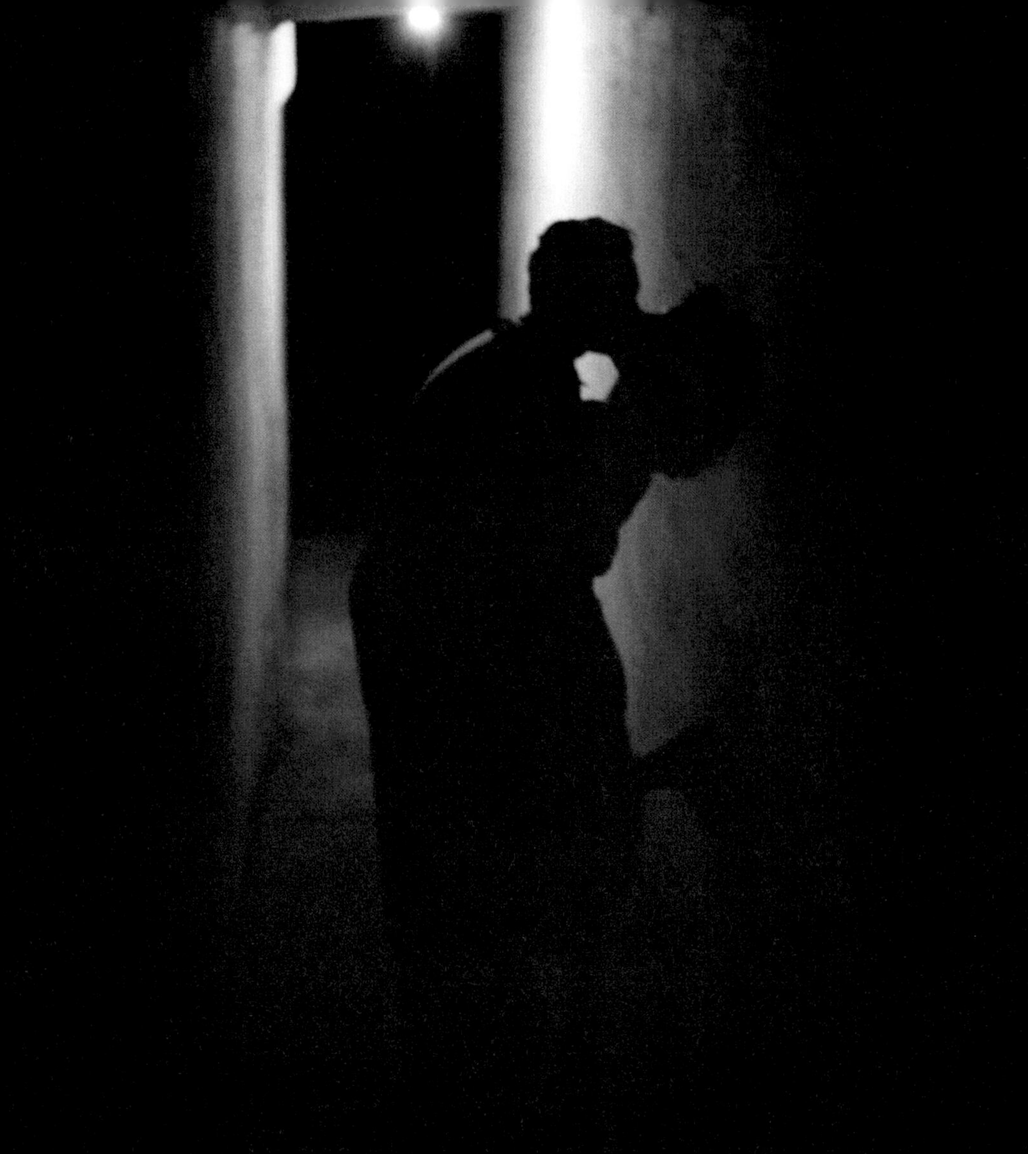

Kissing, c. 1956   Untitled, undated

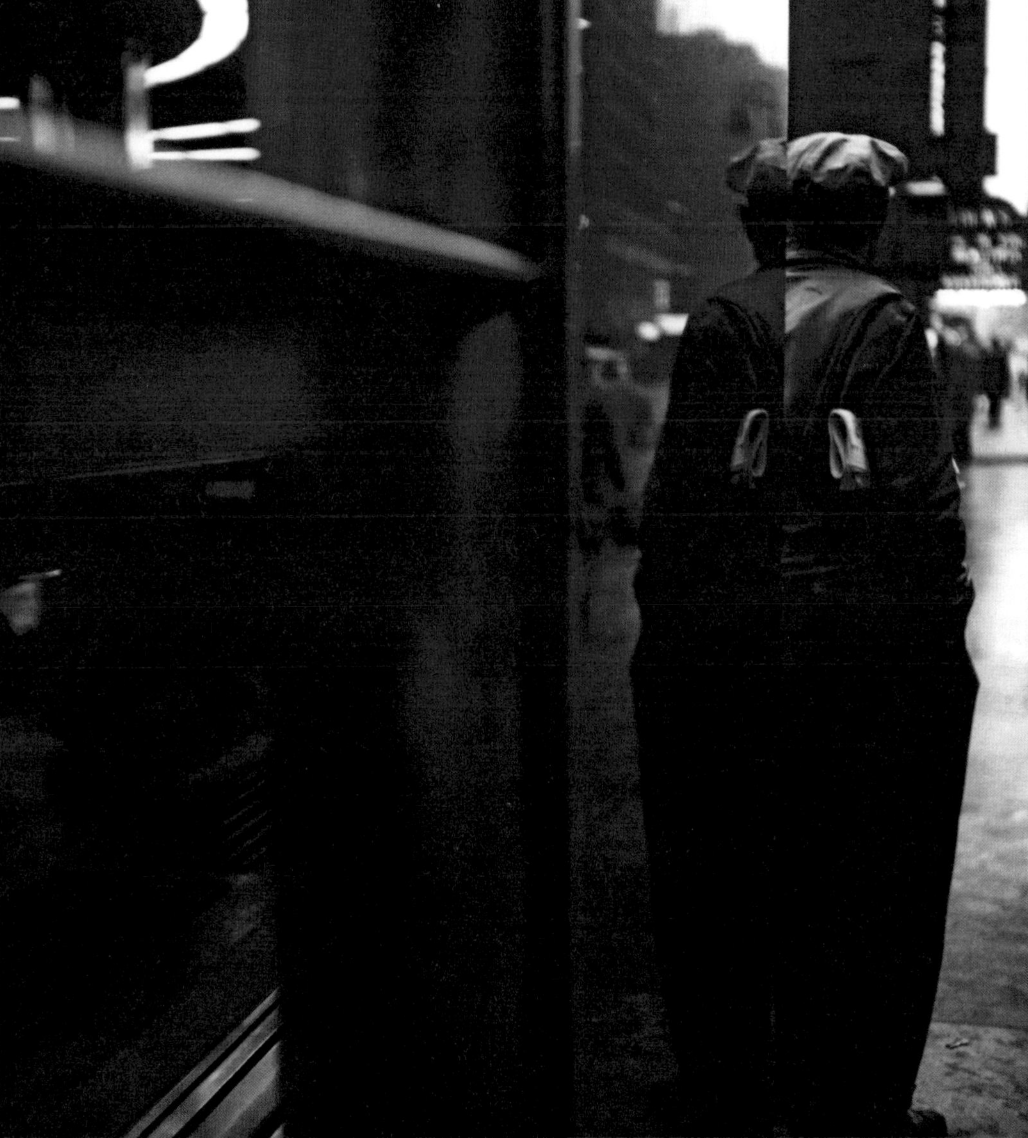

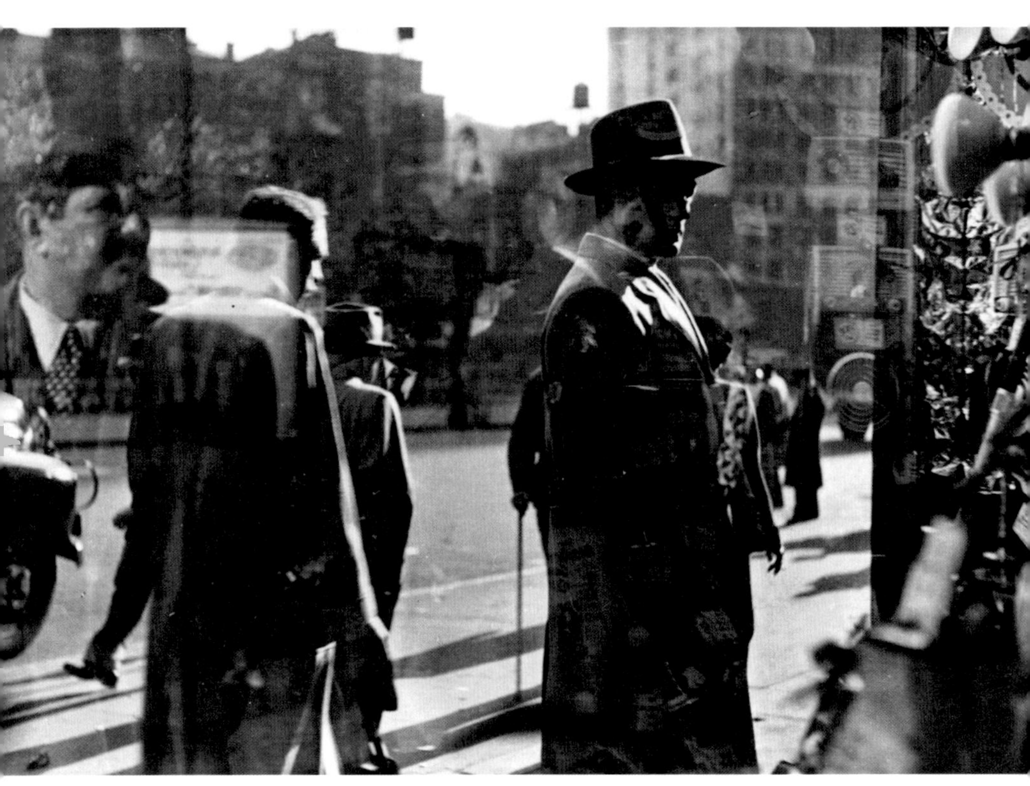

I just take pictures of somebody's window.
That's not such a great achievement.

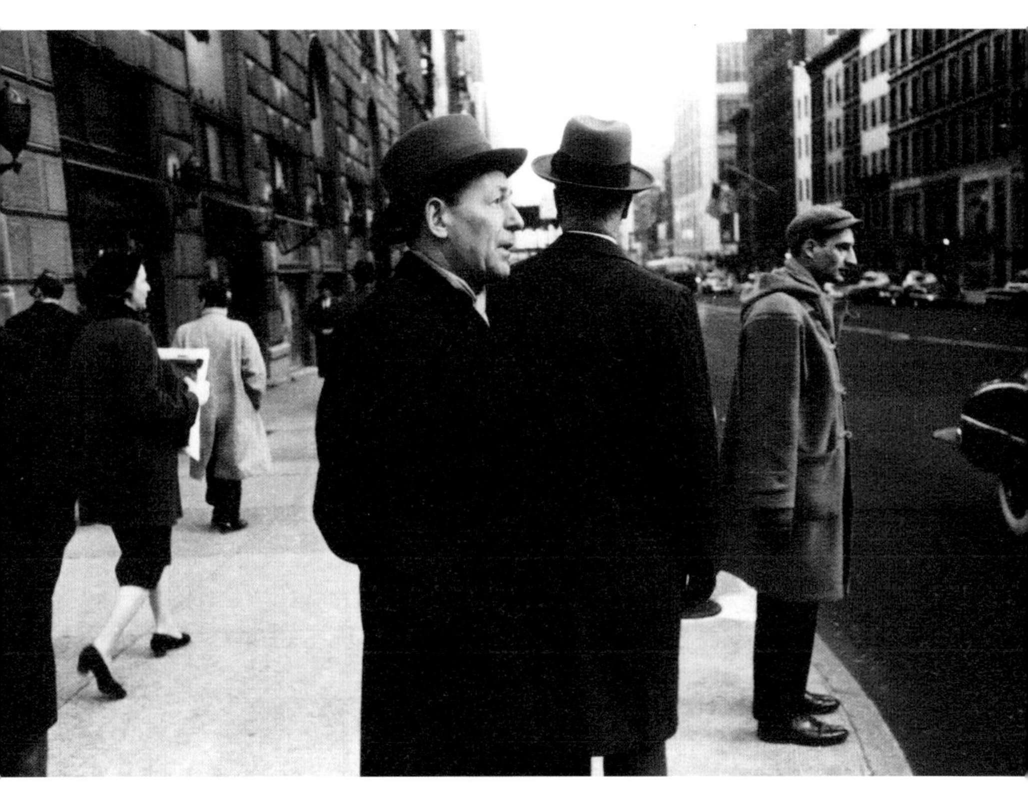

Angelo, c. 1952

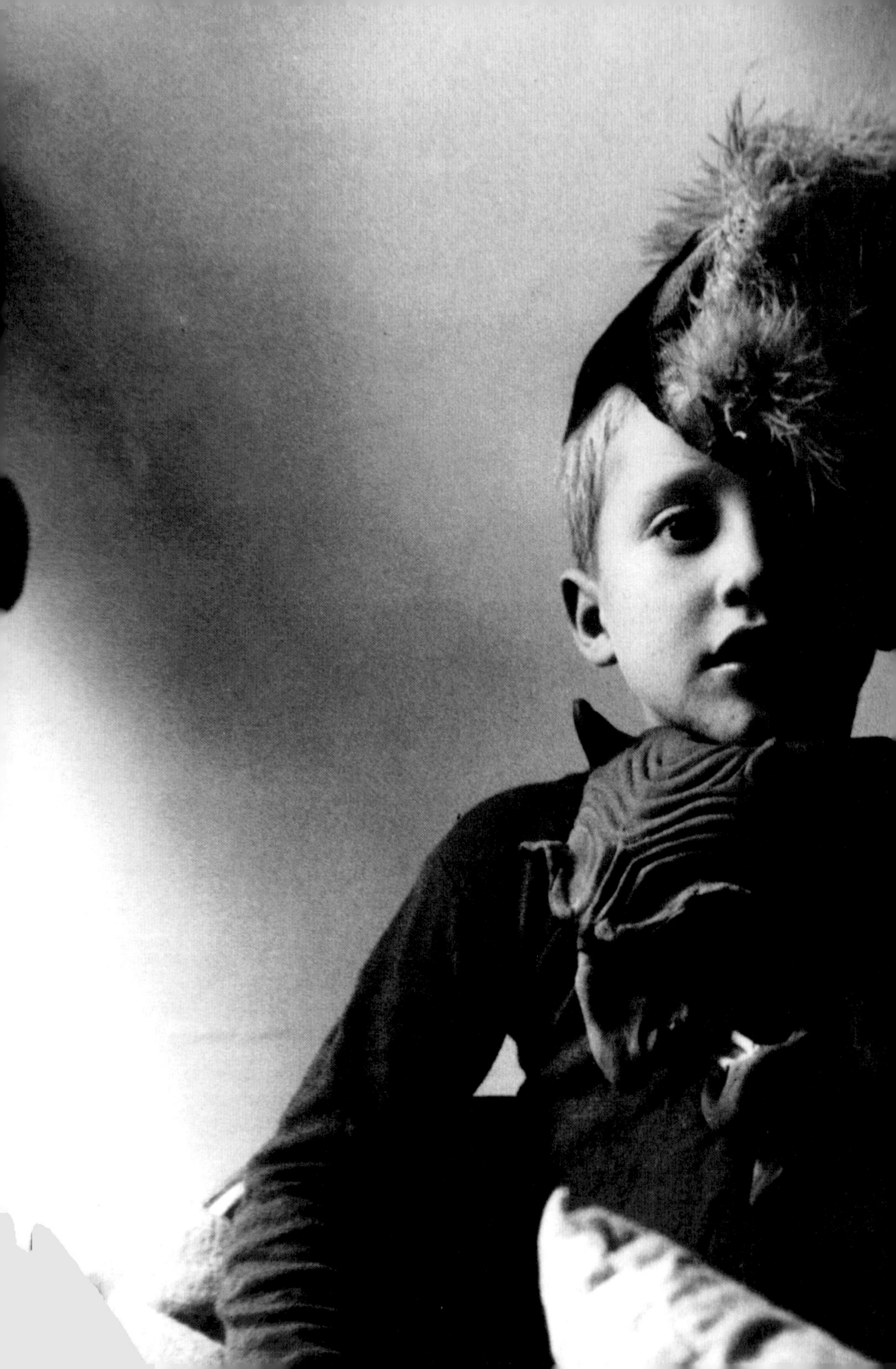

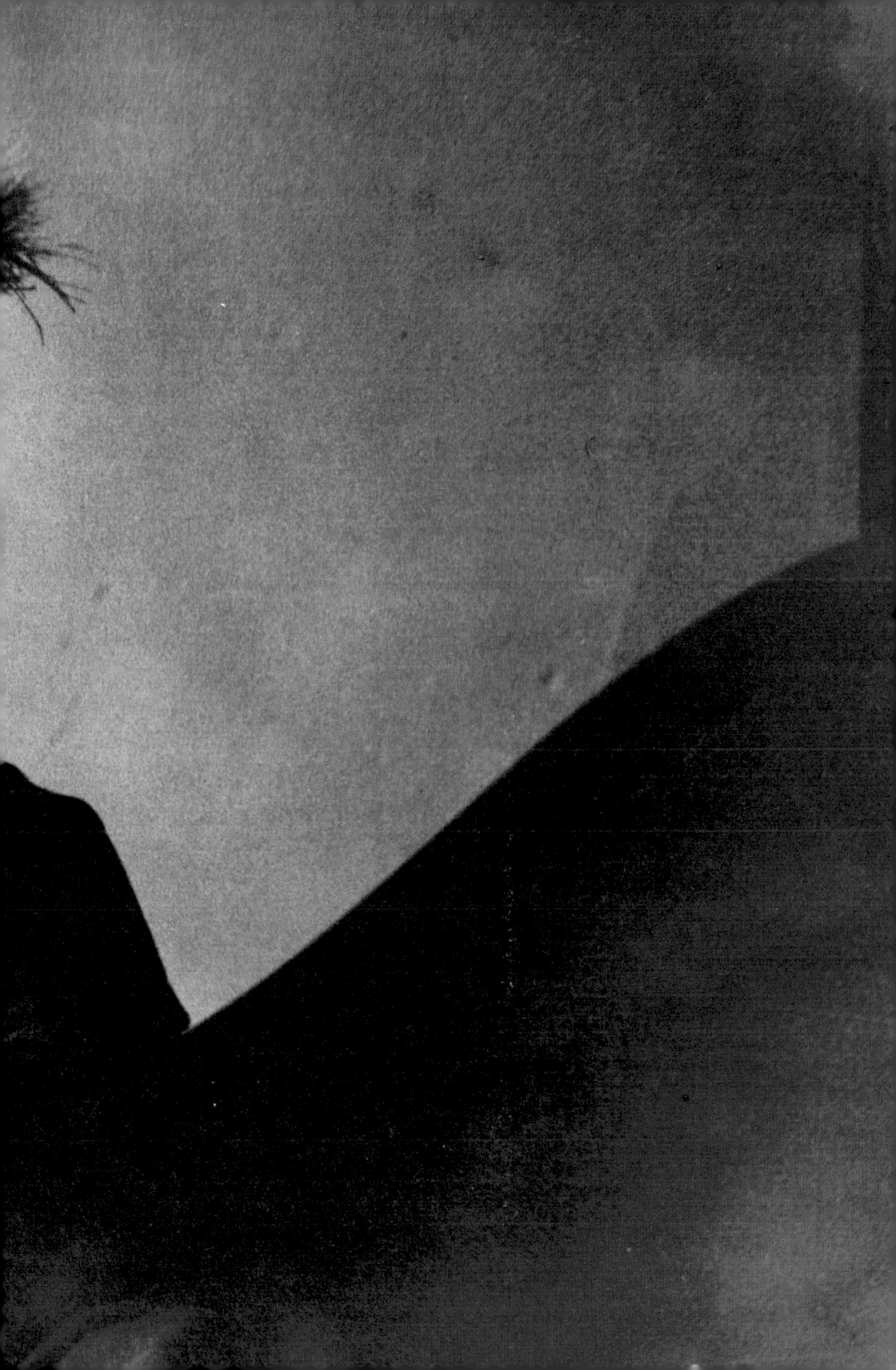

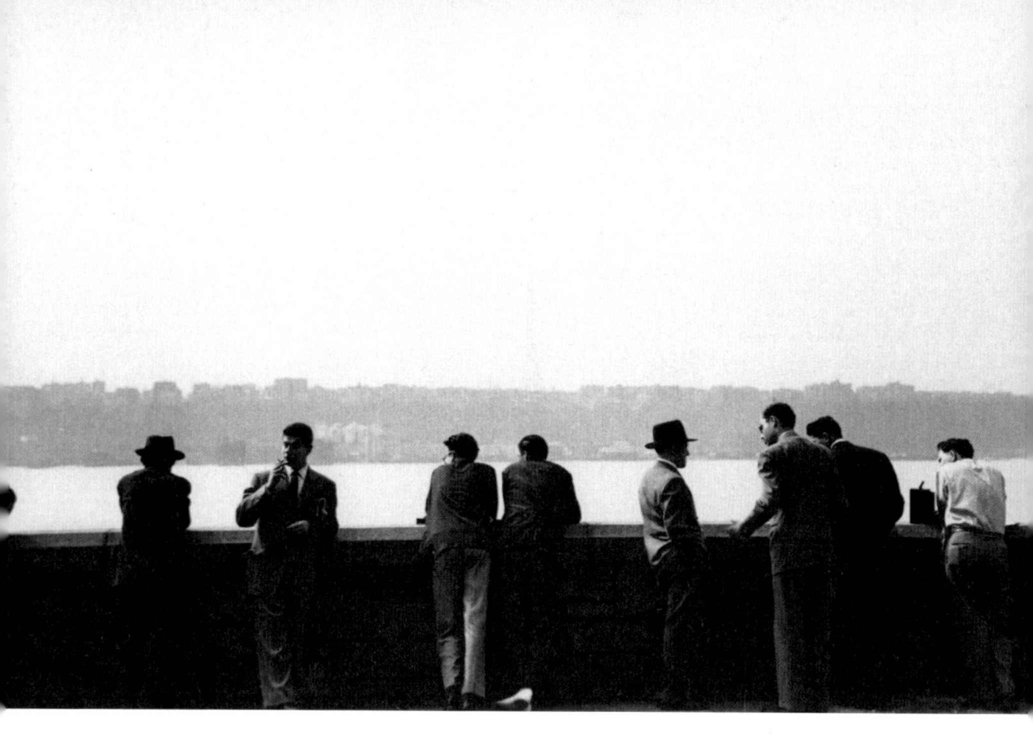

We like to pretend that what is public is what the real world is all about.

                     pp. 166–167: Party, c. 1948   Portrait of Bobby, c. 1948   Walking, c. 1955

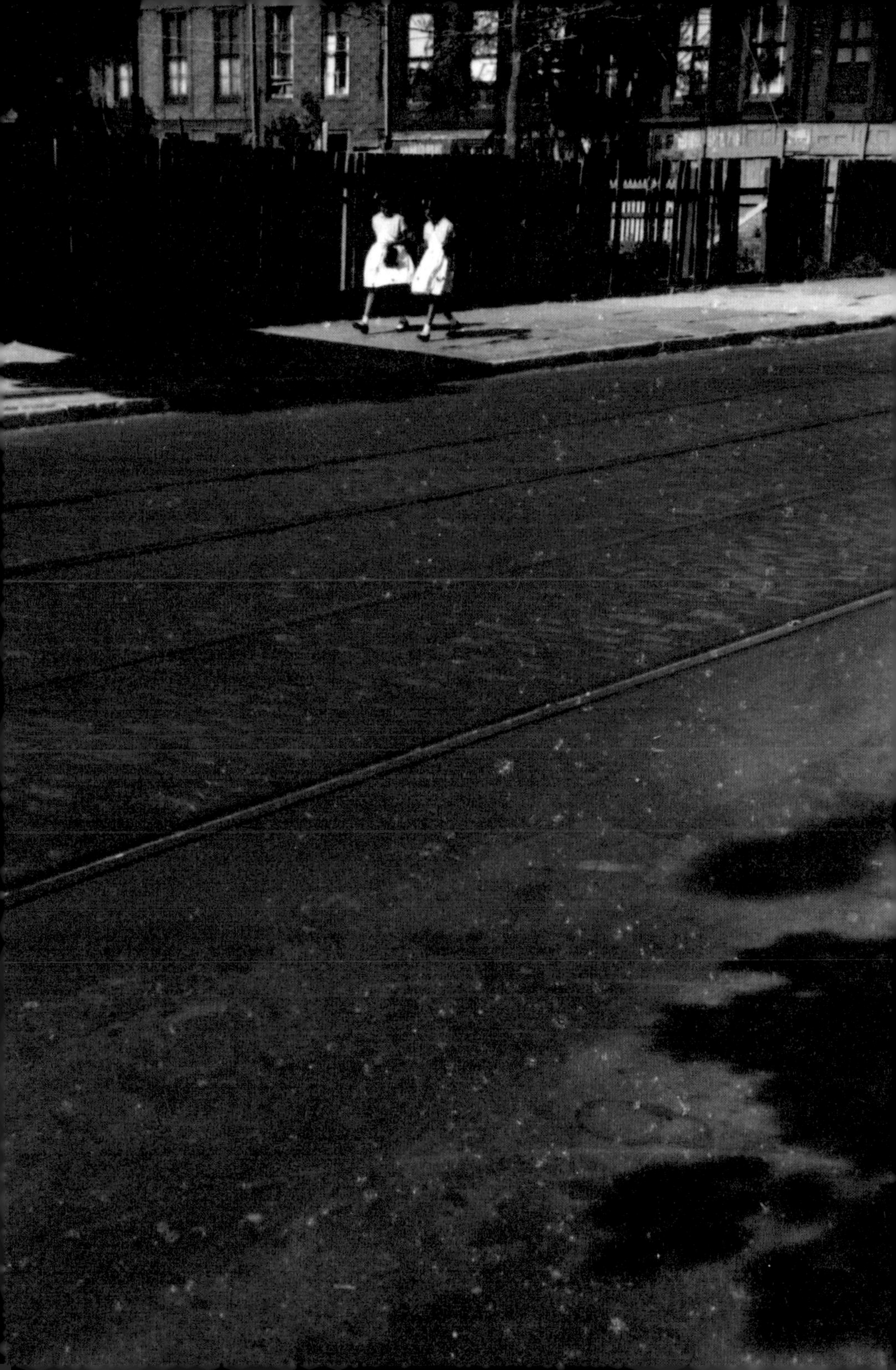

2

Seeking
Saul Leiter

My photographs have not contributed to
the improvement of mankind's condition,
but I'd like to think that the work I do gives
others pleasure.

Self-Portraits

Fittingly, Saul Leiter's self-portraits tend to subvert viewers' expectations much in the way that his other street work does. Some of these photographs, in fact, take a while to reveal themselves as self-portraits, with the realization striking the viewer like the punchline of a joke. It's characteristic of Saul to blend into the scenery, with his own figure seasoning or accentuating the image rather than being its subject.

One of Saul's first self-portraits was made circa 1943, when he was still living in his family home in Pittsburgh (p. 188). He painted his shirt green on the print, so already we see an interest in painting and, one could say, color photography. When he arrived in New York in 1946, shedding his family's expectation that he become a rabbi, Saul found himself in a somewhat shockingly exotic new setting, albeit one holding the promise of a new world. His self-portraits from this era show quiet self-contemplation in an otherwise frenetic city, as if Saul is examining how his new life suits him. He sometimes places friends or lovers in the frame along with him, perhaps seeing how they fit in too.

Self-Portrait, c. 1970

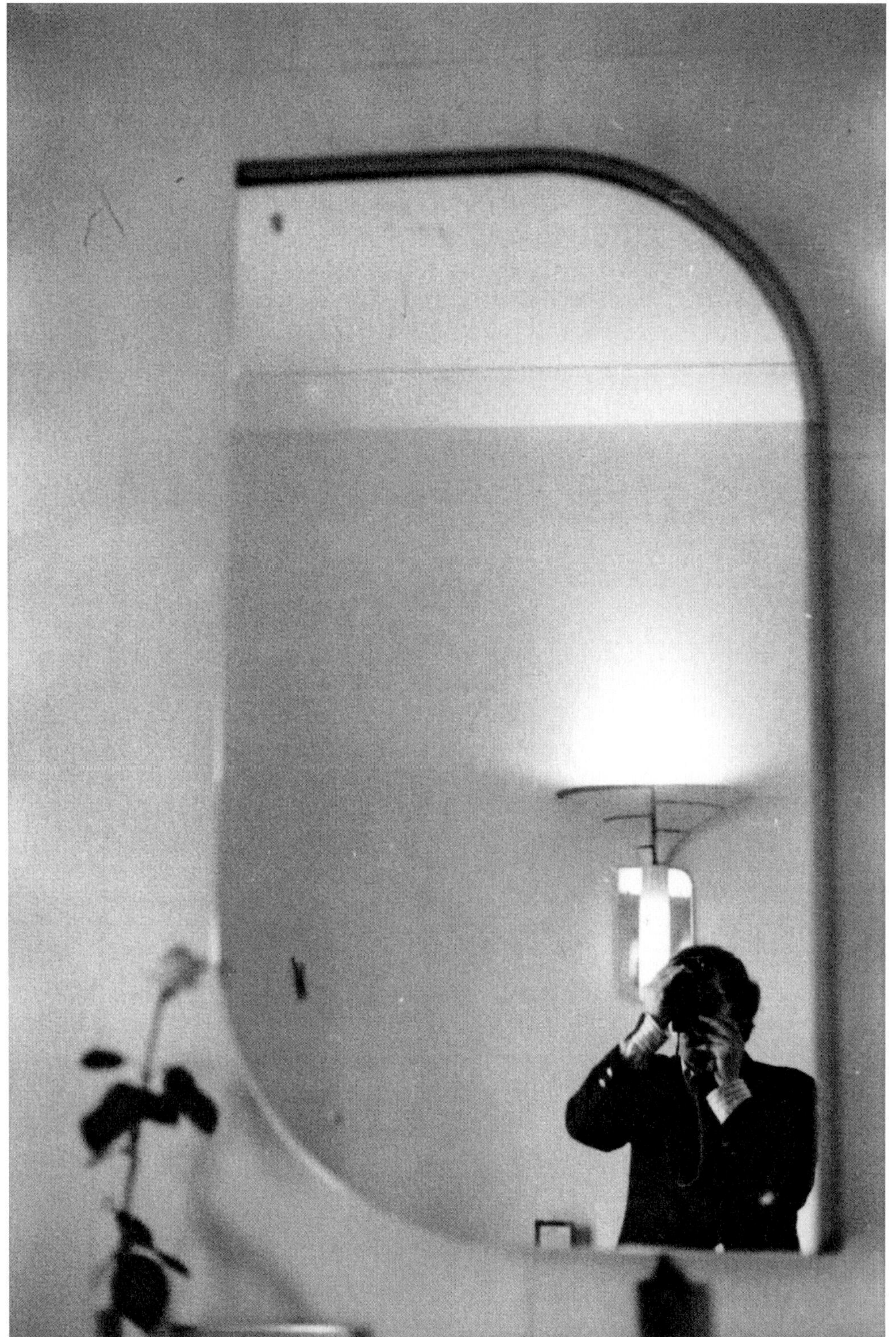

There were periods in my life where no one photographed me,
and now I sit down and people shove their cameras at me.

Untitled, c. 1942

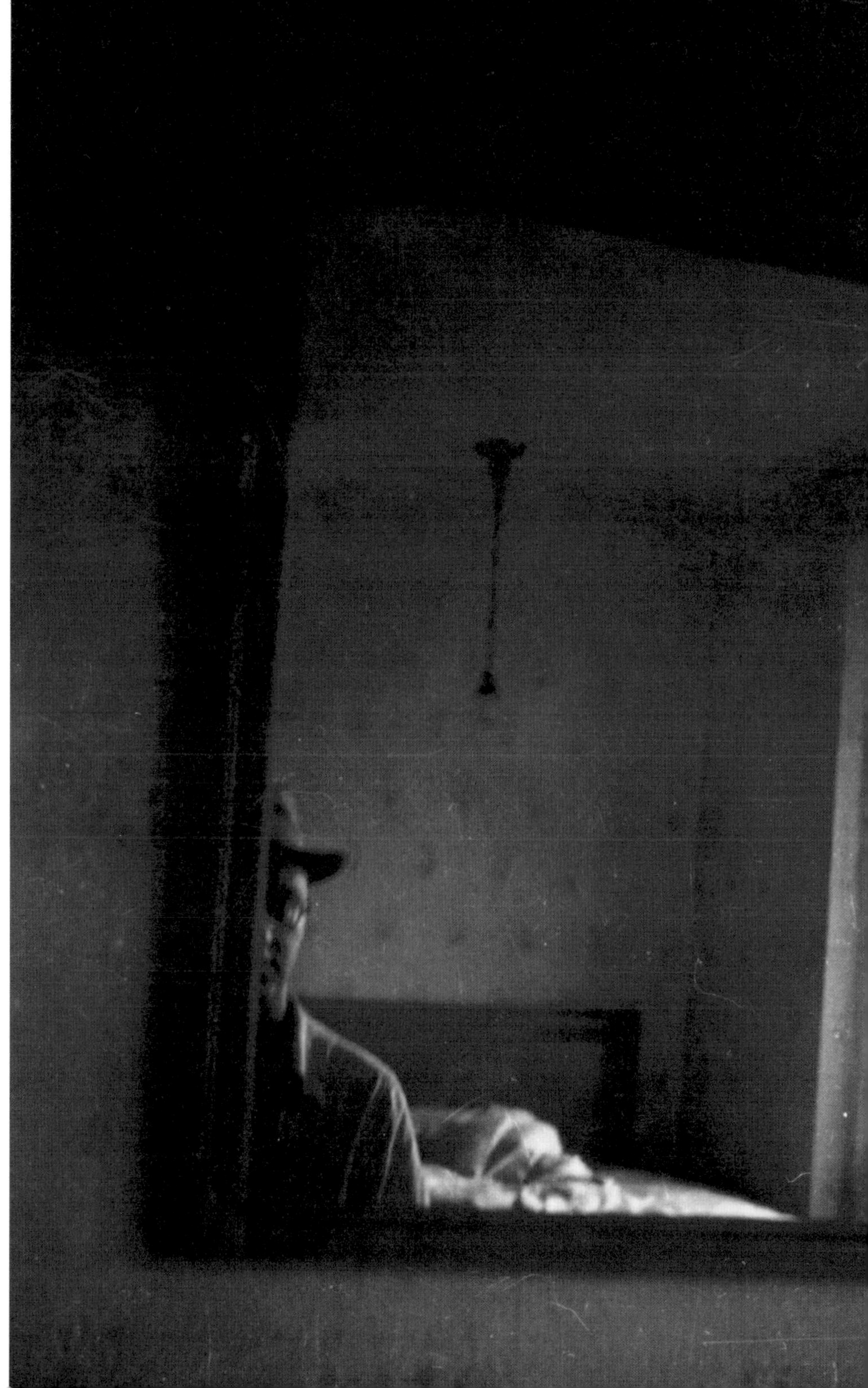

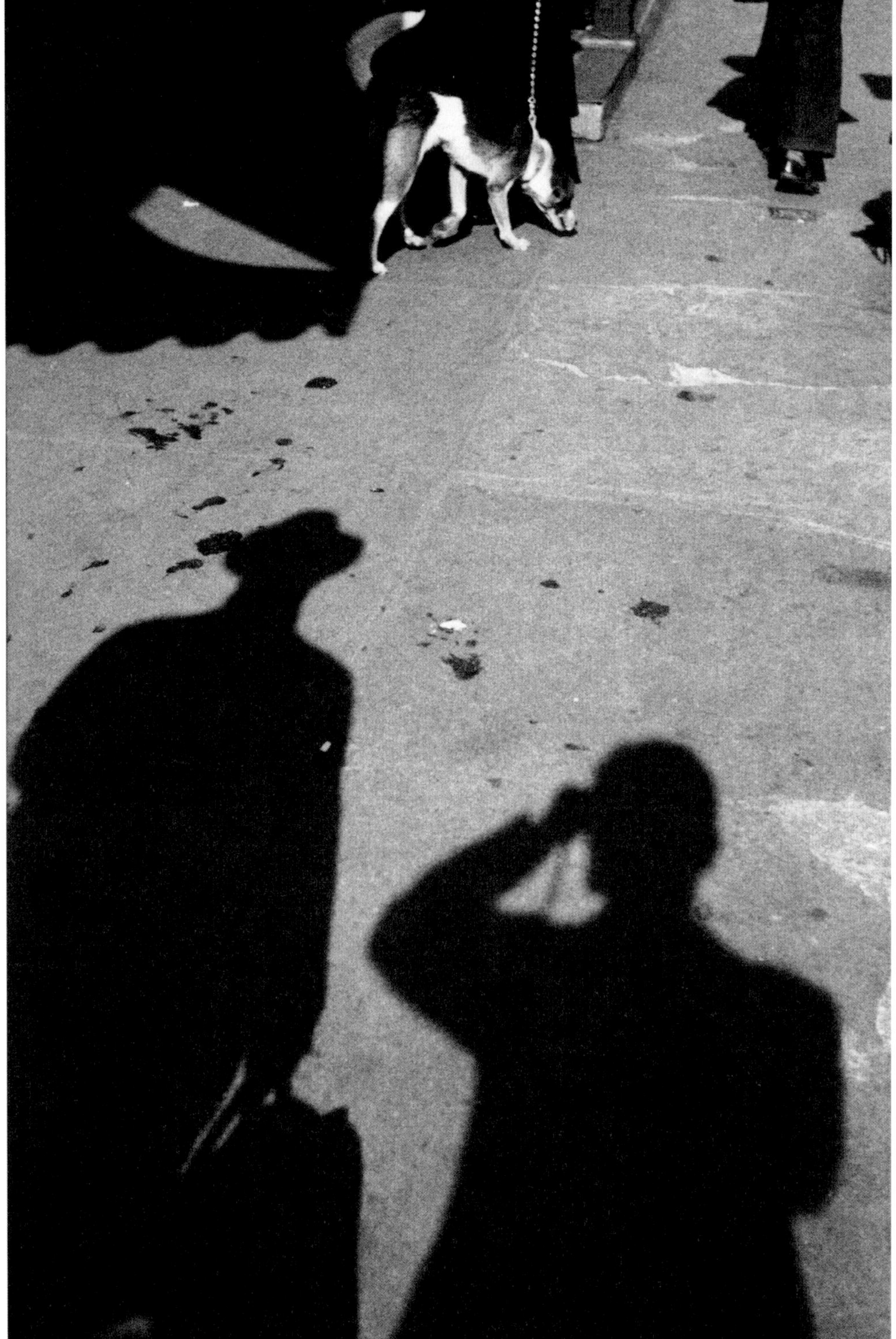

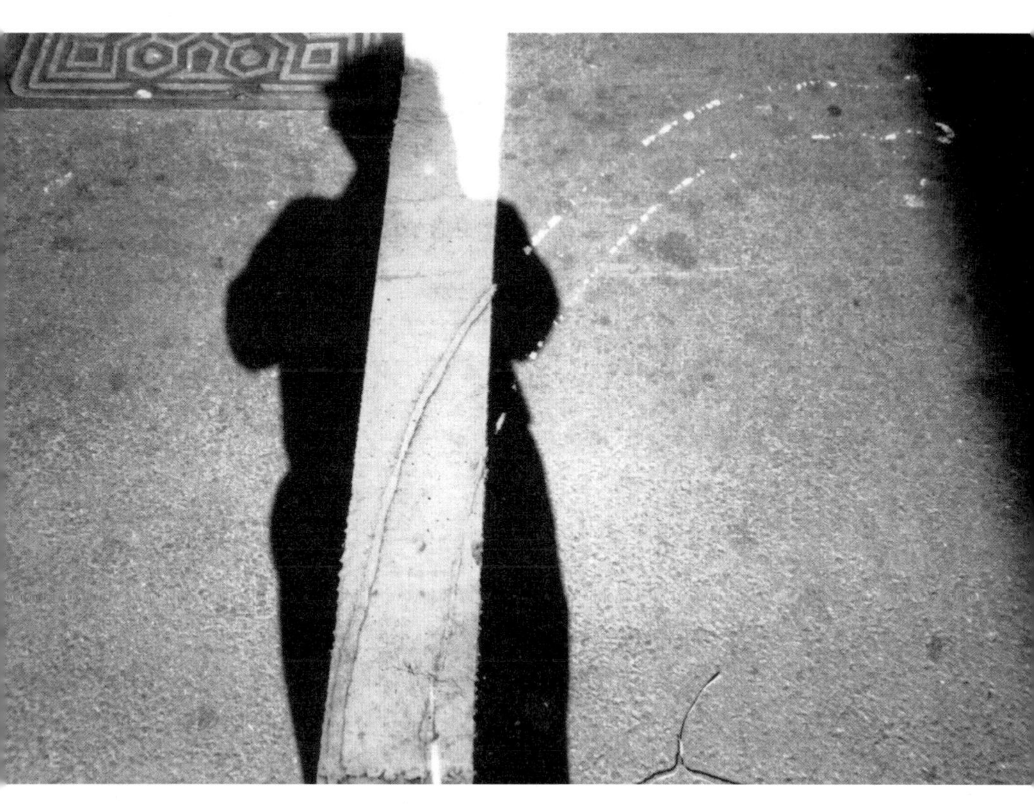

Untitled, 1950s   Self-Portrait, 1950s

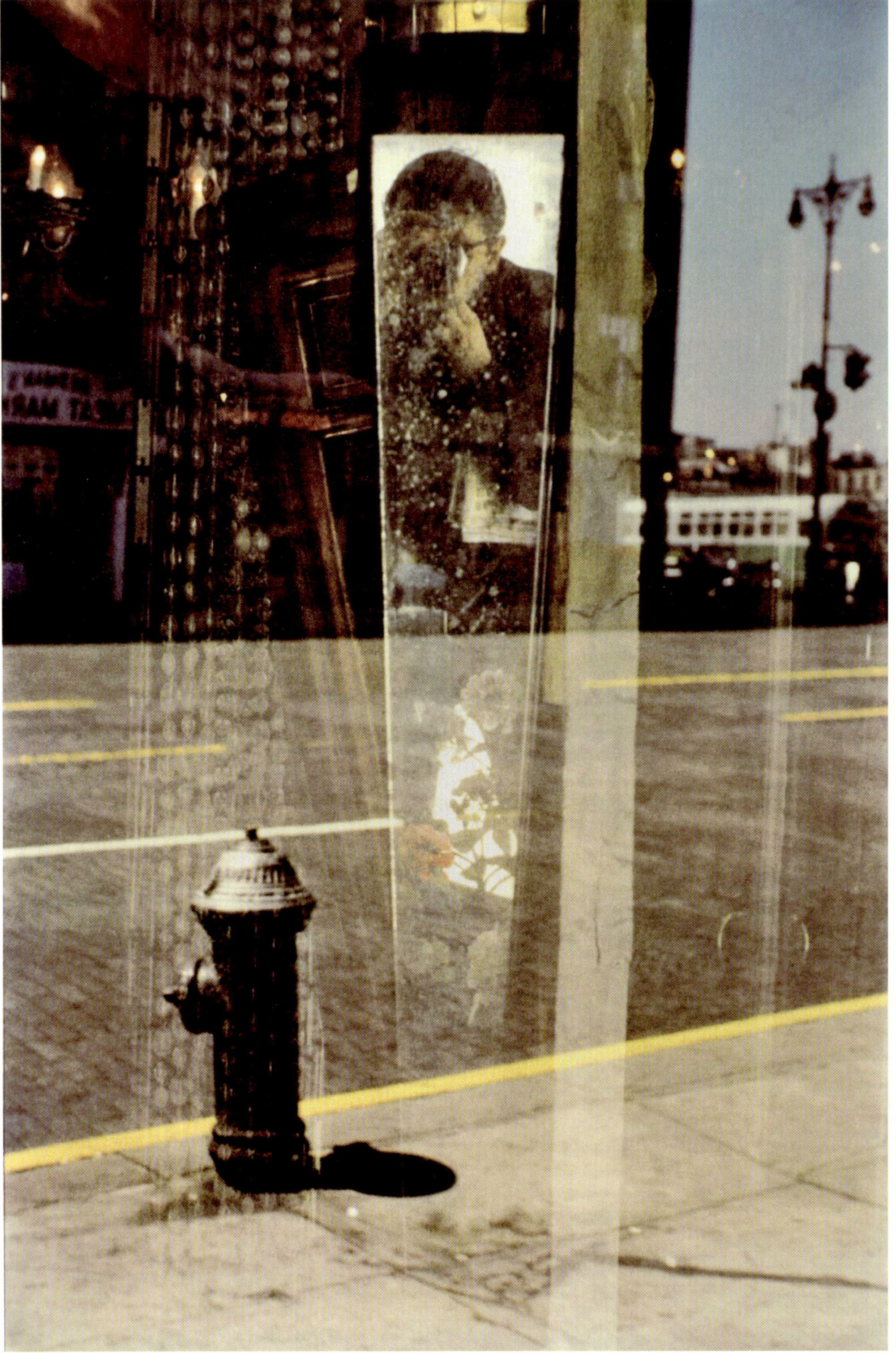

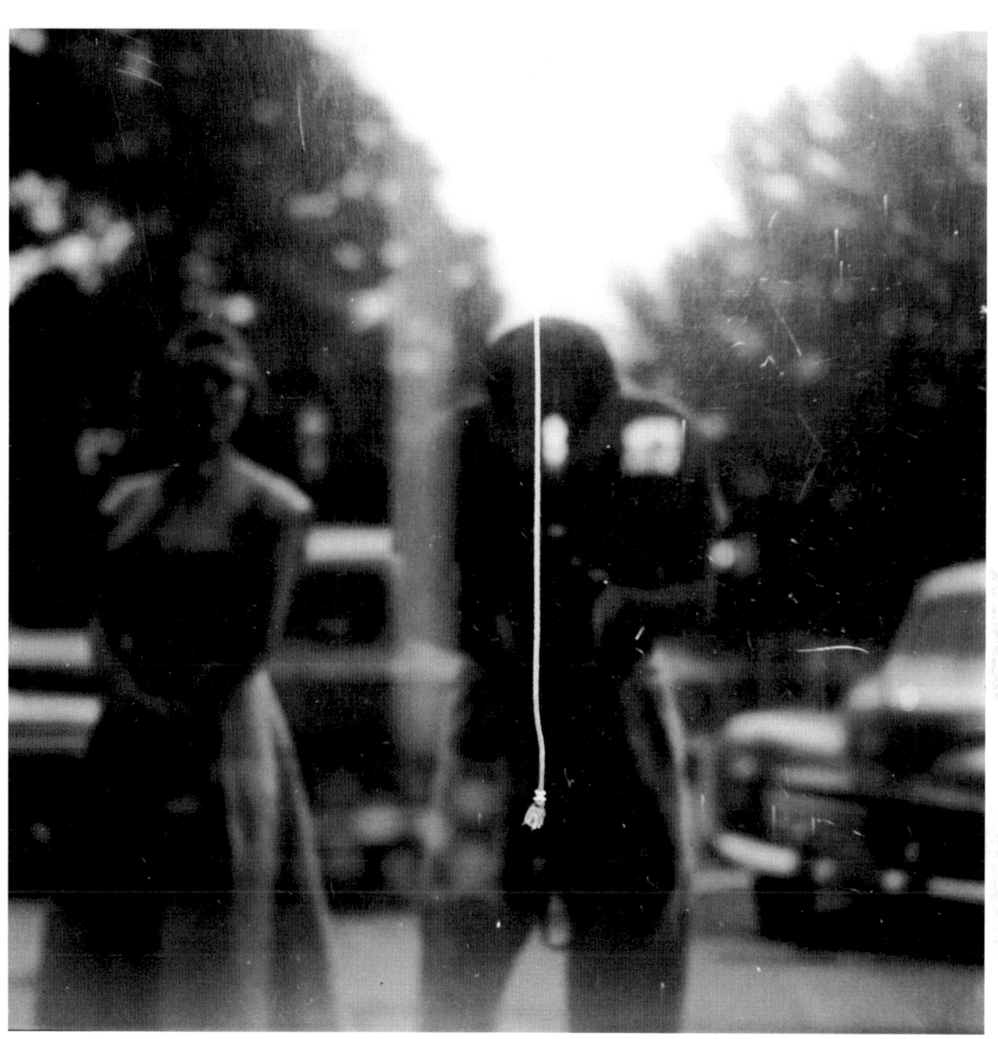

Untitled, undated   String, c. 1955

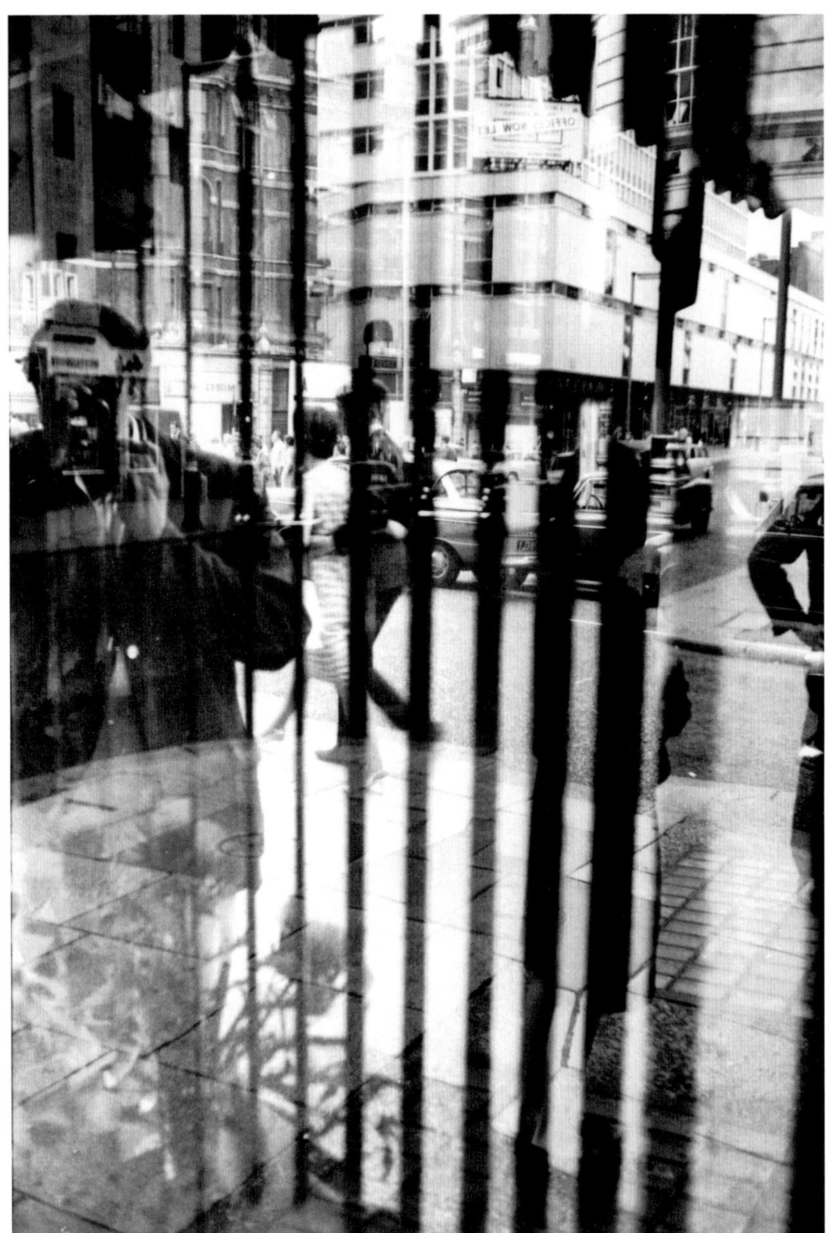

Self-Portrait, 1950s

Self-Portrait, c. 1949

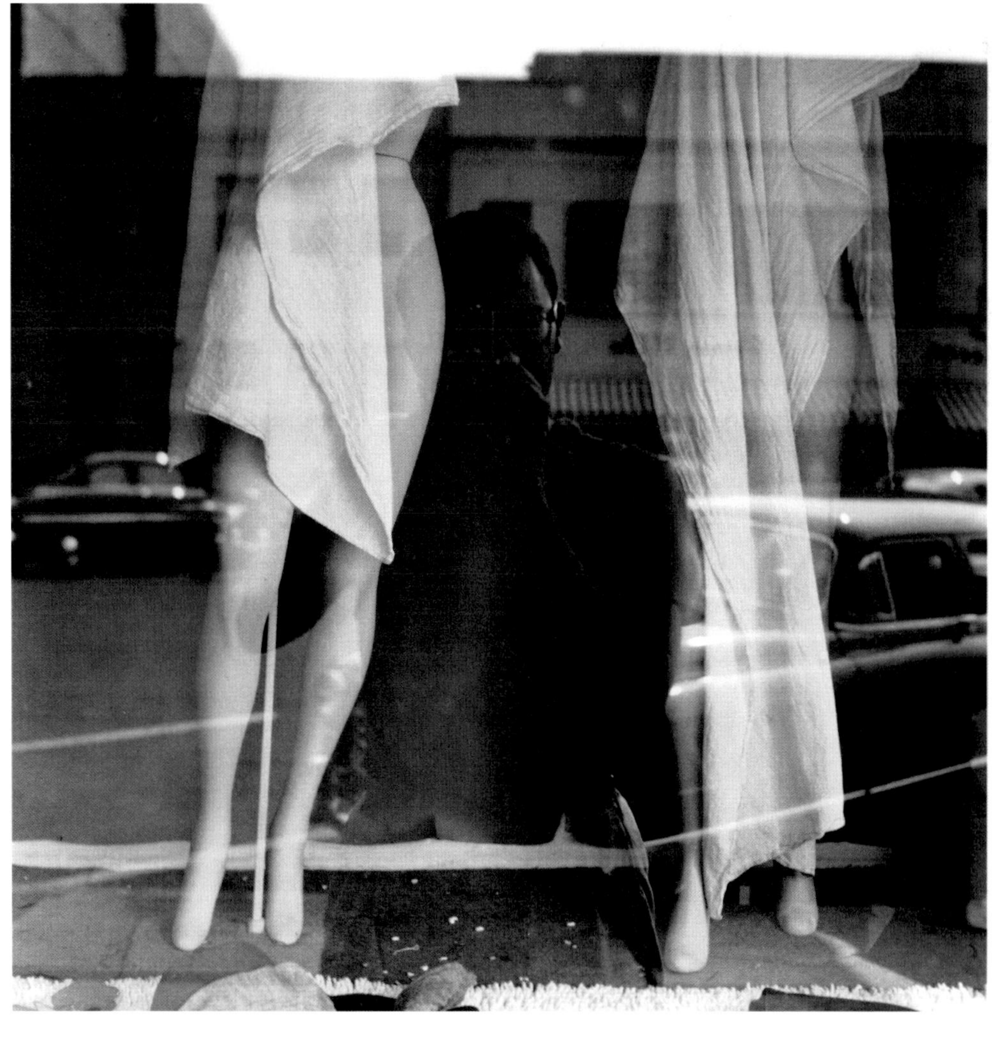

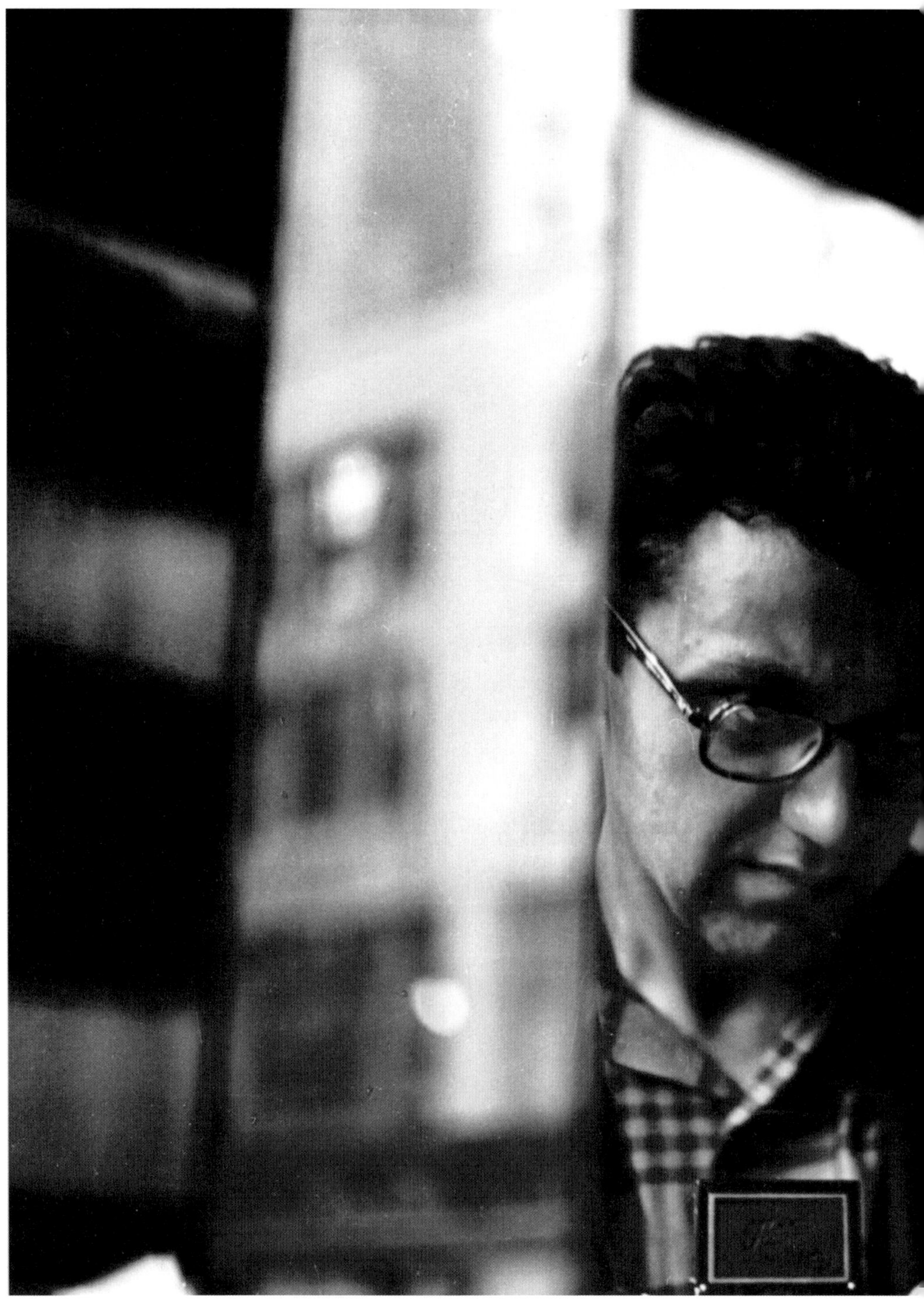

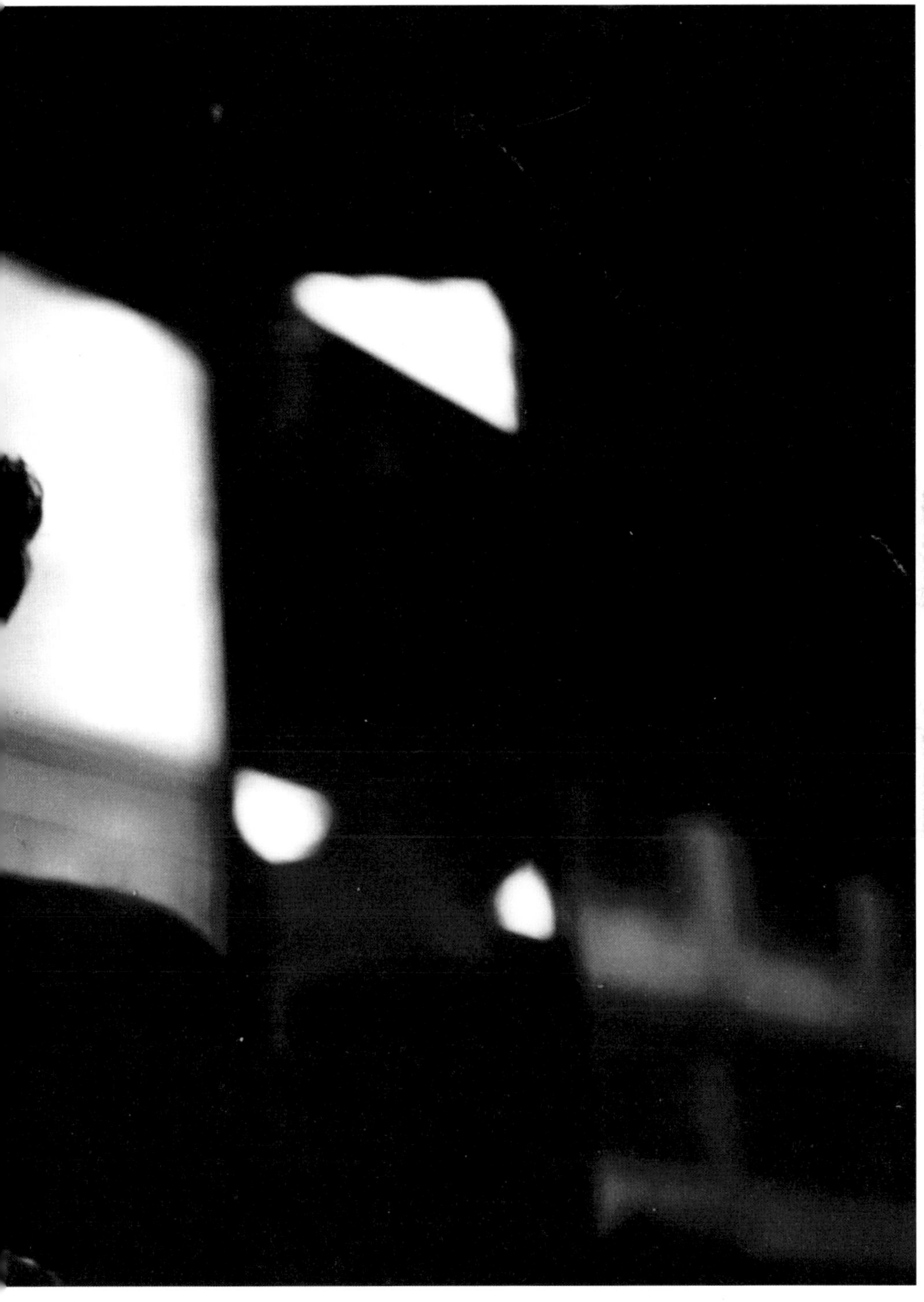

Self-Portrait, c. 1950

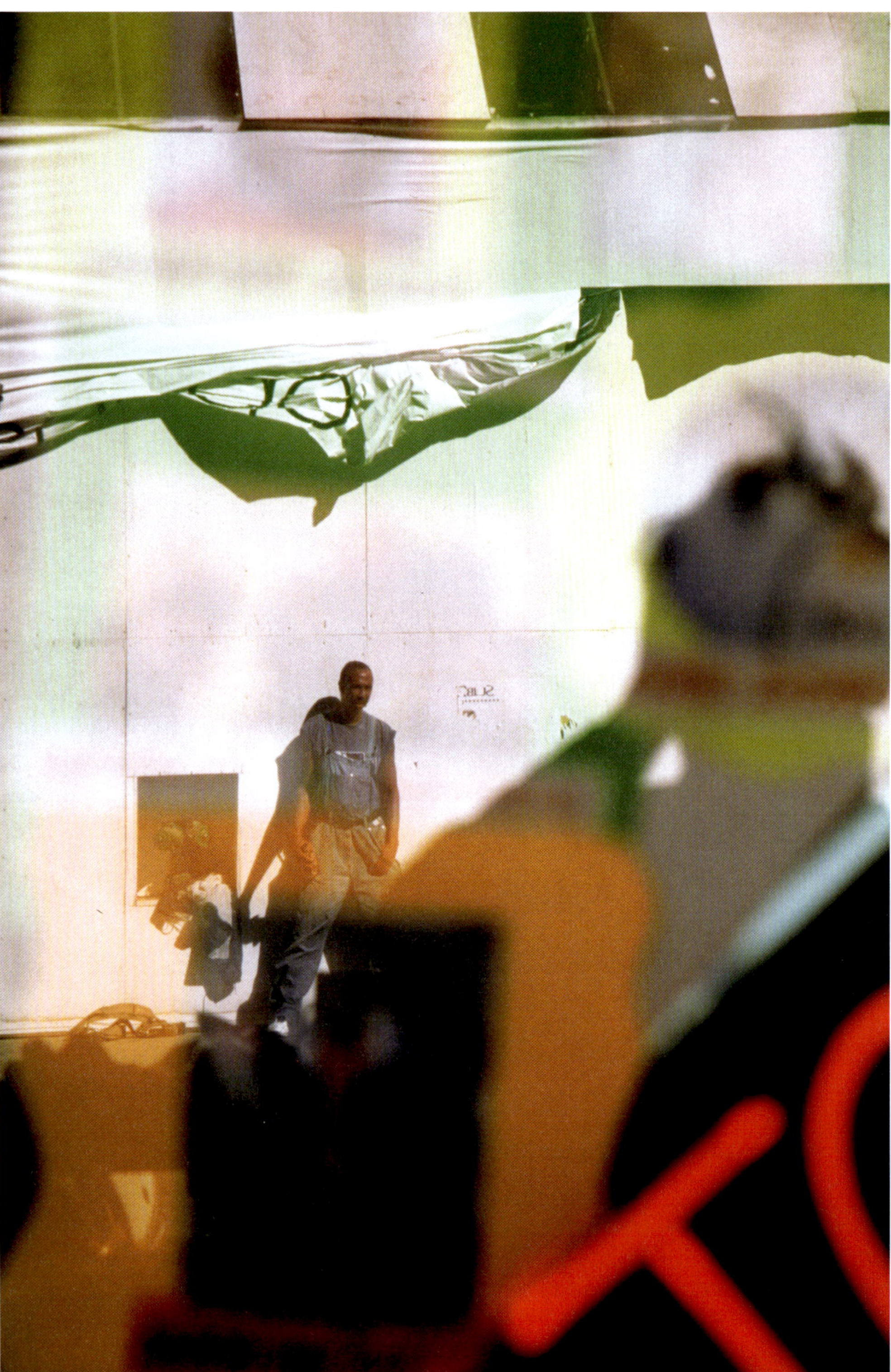

I go out with my camera and I take pictures
because I enjoy catching certain moments.

Sometimes I wake up in the middle of the night and take out
a book on Matisse or Cezanne or Sōtatsu.
A detail that I had not noticed suddenly catches my attention.
Painting is glorious.

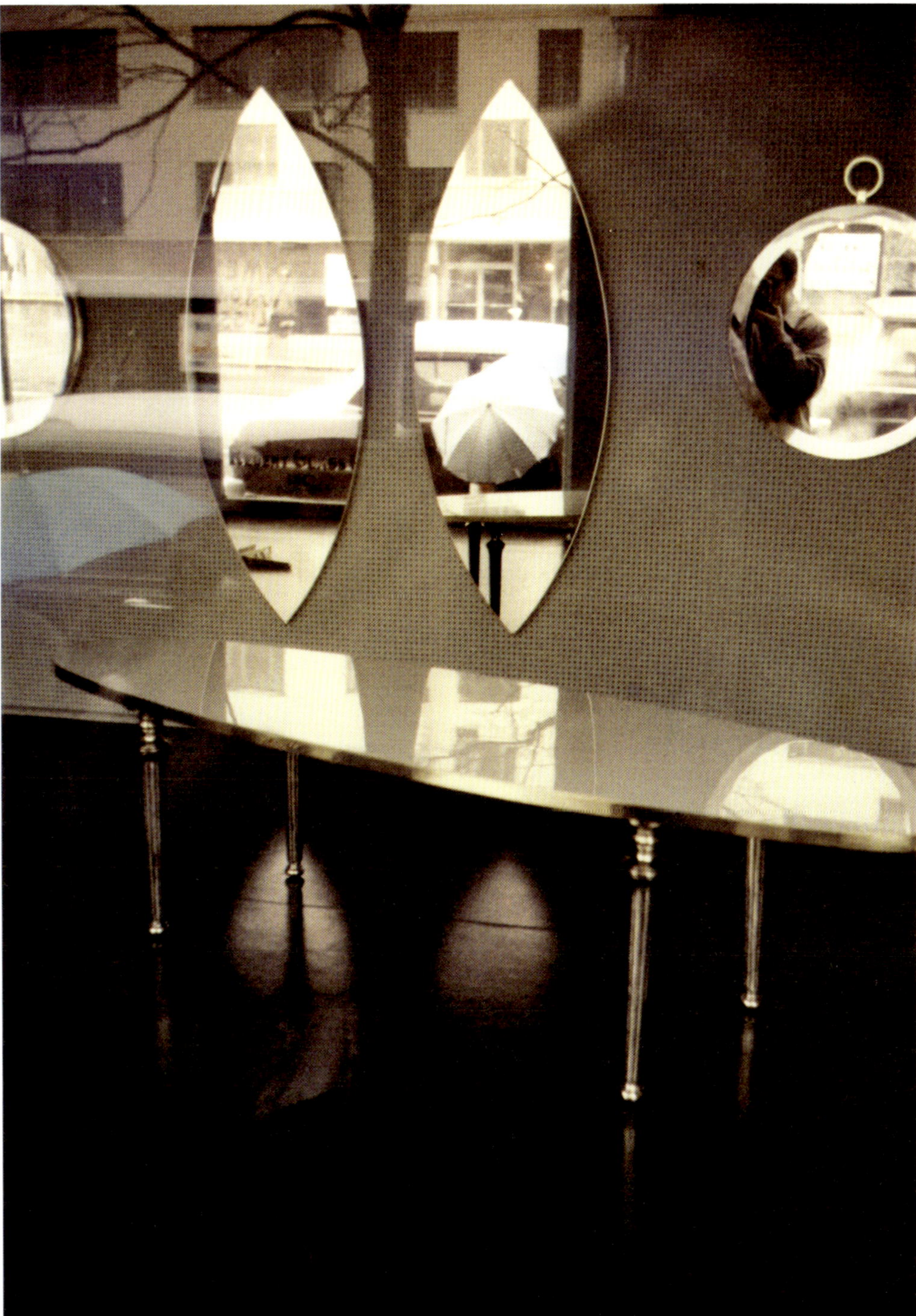

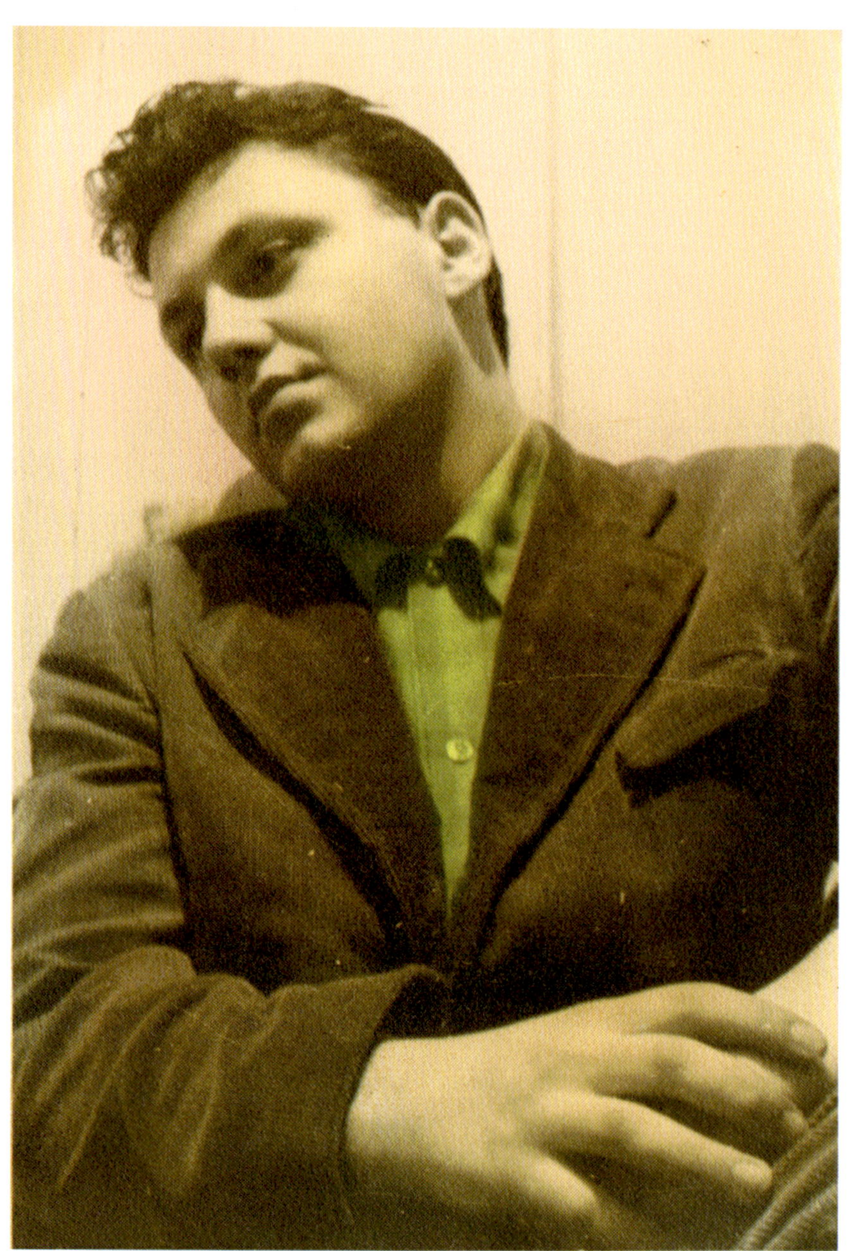

Untitled, c. 1943

Self-Portrait, c. 1946
Self-Portrait, c. 1950

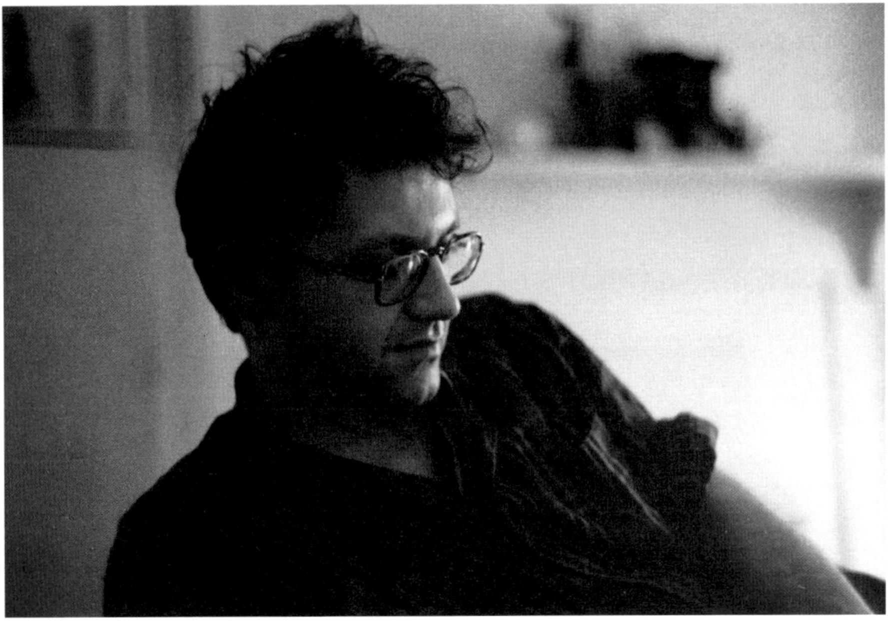

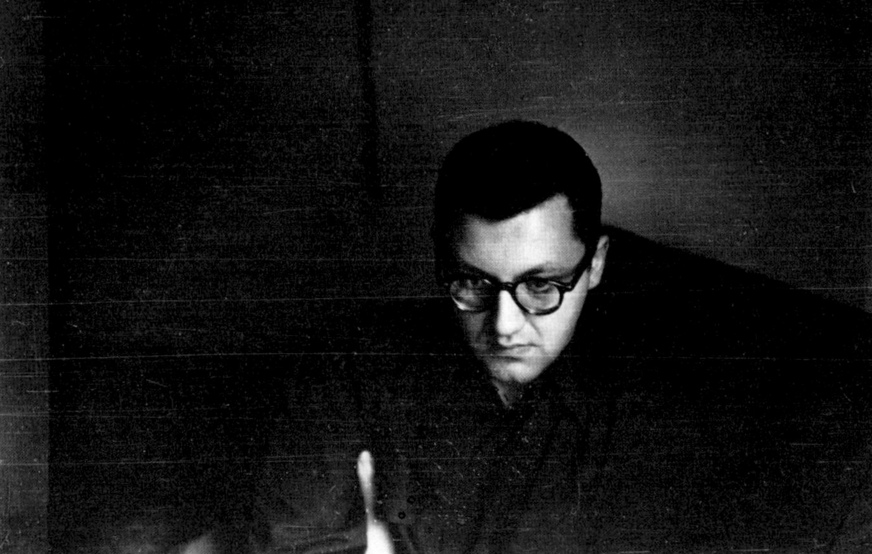

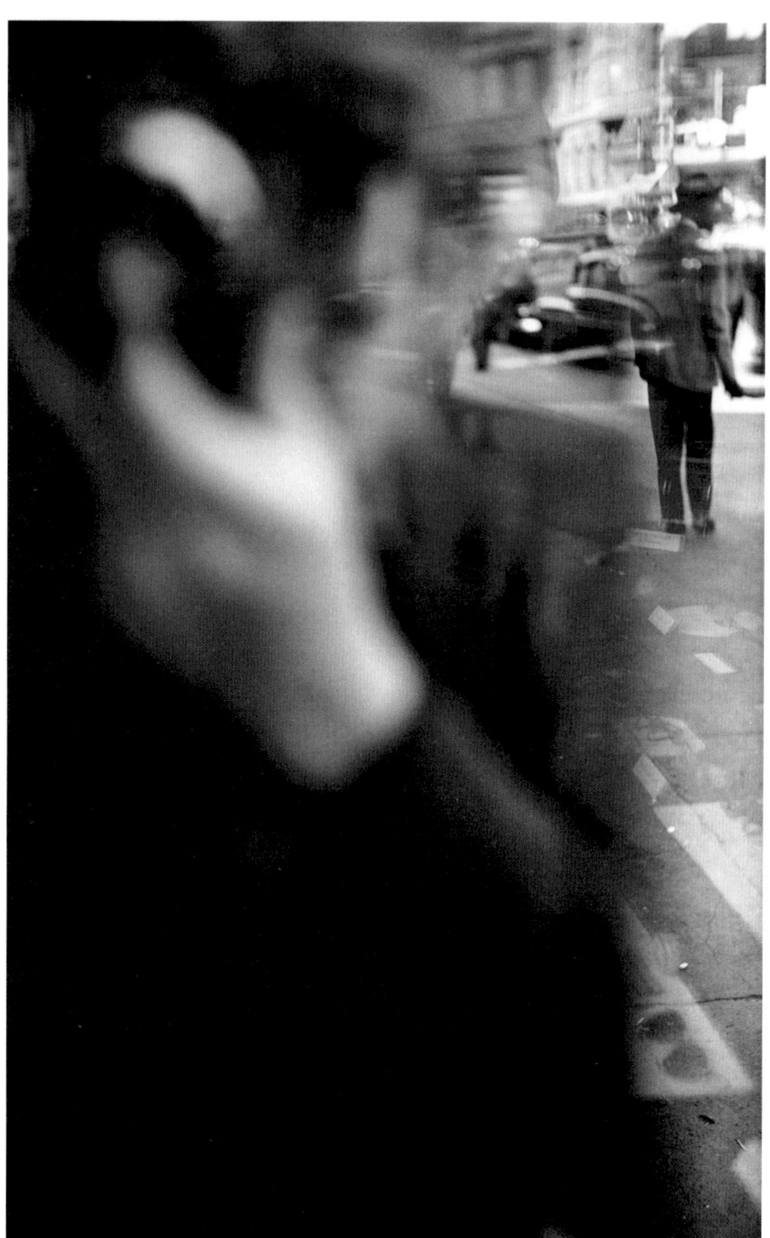

Self-Portrait, c. 1948

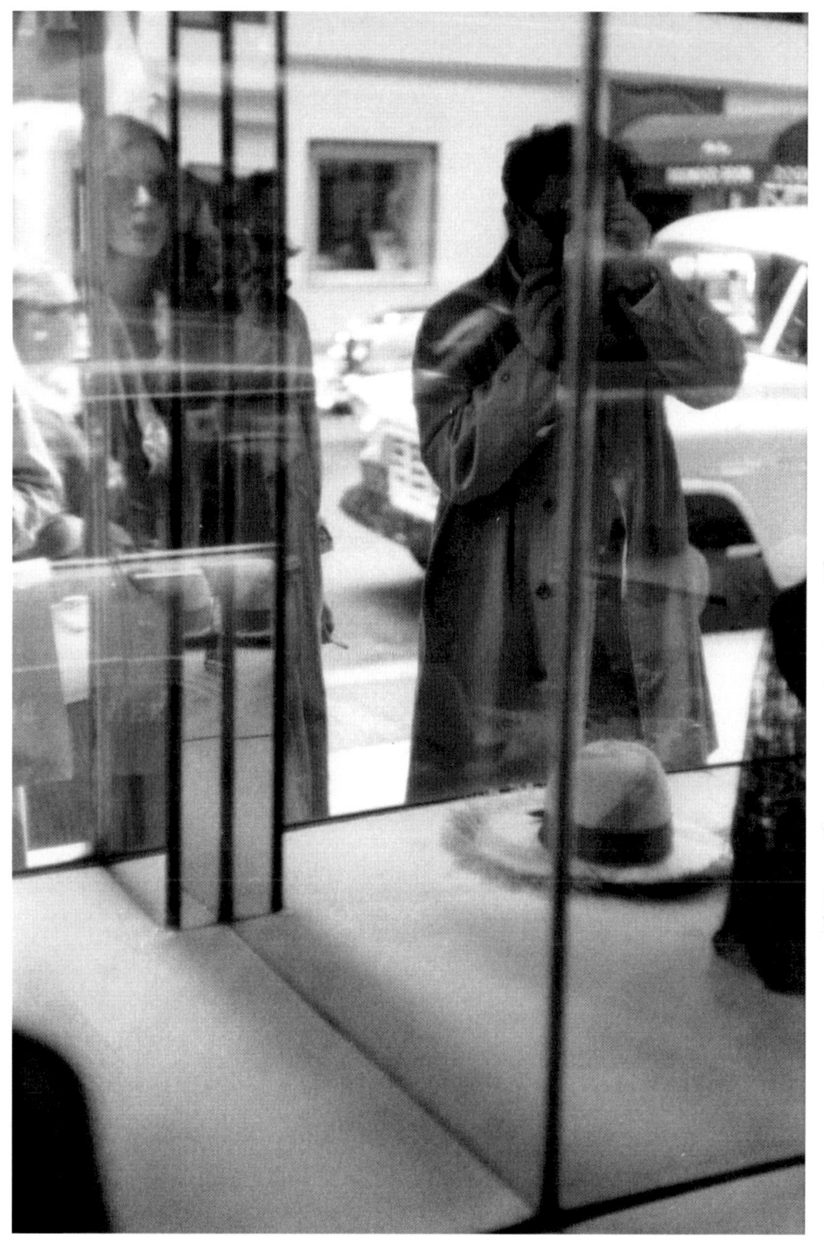

Untitled, 1950s

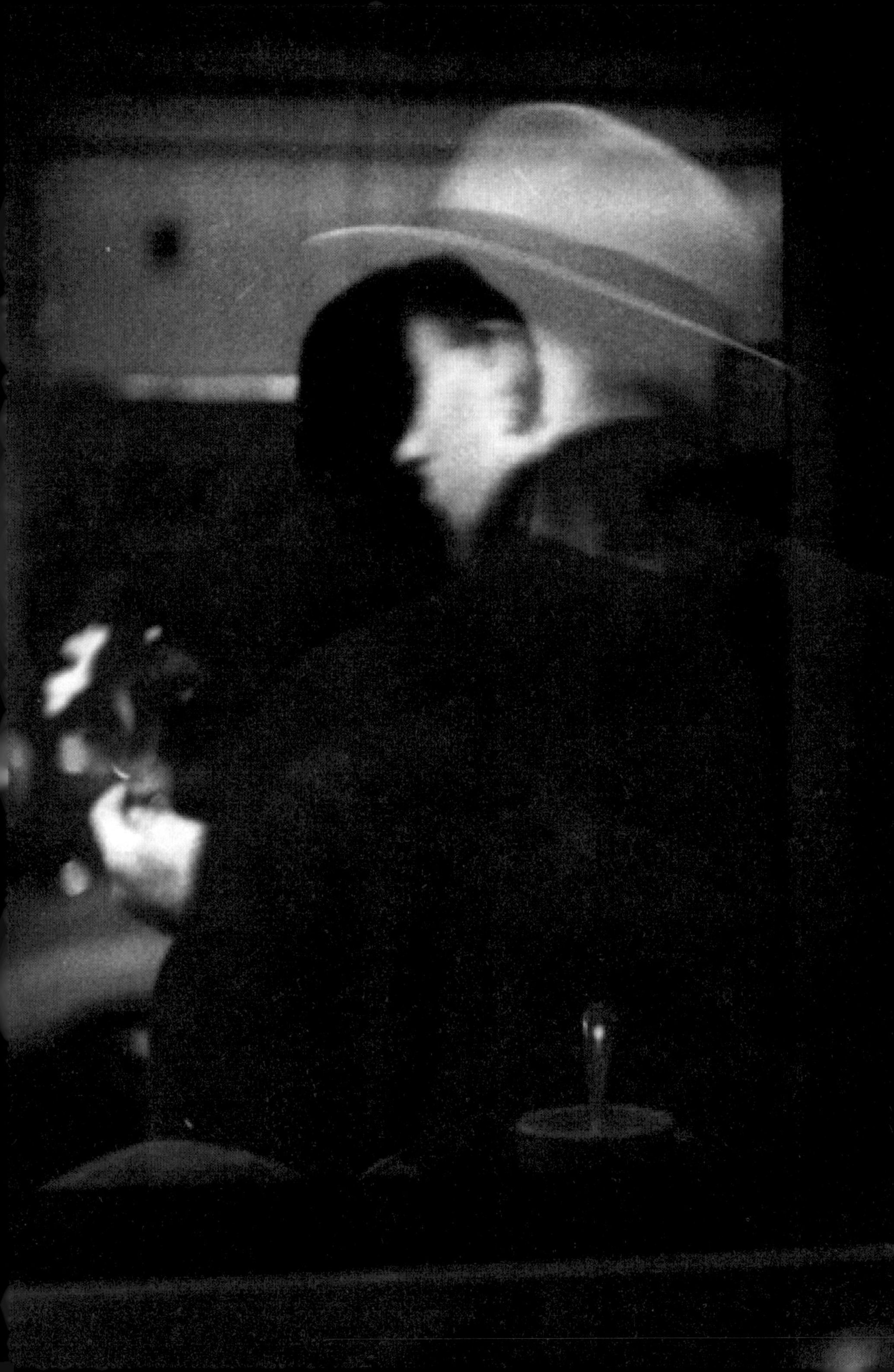

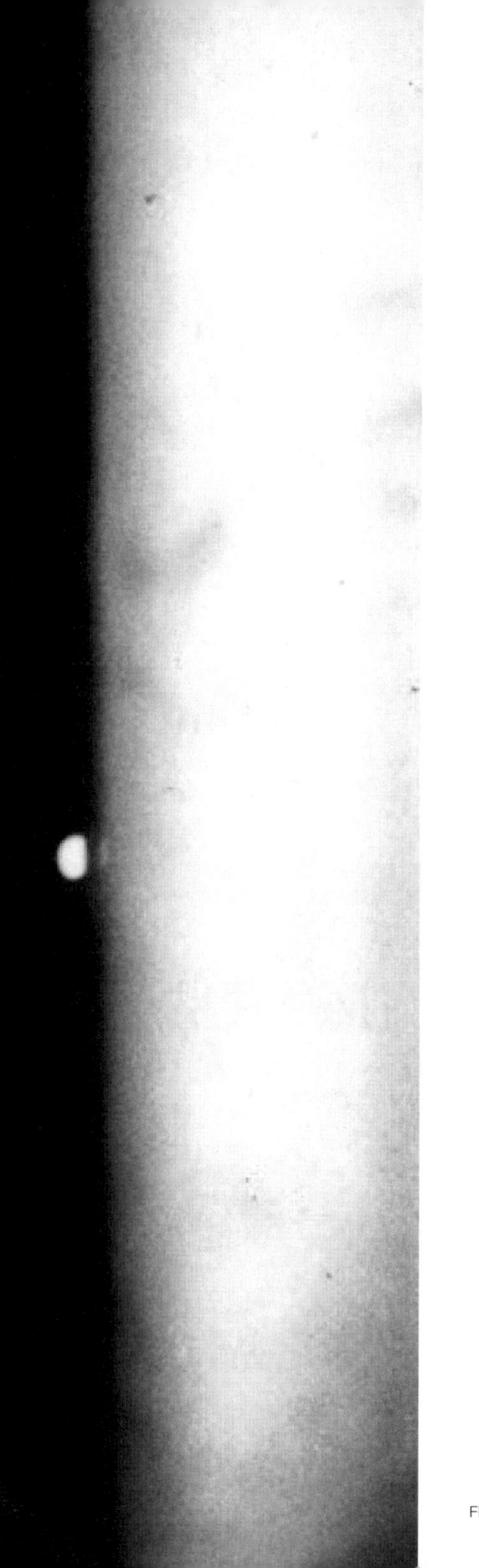

Flower Man, c. 1952

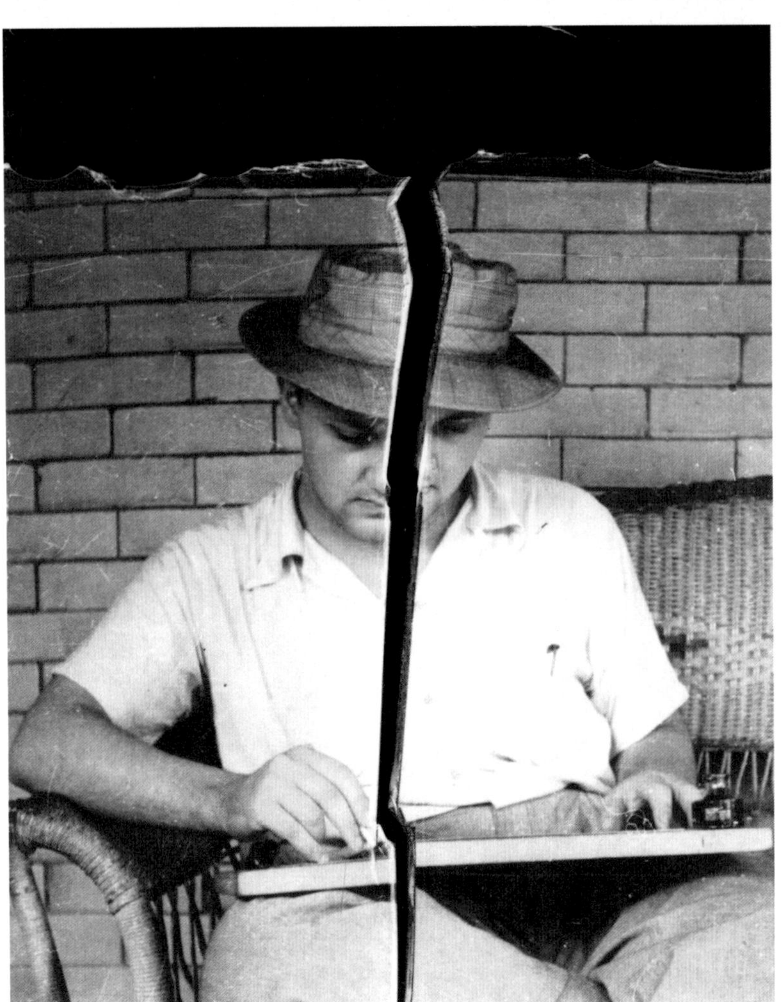

Self-Portrait, 1939   Self-Portrait with Father and Brother, 1940s

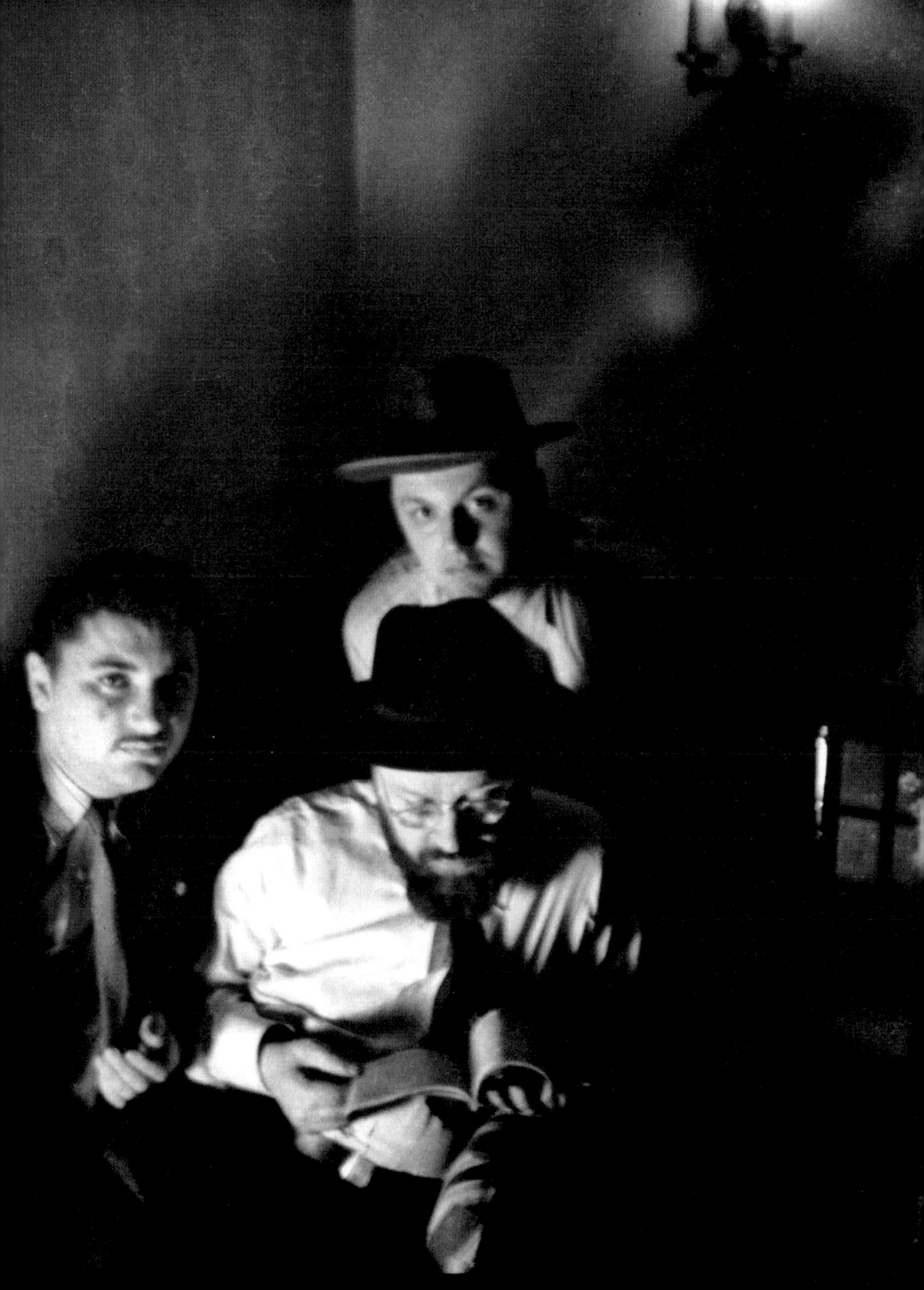

I think that mysterious things happen in familiar places.
We don't always need to run to the other end of the world.

Self-Portrait, 1970s

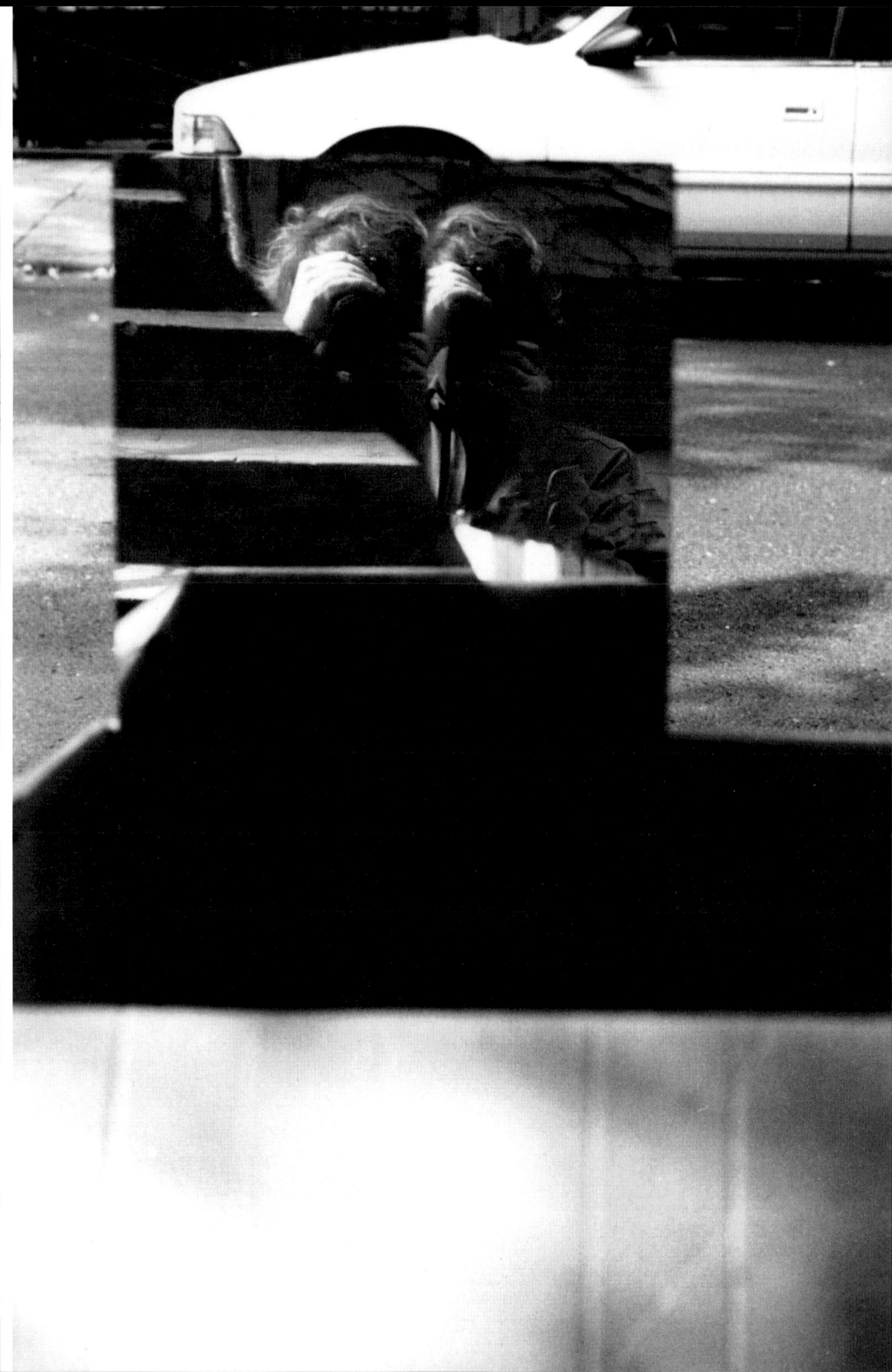

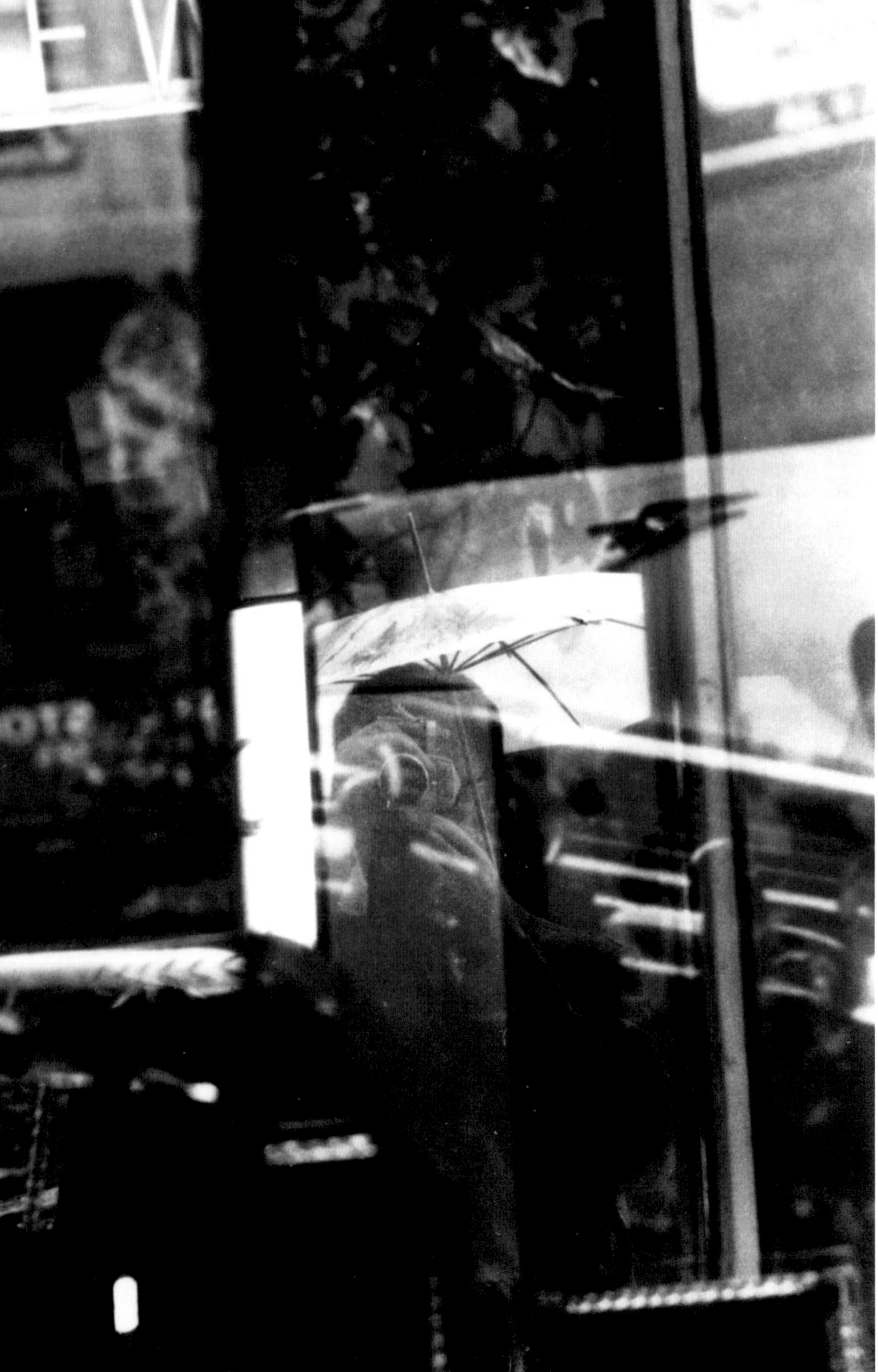

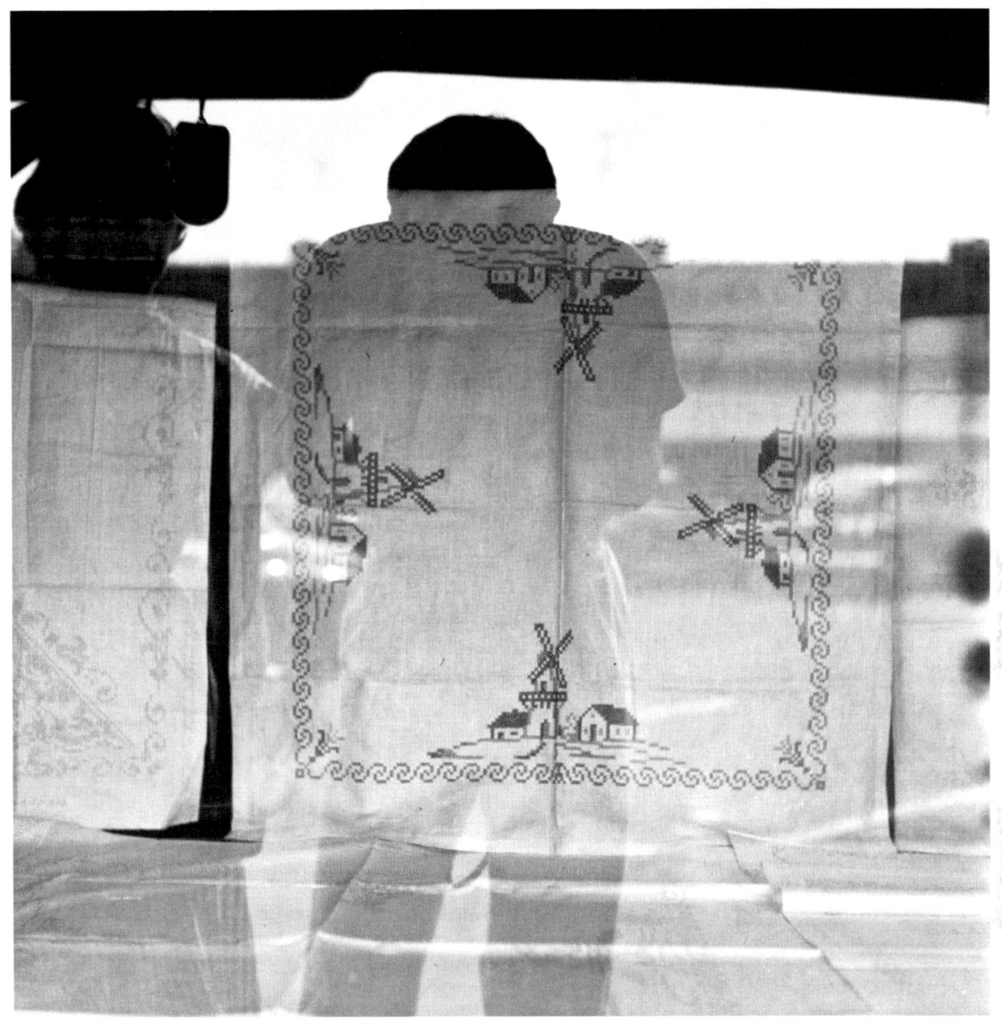

Self-Portrait, 1980s   Self-Portrait with Barbara, c. 1948

Deborah

Deborah Leiter, Saul's sister, was the artist's first model and muse. She was born in 1925, two years after Saul, and is the primary subject of many of his early photographs from the 1940s. These images reveal the mutual affection between the siblings. Deborah, showing intelligence and good humor, is happy to play along as Saul experiments and begins to discover his photographic style.

Deborah at Tante Esther's (p. 225), taken in Brooklyn in 1947, contains several motifs that would appear in countless Leiter photographs in the coming years, including a large expanse of the foreground being occupied by a single surface, in this case the table. Deborah's face is hidden behind a teacup—she's obscured yet also in plain view, a recurring idea in Saul's work. And in this scene of almost complete stillness, there's a sliver of action, as Deborah lifts a saucer with her left hand.

Deborah suffered from mental disorders beginning in her twenties that eventually left her permanently institutionalized, and sadly Saul lost his connection with her. (She passed away around 2007.) We now know that Saul painted and made prints from his negatives of Deborah all the way until the end of his life. To date we've discovered nearly 100 works depicting or inspired by her, showing that she was never far from Saul's heart.

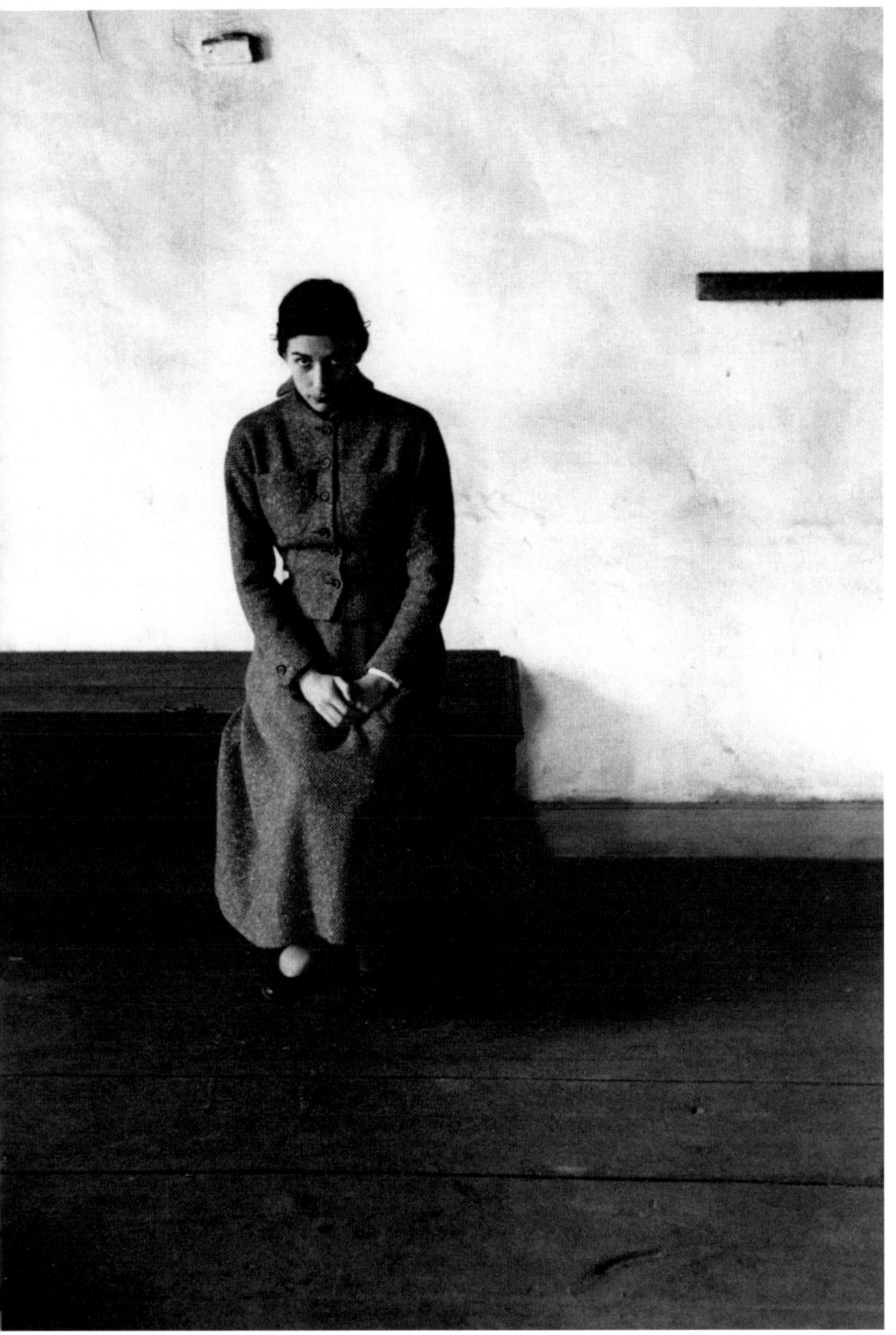

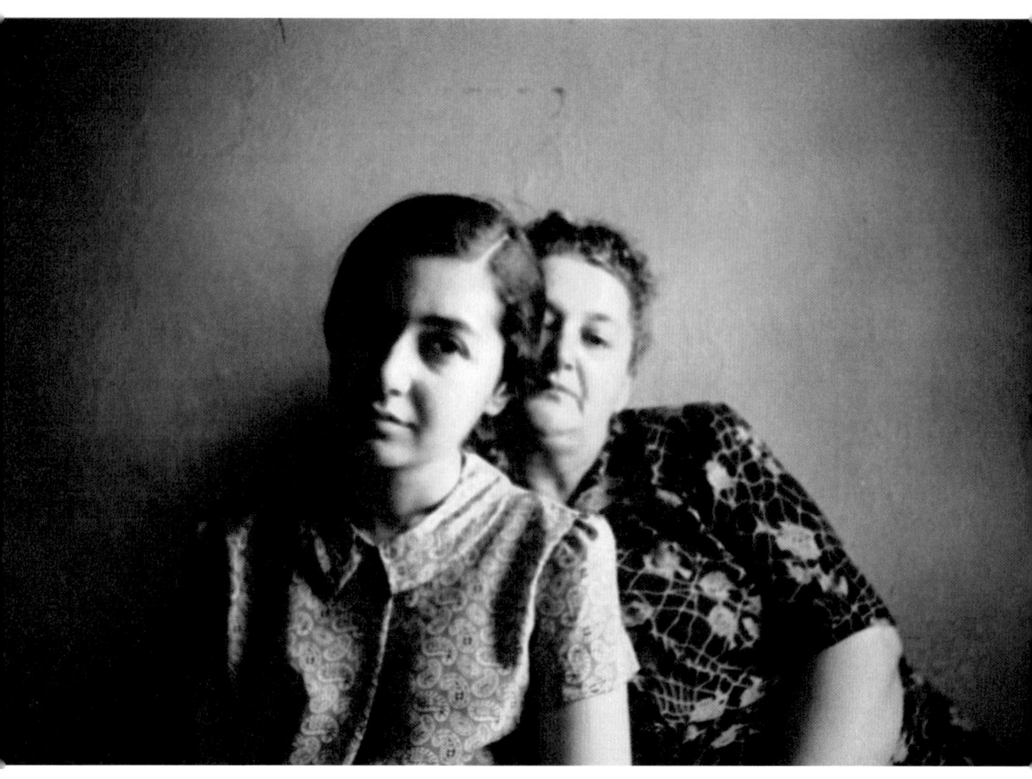

Deborah and Regina, c. 1948

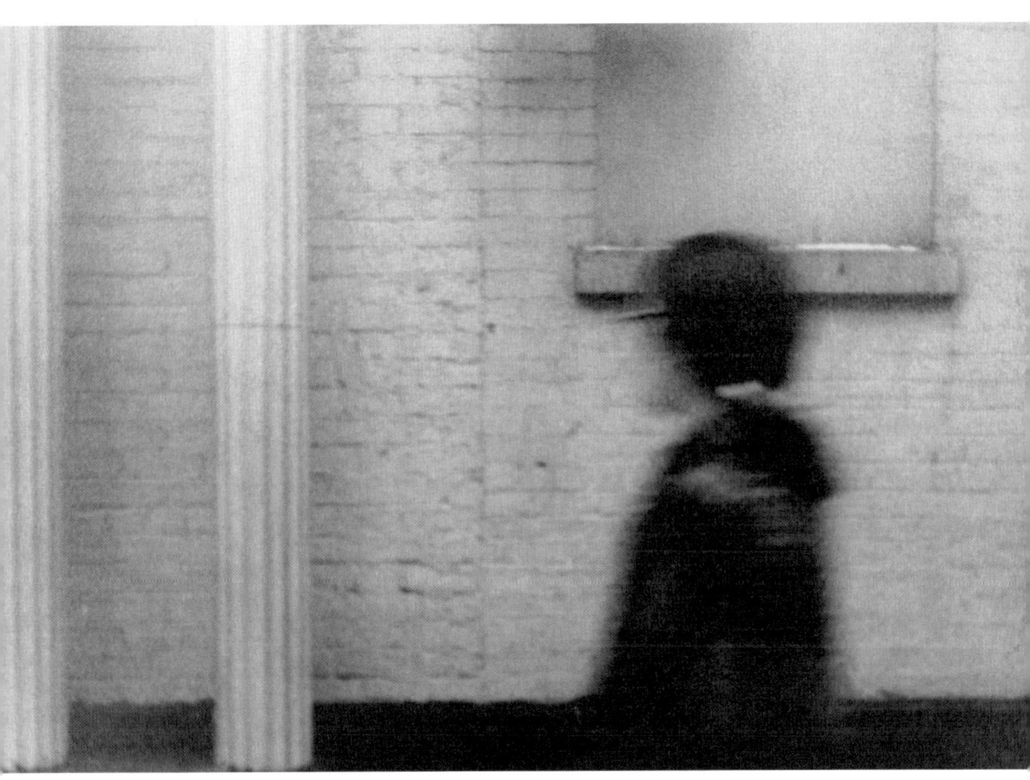

Deborah, c. 1948

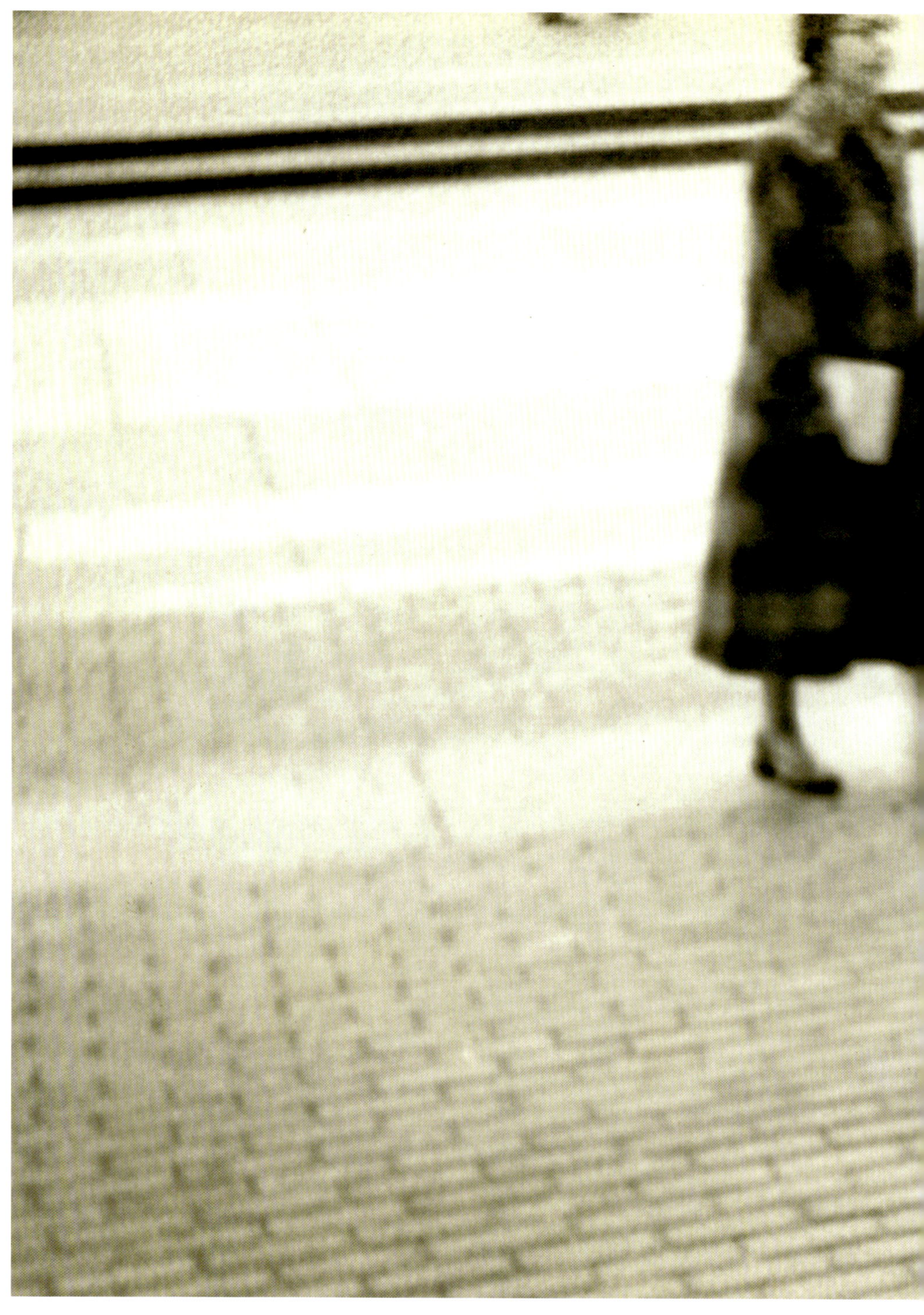

Deborah, c. 1946

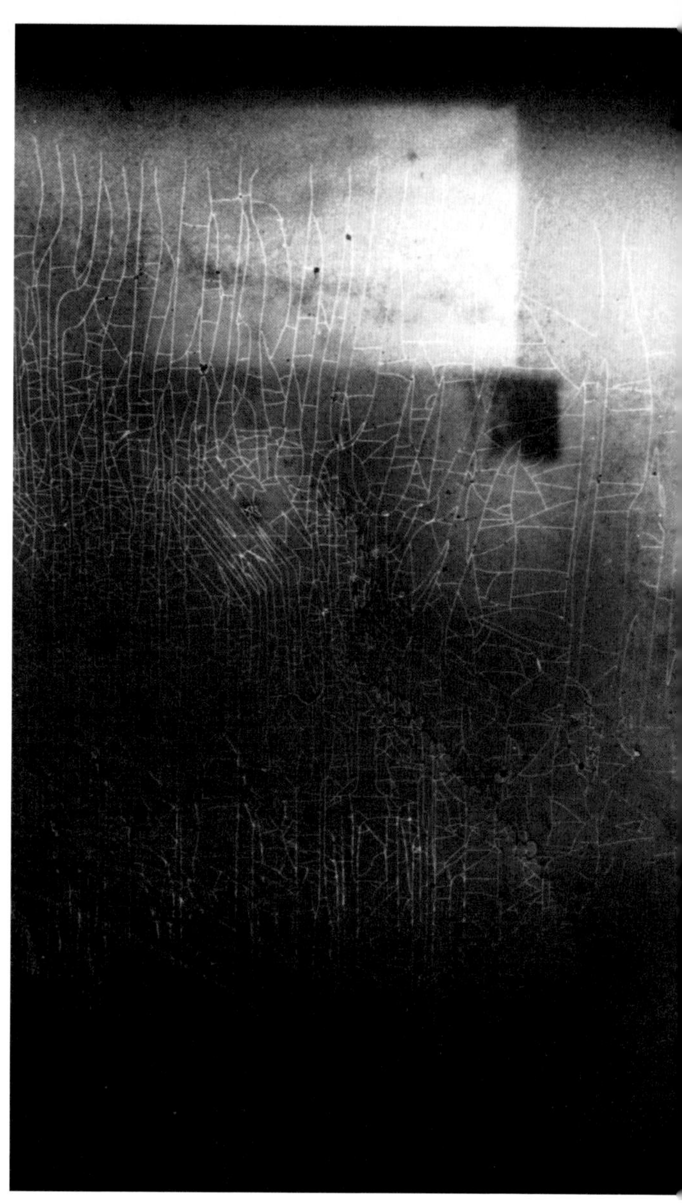

Deborah, 1947

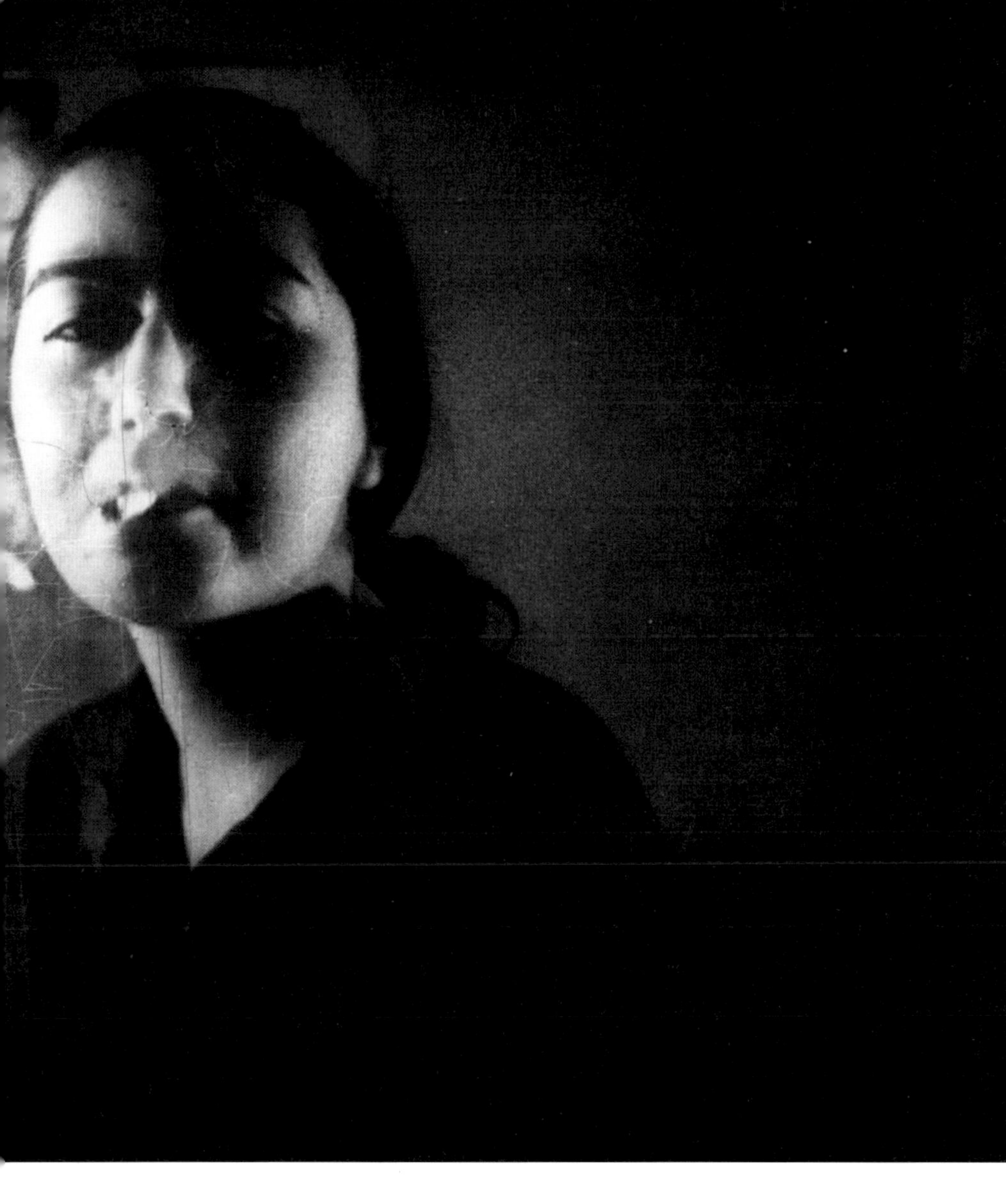

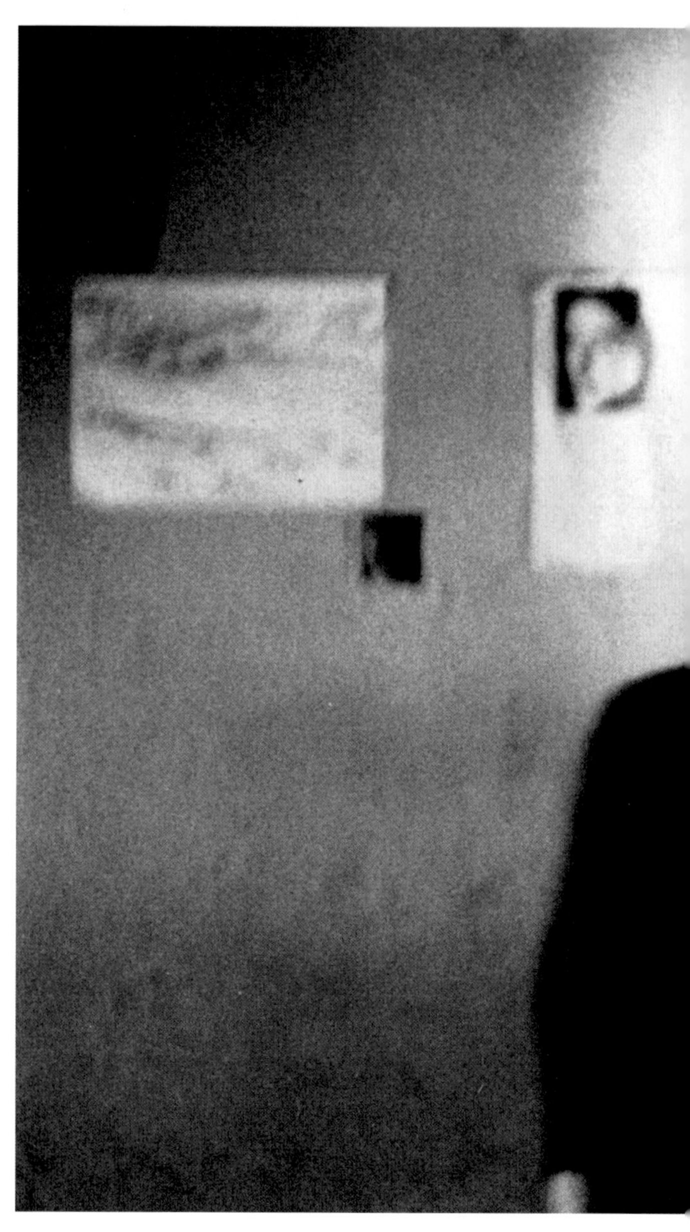

Deborah, c. 1946

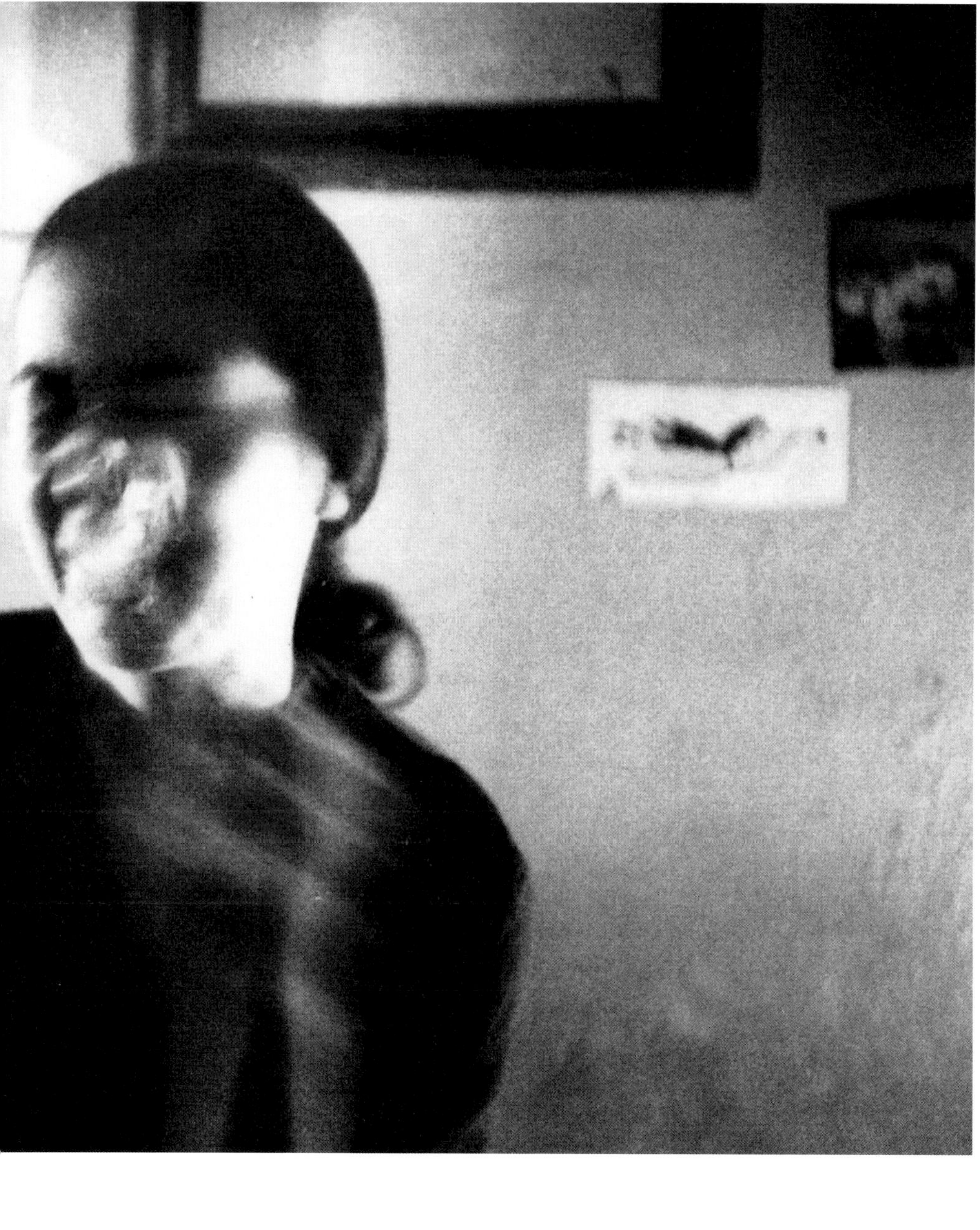

Deborah, 1940s

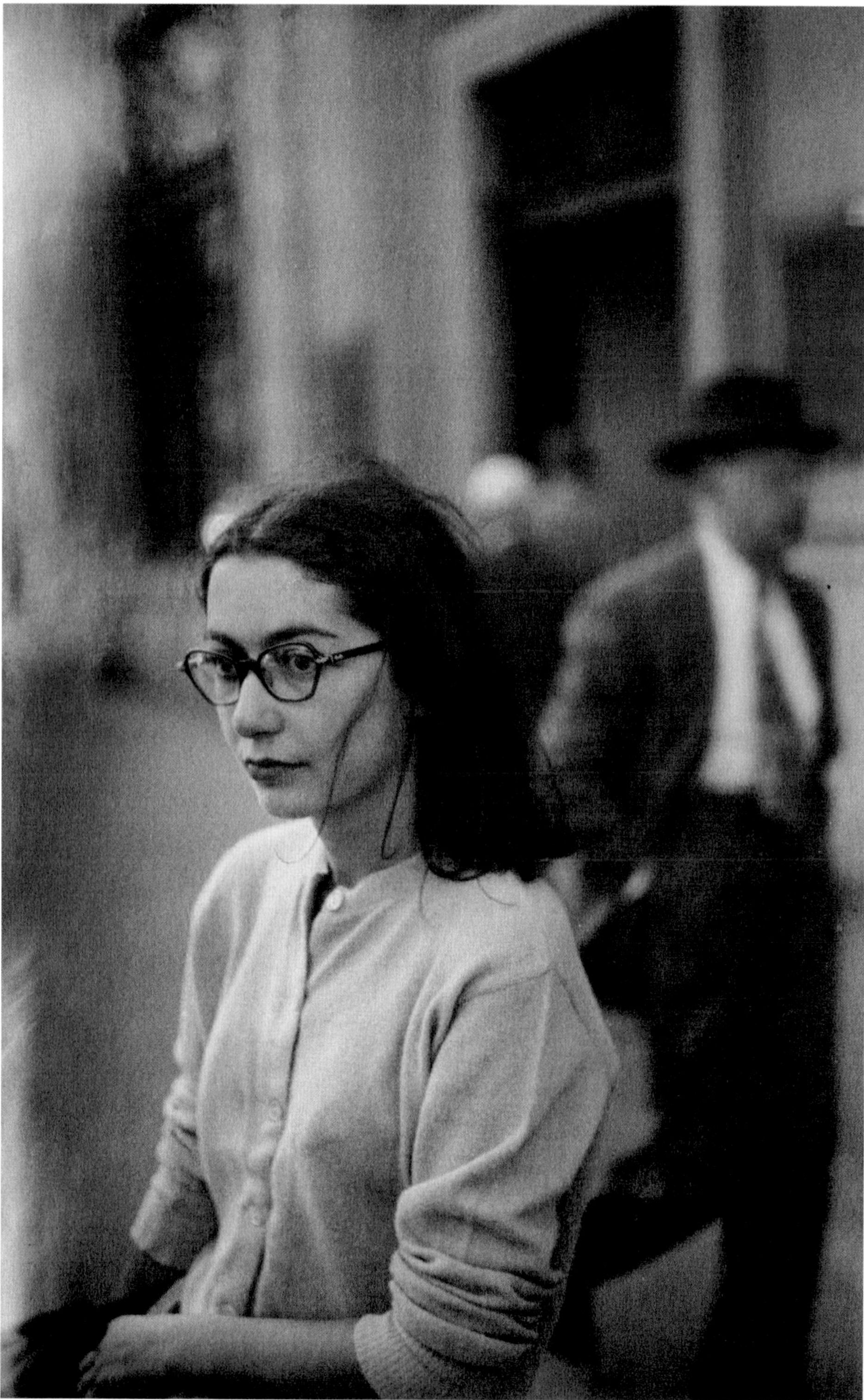

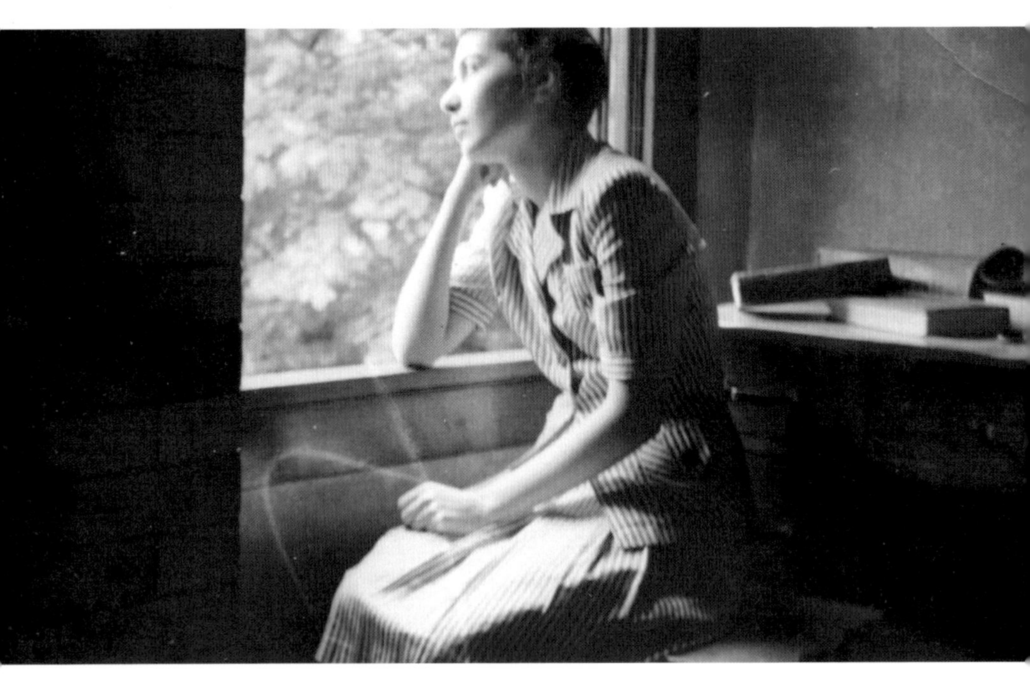

Deborah, May 1943   Deborah, 1940s

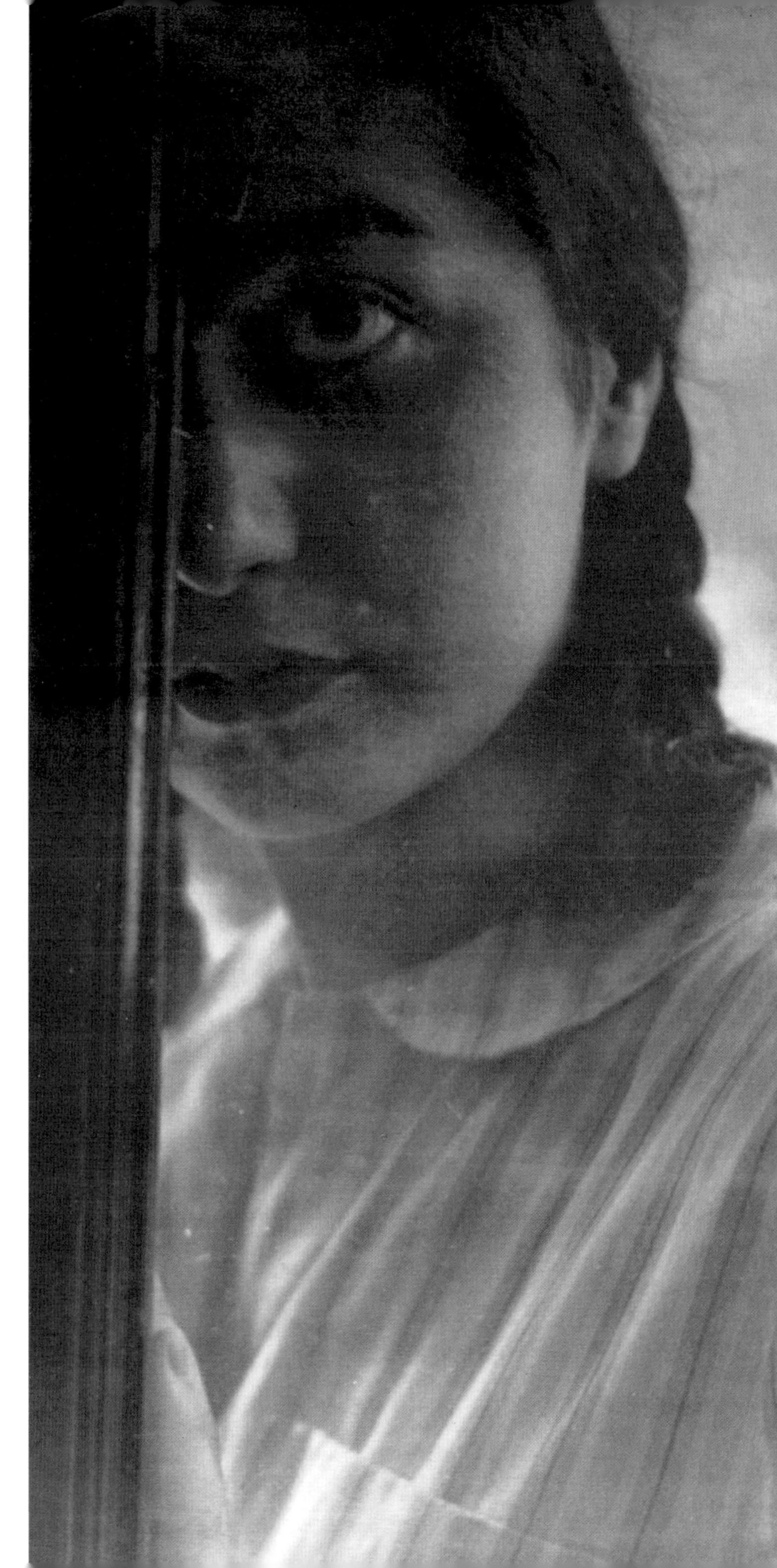

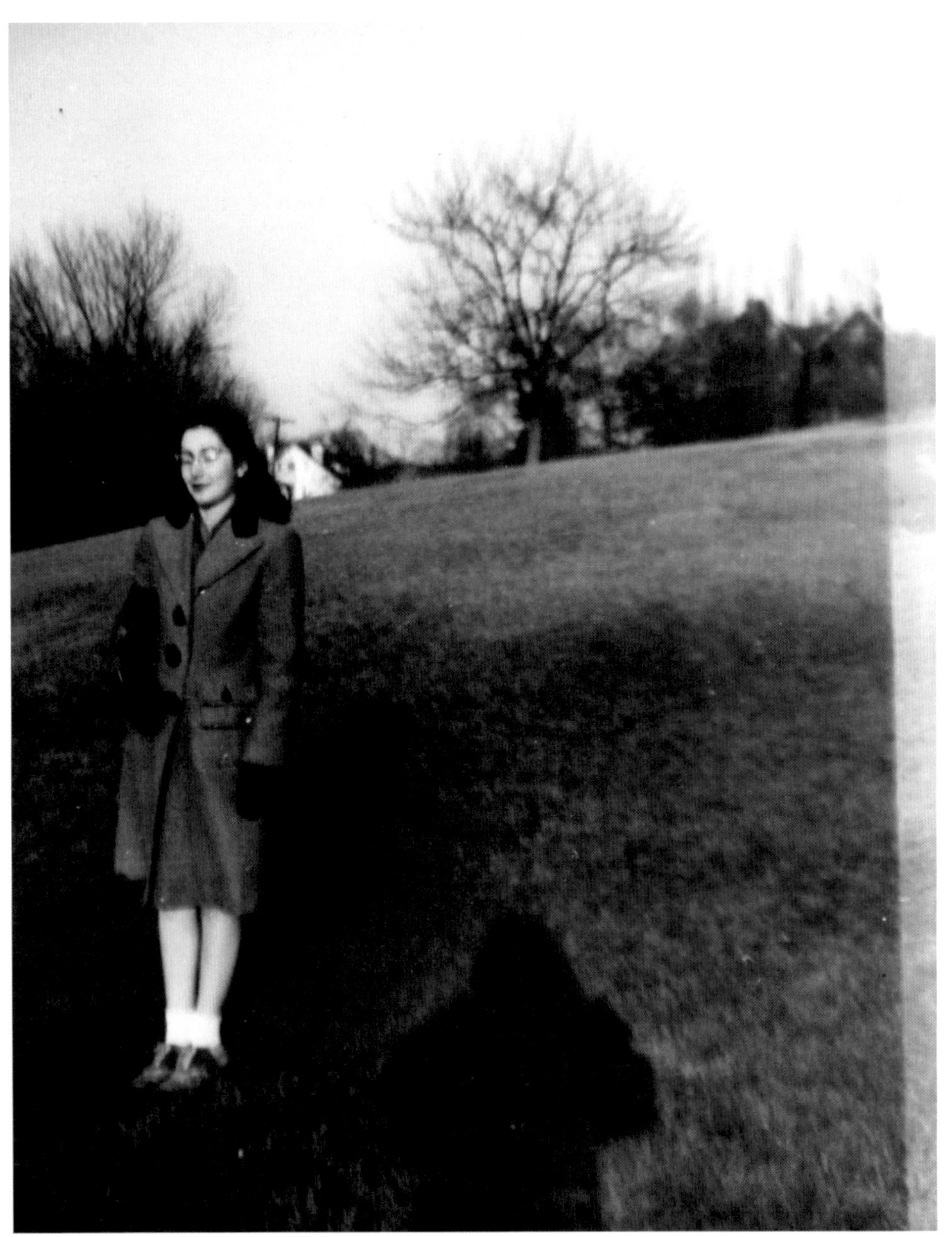

Deborah, March 1946

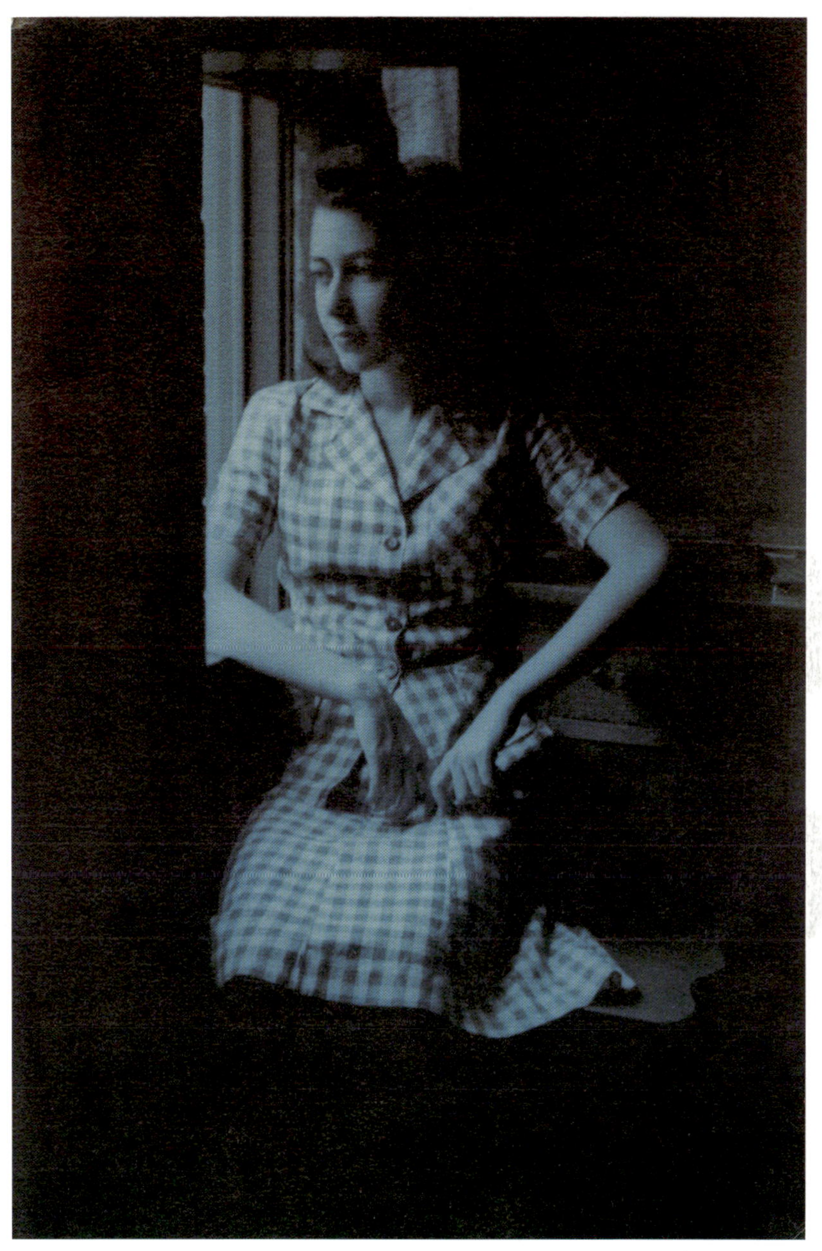

pp. 216–217: Deborah, undated

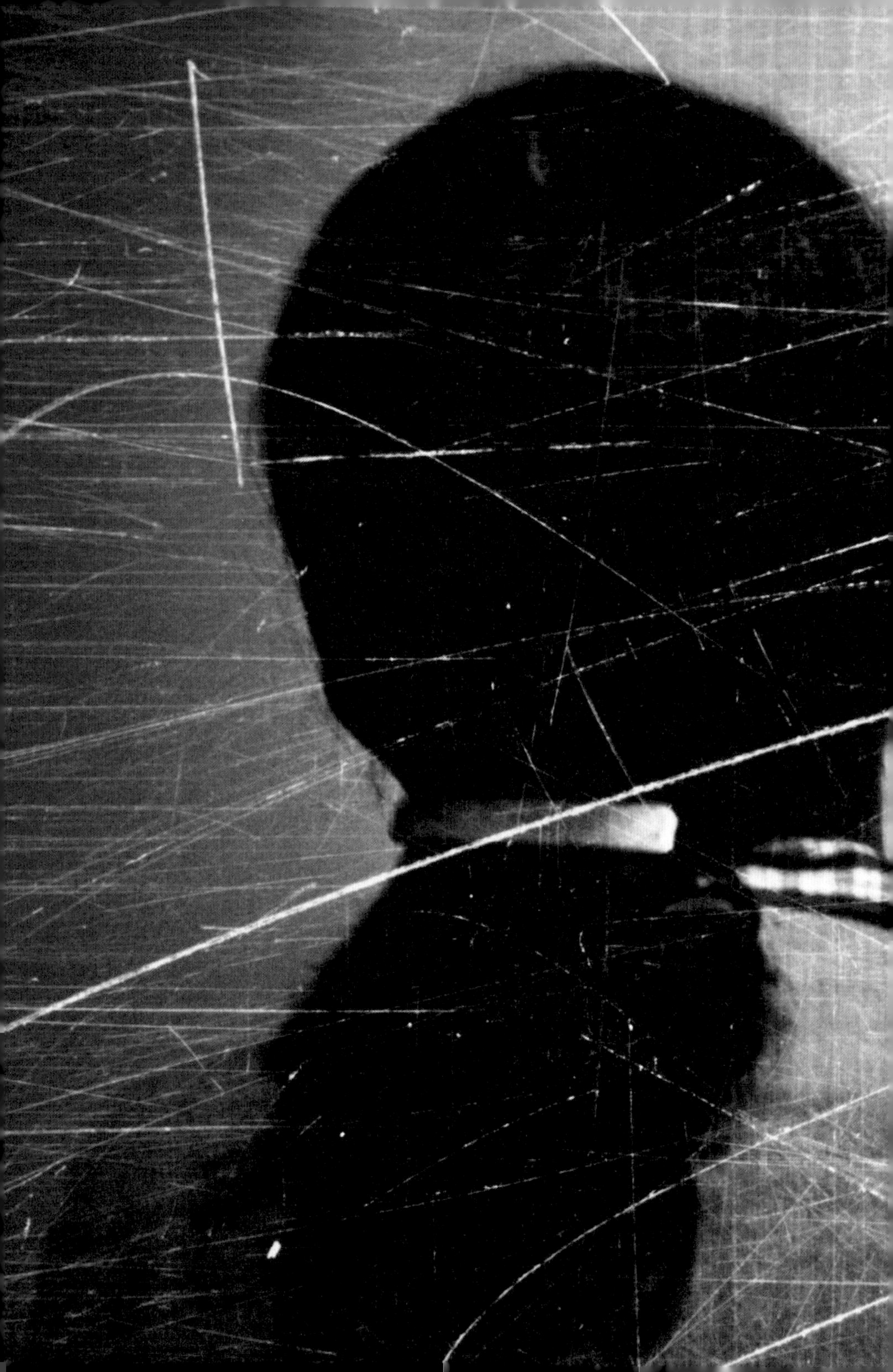

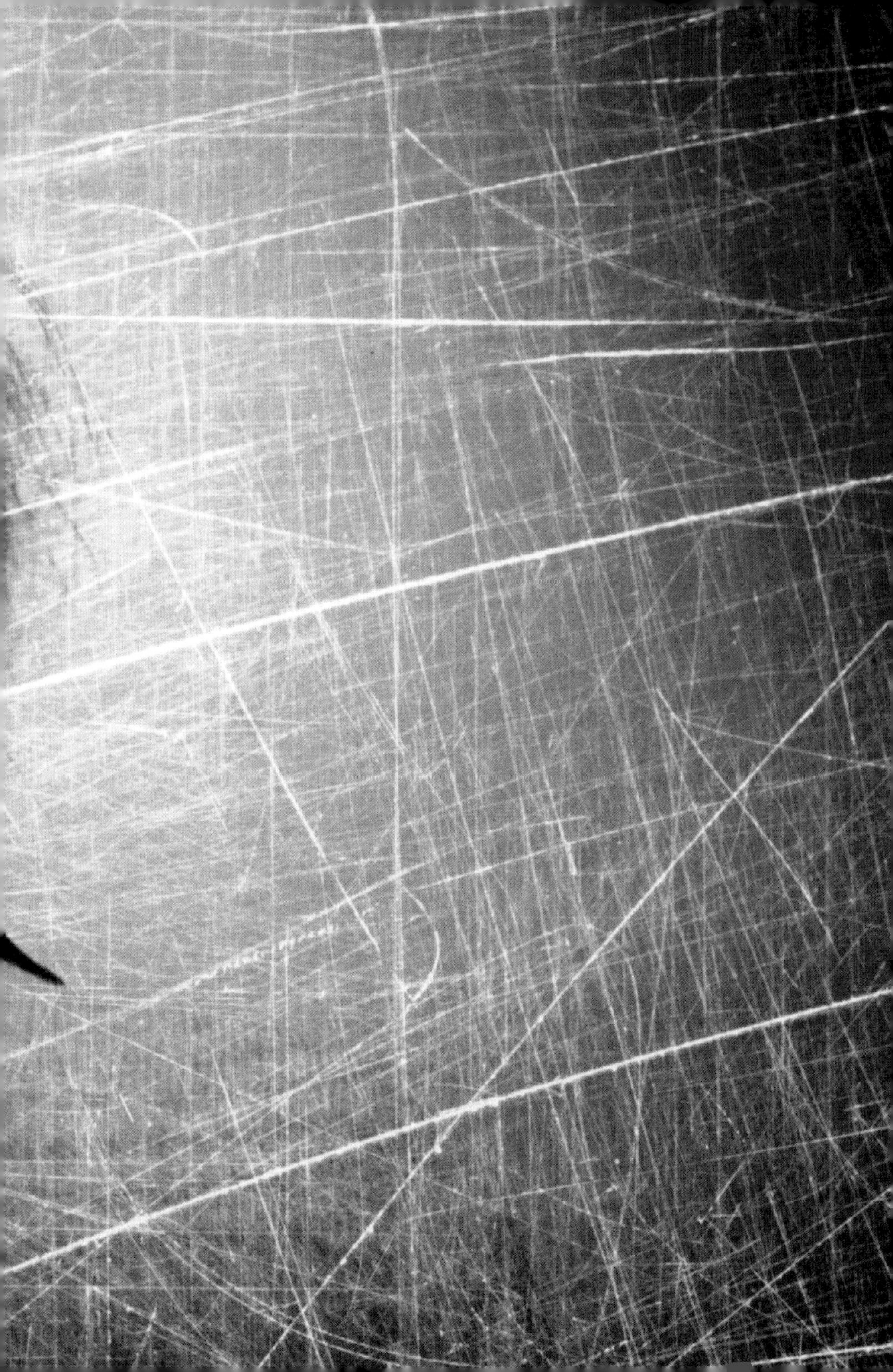

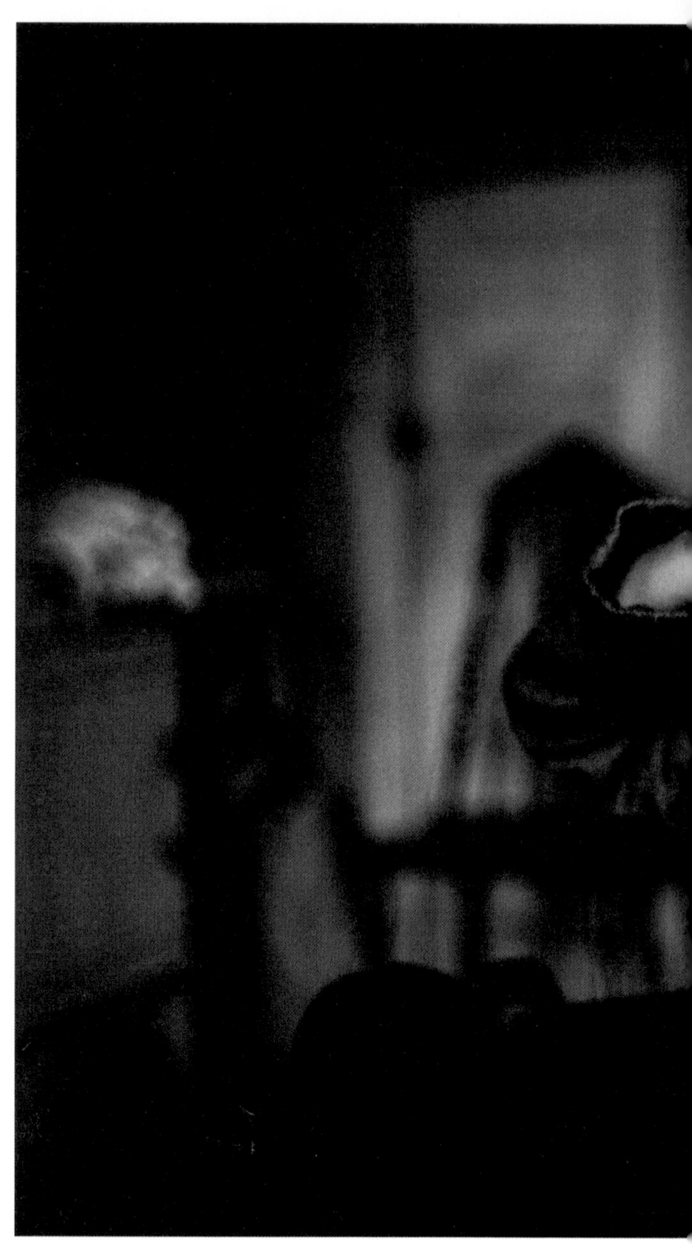

Deborah, c. 1946

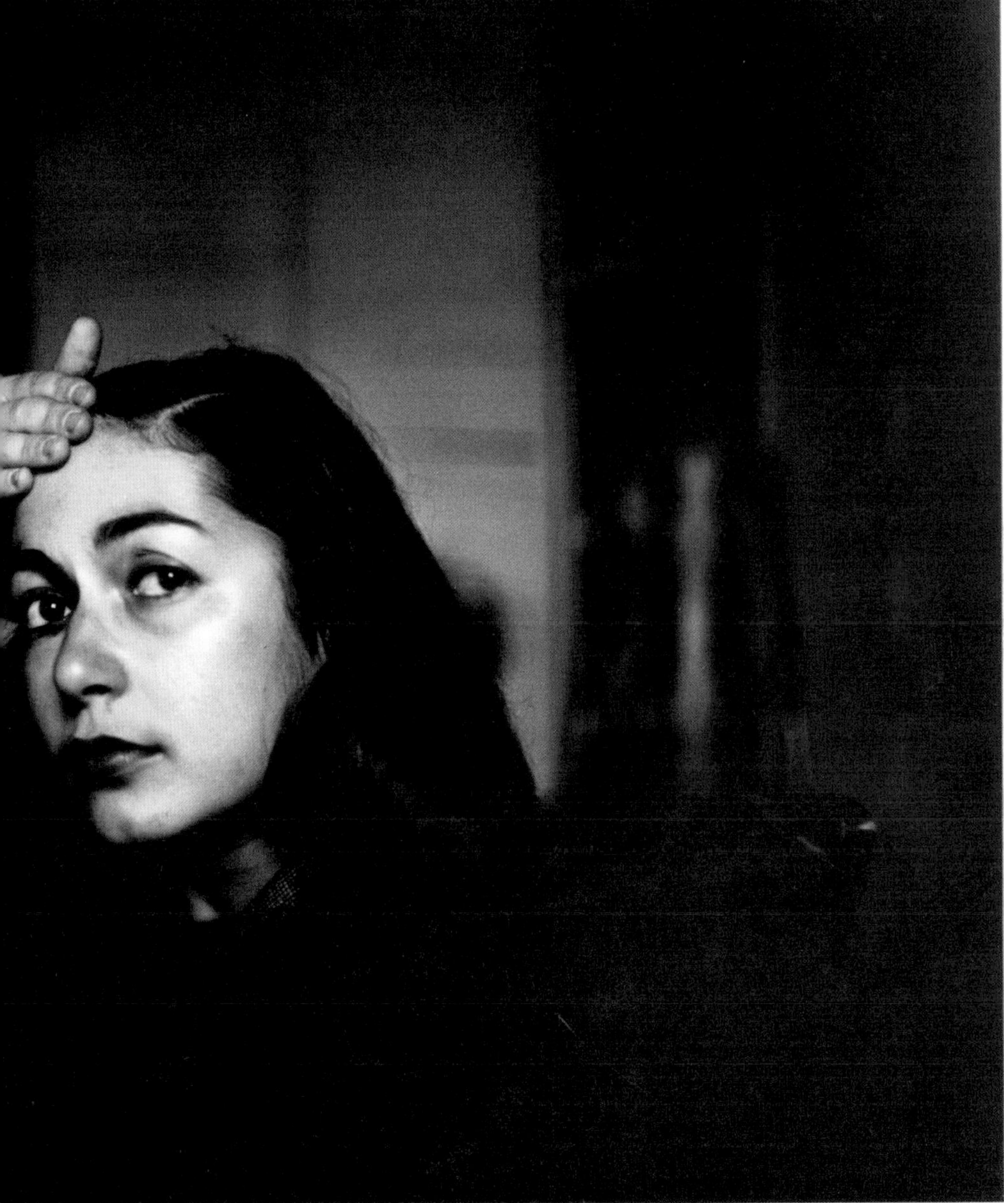

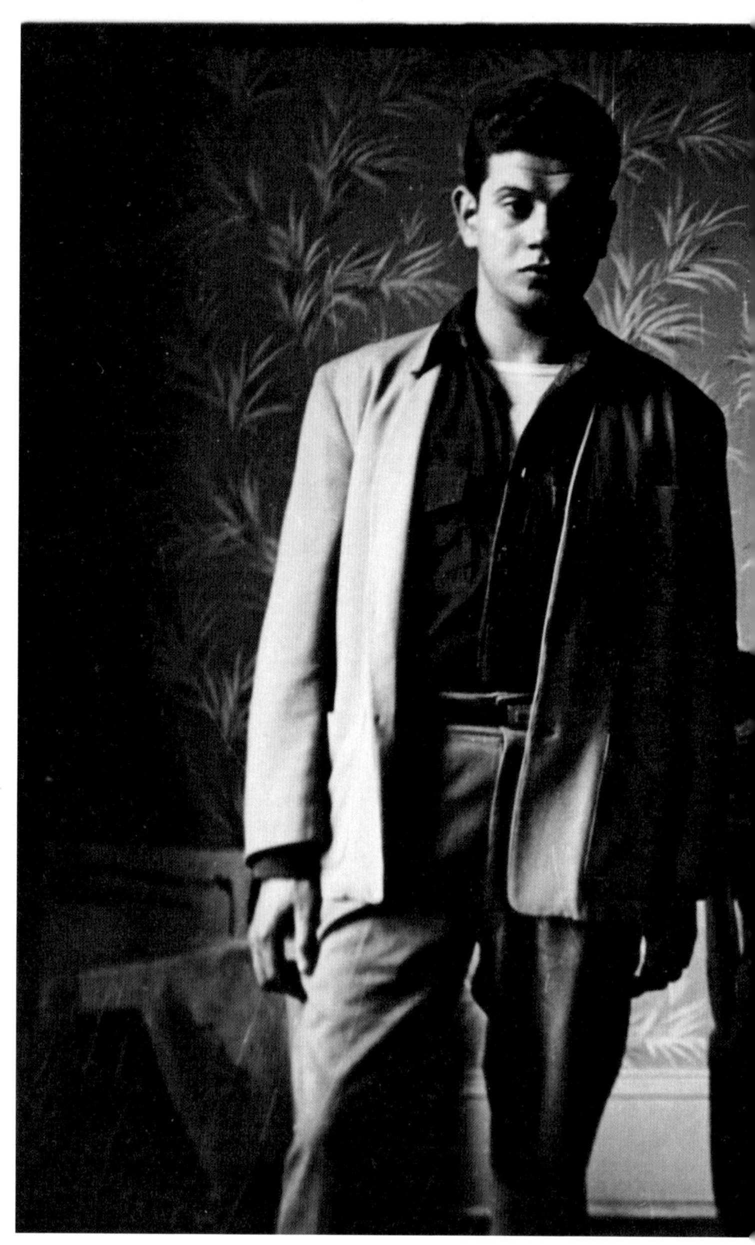

Bobby and Deborah, undated

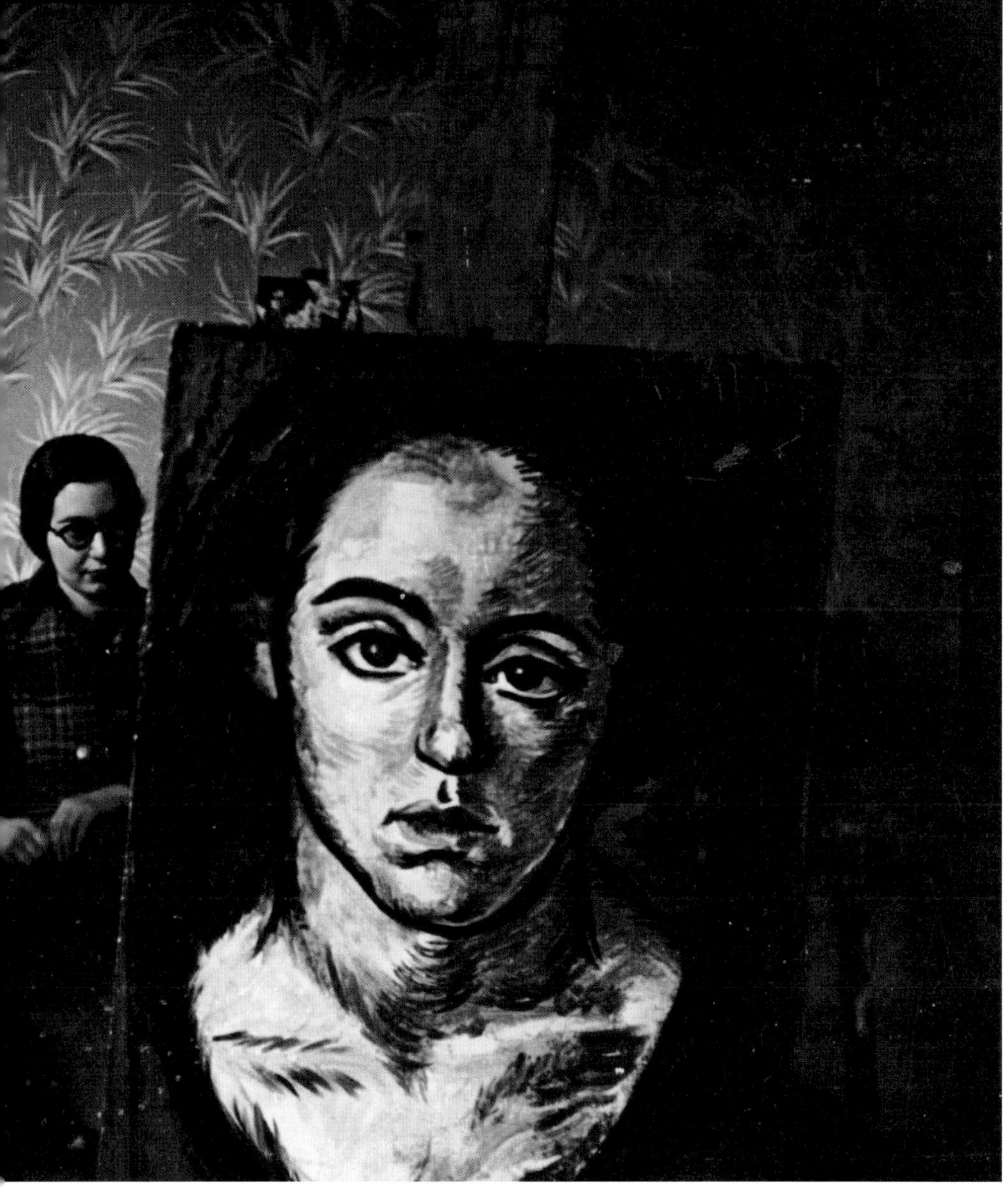

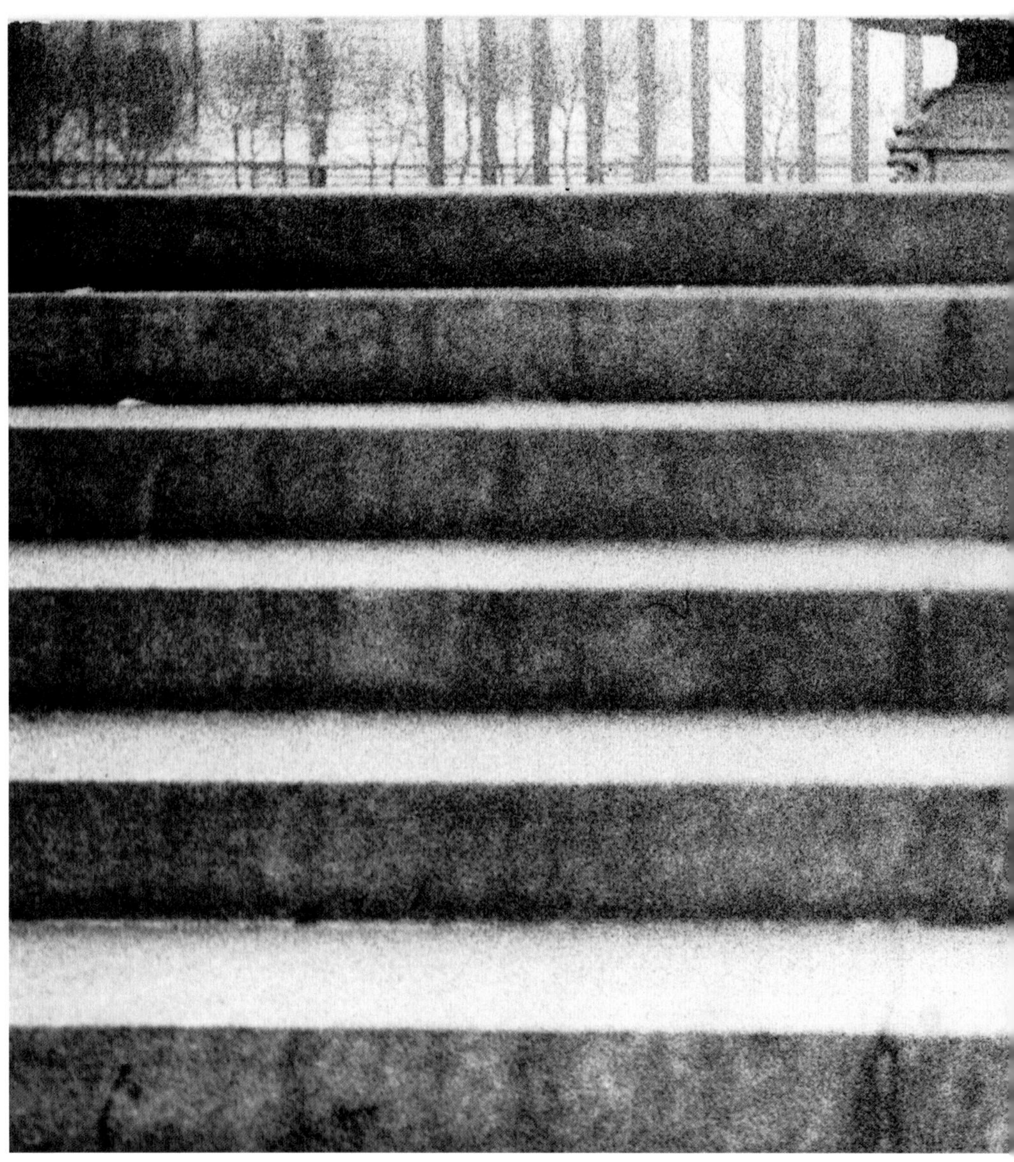

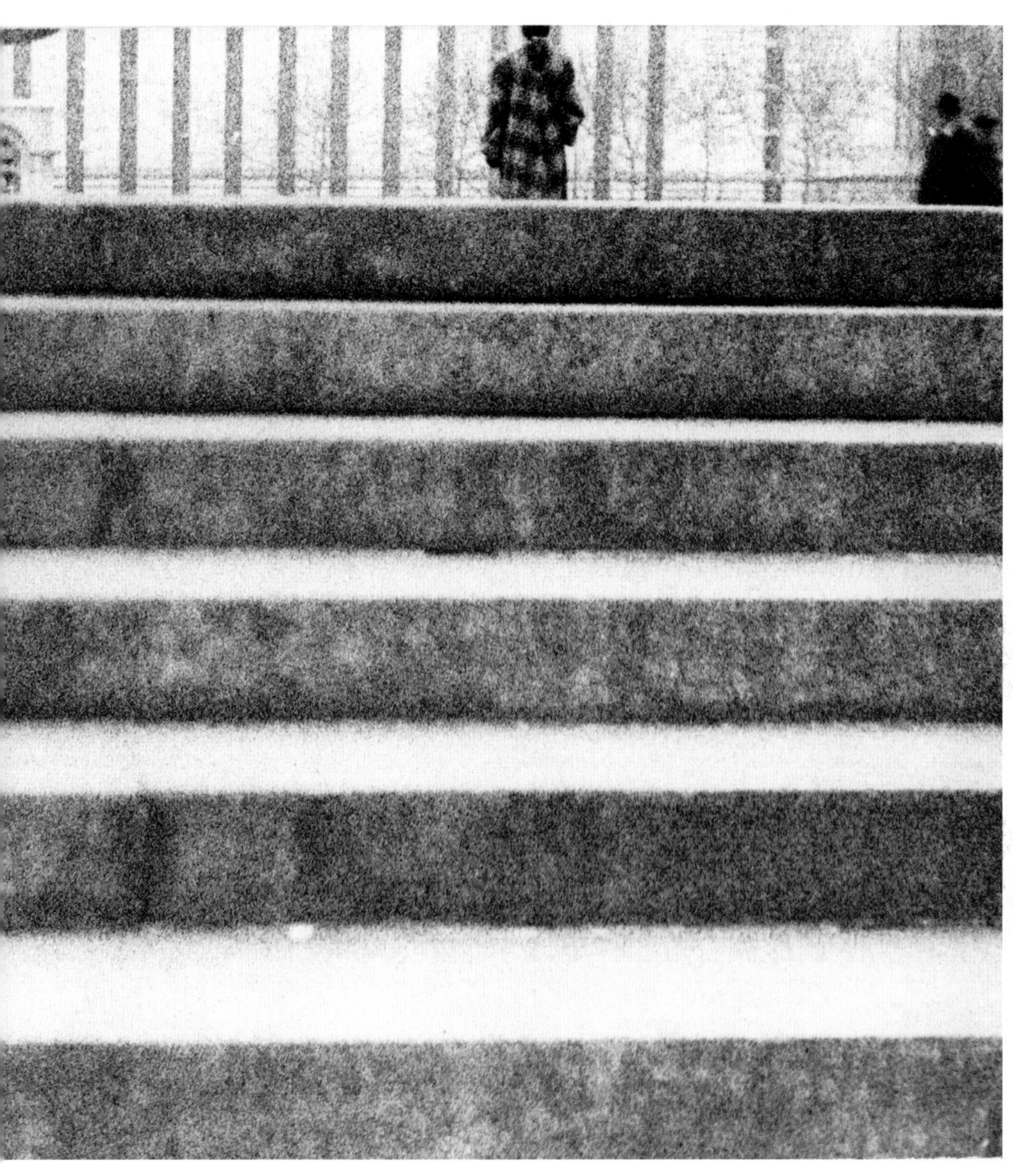

Deborah, 1940s

Deborah at Tante Esther's, 1947

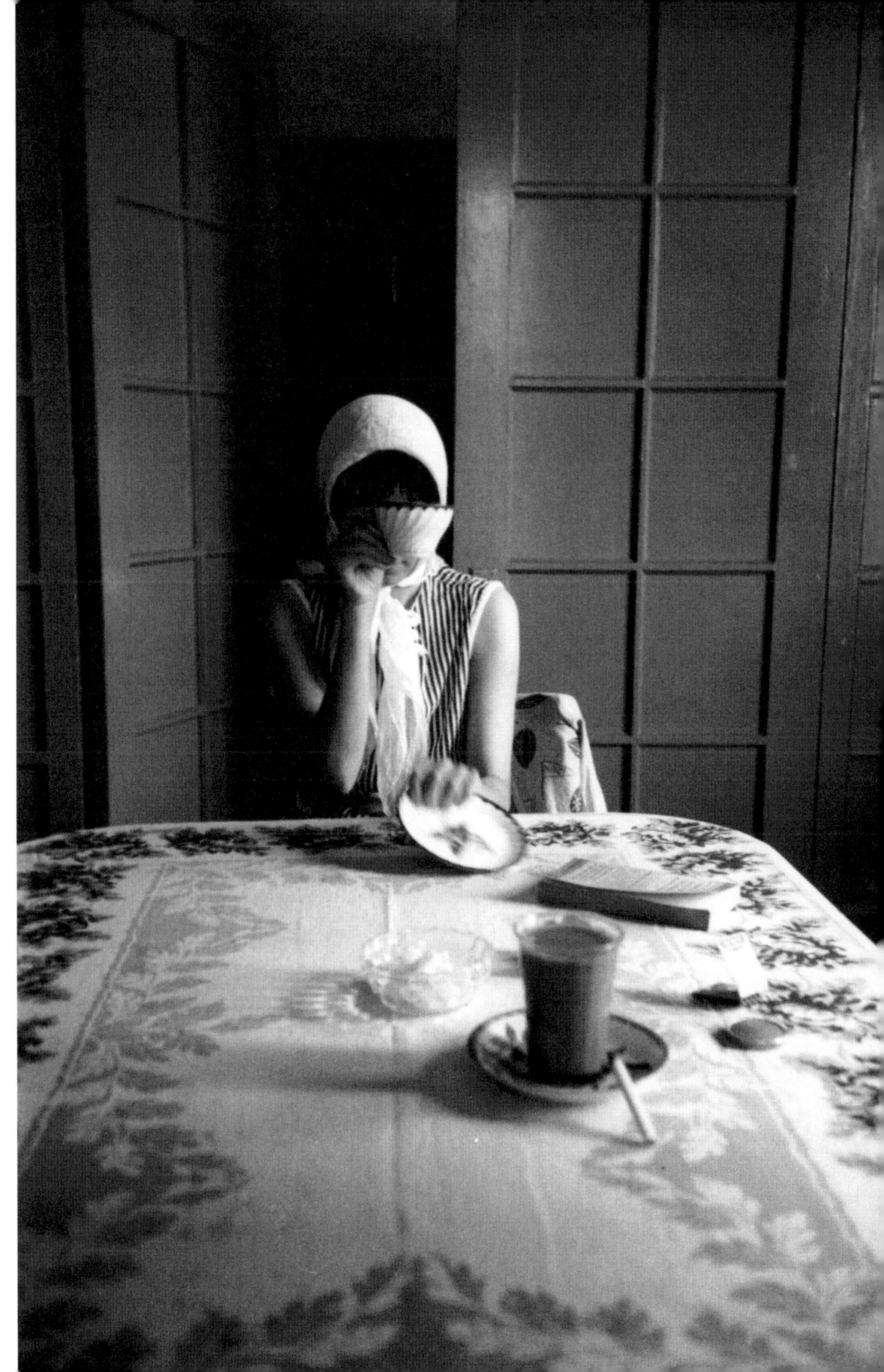

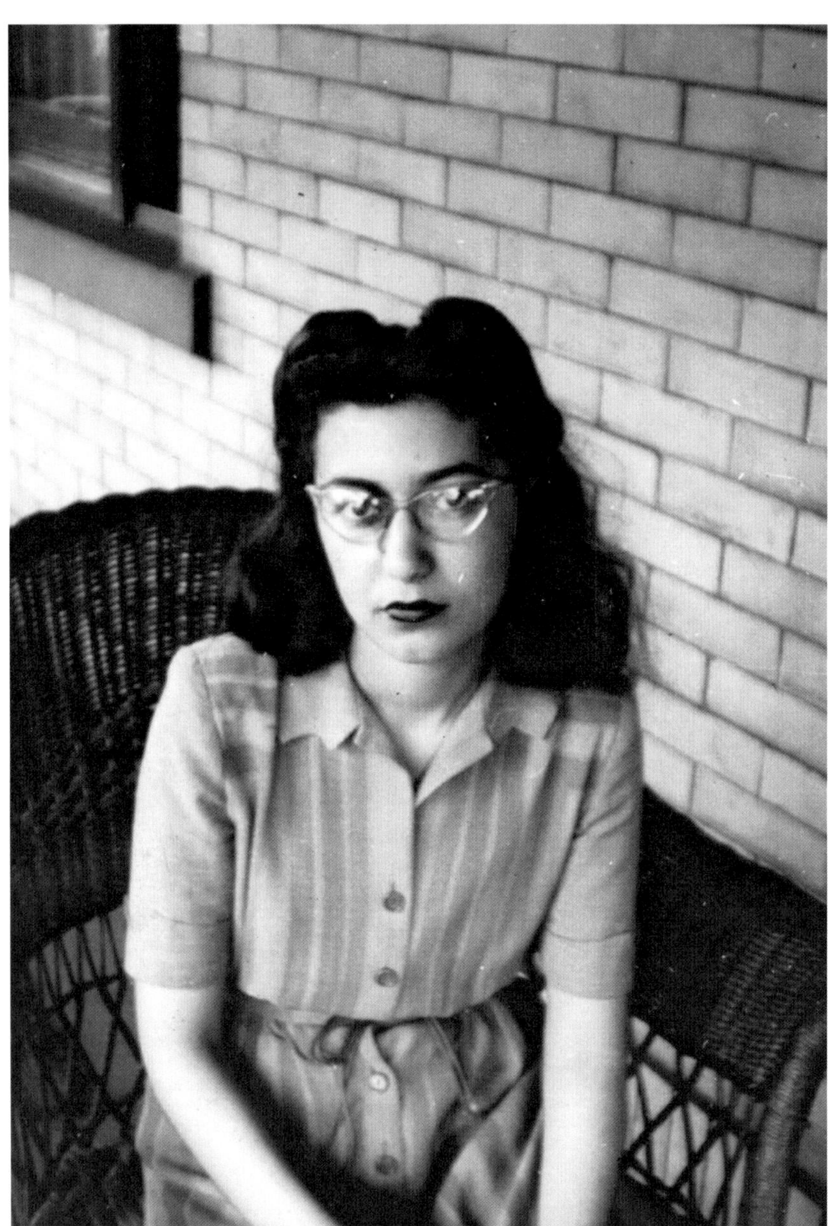

Deborah, May 1944   Deborah, May 1943

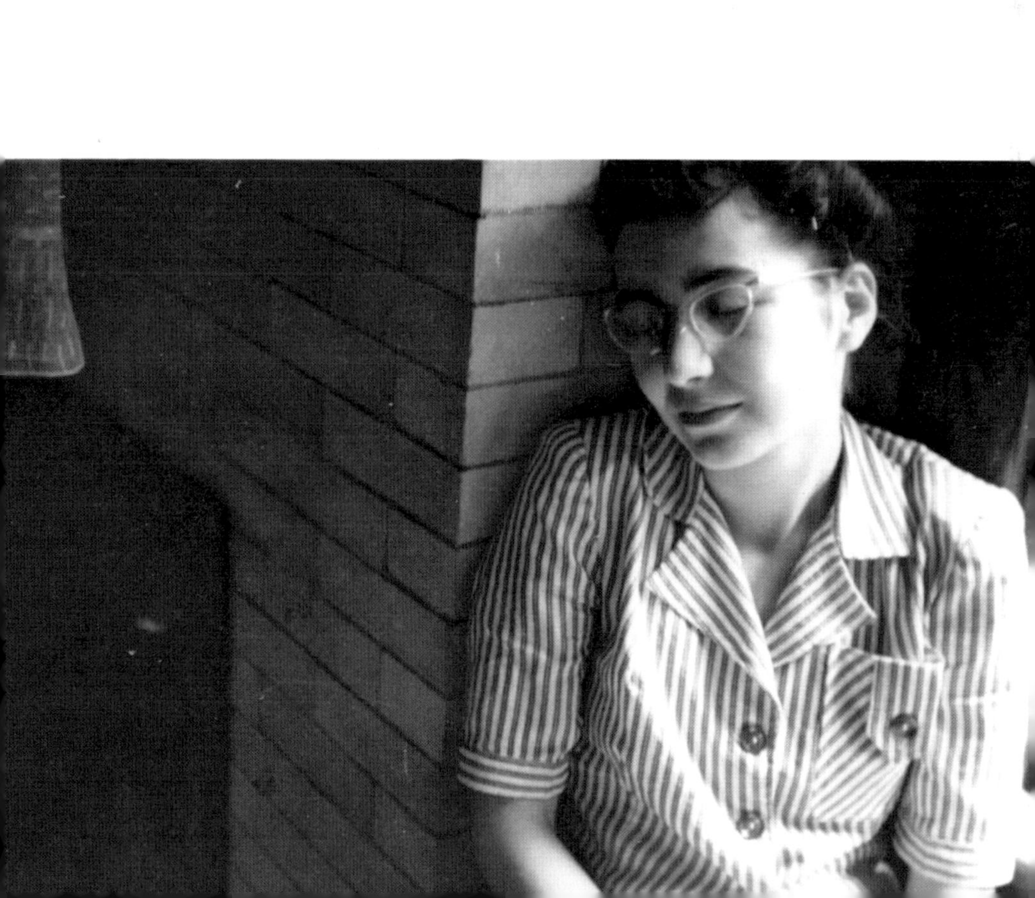

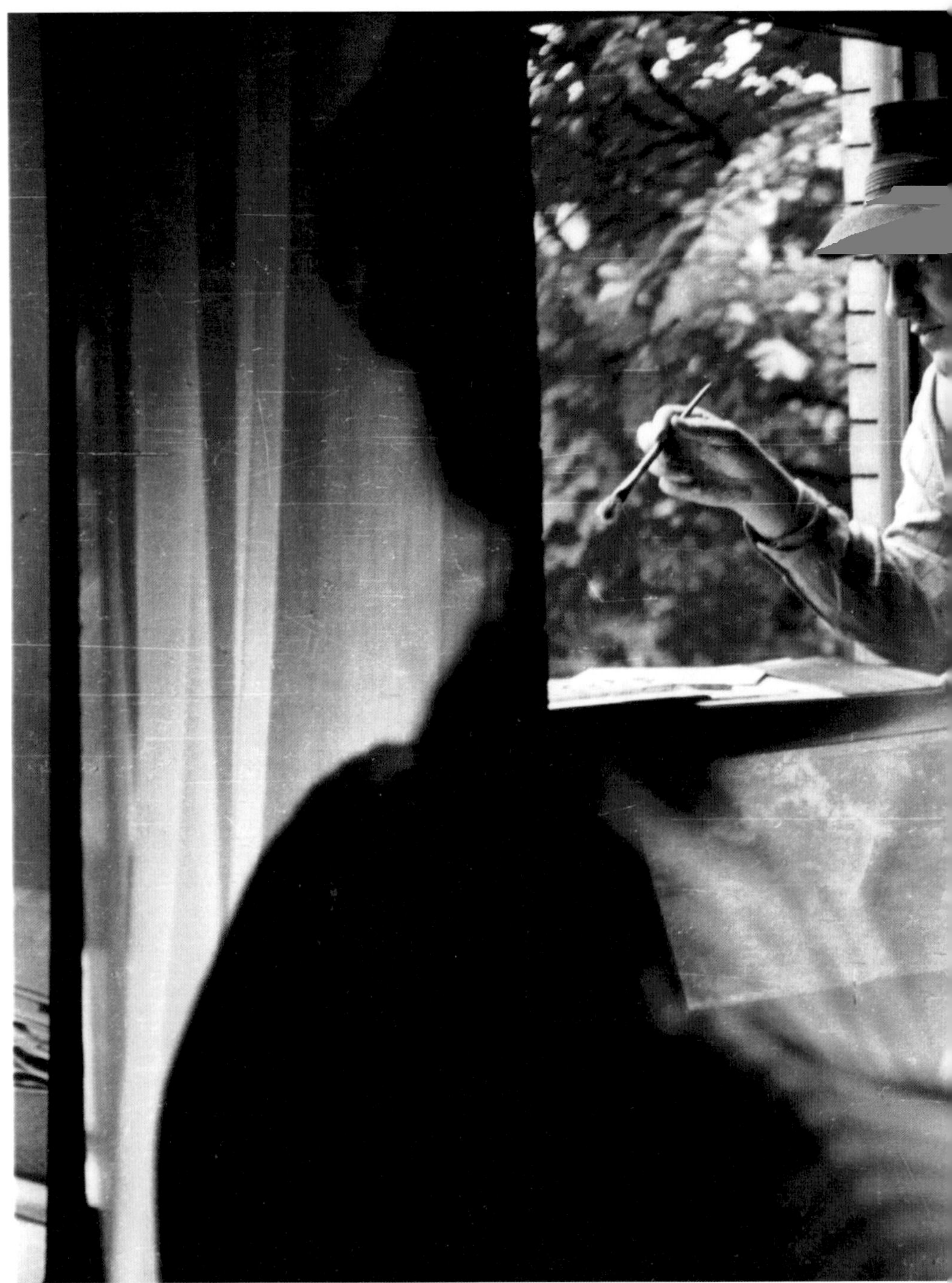

Self-Portrait with Deborah, 1940s

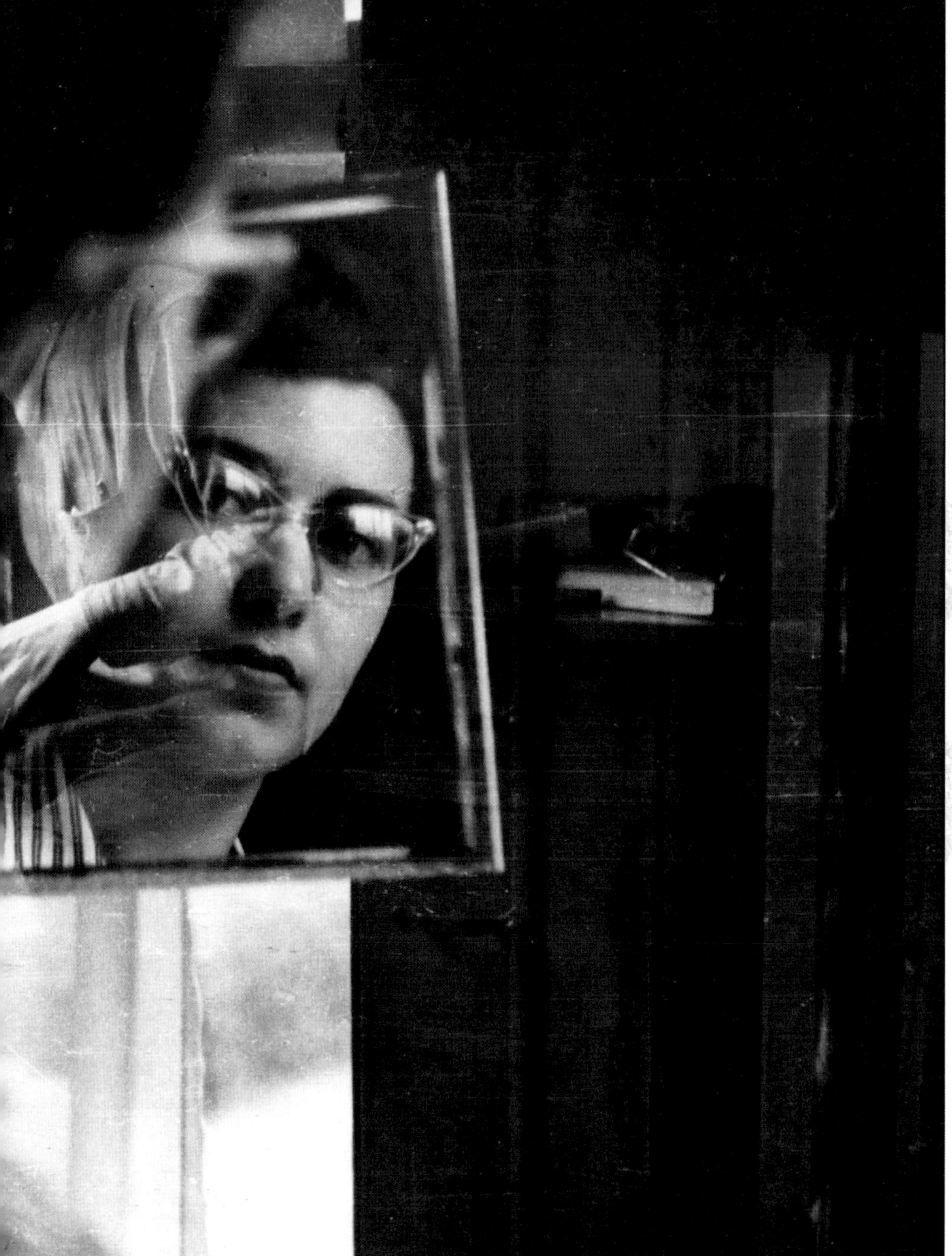

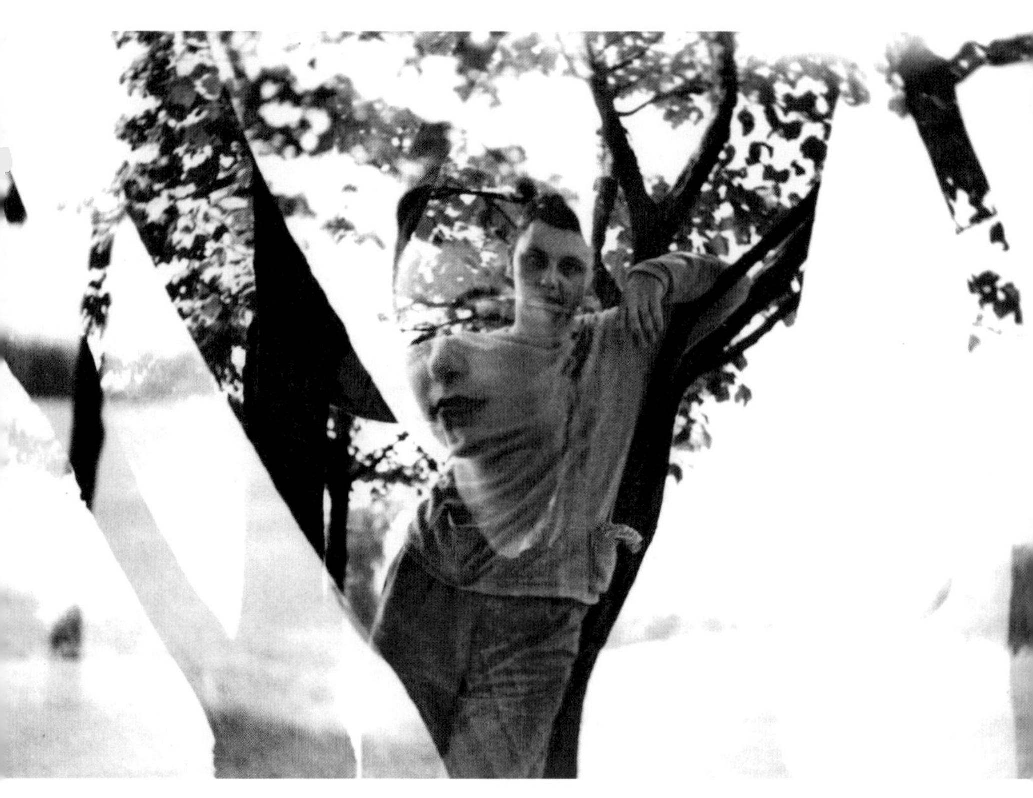

Self-Portrait with Deborah, 1940s

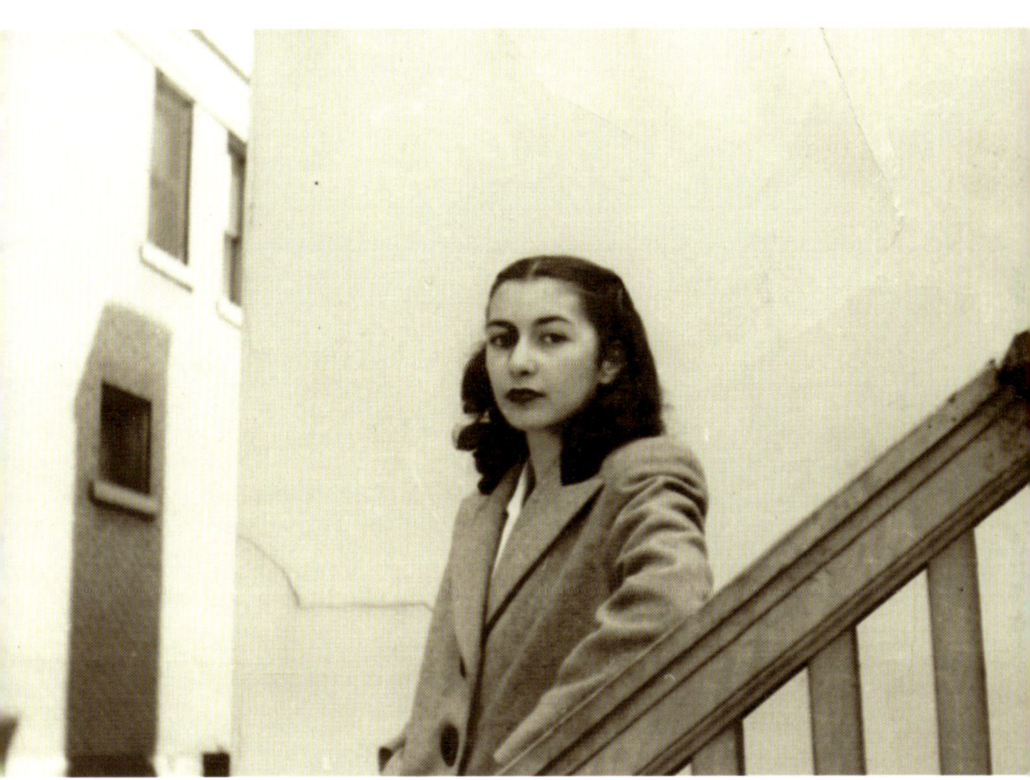

Deborah, April 1945

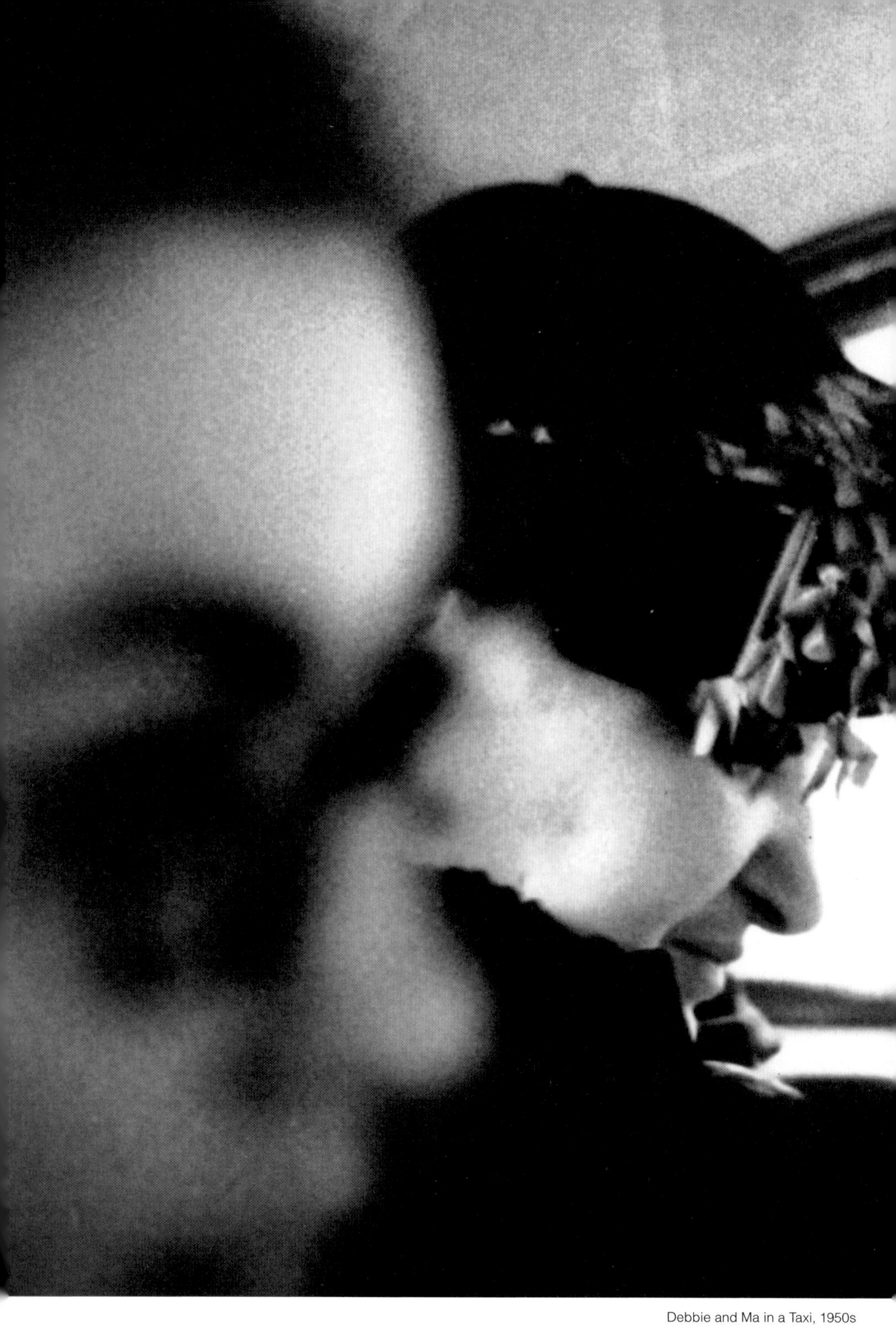

Debbie and Ma in a Taxi, 1950s

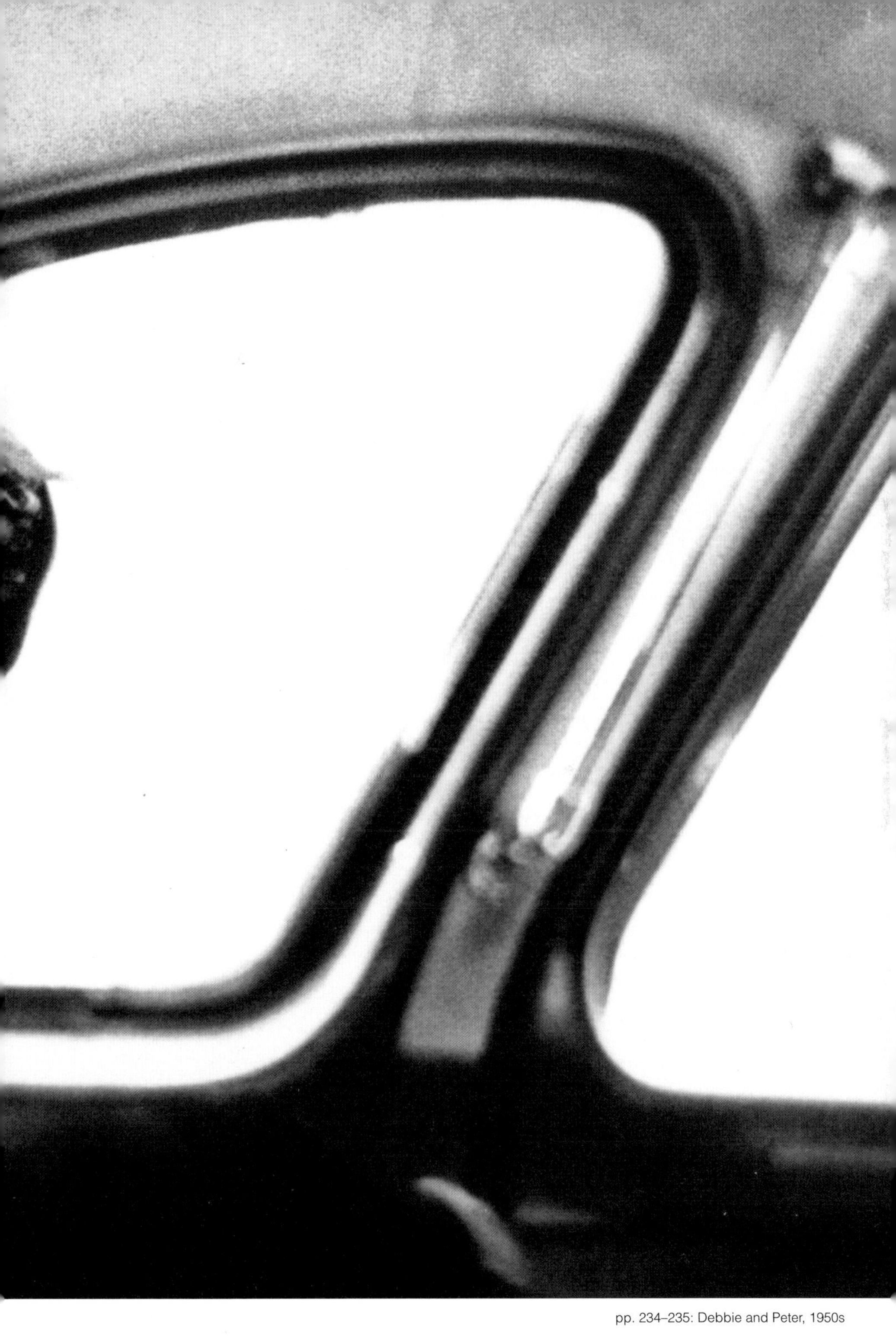

pp. 234–235: Debbie and Peter, 1950s

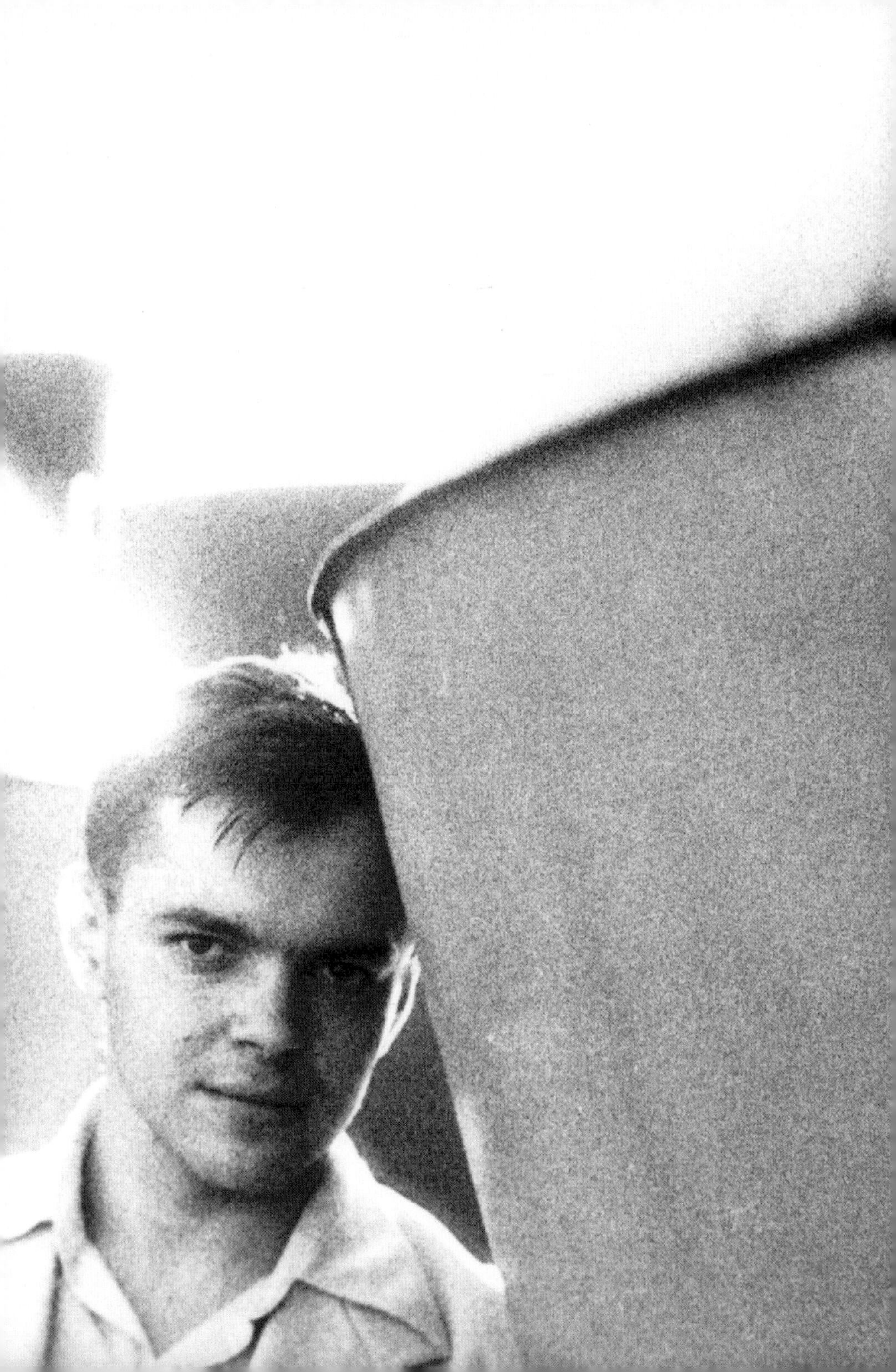

Soames

Soames Bantry was a fashion model when she first met Saul Leiter, in the late 1950s. She would soon become the subject of some of his deepest and most lovely photographs, both commercial and personal, and the two of them would spend more than four decades living together in New York's East Village and traveling extensively on Saul's fashion assignments. "We wasted ourselves in happy foolishness," Saul says in Kehrer's 2012 book *Retrospektive*. The couple shared a passion for making and looking at art, and they adored each other's work. "Quite often I would sit under the skylight, with a cup of coffee or wine in hand, and watch her paint," Saul says. "I very much admired her methods, which were very different from mine, much more controlled, much more patient." Soames Bantry died in 2002, and Saul would often lament the fact that she never got to share in the success he enjoyed after the 2006 publication of *Early Color*.

As the Saul Leiter Foundation continues to unearth treasures from the archive, we're forever discovering new photographs of the artist's most enduring muse—or as he liked to call her in his typically understated way, "my friend Soames."

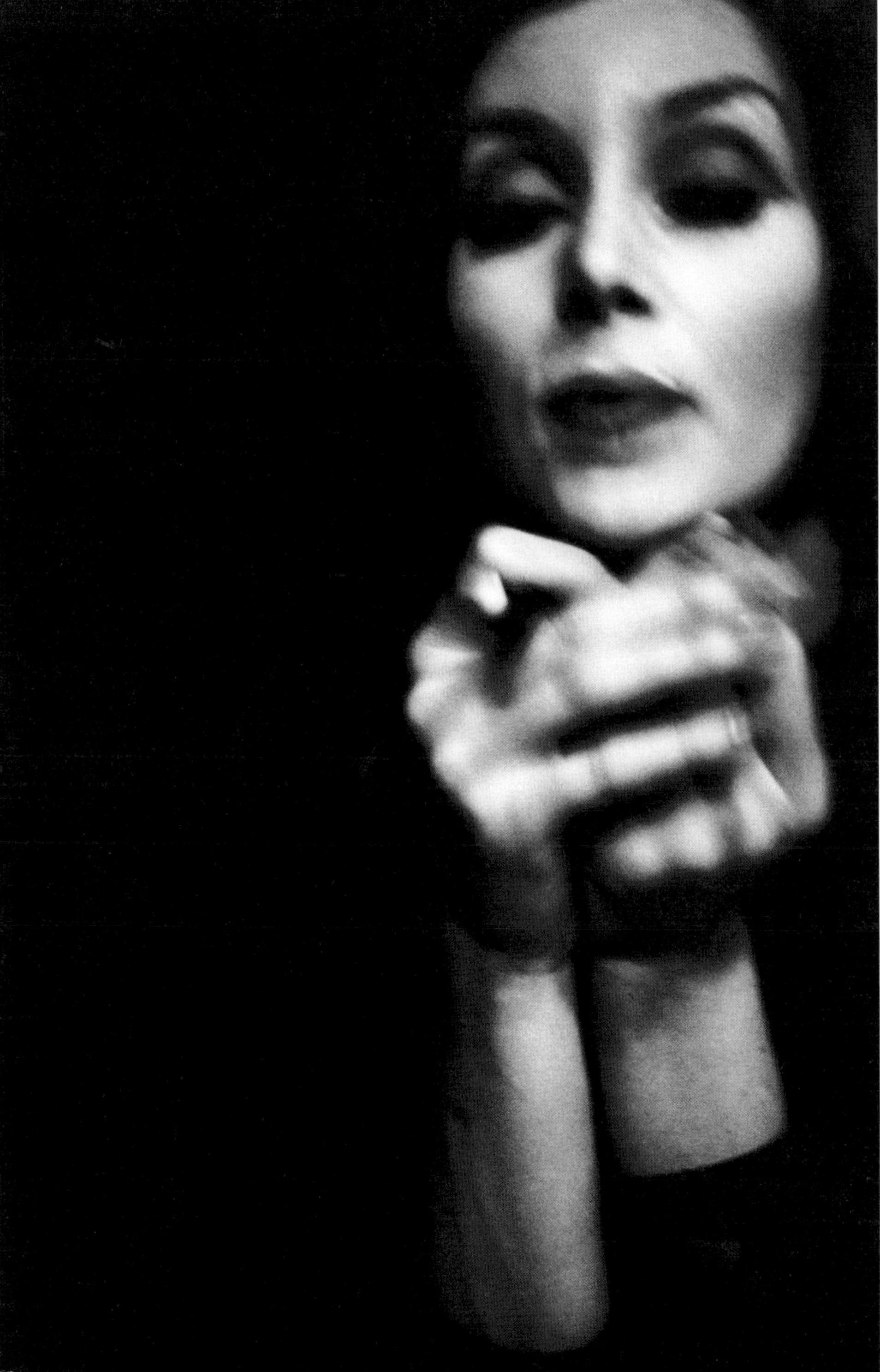

Soames, undated

p. 240: Ireland, for *Nova* magazine, 1960s
p. 241: Soames, undated

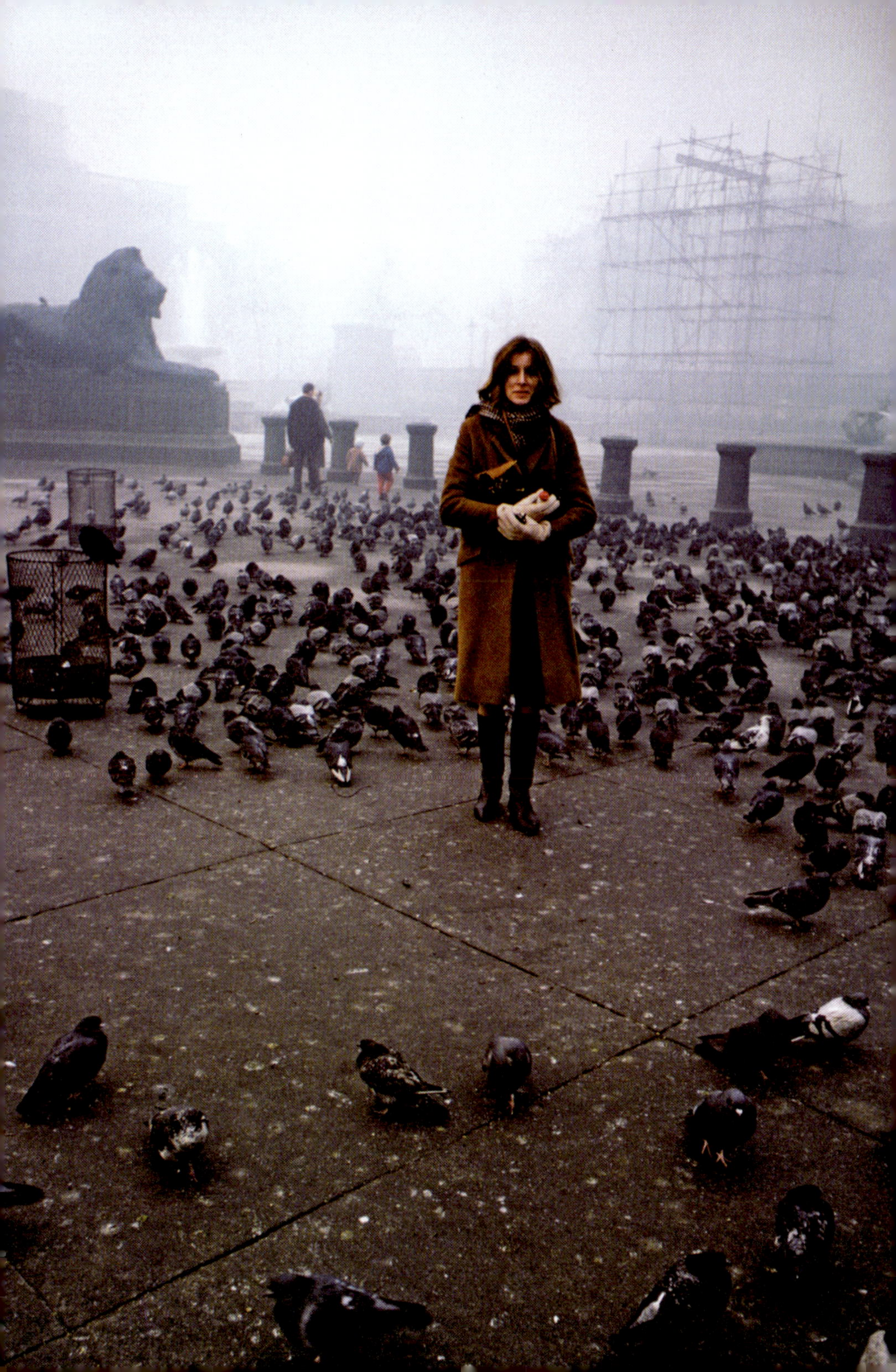

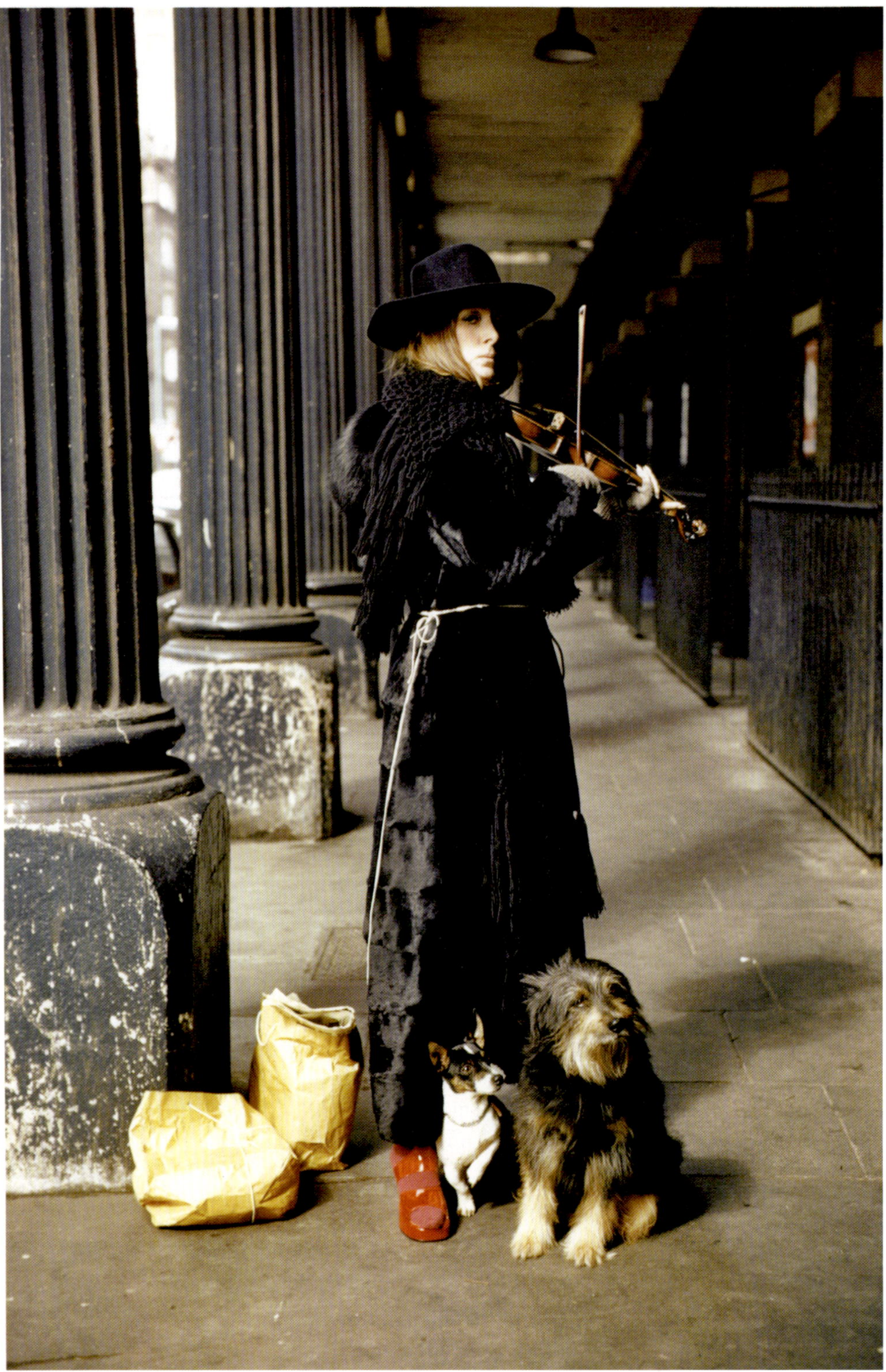

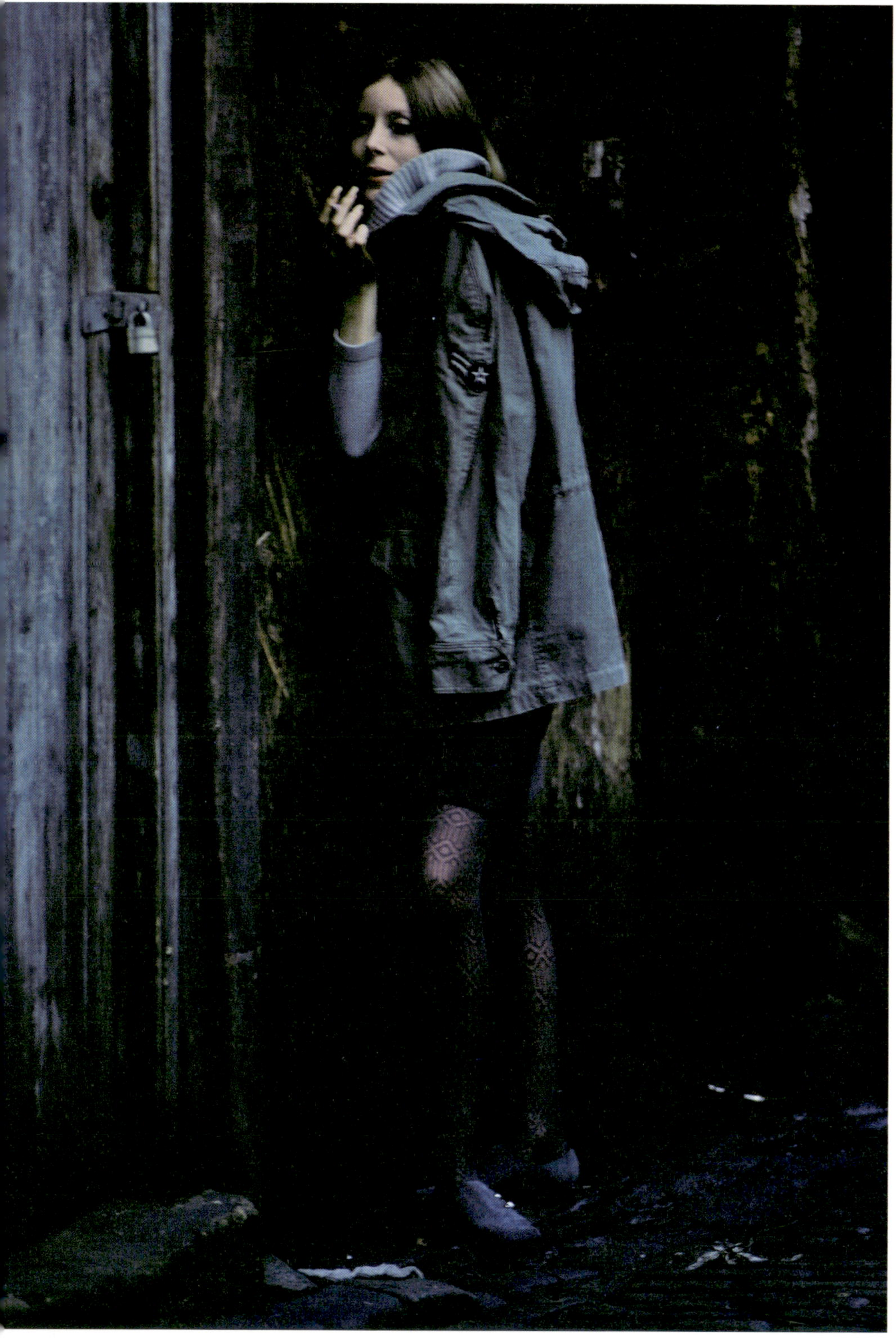

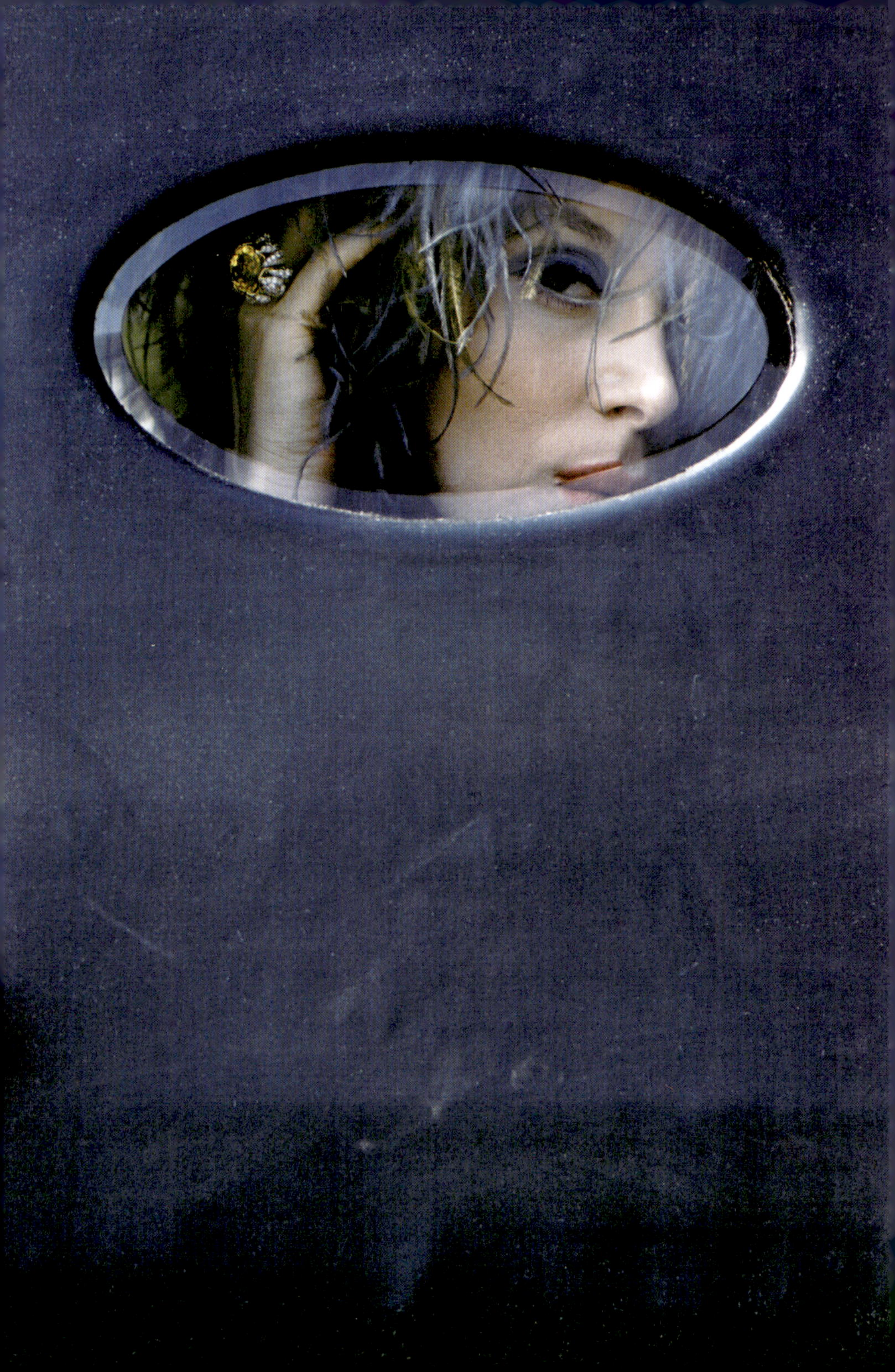

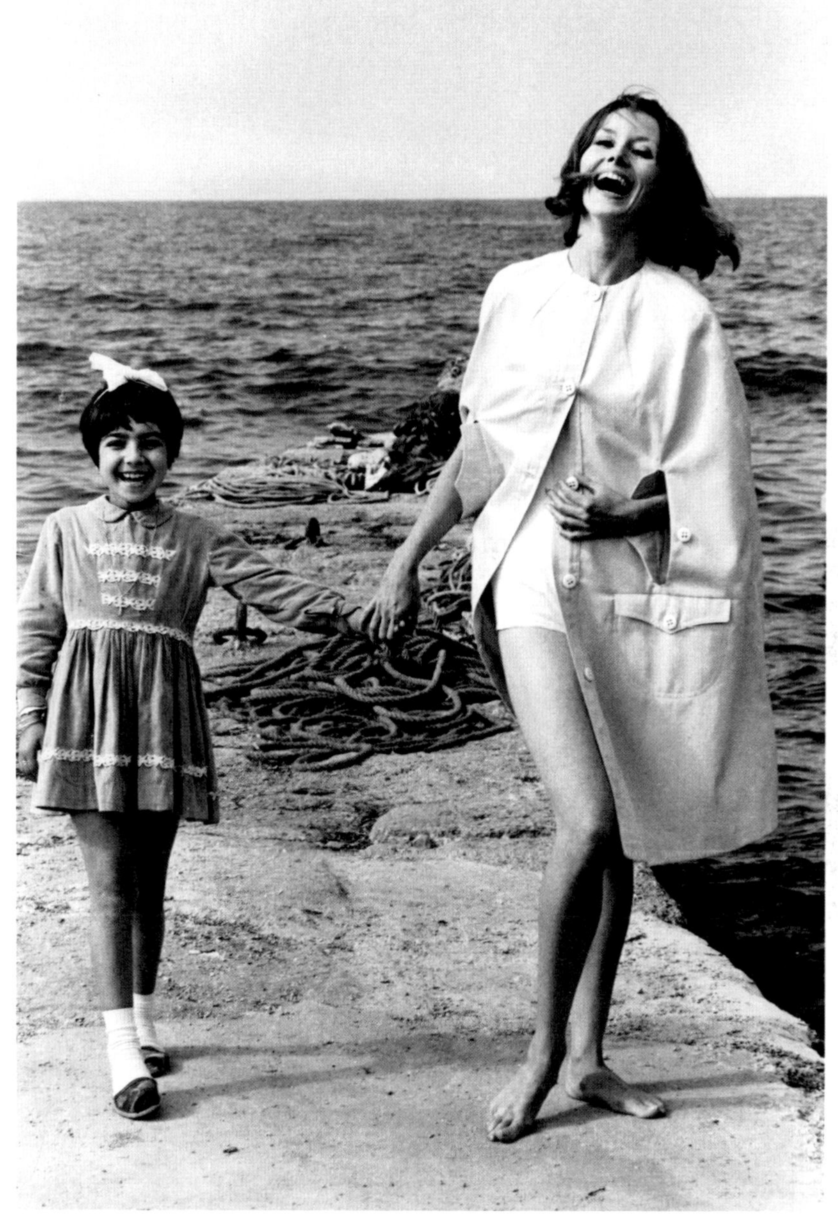

Soames Bantry, *Harper's Bazaar*, c. 1963   Soames, undated

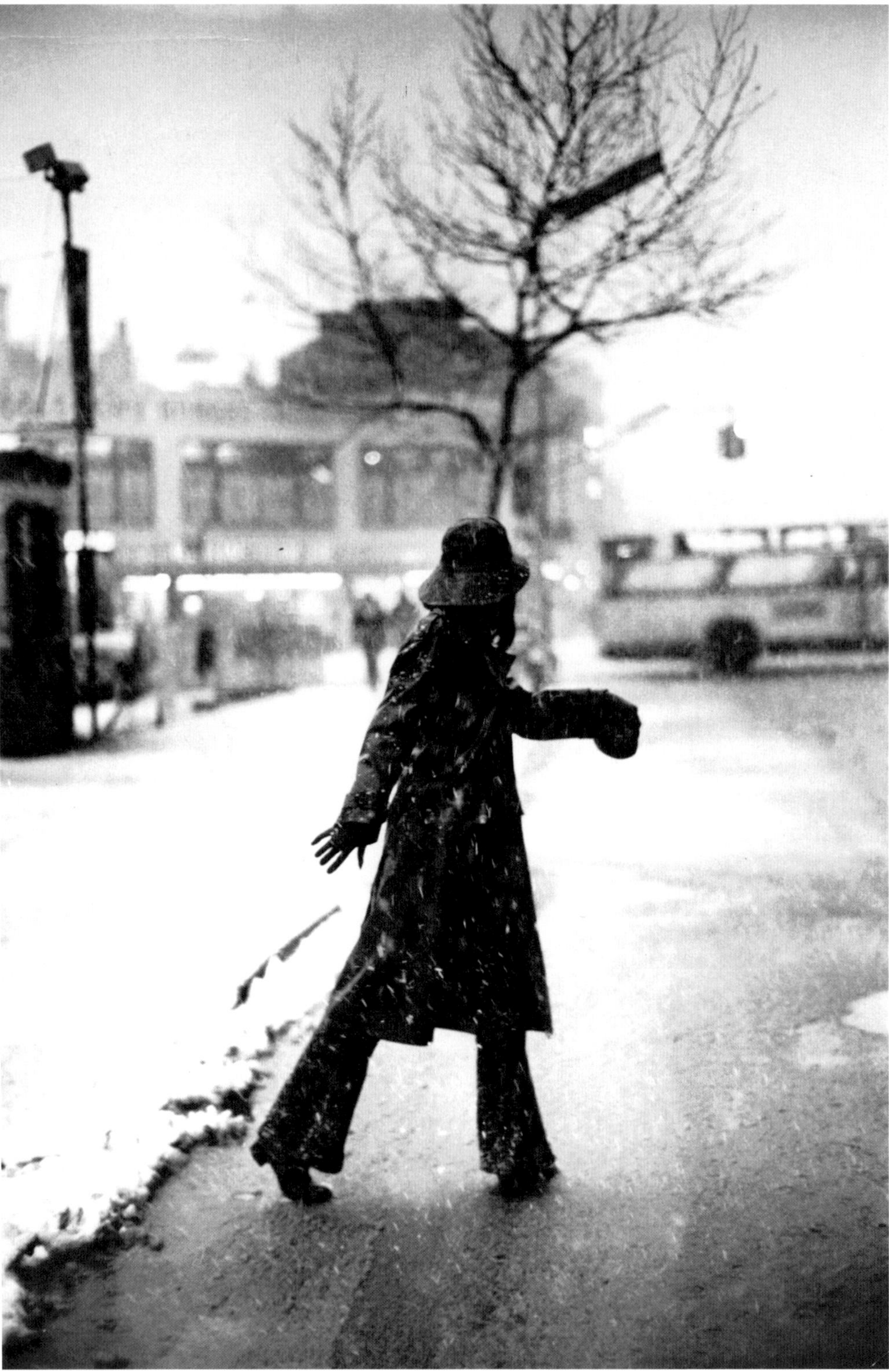

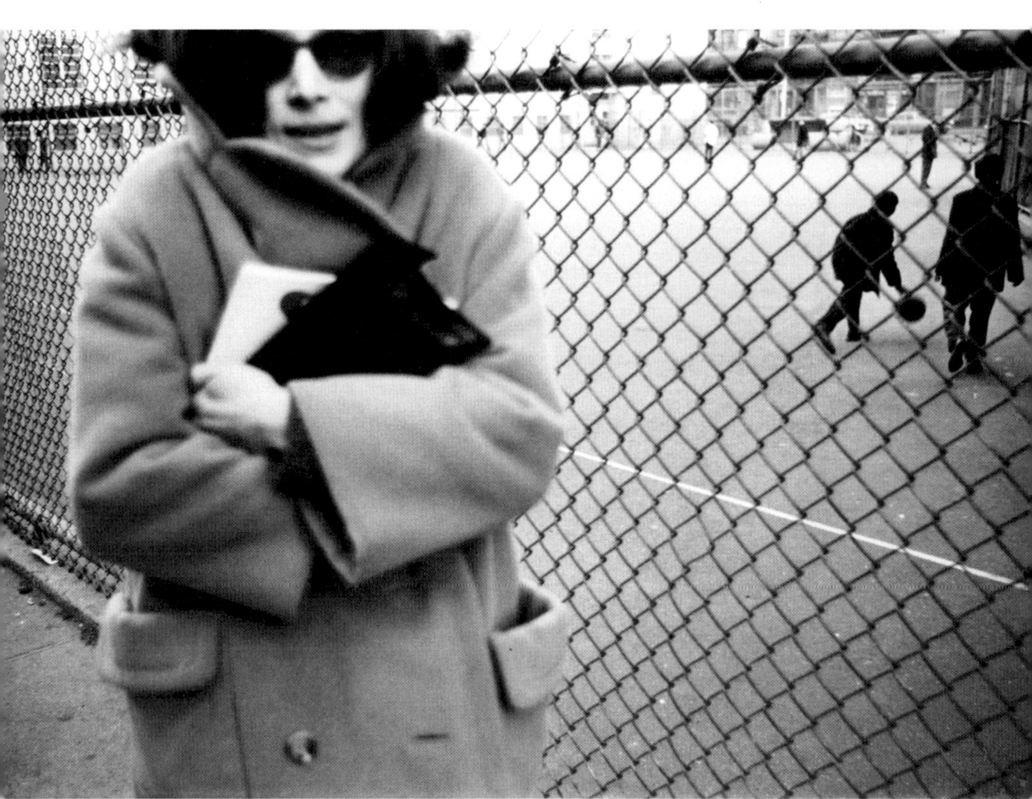

Soames, 1960s

pp. 246–247: Soames, 1960s

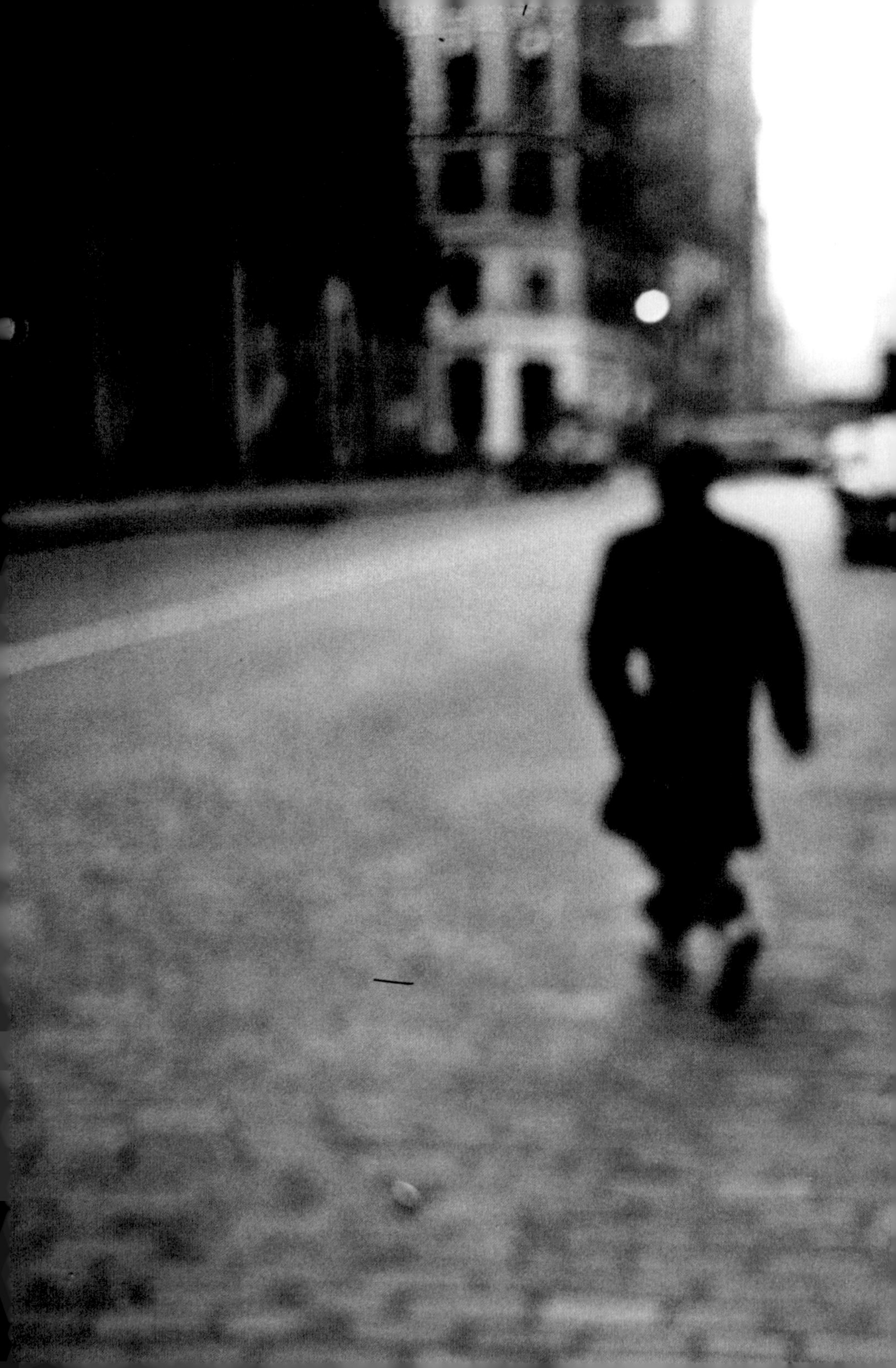

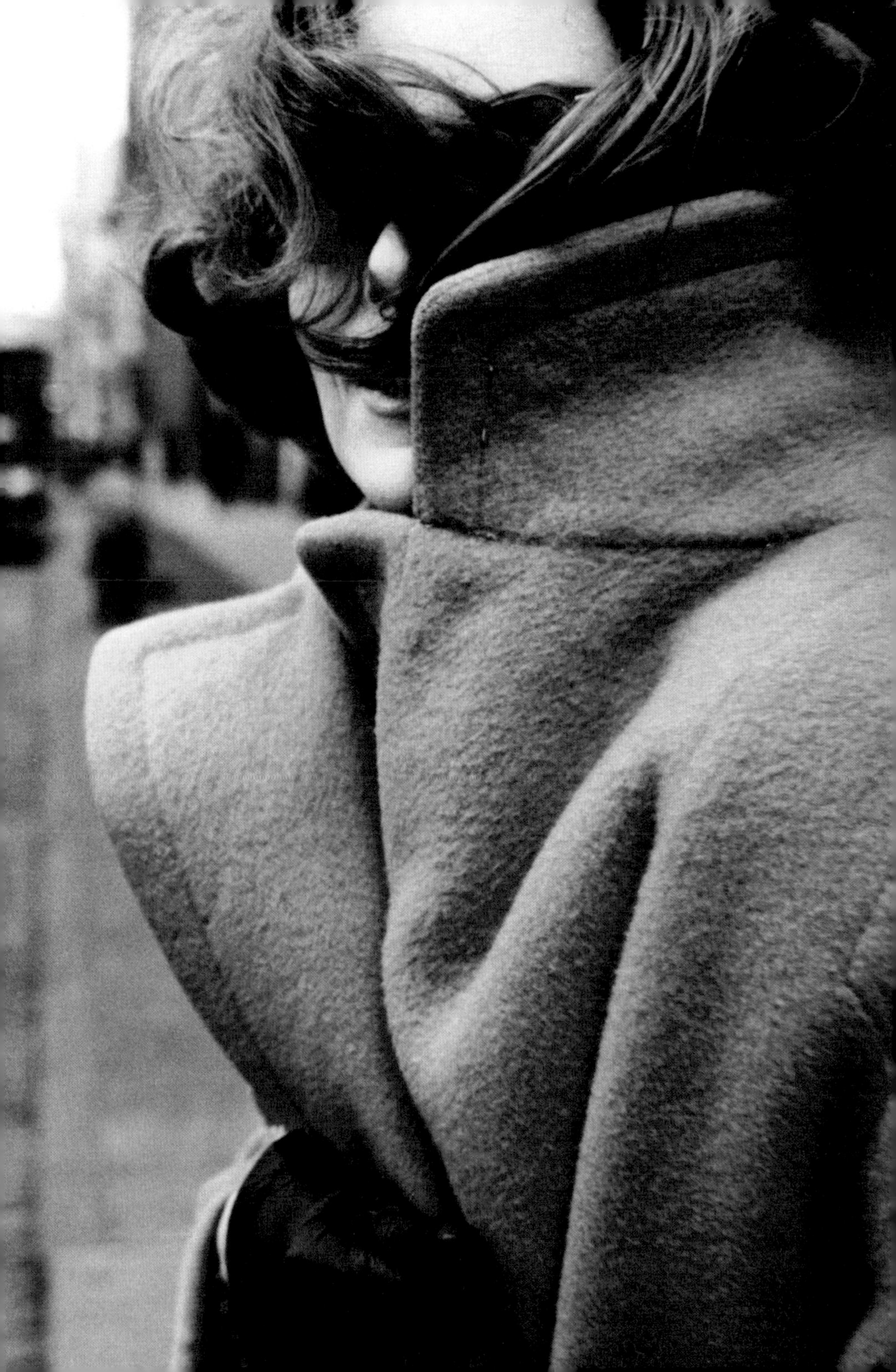

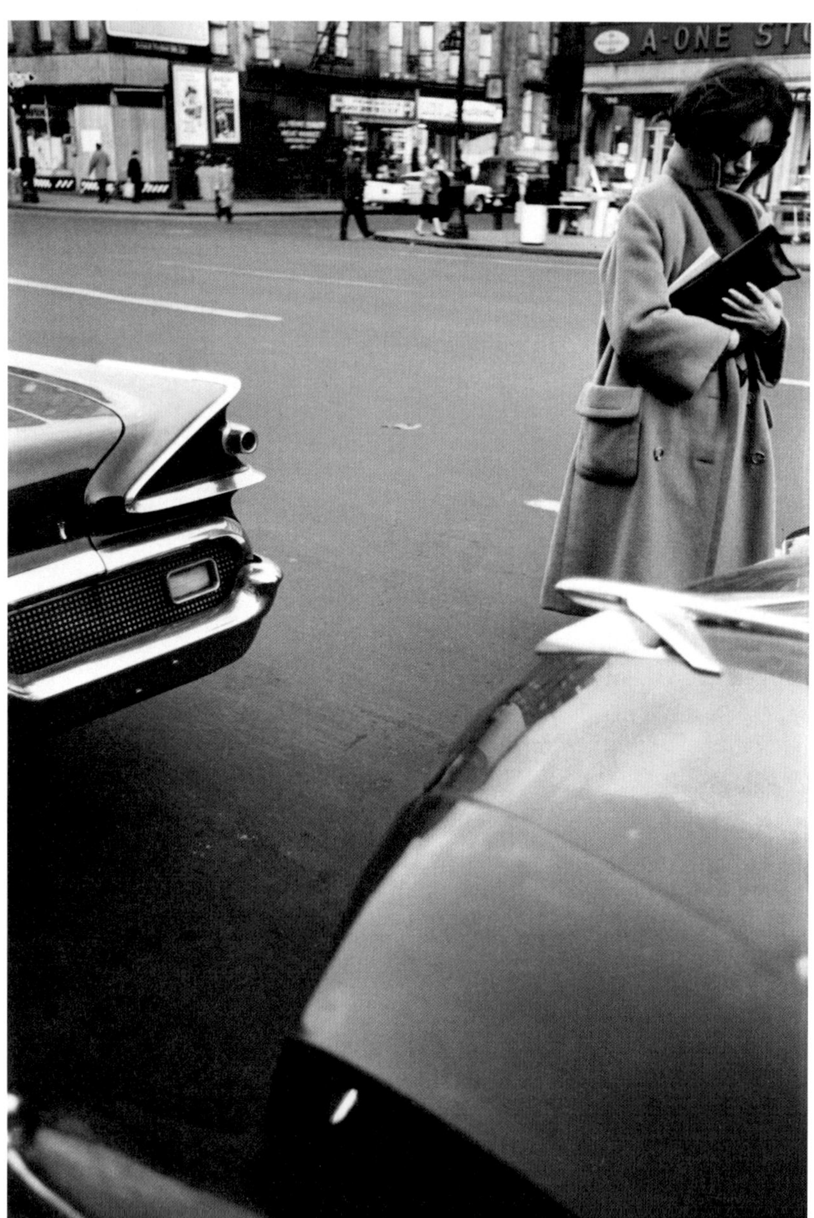

Soames, 1960s   Soames, 1960s

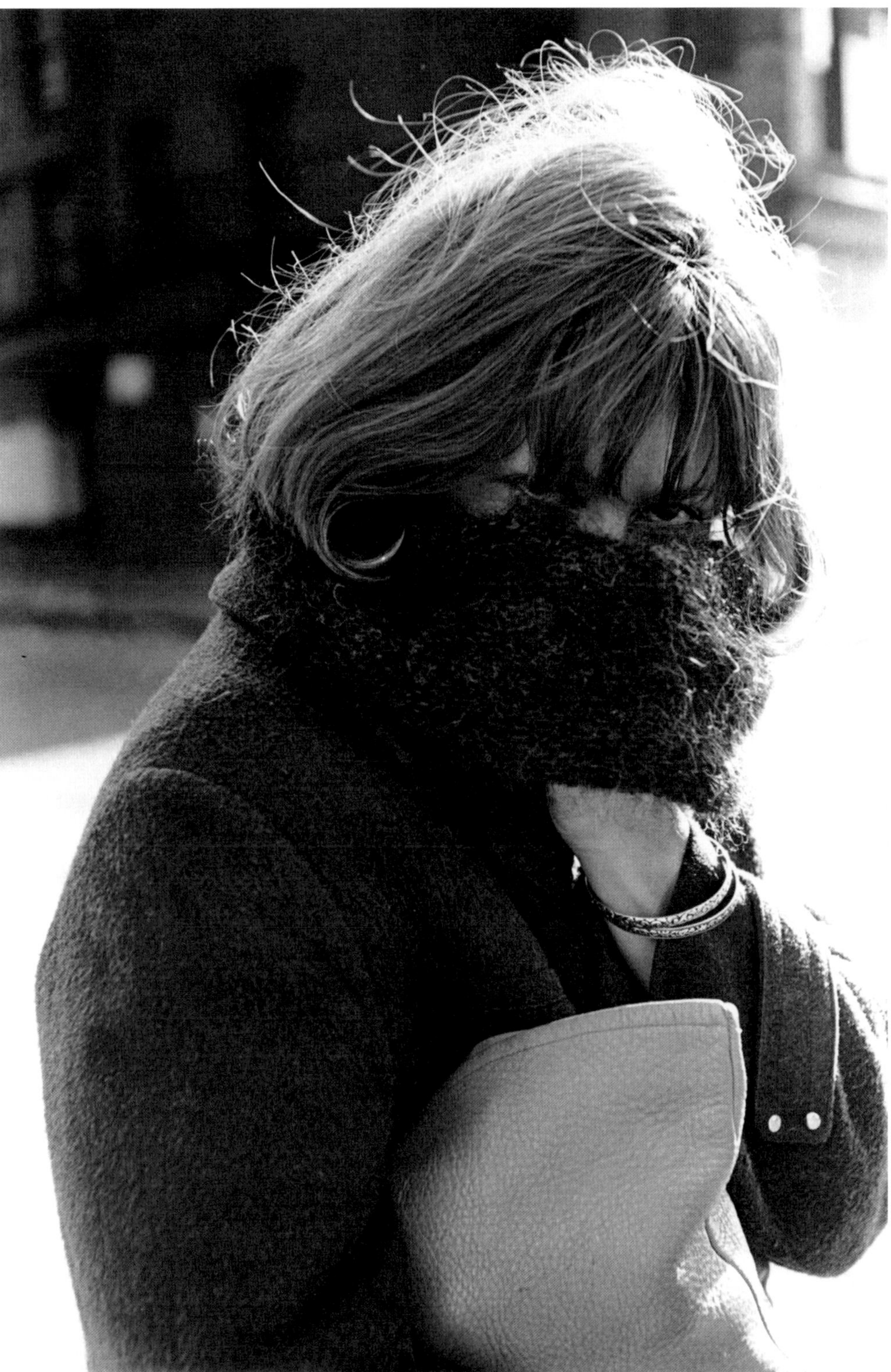

I shared my life with Soames.

We had moments where, in spite of all the problems,

we had an inability to concentrate on misery properly,

and a tendency to enjoy life.

And I don't think that's such a bad thing.

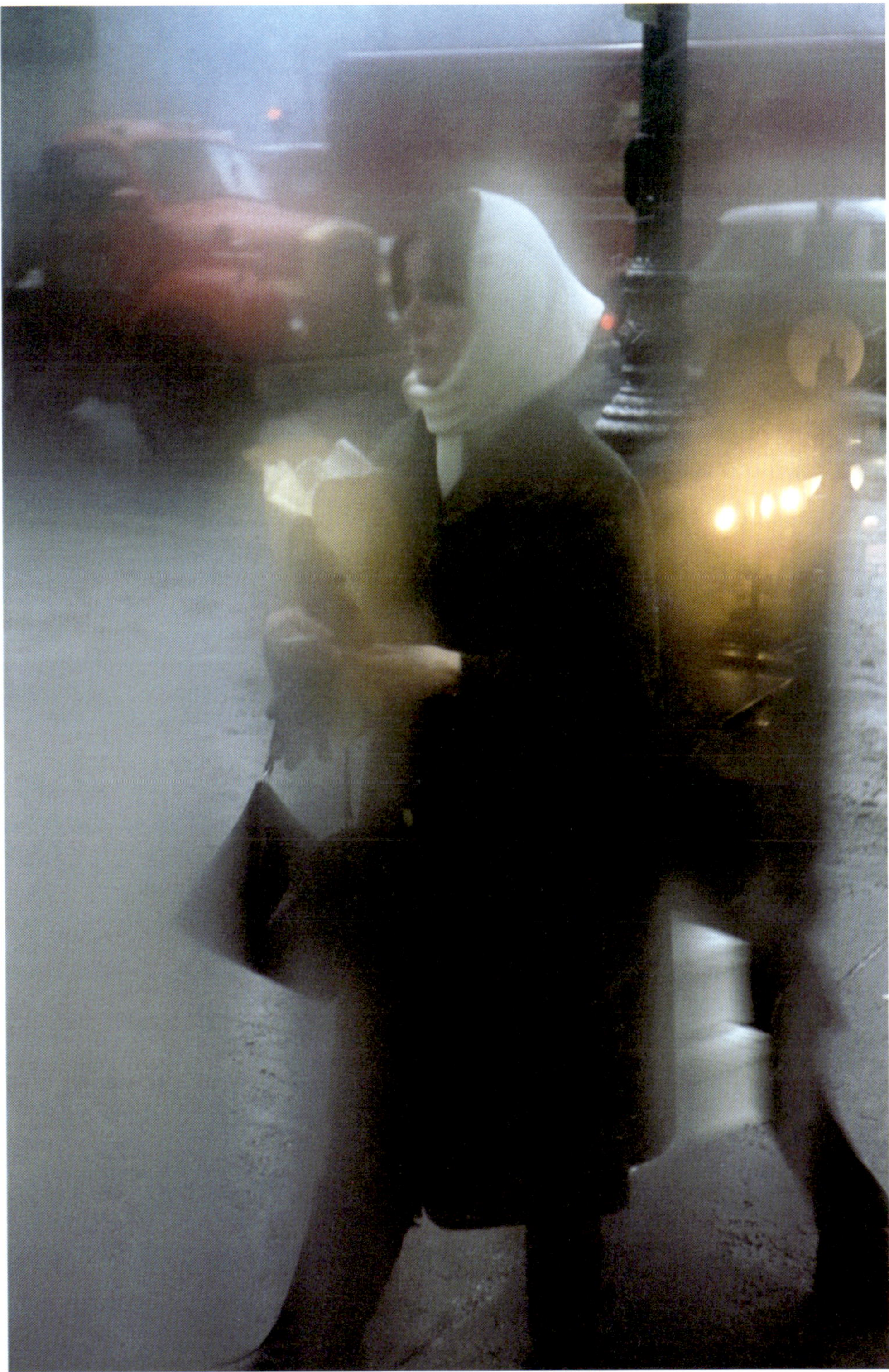

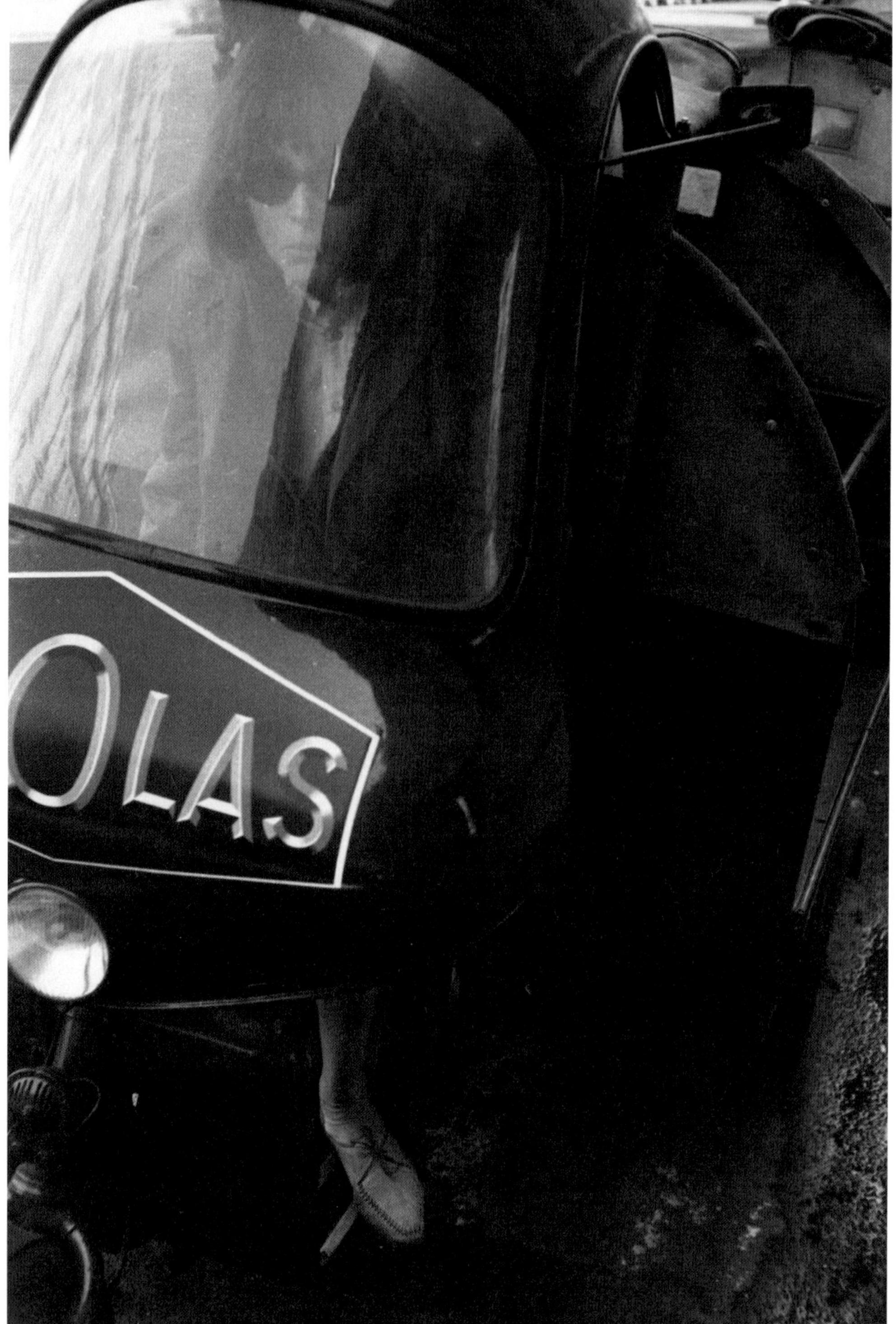

OLAS

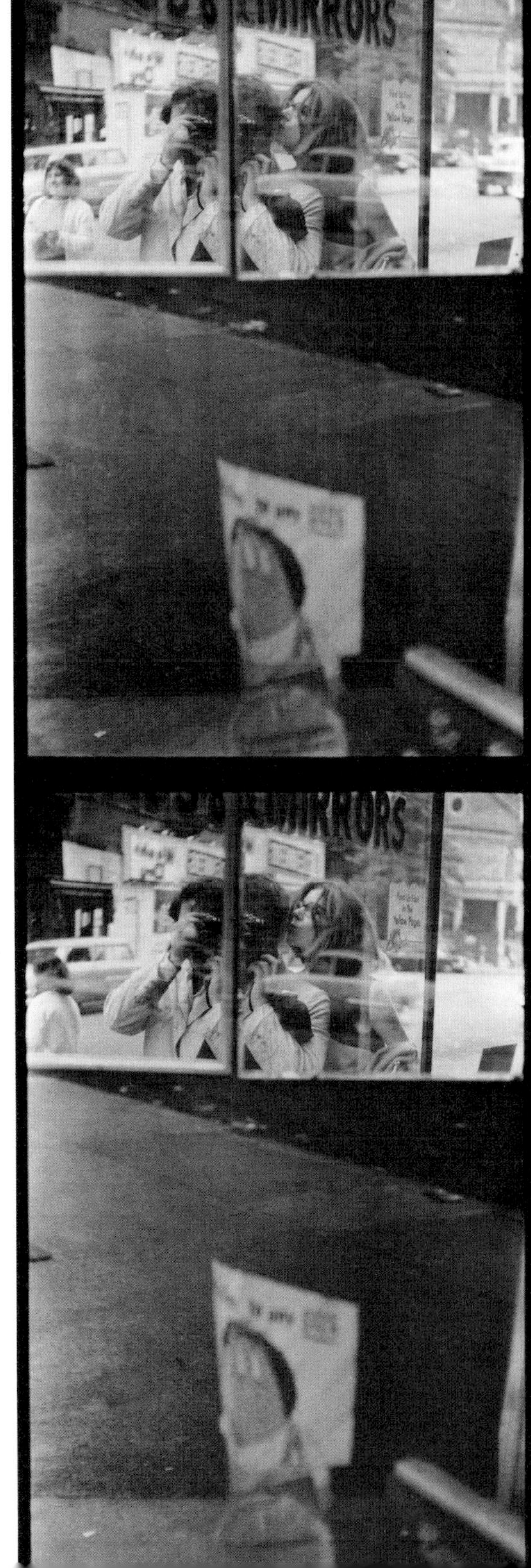

Soames, undated

Self-Portrait with Soames, c. 1960

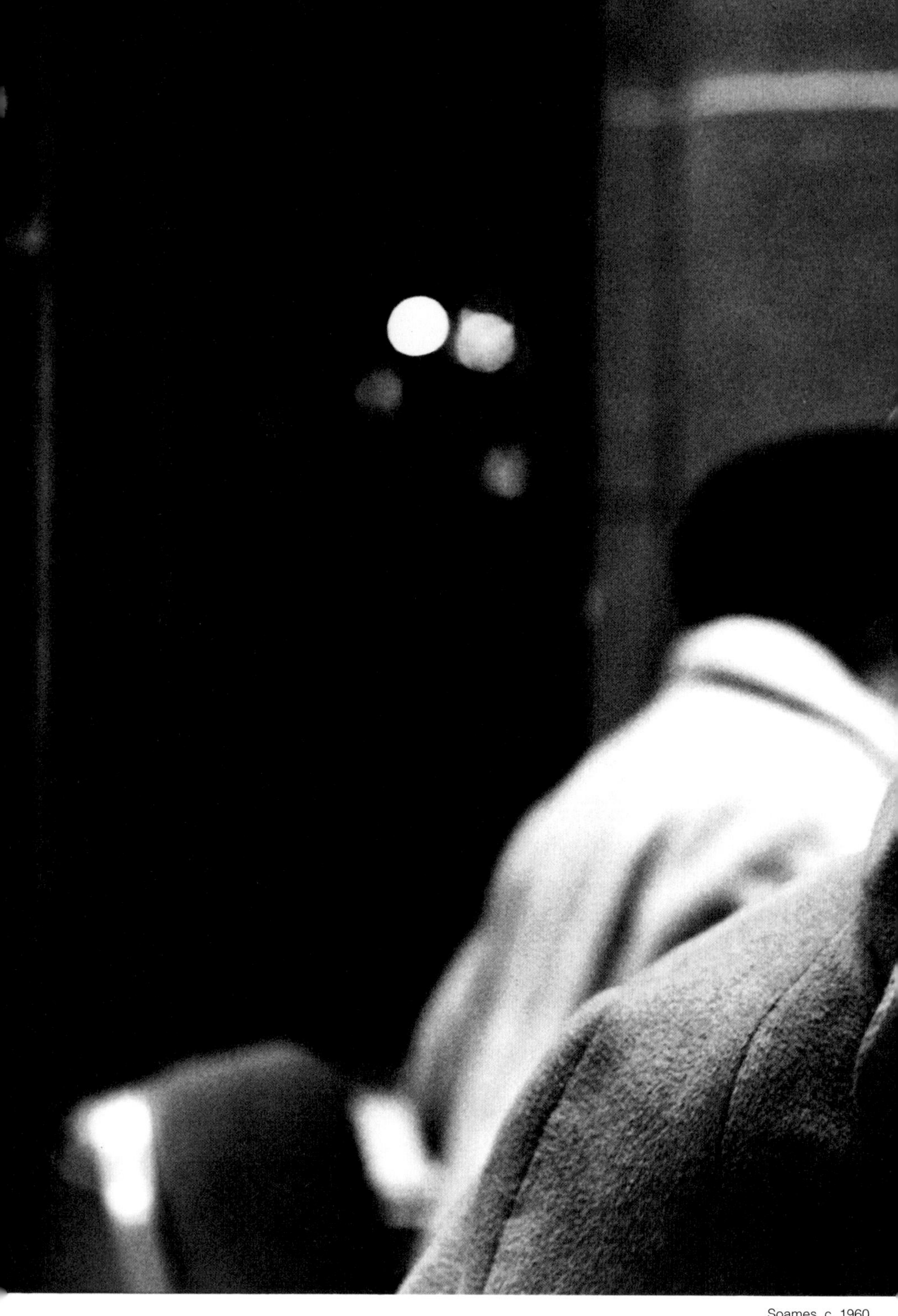

Soames, c. 1960

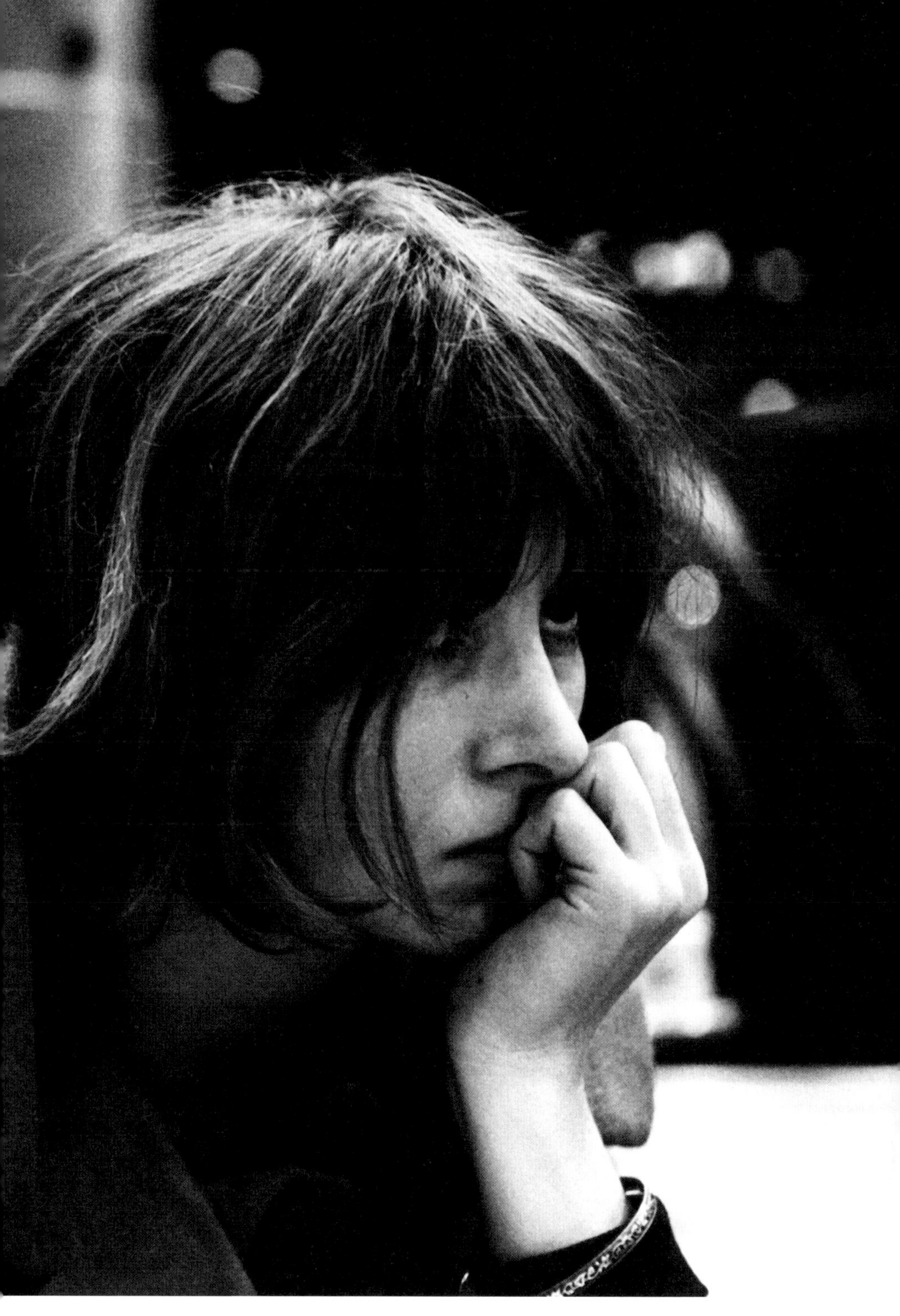

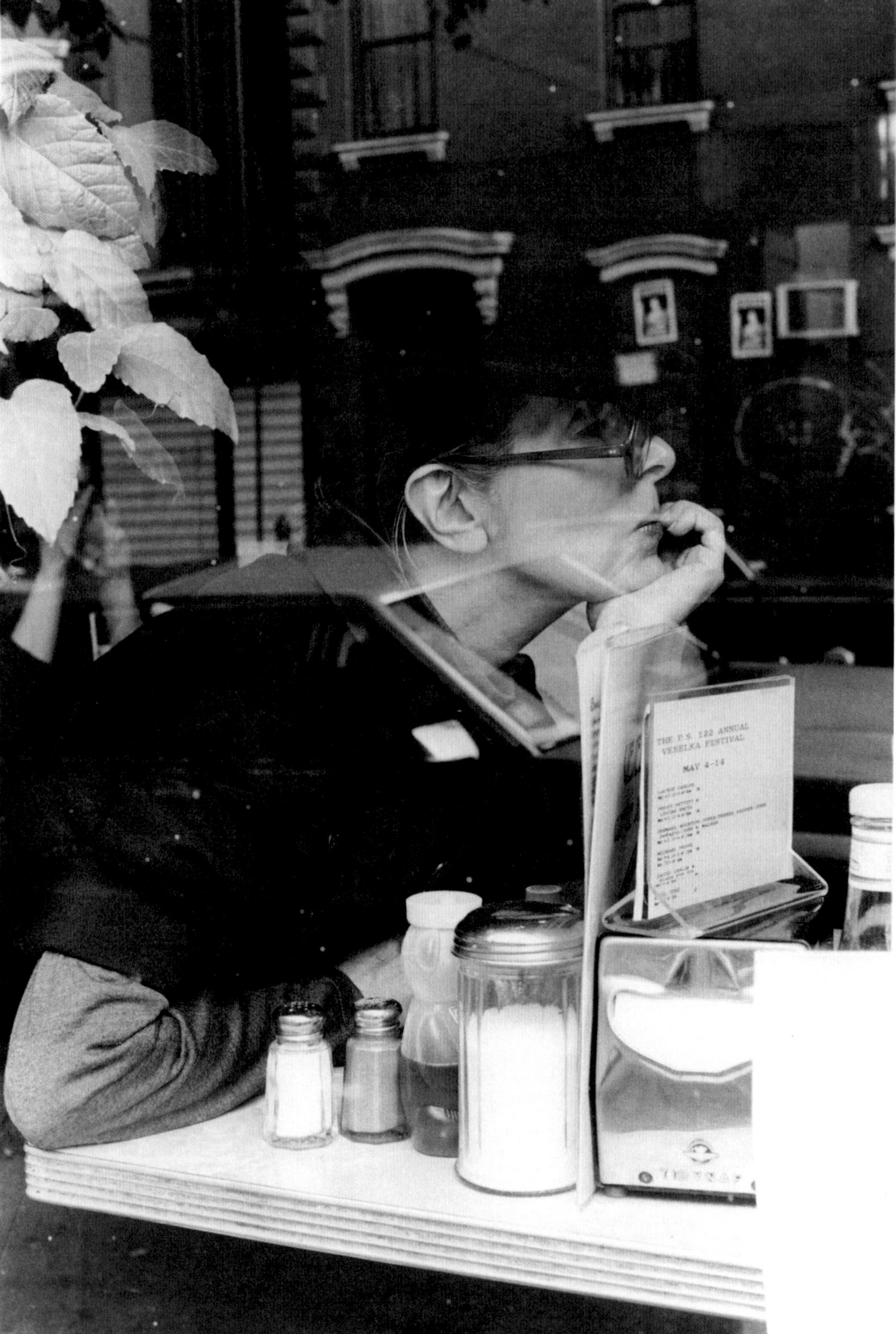
THE P.S. 122 ANNUAL
VESELKA FESTIVAL
MAY 4-14

I liked looking over and seeing Soames rocking away and listening to music.

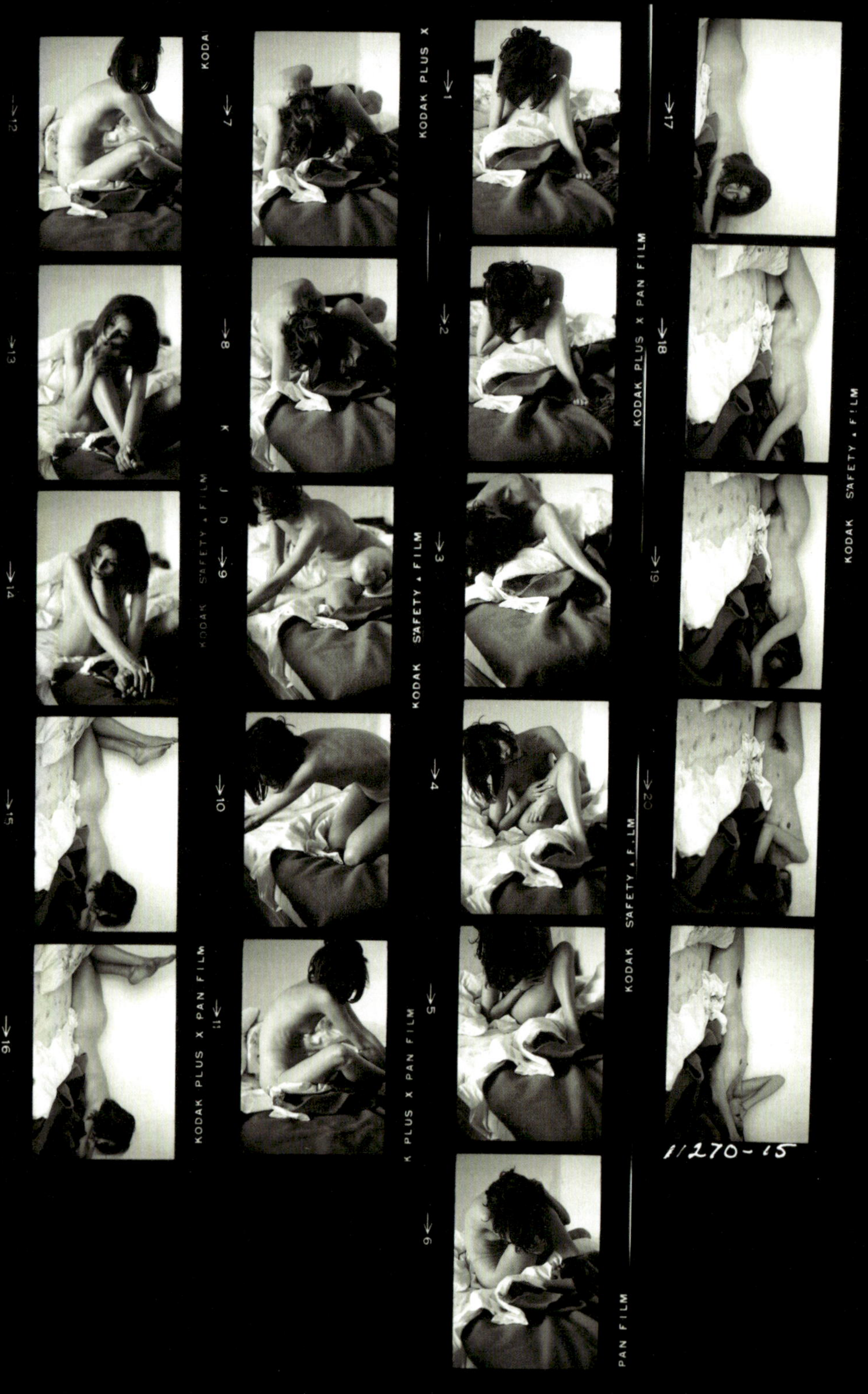
KODAK PLUS X PAN FILM
KODAK SAFETY FILM
11270-15

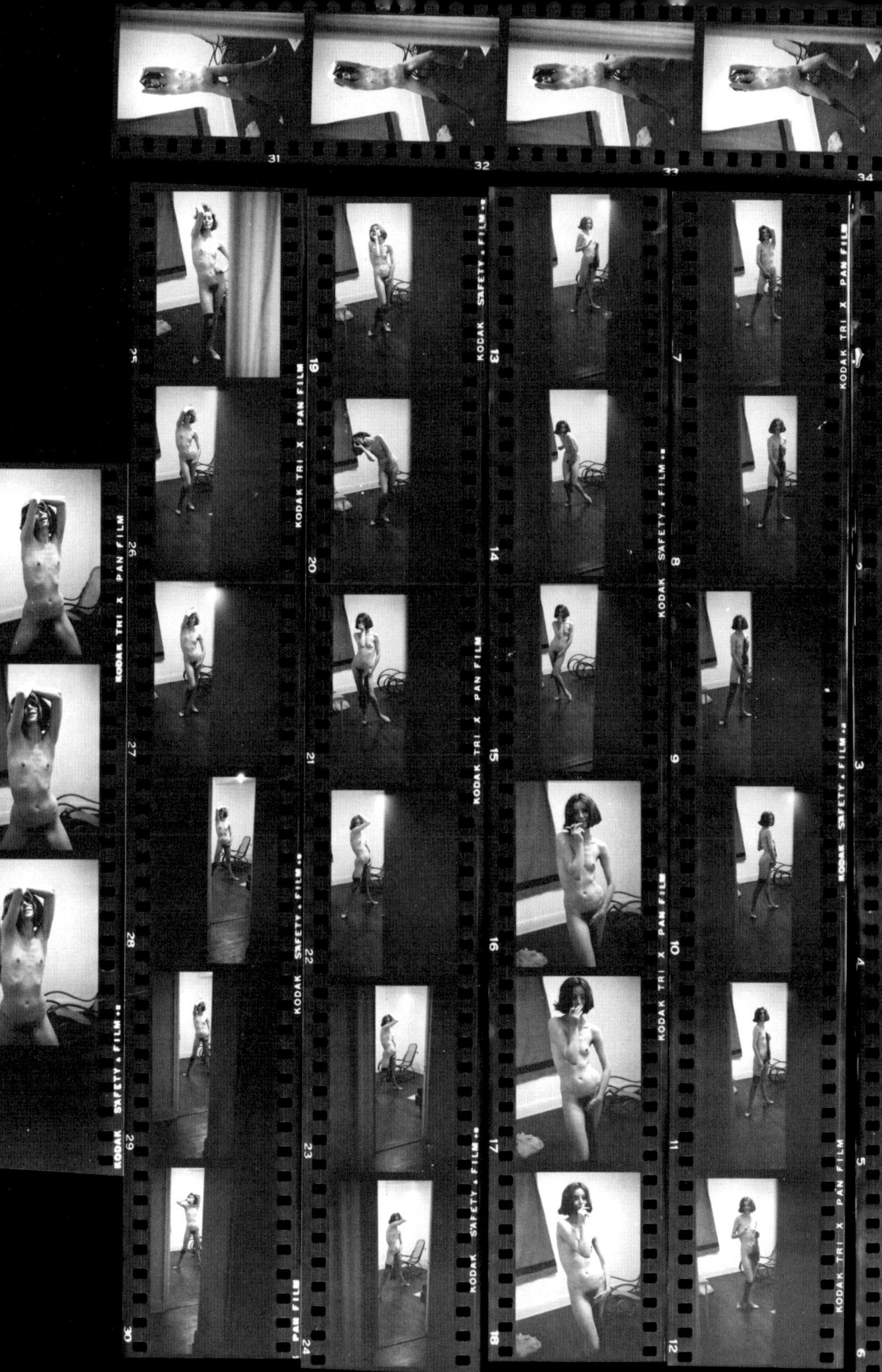

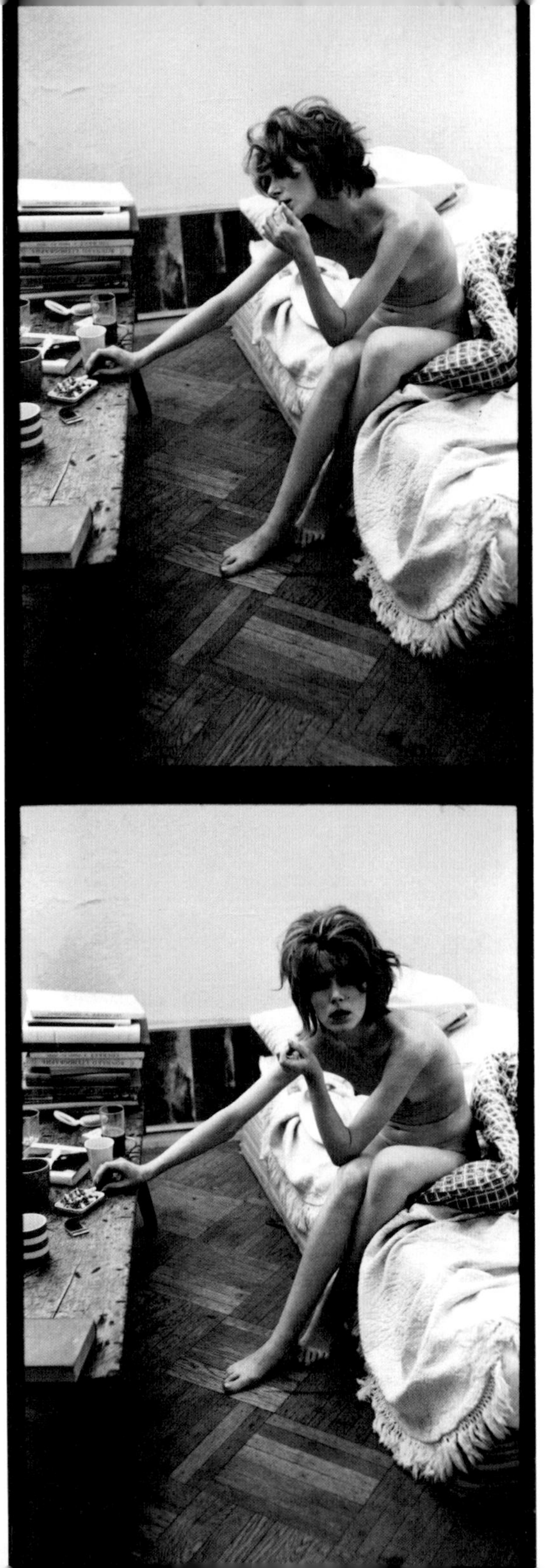

Soames, c. 1965

Soames, 1970s

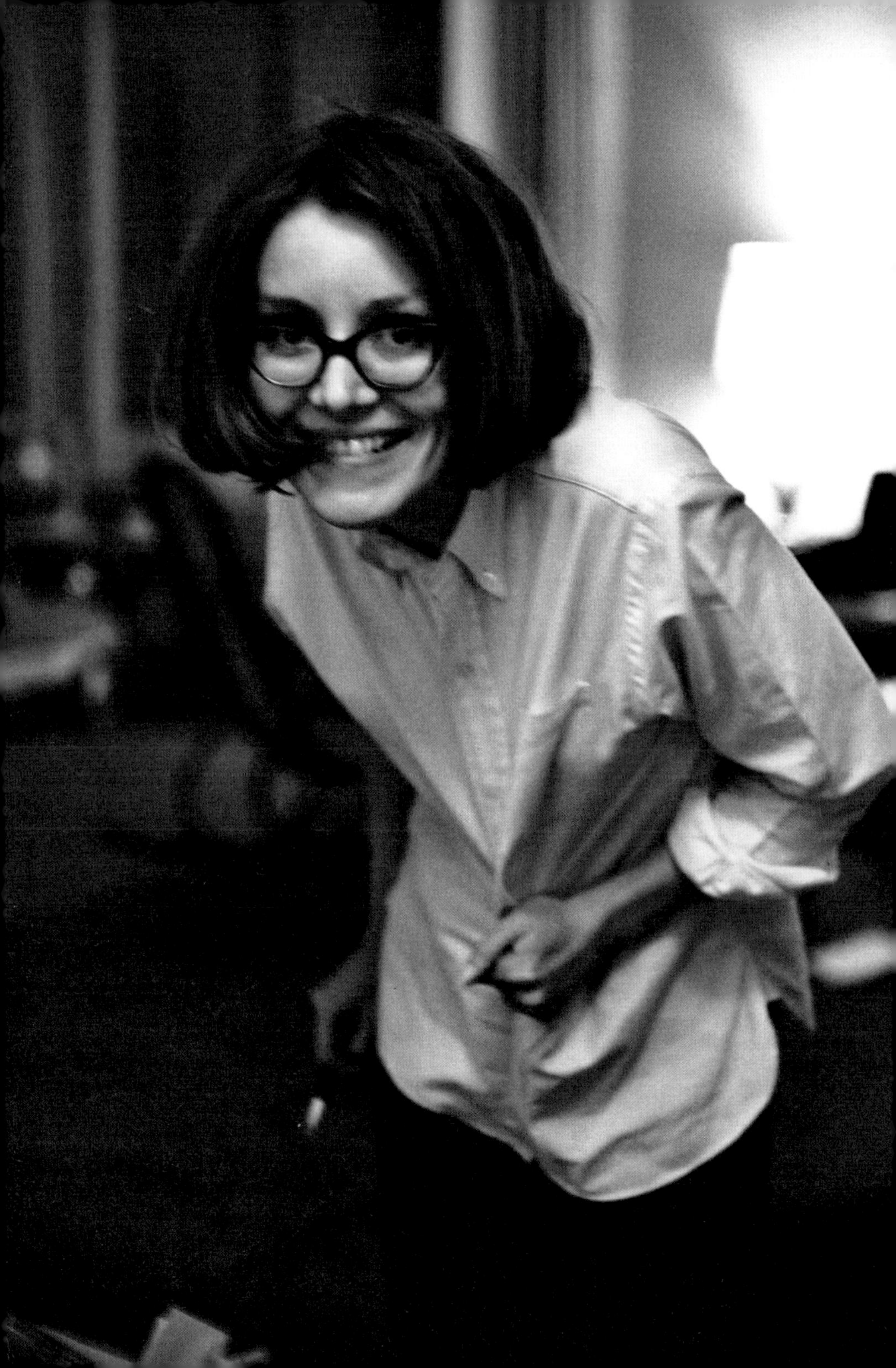

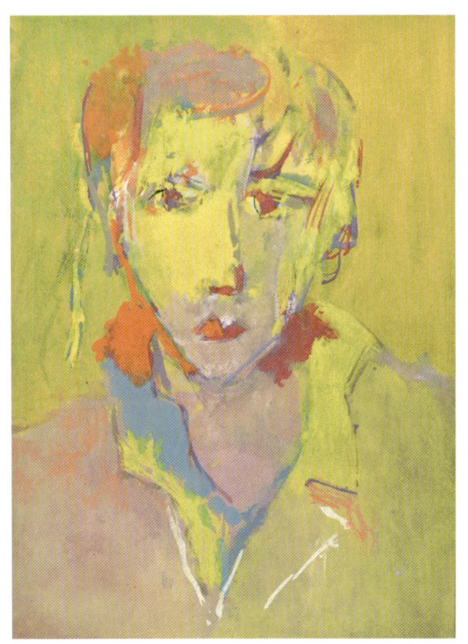

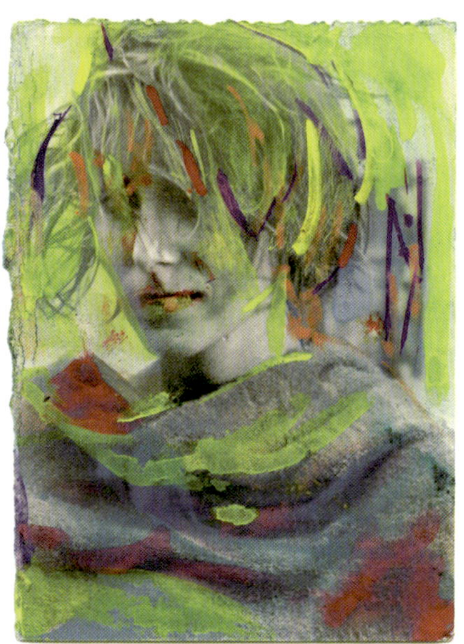

Of Soames, *She Was 7*, undated
Gouache, casein and watercolor on paper

Soames, 1970s–1990s. Gouache, casein
and watercolor on gelatin silver paper

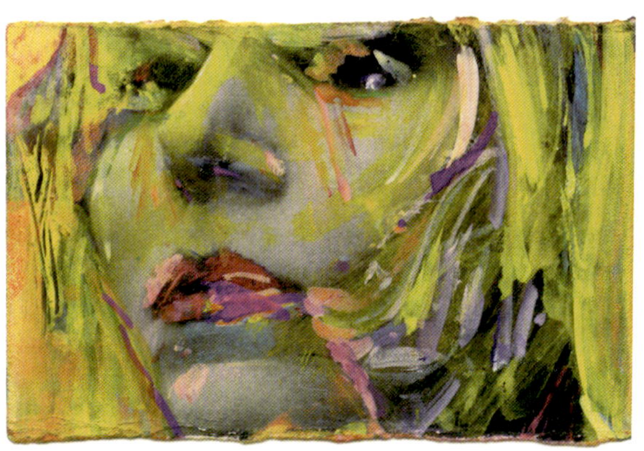

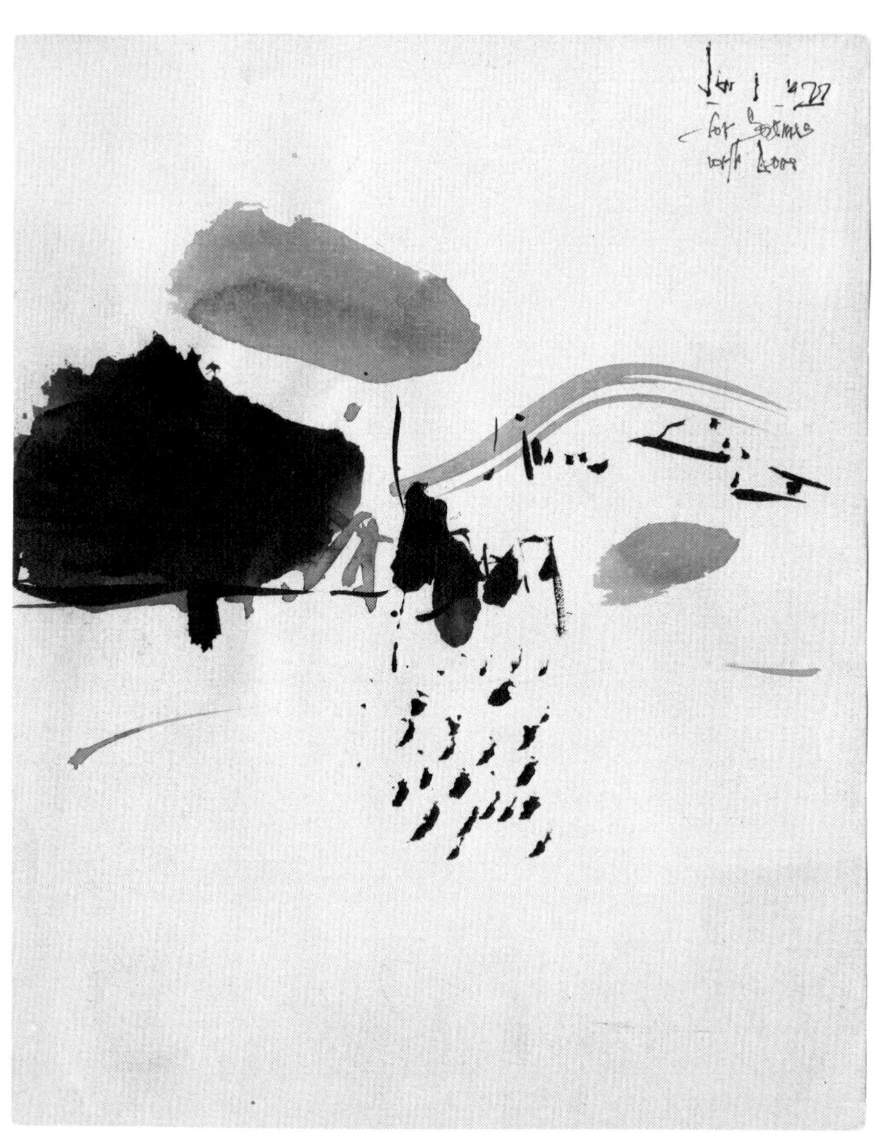

For Soames with Love, January 1, 1977. Ink on paper

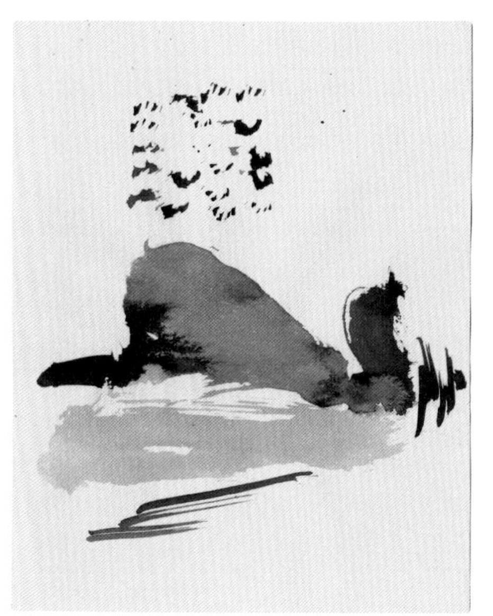

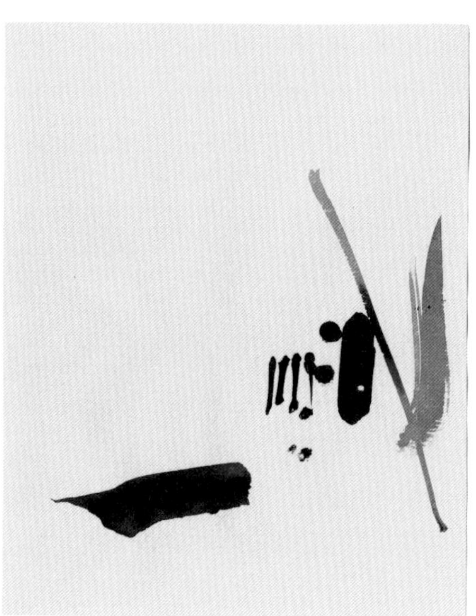

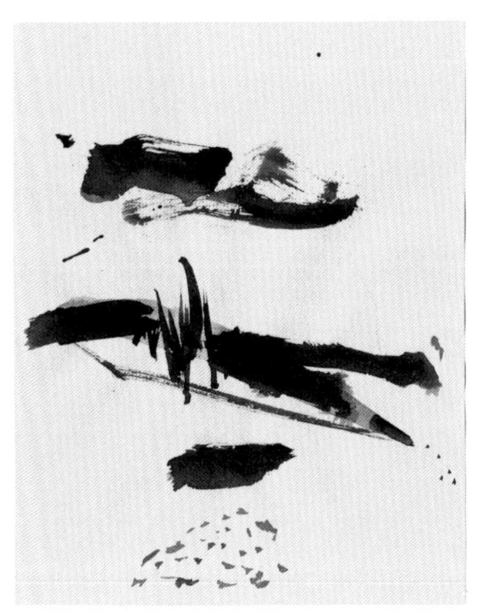

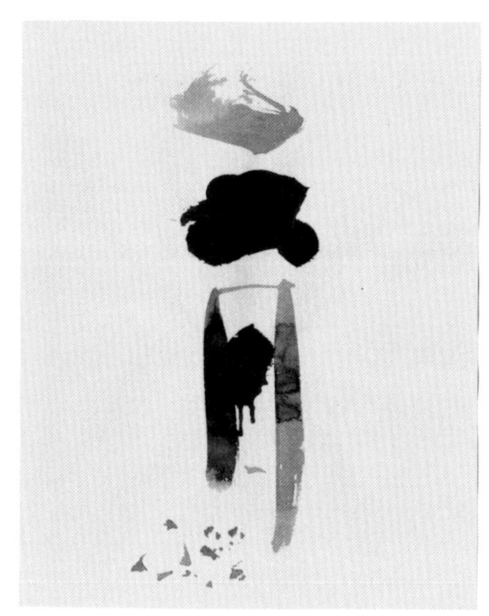

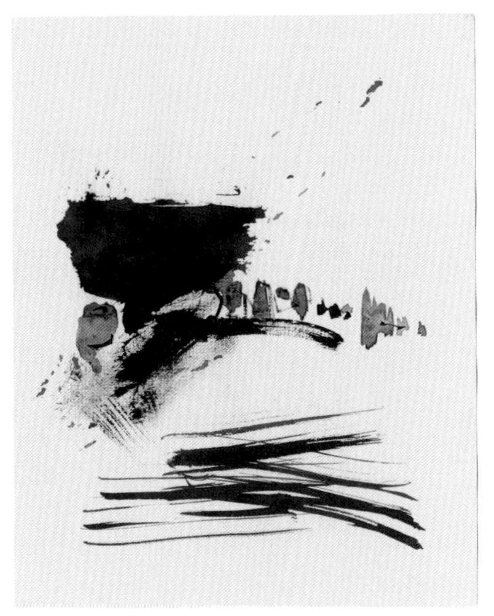
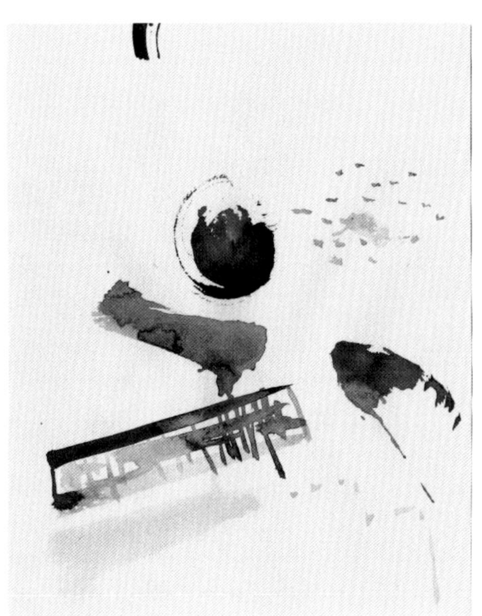
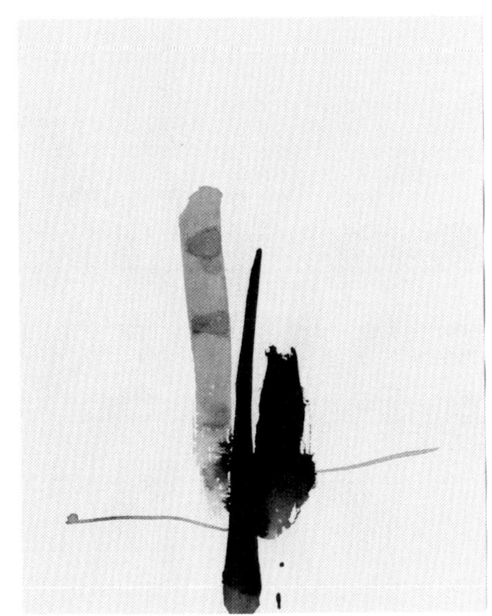
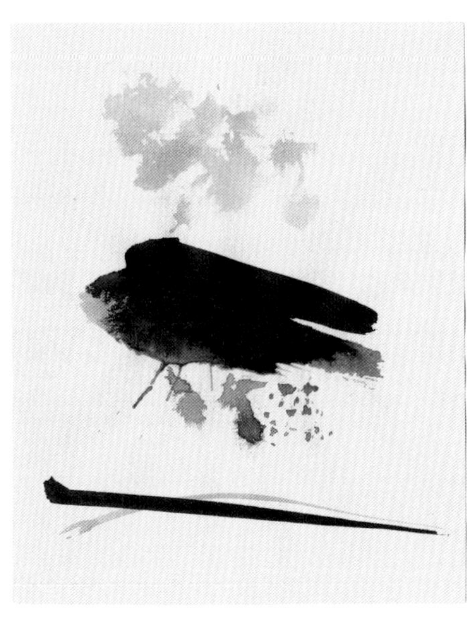

For Soames with Love, January 1, 1977. Ink on paper

Color Slides

"I have thousands of color slides that have never been printed and quite possibly never will be," Saul Leiter told *New Yorker* writer Vince Aletti in a 2013 interview at SVA in New York. Although dozens of his color slides were in the printing queue when he died, Saul indeed left many thousands unseen. It's the goal of the Saul Leiter Foundation to examine them all.

One recent slide project was initiated by a scholar from Berlin, Elena Skarke, who is currently preparing a dissertation on Saul's work in this area. In 2018, Elena began viewing and cataloguing his color slides, mostly Kodachrome, Ektachrome, and Anscochrome, from a total of upwards of 60,000. In his lifetime Saul printed a relatively small percentage of the images that he captured. "The world has seen only the tip of the iceberg," he would say.

"I had a studio on Fifth Avenue, and I kept a lot of stuff there," Saul told Vince Aletti in 2013. "Every now and then someone would say to me, 'What are you keeping all the slides for? There's so many. Why don't you get rid of them? Nothing's going to happen with them.' And I didn't get rid of them." Needless to say, the Saul Leiter Foundation is grateful that he held on to this bounty of beautiful and inventive work, which we'll continue to mine in the days ahead.

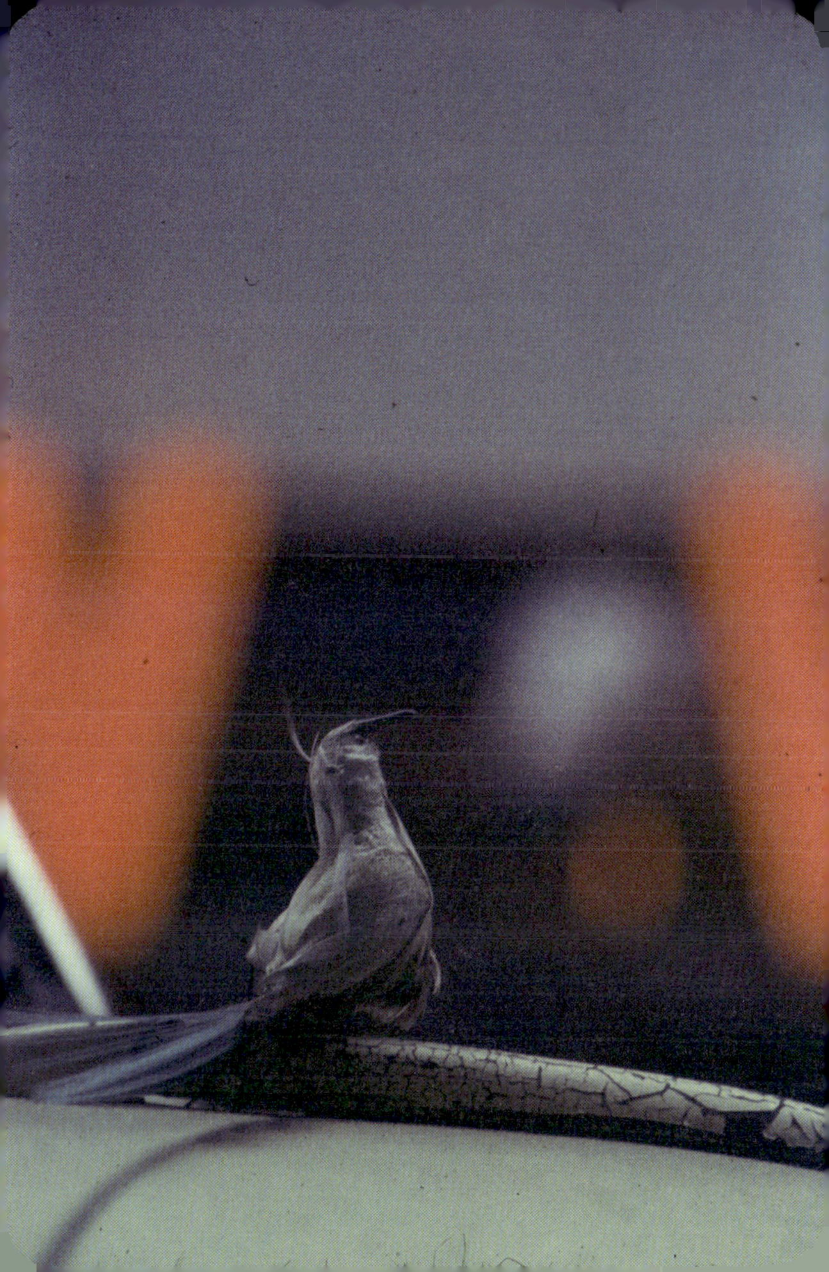

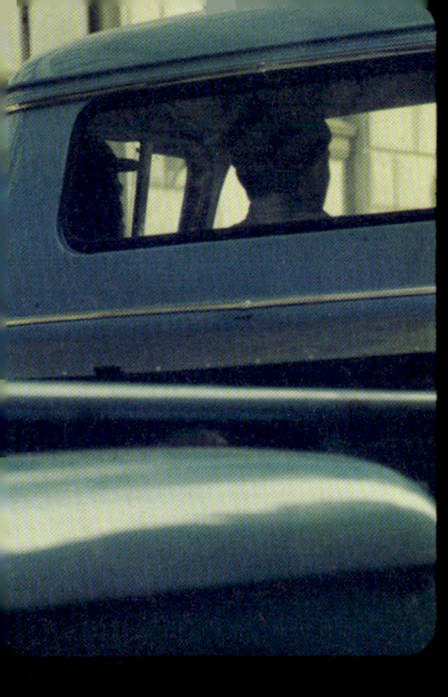
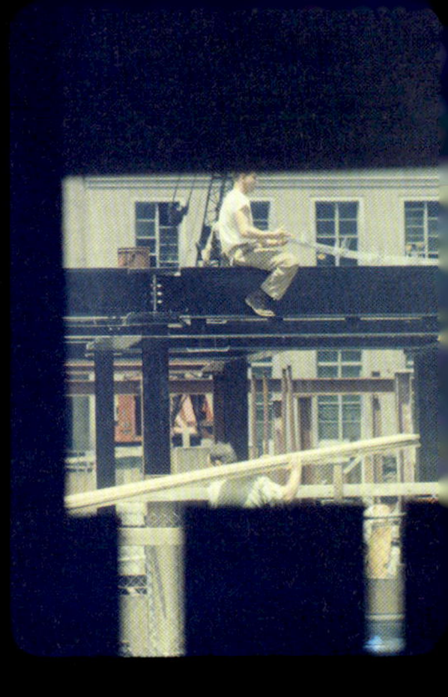
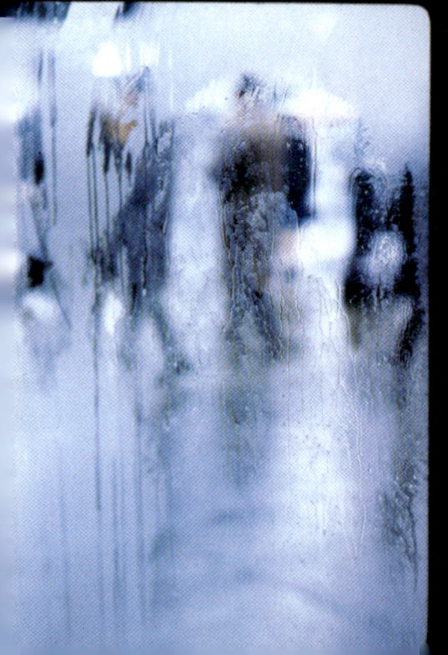
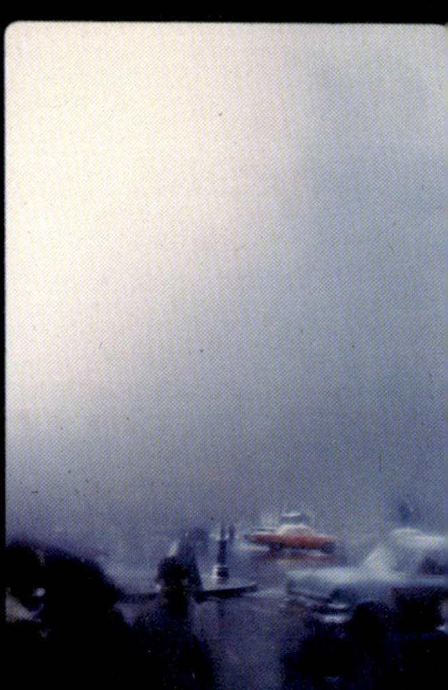

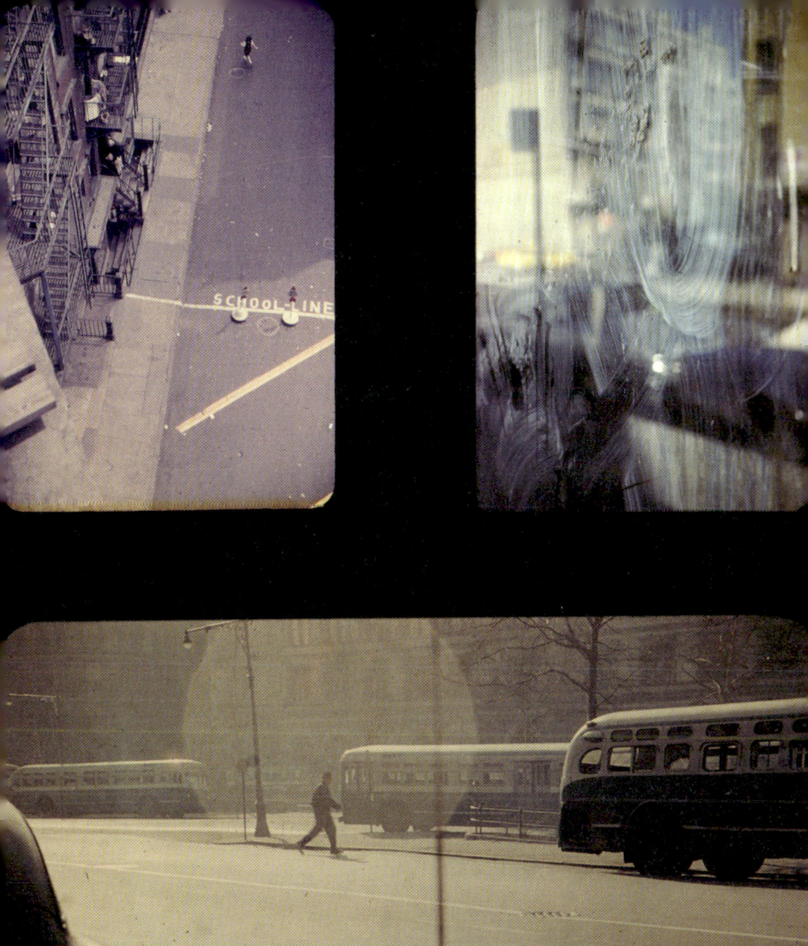
SCHOOL-LINE

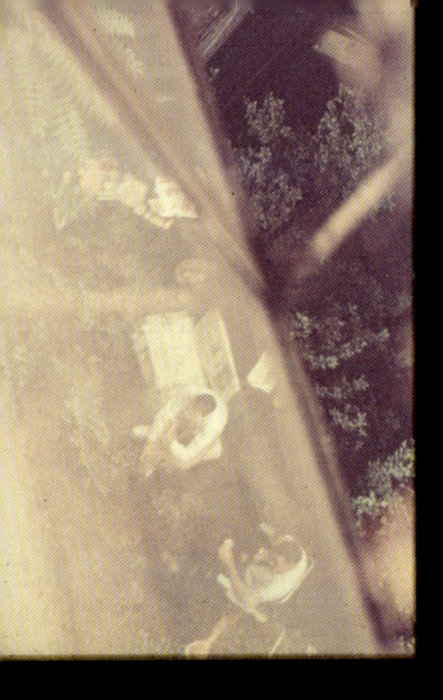
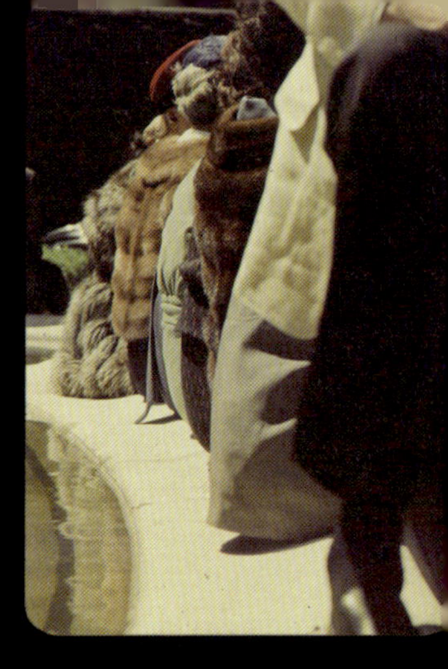
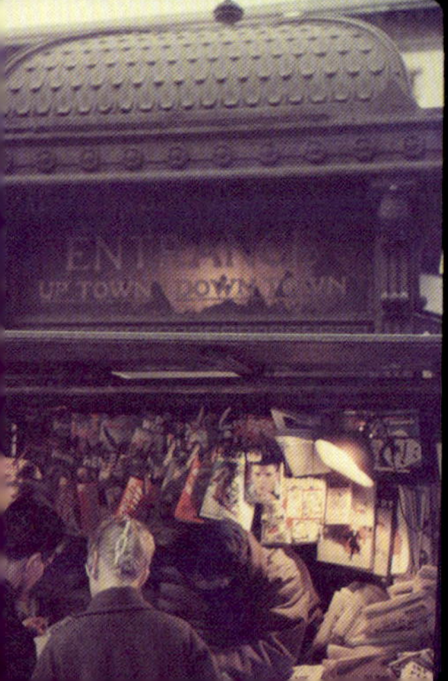
ENTRANCE
UPTOWN   DOWNTOWN
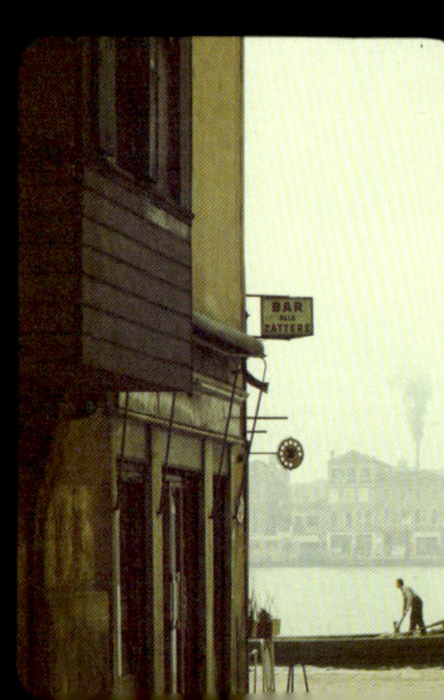
BAR
ALLE
ZATTERE

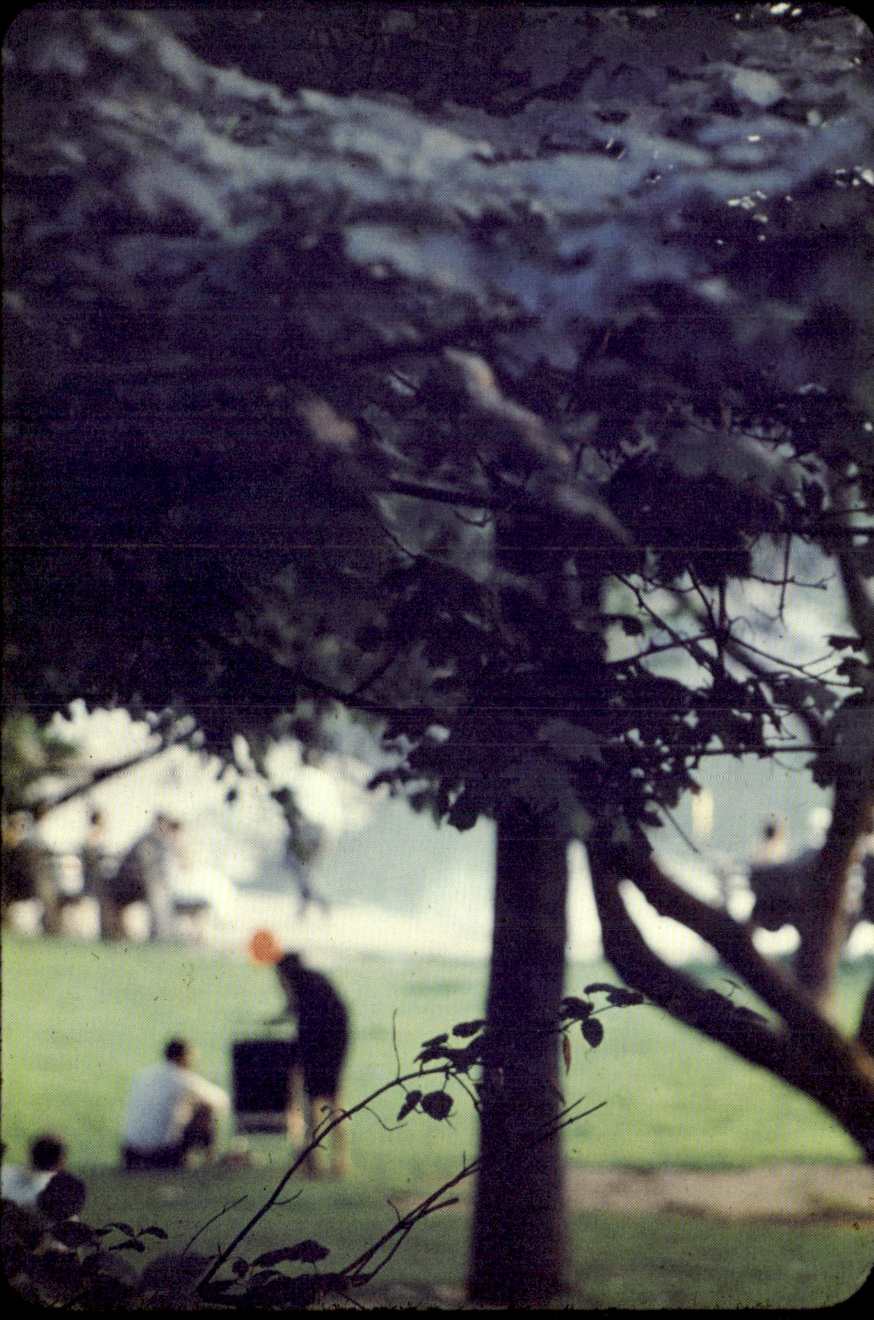

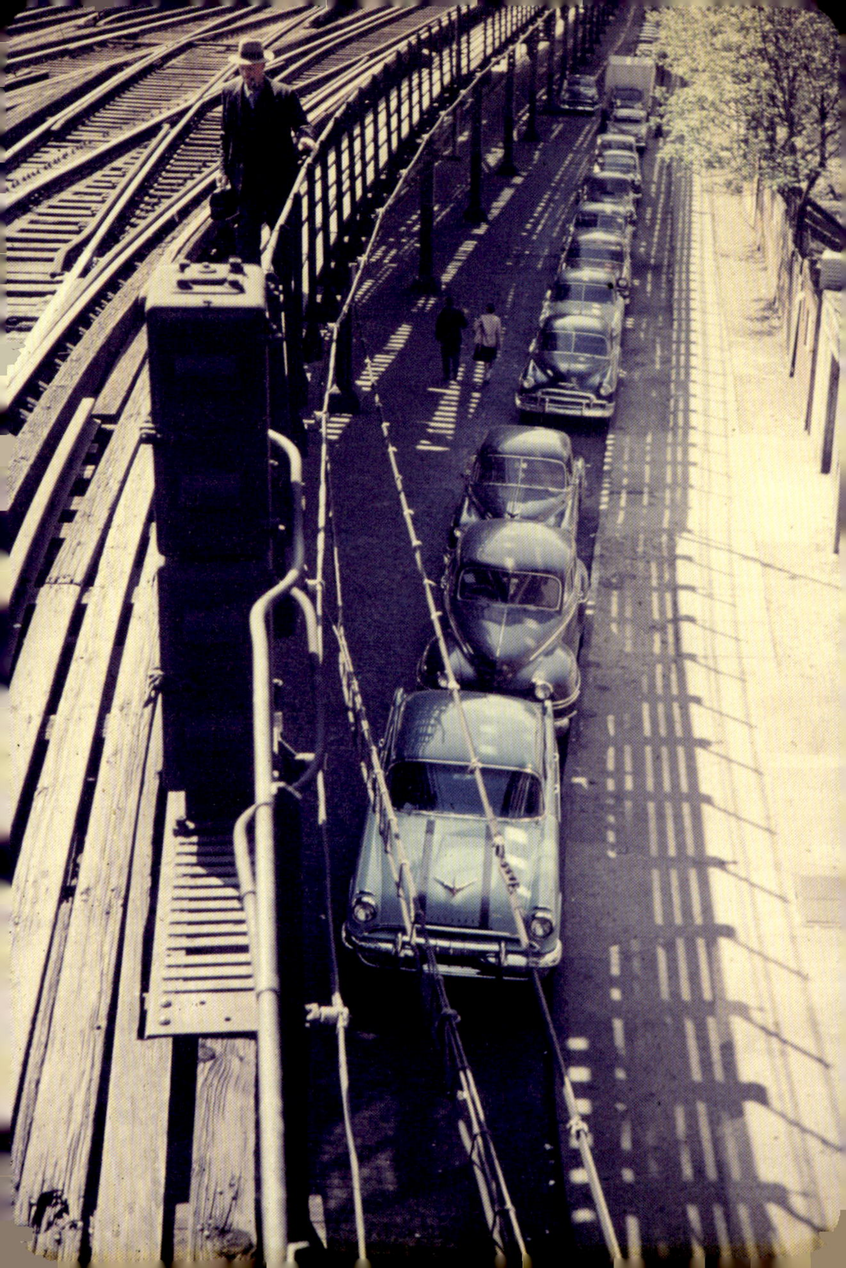

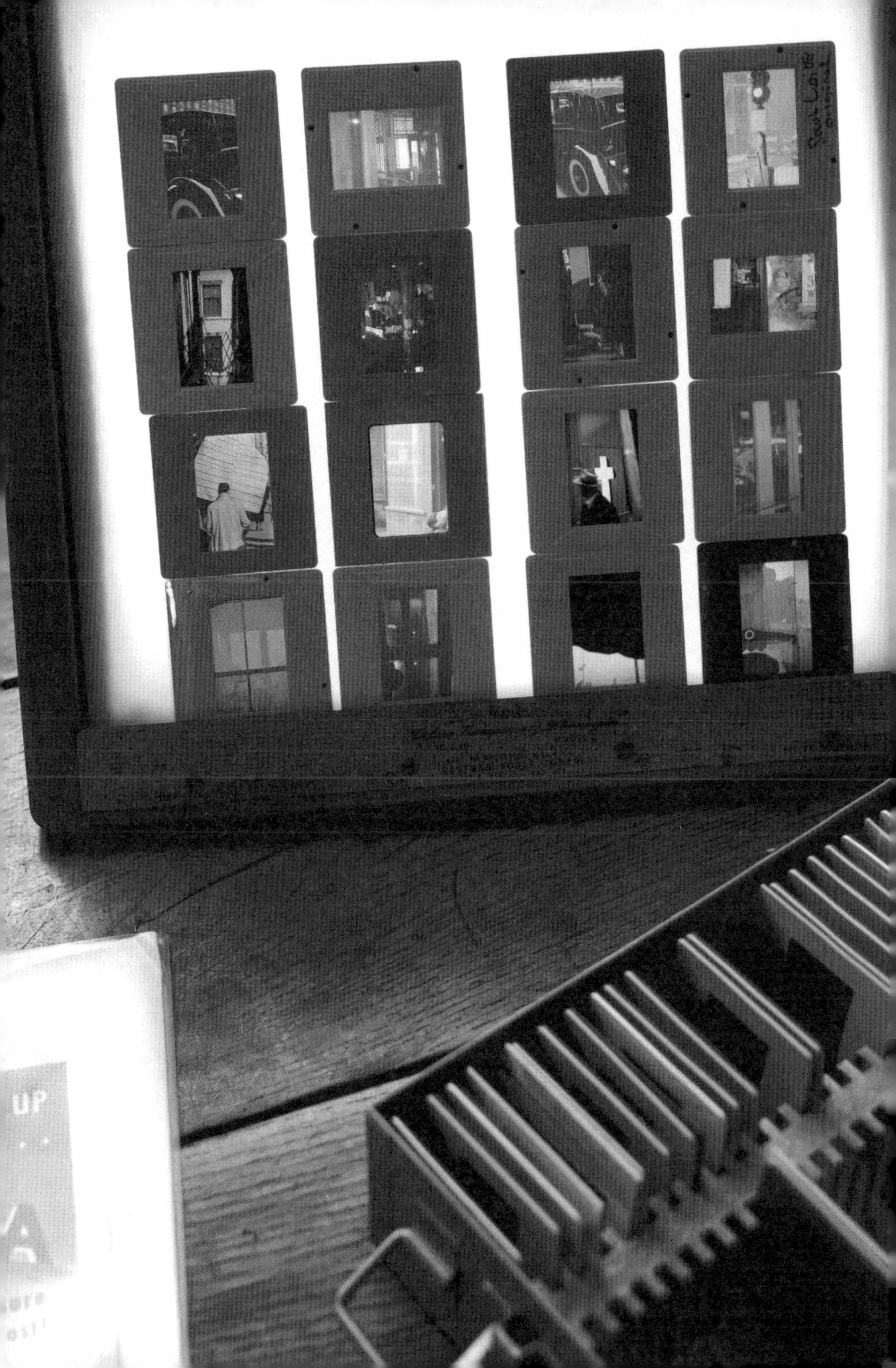

Snippets

Saul Leiter had a predilection for business-card-sized photos, which he printed on paper, tore apart, and made into what he called "snippets": photographic fragments with unique textures. Most of these works show his family, lovers, and other women he knew, and speak of his affection for these people. The snippets, which number several hundred, form something of a miniature galaxy of their own.

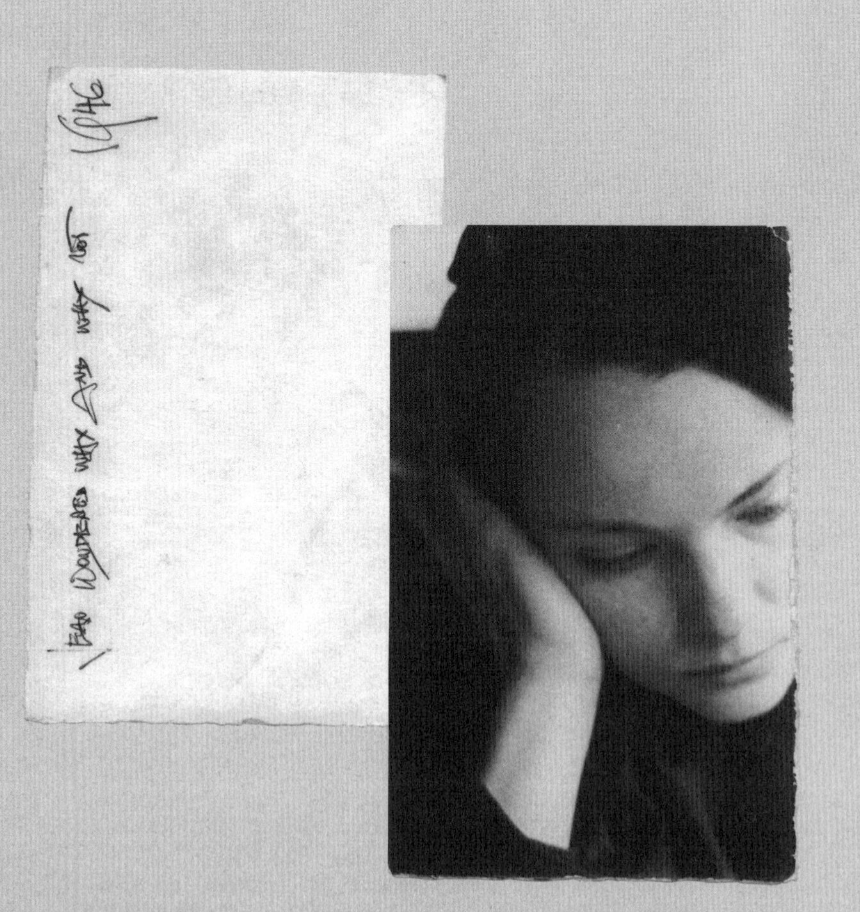

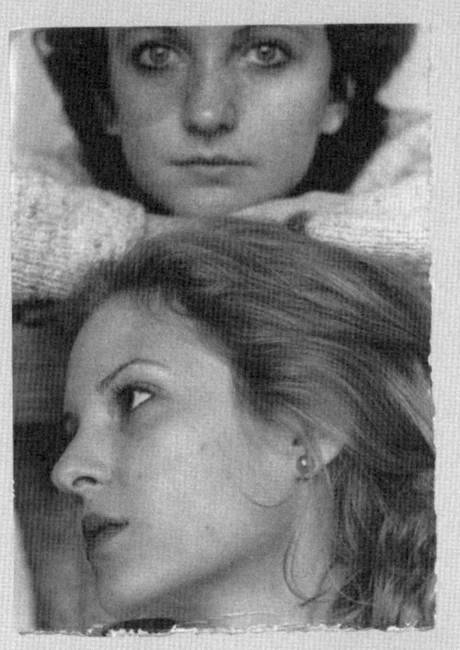
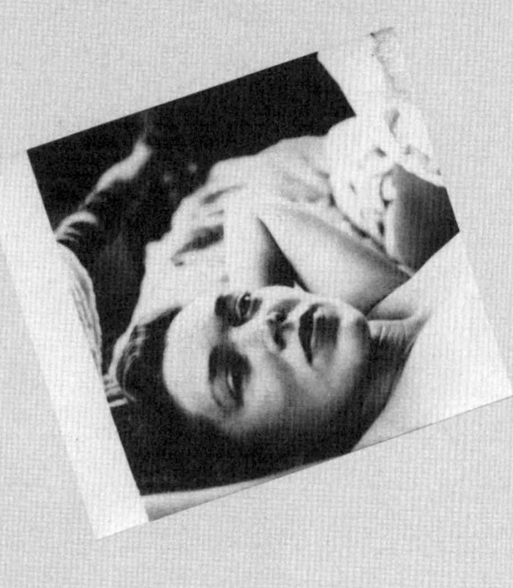
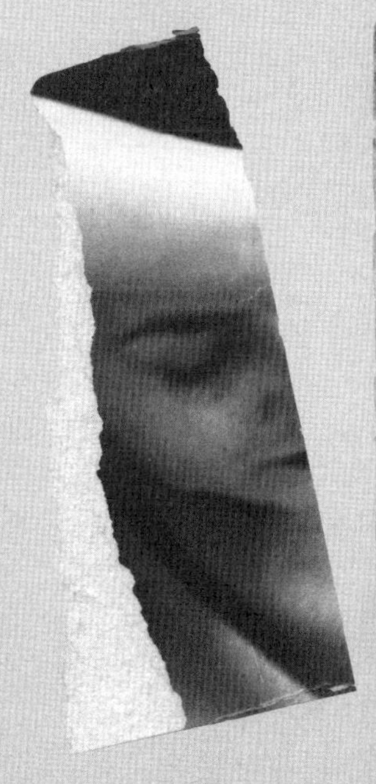
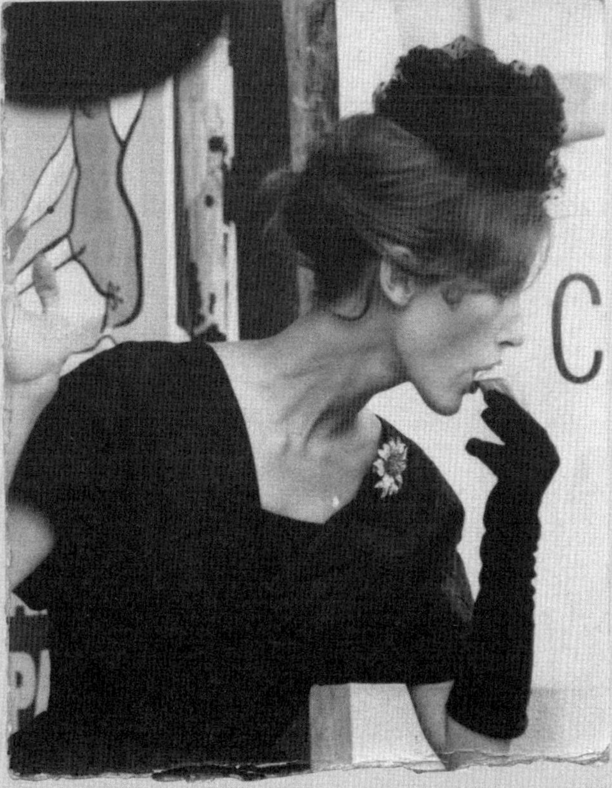
C

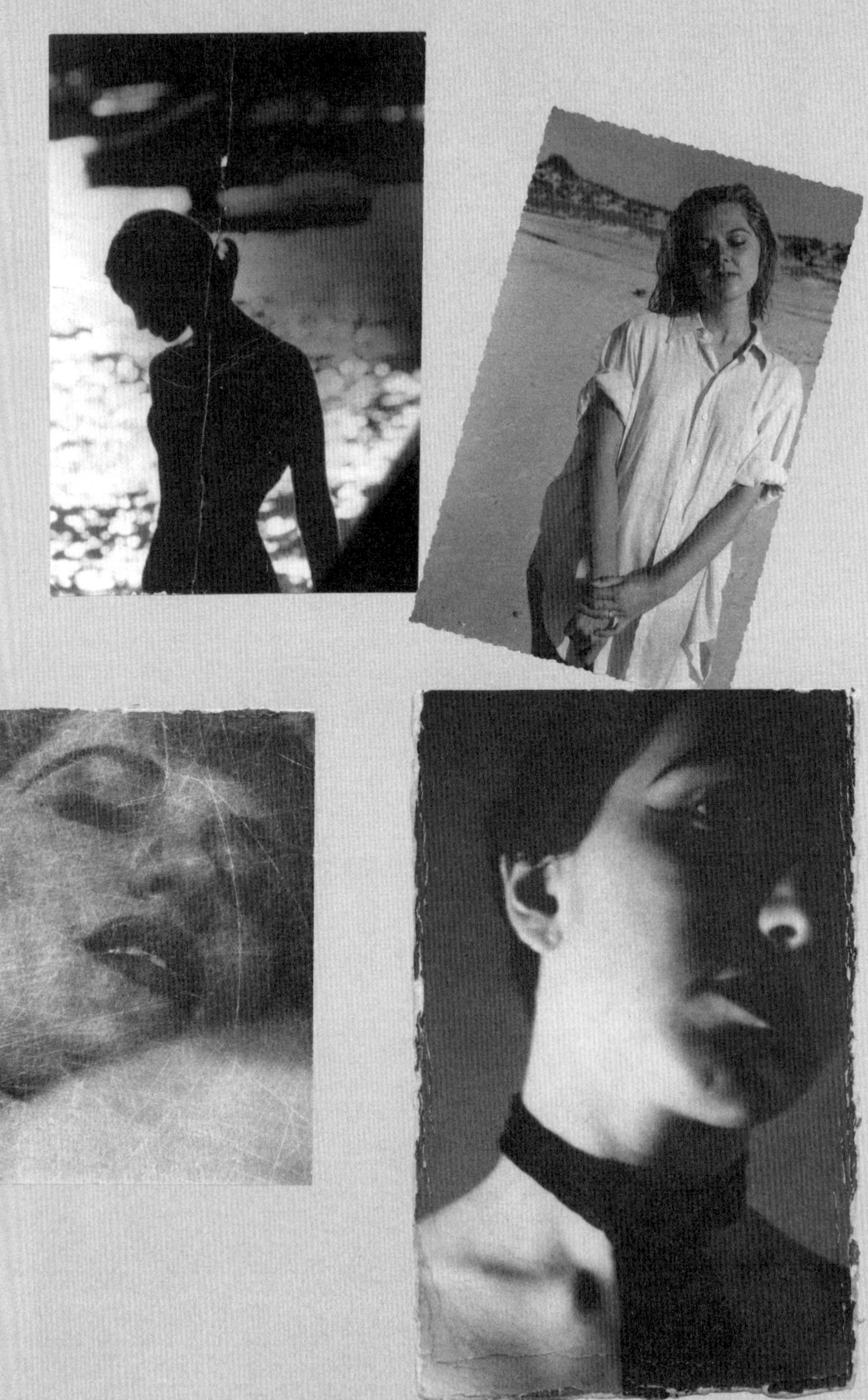

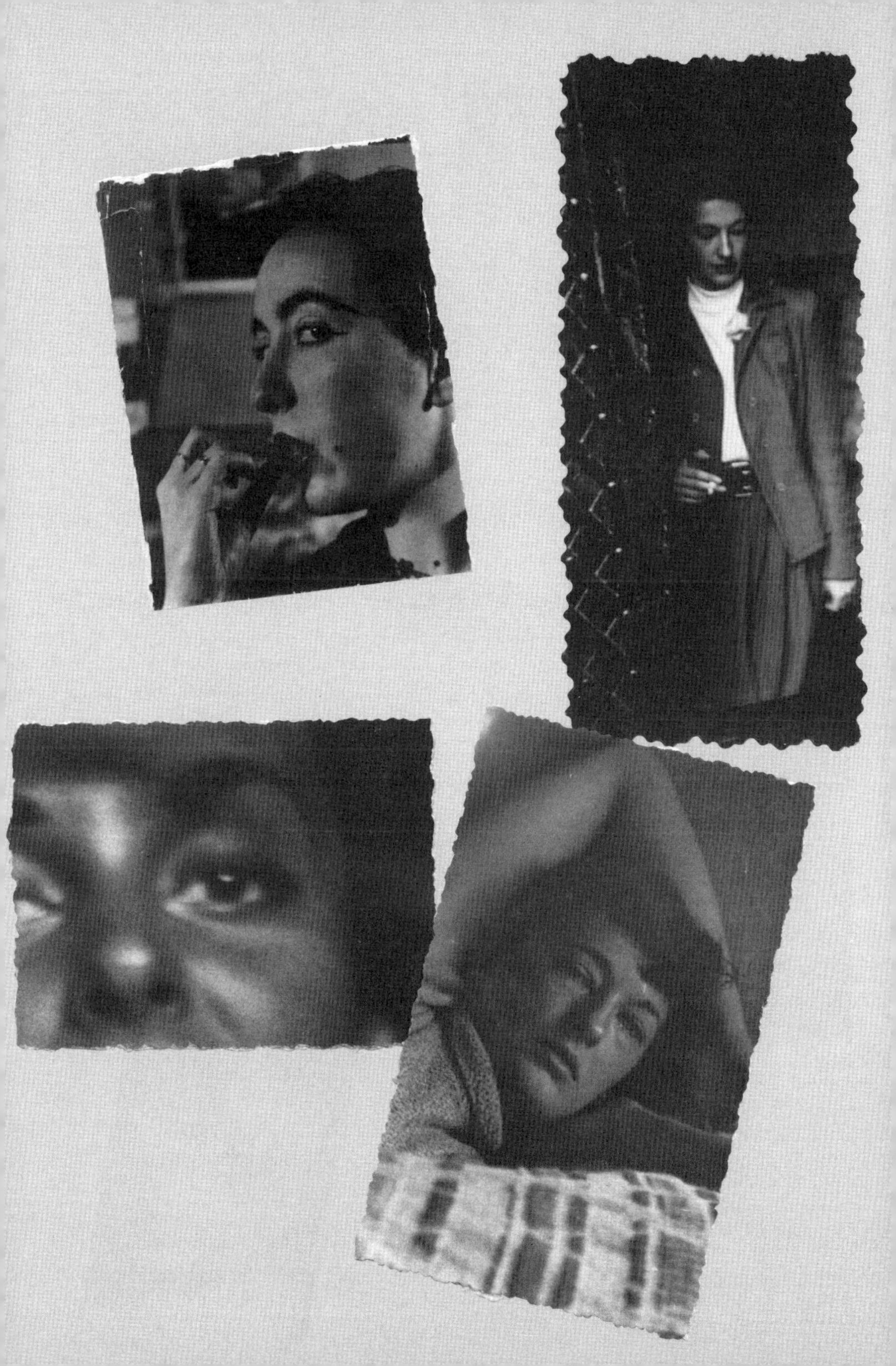

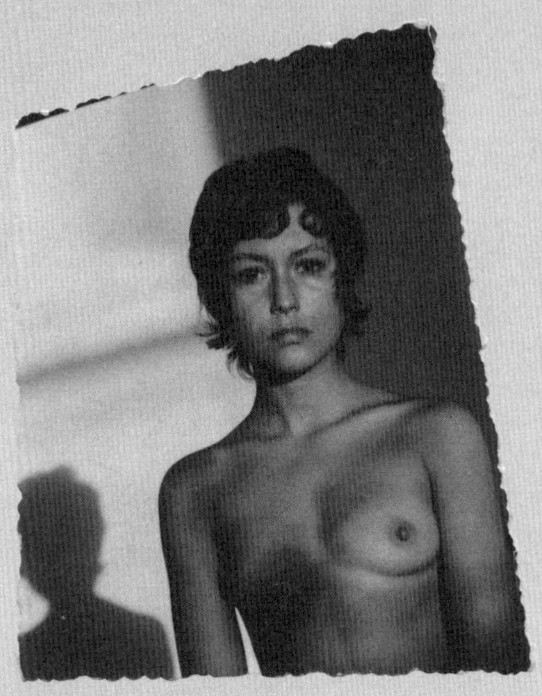
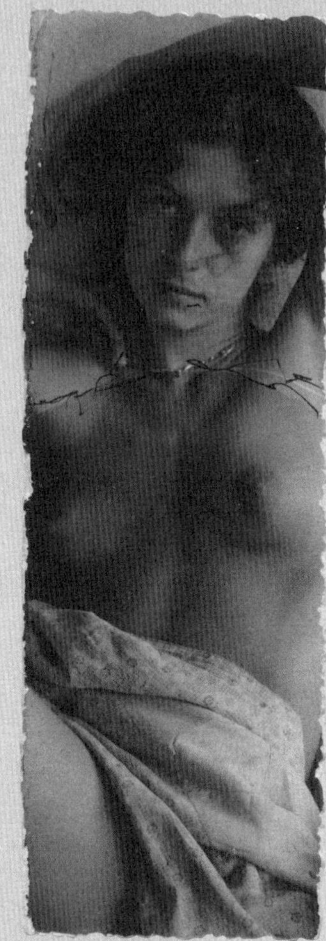
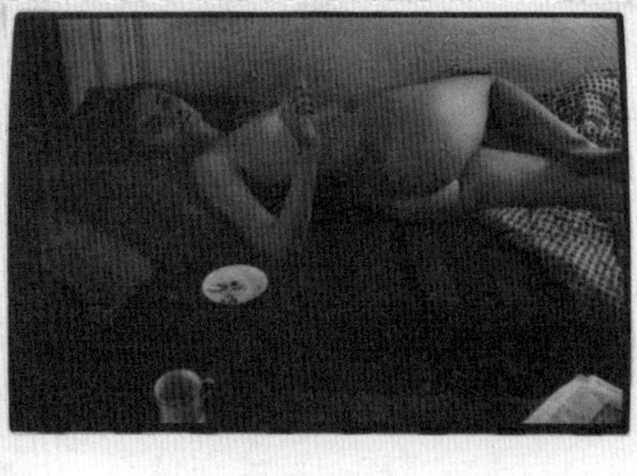
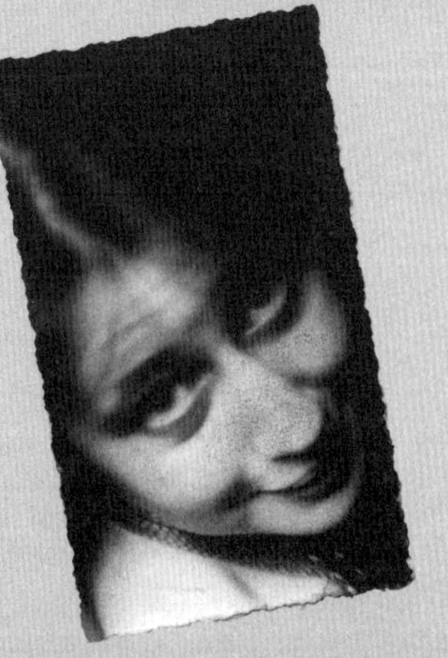

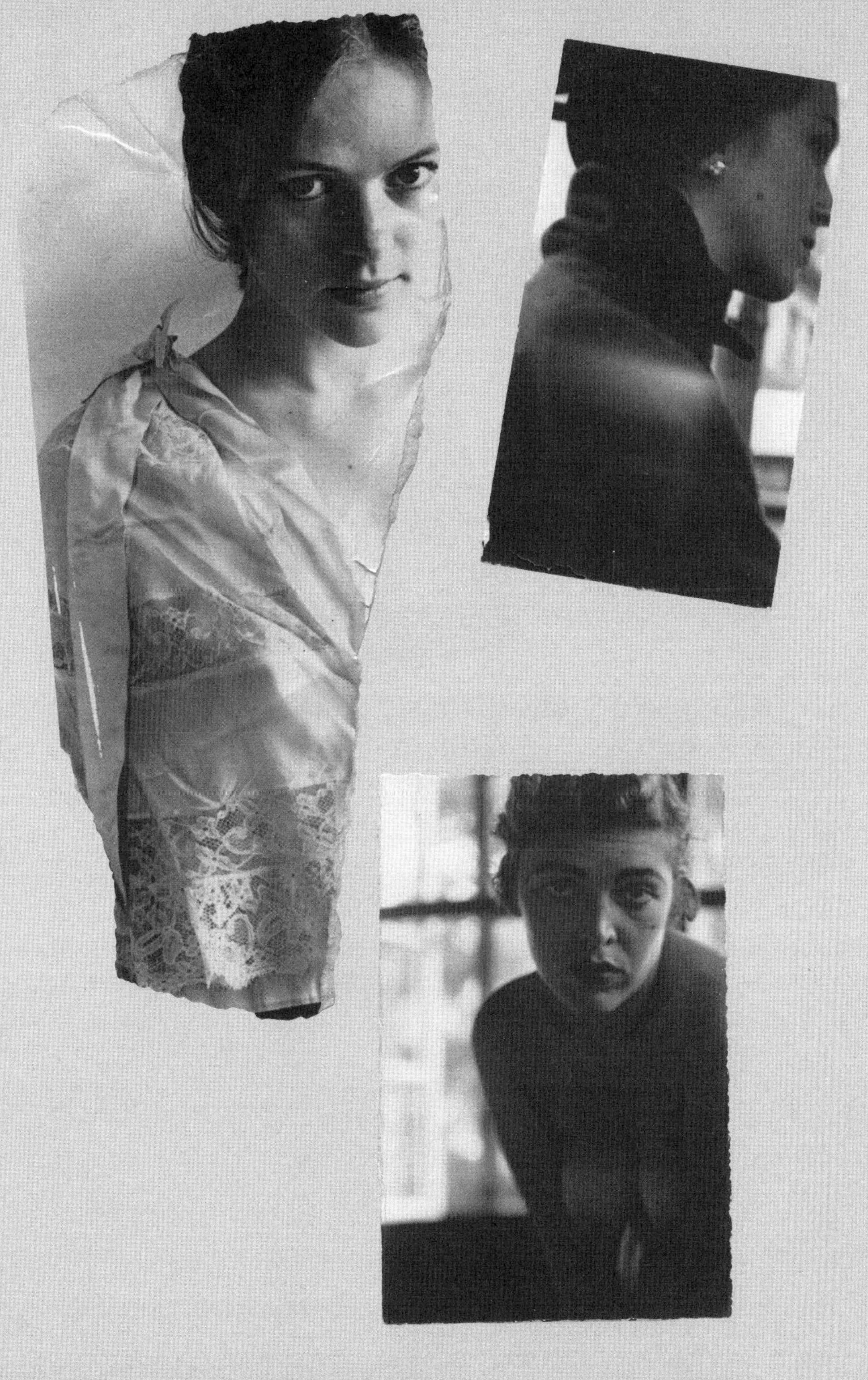

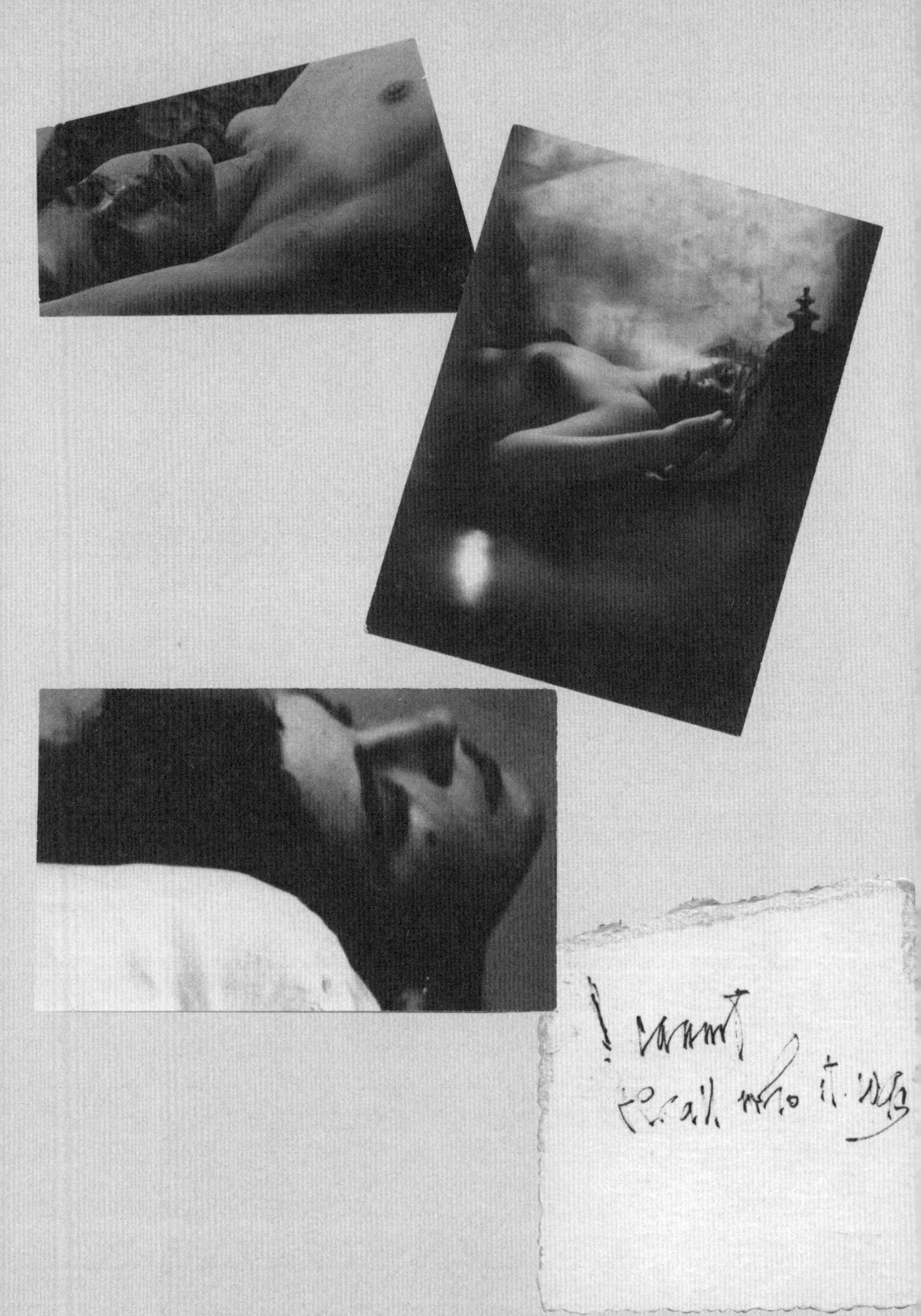

212 888
660

Kenneth
Rubenstein
protect your assets

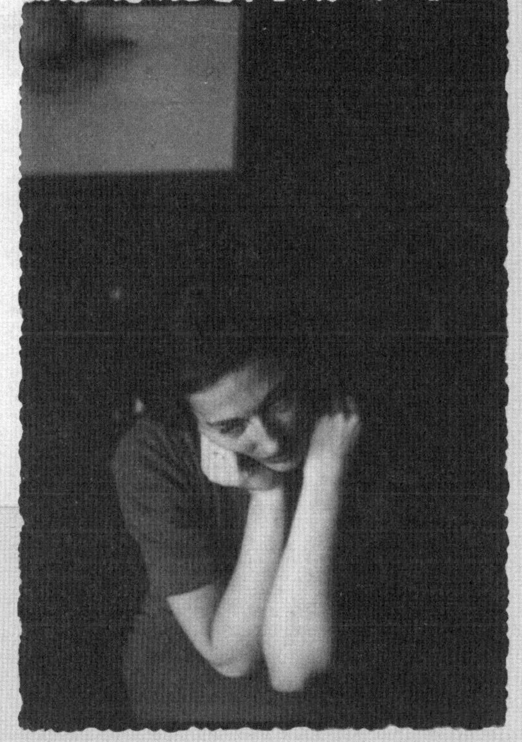

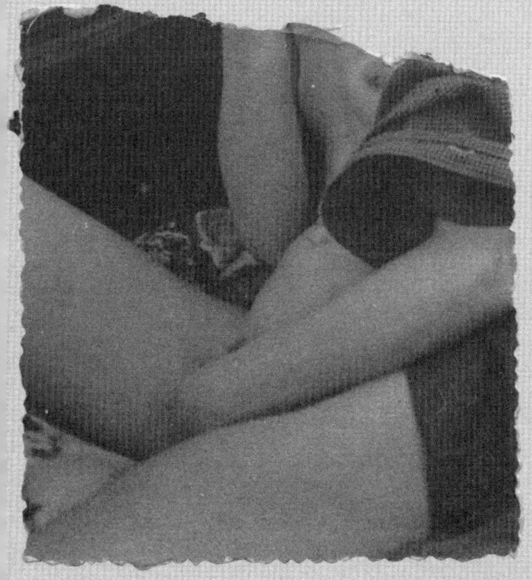

Sources of Saul Leiter quotations

pp. 1, 5, 44, 54, 67, 103, 171, 186, 196:

Saul Leiter: Colors, Idpure Éditions, Lausanne,

Switzerland, 2011

pp. 9, 18, 35, 60, 64, 78, 88, 97, 122, 158, 174, 250:

Interview with Vince Aletti at SVA Theatre, New York City,

for *Dear Dave* magazine, May 2013

pp. 14, 24, 38, 39, 74, 115, 136, 155, 164, 165, 168,

185, 257:

In No Great Hurry: 13 Lessons in Life with Saul Leiter

directed by Tomas Leach, 2013

pp. 29, 116:

Interview with Mitch Teich on WUWM's *Lake Effect*

radio show, Milwaukee, 2006

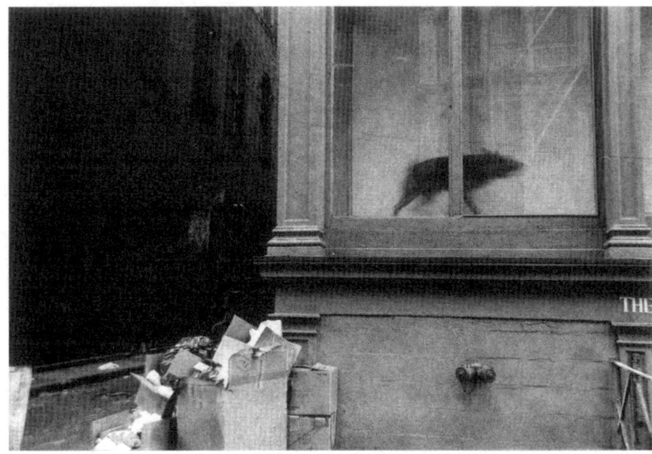

SOHO DOG by Akiko Otake

In the Ordinary World Where Nothing Happens... Something Appears Unexpectedly

Akiko Otake

It hasn't been that long since I first became aware of Saul Leiter. There was the 2015 Japan release of Tomas Leach's documentary *In No Great Hurry: 13 Lessons in Life with Saul Leiter* and the exhibition in 2017 at the Bunkamura Museum of Art. Through them, I became aware of the existence of this photographer, whose name I had never even heard before.

And I was taken by surprise at the time by two things.

One was the fact that he resided on East 10th Street. When I learned that it was 10th Street between 2nd and 3rd Avenues, I could instantly recreate the streetscape in my mind. From 1979 to the early 1980s, I lived right nearby. On the corner of 2nd Avenue, there was a small, triangular park on a diagonal street angling off toward Broadway and at its entrance were rows of elegant apartment buildings, with steps leading up, and St. Mark's Church—with its poetry readings and dance performances—nearby.

At the time, New York was known for being dangerous. Even by that standard, the entire area called the East Village was of a different league—you had to have a certain innate sense to safely navigate its streets. However, that block on East 10th Street was the exception. Even though just over in the next block junkies were hanging out, I remember that there it was always peaceful with shade trees giving an air of calm.

Saul Leiter moved into his apartment on 10th Street in 1952 when he was 28 and that is where his life ended. He had in fact resided in the same place for more than 60 years. When I lived in the neighborhood, there was a Ukrainian cafe called Veselka on the corner of 9th, which was a kind of local hangout (according to Google Maps it's still there). People with an aura like Saul Leiter—not burning with ambition but more bohemian—would be there drinking weak coffee and reading papers they picked up at the newsstand. It occurs to me now that I may have glimpsed Saul's silhouette among them.

The second thing that took me by surprise was Leiter's photographic style.

Soon after moving to New York, I got a yearning to shoot street photography and bought a single lens reflex. At one point I was so obsessed with photographs that I thought of them while sleeping and when awake. The unusual angles in Leiter's photographs are very similar to my images of that period. It may sound bold, but compared to any other photographer I felt an unbelievable affinity when I gazed at his work. I kept nodding and saying, "That's it. Yes. I get it."

In Leiter's photography there are scores of shots through glass—especially car and building windows—peeking through door cracks, taken from high places looking down, and gazing at virtual images in mirror reflections. Rarely engaging his subjects directly (with the exception of children, as well as family and close friends), most of his images feel like quietly stolen glimpses. A foreground dominated by a large shadow with a solitary figure walking ahead. An umbrella so large you can barely make out the person swallowed beneath it. These were his kind of indelible images. Even when something catches his eye, he never moves in on the subject

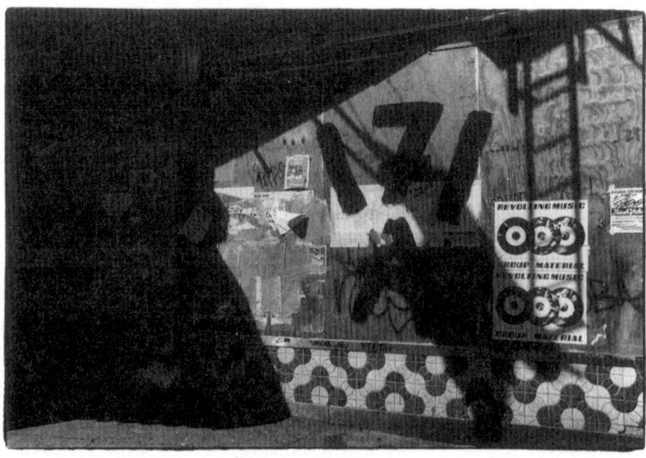

171 Avenue A by Akiko Otake

and prefers glancing at it, always keeping a distance. The objects of his interest are rarely shot in close-up and if they are, they're out of focus.

When I was in New York, that pretty much matched my approach to photography. Aiming my camera without being noticed, I'd enjoy the beautiful image all to myself. And in so doing, a feeling of quiet joy would well up in me, for I had discovered myself in my own little story in the city. This fiction was modest, transient and left a slightly melancholic feel, which perfectly suited my mood.

This may have been a reaction to my state of being at the time—feeling like a nobody, just dangling in the air, not knowing what I wanted to do or what avenue to pursue. New York's atmosphere was electric and stimulating, but that seemed to only deepen my sense of frustration as, unable to connect with it, I continued to float.

When I was photographing I could retreat from this emotional instability. It was like an affirmation, as I could shed my awkward self-consciousness and feel connected and at one with the world. It was a feeling of bliss that I had never experienced with anything else.

Many of Leiter's images are striking for being shot on snowy and rainy days. This also deeply resonated with me. First of all, I never felt compelled to go out shooting when the sky was bright and clear. Instead I was most motivated when dense shadows formed in the slanting light, when snow drained the world of vivid colors, when people and objects were covered in raindrops on rainy days. Direct sunshine tends to expose the garish nature of human ambition and will. However, the moment these are hidden in a curtain of snow or raindrops, people and

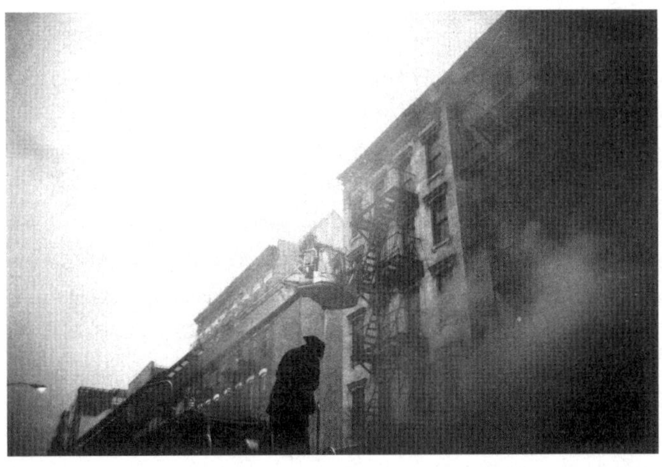

Firefighter by Akiko Otake

landscapes are evened out, creating a harmony. For me, holding my breath while waiting for the moment when the rawness of the everyday world would lift away to be replaced with surrealistic scenes, was as thrilling as stepping into a big city forest.

"I have a great respect for people who do nothing." "The secret of happiness is for nothing to happen." "There is a tremendous advantage of being unimportant." Those words that Leiter left behind completely embody my mental state at the time. In my twenties, my ideal was to live with the minimum, minimally. Whether it would be possible to live without becoming anybody or would it all end before I did anything… I constantly questioned myself.

The person I am today admires people who have achieved something, feels joy at the differences a day brings, and is pleased when my works are praised. The minimalism of my youth is hidden in the shadows… I've become an ordinary person who pursues the spice of life and has a tiny spark of ambition. When I pore over my old photographs I feel nostalgic. But I realize I will never be able to shoot that way again and sometimes I even wonder who that person could be who had no control over her insecurities.

From his mid-thirties through his fifties, Leiter shot a great deal of fashion and advertising photographs. And the work is infused with his distinctive shooting style. I can't help feeling that he stubbornly maintained his style, his stance. For instance, take the frontal fashion photograph of a model on page 55. Around an elegant woman, standing as if she hasn't a care in the world, is the imposed giant shadow of a man. The fact that she seems oblivious of it is what elevates this from simply an image of dignified beauty to a more complex narrative. Leiter's images often feature peering out from behind, blurring and obscuring, and the multi-layering of materials, in a way that seems to avoid supplying any explanation or conclusion. For him, nothing was more discouraging than a banal story.

He preferred shooting his commercial assignments out in the streets and not in the studio. And in this there is something very Leiter-esque. Usually it's the opposite, as the photographer can smoothly control the lighting and models' movements in a studio, making it easier to change things around. Of course chance meetings and discoveries may be less likely to occur, but having everything fall neatly into place has its advantages, which is especially true with commercial photography. But for Leiter, this kind of confined space would not have been a welcoming place. In contrast to street photography, happenings and the unpredictable are less likely to occur there, and all the materials necessary for the photographer's direction are ready at hand. With no interest in efficiency or rationality and not possessing a controlling ego, for him the studio would have been an incredibly dull workspace with little room for inspiration.

Leiter never envisioned life as climbing a ladder. He had no interest in that model of the "American Dream," where you doggedly work your way up. He was simply turning it off to allow "for nothing to happen." His friend, the art director Henry Wolf commented: "He has a talent for avoiding opportunities."

If you seek change, good things happen and bad things happen. By gaining something, you might also lose something. Which way it will tumble is unknown and for those who like a challenge, it's that gamble that captivates them. Leiter was completely the opposite. Since eschewing earthly distractions and trying to live as ordinarily as possible were his tenets, he never altered his position as if fixed on a compass. And that's perhaps why, even when he had influence in his commercial work years, and could have moved to a better place had he so desired, he stayed on at East 10th Street. Leiter, who had no connection to ambition, must have felt right at home in the East Village's diverse atmosphere of young artists, forgotten older artists, homeless people, immigrants, and the lonely elderly.

Born to Jewish parents, from a young age he attended a Jewish school in accordance with his rabbi father's wishes. But deciding against following in his father's footsteps, he dropped out of his religious studies and pursued the path of an artist.

About his father, he once said: "Maybe because my father disapproved of almost everything I did—in some secret place in my being was a desire to avoid success."

Instead of passionately trying to prove himself after rebelling, he made a kind of compromise by denying himself success. This may have stemmed from the stoicism that seeped into his bone marrow due to his strict upbringing. Or perhaps by not seeking fame, he was showing a filial loyalty. By reading into his photographs, you sense his personality—shy, moderate, not pushy, and observant rather than assertive—traits that may also have been reinforced through his relationship with his father.

In his last years, a solo exhibition of his paintings spanning thirty years was held. A fluid single brushstroke feel—rather in the spirit of *haiga* paintings—characterizes his style. At a time when people were more familiar with paintbrushes, it wasn't rare to see an artist doing both painting and photography or switching over from painting to photography. Leiter was one of them. Indeed, Henri Cartier-Bresson, whom Leiter highly respected, saw painting as a form of meditation late in his own life.

I would conjecture that when Leiter wanted to be out and about he reached for his camera. When he didn't want to go anywhere he would grab his paintbrush. In either case, he wasn't taking a position; he went back and forth between the two disciplines, following some kind of unconscious flow. Though the media were different, the idea of creating a little story within a square format remained. The two forms were seamlessly intertwined inside him.

That said, there is in fact an obvious difference between the brush as an extension of the arm and the camera as an extension of the arm. The camera, unlike the brush, isn't directly influenced by the arm, which means there is greater distance between the "self" in photography than in painting. And so unconscious action becomes more pronounced in this discipline. Even though a person has taken the image, there is no direct trace back to the hand. And this, you could argue, is a defining quality of photography.

I think this is probably one of the reasons Leiter was drawn to the medium. While his framing has signature qualities, you never get the sense he's pursuing an image. Instead you have the impression that he is capturing something transcendent and independent of intention. The beauty emerging in the photograph is not created by the "self" but rather is the result of a connection between something other and the "self." I am certain he felt he just simply happened to be there.

Not rising, not falling—suspended in the ordinary world where nothing happens, but the unexpected appears. Life is the process of bearing witness… I can hear Saul Leiter whisper as much from his countless silent photographs.

Akiko Otake Biography

Writer Akiko Otake lived in New York in the early 1980s, where she began her writing career. Her work is not confined by genre and includes essays, novels and criticism. She is also a photographer and has published a collection of her images with Akaaka-sha, under the title *New York 1980*.

She has written extensively on photography, including *Karera Ga Shashin wo Te ni Shita Setsujitsusa wo* (Heibon-sha), *Kono Shashin ga Sugoi* (Asahi Press) and *Dekigoto to Shashin* (co-authored, Akaaka-sha).

Other publications include *Tokyo Dekoboko Sanpo* and *Madori to Moso* (Aki Shobo). She also hosts "katarikoko," a series of talk events and readings held at various second-hand bookshops around Tokyo: http://katarikoko.blog40.fc2.com

Explorations

Margit Erb and Michael Parillo, Saul Leiter Foundation

The two of us were touched and delighted by the warm reception for Saul's first solo exhibition in Japan, *Photographer Saul Leiter: A Retrospective*, which opened at the Bunkamura Museum of Art in Tokyo in April 2017 and then traveled to Itami and Niigata. Saul owned dozens of books on subjects like *ukiyo-e*, ink-wash painting (*sumi-e*), and calligraphy, and his love for and kinship with Japanese art is evident in his photographs and paintings alike. Still, he would be tickled to no end to see the instant connection he made in this country so far from home. Less than three years later came *Forever Saul Leiter*, a second exhibition at the same venue, which this book was designed to accompany. We're pleased to give you a peek inside Saul's archive and our ongoing efforts to nurture his legacy.

Running the Saul Leiter Foundation is a big job. Our mission began shortly after Saul's passing on November 26, 2013; these were sad days, but the work was a balm against the pain of losing a dear friend. It was inspiring to begin sorting through all that Saul left behind—a necessary distraction at the time, and a process that continues to offer daily wonders. Although we knew Saul for many years, we've found that compiling his work, library, and personal effects has filled gaps in our knowledge of his life and his art, deepening our understanding of a body of work that has turned out to be even more vast and far-reaching than we realized during his lifetime.

The sheer volume of material before us reinforced what was already evident: Saul never stopped working. Between his studio storage in New York City's East Village and the work housed by his primary dealer, Howard Greenberg Gallery in midtown Manhattan, Saul bequeathed to the foundation thousands of prints in color and black and white plus tens of thousands of slides and negatives, along with hundreds of paintings and handpainted photographs. The accompanying exhibition included a number of works that were seen for the very first time, in addition to a newly curated selection of street and fashion photography (including rarely seen street images taken during the last decade of Saul's life), intimate portraits, contact sheets, paintings, and ephemera such as his painting palette and Leiter family photos.

We were especially excited to unveil a slide show bursting with brand-new discoveries, which was the result of a research project begun in 2018. Sifting through hundreds of little yellow slide boxes, we saw the widening of Saul's contributions to mid-twentieth-century color photography, a field where he is already considered a pioneer thanks to his groundbreaking 2006 monograph,

Early Color, in which all of the images were shot using 35-millimeter slide film. In the late 1940s and the 1950s, when most of the book's photographs were taken, Saul would show his work to friends by projecting his slides on the walls of his apartment.

Revelations from our recent slide studies show trusty Leiter motifs like snow, car windows, and the Third Avenue elevated train, along with fresh ideas and perspectives. Although Saul's eye was remarkably consistent, which you'll see in the late-period prints presented here, the slides also reveal the spirit of relentless experimentation. "I would try different things," Saul told *New Yorker* writer Vince Aletti in a 2013 interview at the School of Visual Arts in New York City. "Sometimes I failed, and sometimes I didn't fail. Sometimes something worked out."

Whether you saw the earlier book, *All about Saul Leiter*, or this is your first journey to the land of Leiter, we invite you to have fun in your explorations and come away feeling the unique aesthetic of an artist who said, "I see this world simply. It is a source of endless delight."

Margit Erb Biography

Margit Erb is the director of the Saul Leiter Foundation. She worked for Howard Greenberg Gallery for eighteen years, during which she assisted Leiter in his studio with the organization of his archive. She helped produce his first book, *Early Color* (2006), as well as many other books on his work. She also co-produced the film *In No Great Hurry: 13 Lessons in Life with Saul Leiter* (2013). In 2014, she helped establish the Saul Leiter Foundation.

Michael Parillo Biography

Michael Parillo is the associate director of the Saul Leiter Foundation and the president of its board. He joined the foundation in 2015, after spending twenty years as an editor and writer. He has worked on the Leiter books *All about Saul Leiter* (2017), *Travel Eye: New York* (2017), *Women* (2018), and *In My Room* (2018), among others, and is the executive producer of the short film *Seeing Is a Neglected Enterprise: The Saul Leiter Foundation*.

1923	Born in Pittsburgh, Pennsylvania, on December 3. Parents are Rabbi Wolf Leiter and Regina *née* Goldberg.
1924–25	Compact cameras appear on the market, such as the Ermanox by Ernemann-Werke (GER) and the Leica I (A) by Ernst Leitz (GER).
1930s	Attends Talmudic Academy in New York City.
1933	Eastman Kodak (USA) starts selling the first panchromatic roll film, Panatomic-X.
circa 1935	Is given a Detrola camera by his mother and begins photographing.
1936	Eastman Kodak starts selling 35mm Kodachrome, the world's first 35mm color reversal film. Agfa (GER) releases Agfacolor Neu, a pioneering color reversal film of the type still in use, which later became known as Agfachrome.
1940	The Department of Photography is established at The Museum of Modern Art (MoMA), New York.
early 1940s	Attends Telshe Yeshiva Rabbinical College, Cleveland.
1944	Paintings exhibited at Ten-Thirty Gallery, Cleveland.
1945	Paintings exhibited at Outlines Gallery, Pittsburgh, and at Gump's department store, San Francisco.
1946	Leaves Telshe Yeshiva Rabbinical College and moves to New York. Befriends Abstract Expressionist painter Richard Pousette-Dart, who encourages Leiter to take photographs.
	Eastman Kodak releases Ektachrome, a 35mm color reversal film.
1947	Attends Henri Cartier-Bresson's exhibition at the Museum of Modern Art. Befriends W. Eugene Smith, who gives him Alexey Brodovitch's book *Ballet*. One of Leiter's paintings is included in *Abstract and Surrealist American Art* at the Art Institute of Chicago. Paintings exhibited at the Butler Institute of American Art, Youngstown, Ohio.
circa 1948	Begins working with color reversal film. Uses cameras such as the Argus C3, Auto Graflex Junior and an early Rolleiflex.
1950	The world's first pentaprism single lens reflex camera, the Contax S by VEB Zeiss Ikon (GDR), is released. This type of camera finds a ready market.

1951	*LIFE* publishes his black-and-white series *The Wedding as a Funeral* in its September 3 issue. More work is featured in the November 26 issue of *LIFE* (*Shoes of the Shoeshine Man*).
1952	Moves to East 10th Street in East Village.
1953	Black-and-white photographs are included in *Always the Young Strangers* at the Museum of Modern Art and in *Contemporary Photography* at the National Museum of Modern Art, Tokyo.
1956	Solo exhibition at the Tanager Gallery, New York.
late 1950s	Gives slide talk about color work at "The Club," an art space in the East Village. Exhibits color work at Samuel Kootz Gallery, New York.
1957	Steichen includes twenty of Leiter's color photographs in his slide talk, "Experimental Photography in Color," at the Museum of Modern Art, New York. Henry Wolf, art director at *Esquire*, publishes some of Leiter's fashion photographs.
1958	Begins to photograph for *Harper's Bazaar* when Henry Wolf becomes art director.
1959	Travels to Europe on assignment for *Esquire* to photograph Gina Lollobrigida during the making of *Solomon and Sheba*.
1960–80s	Continues to take fashion photographs and do other commercial work. His fashion work is published in *Harper's Bazaar, Elle, Show, Vogue (UK), Queen,* and *Nova*. His photographs are also included in *LIFE, U.S. Camera, Photography Annual,* and *Infinity* magazines.
1976	The Museum of Modern Art (MoMA), New York, holds *Photographs by William Eggleston*, its first exhibition of color photographs, organized by John Szarkowski.
1981	Closes commercial studio at 156 5th Avenue.
	International Center of Photography, New York, holds the group exhibition *New Color*, which is dedicated to color photography and accompanied by a book with the same title.
1991	Fashion work included in group exhibition *Appearances* at the Victoria and Albert Museum, London.

1992	Black-and-white work included in Jane Livingston's book *The New York School: Photographs 1936–1963*.
1993–94	Black-and-white photographs exhibited at Howard Greenberg Gallery, New York. Receives funding from Ilford Paper Company to begin printing color work as Cibachromes with Laumont Labs in New York.
1997	Exhibition of color photographs at Howard Greenberg Gallery, New York. (Color works exhibited at Howard Greenberg Gallery again in 2005.)
2006	First monograph *Early Color* is published by Steidl, Göttingen, Germany. First solo museum show, at Milwaukee Art Museum.
2008	First solo museum show in Europe at the Fondation Henri Cartier-Bresson, Paris, with accompanying book.
2009	First painting exhibition in over 30 years at Knoedler Gallery, New York.
2012	Major retrospective at Deichtorhallen, Hamburg, Germany.
2013	Saul Leiter dies at the age of 89 on November 26, in New York. Release of the documentary film *In No Great Hurry: 13 Lessons in Life with Saul Leiter*, directed by Tomas Leach.
2014	Second monograph, *Early Black & White,* is published by Steidl, Göttingen, Germany. The Saul Leiter Foundation is founded.
2017	First solo exhibition in Japan at the Bunkamura Museum of Art, which was also shown at Itami City Museum of Art in 2018 and at the Niigata Bandaijima Art Museum in 2019. These exhibitions were accompanied by the book *All about Saul Leiter*, first published by Seigensha, Tokyo.
2018	The monograph *In My Room* is published by Steidl, Göttingen, Germany. International editions of *All about Saul Leiter* are published in the UK, France, Spain, and South Korea.
2019	His nude work is included in the group exhibition *Saul Leiter/David Lynch/Helmut Newton: Nudes* at Helmut Newton Foundation, Berlin.
2020	Second solo exhibition in Japan, *Forever Saul Leiter,* at the Bunkamura Museum of Art, with accompanying book published by Shogakukan. This exhibition was also shown at Museum EKi KYOTO.

Photo Credit:
p. 273: Kakuta Miho

Translated from the Japanese by Kate Klippensteen

First published in the United Kingdom in 2021
by Thames & Hudson Ltd, 6-24 Britannia Street,
London WC1X 9JD

First published in the United States of America in
2022 by Thames & Hudson Inc., 500 Fifth Avenue,
New York, New York 10110

Reprinted 2022, 2024, 2025

Produced by Masako Sato (Contact)
Designed by Osamu Ouchi (nano/nano graphics)

EU Authorized Representative: Interart S.A.R.L.
19 rue Charles Auray, 93500 Pantin, Paris, France
productsafety@thameshudson.co.uk
interart.fr

A CIP catalogue record for this book is available
from the British Library

Library of Congress Control Number 2022932723

ISBN 978-0-500-29643-1
04

Printed and bound in Singapore

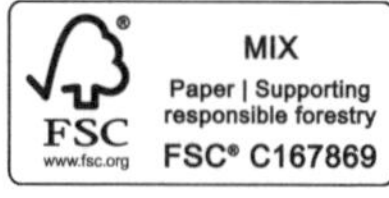

Be the first to know about our new releases,
exclusive content and author events by visiting
thamesandhudson.com
thamesandhudsonusa.com
thamesandhudson.com.au

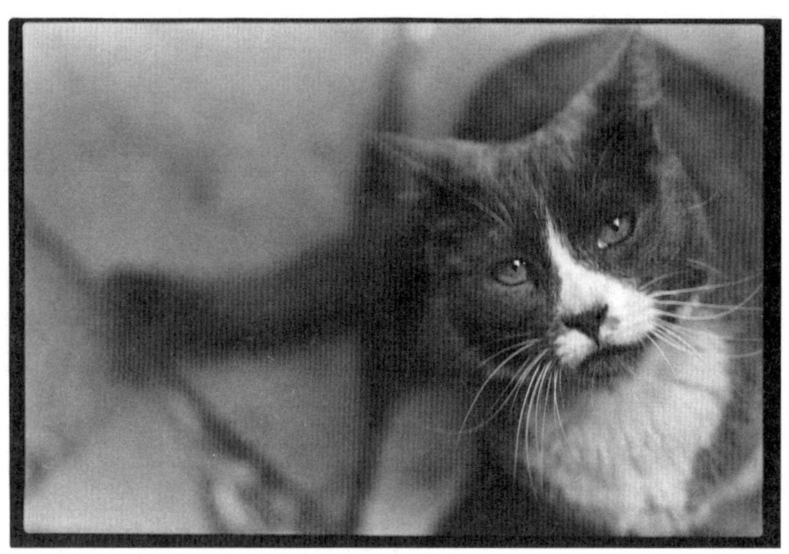

Alice, 1980s